Utopophobia

ON THE LIMITS (IF ANY) OF POLITICAL PHILOSOPHY

David Estlund

PRINCETON UNIVERSITY PRESS

PRINCETON & OXFORD

Published by Princeton University Press
41 William Street, Princeton, New Jersey 08540
6 Oxford Street, Woodstock, Oxfordshire OX20 1TR

press.princeton.edu

First paperback printing, 2022
Paperback ISBN 9780691235172

The Library of Congress has cataloged the cloth edition of this book as follows:

Names: Estlund, David M., author.
Title: Utopophobia : on the limits (if any) of political philosophy / David Estlund.
Description: Princeton, New Jersey : Princeton University Press, 2020. |
    Includes bibliographical references and index.
Identifiers: LCCN 2019024586 (print) | LCCN 2019024587 (ebook) | ISBN
    9780691147161 (hardback) | ISBN 9780691197500 (ebook)
Subjects: LCSH: Justice (Philosophy) | Idealism. | Realism. | Political
    science—Philosophy.
Classification: LCC B105.J87 E77 2020 (print) | LCC B105.J87 (ebook) |
    DDC 320.01/1–dc23
LC record available at https://lccn.loc.gov/2019024586
LC ebook record available at https://lccn.loc.gov/2019024587

British Library Cataloging-in-Publication Data is available

Editorial: Rob Tempio and Matt Rohal
Production Editorial: Kathleen Cioffi
Cover Design: Chris Ferrante
Production: Merli Guerra and Brigid Ackerman
Publicity: Nathalie Levine and Julia Hall
Copyeditor: Mark Epstein

This book has been composed in Miller

For Corey, Marshall, and Hannah

The sea rises, the light fails, lovers cling to each other, and children cling to us. The moment we cease to hold each other, the moment we break faith with one another, the sea engulfs us and the light goes out.

—JAMES BALDWIN, *NOTHING PERSONAL*

CONTENTS

PART V. THE PRACTICAL AND THE IDEALISTIC

THE INSCRIPTION I HAVE CHOSEN for the book—from James Baldwin's collaboration with photographer and activist Richard Avedon—verbally develops a still image, almost photographic—not coincidentally, perhaps. In this image, nature (including our own) both looms and tantalizes, our potential and our proclivities are black and white and in between. But keeping faith is the linchpin—the moral organizes the picture. The elements appear but so does agency, as well as the continuum of value between thriving and tragedy. Baldwin's eyes seem moist but wide open. The light may indeed finally go out, but not necessarily. The image is not blinkered by optimism or even by any clear hope. And yet whatever it would take not to "break faith," it is hard to believe that it is not deeply political in part—his full text is pervasively political—and impossible to believe that a political failure to do so would not be a profound moral failure. We could keep the roiling sea at bay, and yet we might not.

The image of holding each other and not letting go evokes an almost lurid idealism about what is needed, framed by an unmistakable realism that holds hope at arm's length. On the one hand, the evocation of high standards we are called to is anthemic. On the other hand, knowing what we know, we might fall tragically short. It can often be hard to see both aspects at once, though we can in the Baldwin passage, as integrated features of a single scene. Closing one eye, the scene, while not static, hardens and clarifies into what seem to be the cold facts, the way things are and have been and are becoming, and that is all.[1] If we change eyes, closing the first, the scene may be anything but clear, hardly a single scene at all, yet now it is good. If we walk like this, with only this eye open, we will hit walls and fall over cliffs. But on the first view there was no pull at all, nowhere to go and nothing admired or lamented, just a passing indifferent scene. The difficulty in keeping both eyes open may be that then we see not just the real facts and forces—or at least seem to—and also much beauty, but also real deficiency, even tragedy. Of course, our eyes can deceive us—that goes for each, and both, eyes. Even if this visual metaphor has some resonance, that is no proof that our eyes are onto something.

In an oft-quoted early reference to nonideal theory, Aristotle writes, "The best is often unattainable, and therefore the true legislator and statesman ought to be acquainted, not only with that which is best in the abstract, but also with that which is best relatively to circumstances."[2] It expresses a stereoscopic view, taking the value of understanding the unattainable best almost for granted before insisting that realistic nonideal thought that concedes injustice and works from there is also important. It seems sometimes to be read as a corrective to some previous thinkers, Plato perhaps, who may seem to neglect the realistic in their focus on the ideal. But Plato wrote in the Laws that,

> [C]alculation and experience suggests that the city we are founding will not be absolutely the best possible. And you might be inclined to reject this second-best city, if your only experience is of law givers with tyrannical powers. . . . [T]he number one city and political system, and the best laws, are those where . . . every possible contrivance has been used to bring about the total eradication of what is called private from every corner of our life. . . . A city of that kind—I don't know if its inhabitants are gods or a number of sons of Gods. . . . The one we have made a start on today, . . . would come second in terms of unity.[3]

It is no surprise about Plato that his idea of the best city strikes us as highly idealistic. But in almost the same breath he says how obvious it is to anyone using both "calculation and experience" that this is not the city that is to be constructed. Is Plato a realist or an idealist? Is there any divide here between him and Aristotle? Or do we have less than a clear understanding of what the question is?

This aspiration to the stereoscopic is not an artifact of an academic philosophical bent. I think many can recognize Baldwin's unease when he writes, elsewhere, "It began to seem that one would have to hold in the mind forever two ideas which seemed to be in opposition. The first idea was acceptance, the acceptance, totally without rancor, of life as it is, and men as they are: in the light of this idea, it goes without saying that injustice is a commonplace. But this did not mean that one could be complacent, for the second idea was of equal power: that one must never, in one's own life, accept these injustices as commonplace but must fight them with all one's strength."[4]

There is really very little one-eyed political philosophy. No one, not even Plato, recommends moving ahead without a clear eye on all the facts that can help us, though that missing faction nevertheless has vociferous opponents. And not even Machiavelli denies that how we ought to live is very different from how we do live.[5] Nor do many hold (though some seem to, as we will see) that no way forward is really any better or worse than any other. We mostly struggle to pull these together in an integrated perspective. Even then, one possible theoretical task is exploring only paths we might actually follow. A different task is to look beyond the space we might inhabit, and try to see things more broadly, but still aright. Partisans of those different projects sometimes seem incredulous about each other, which suggests that there may be, as I think there are, some misunderstandings between them. I hope this conveys, in a general way, the topics that come in for a closer look in the chapters to follow.

This book is not devoted to pressing practical matters, but to a large methodological issue about normative political philosophy and theory: whether—to put it roughly—theories of such things as justice are incorrect, or are in some way a failure, if there is no realistic expectation of justice, as understood by the theory, being achieved. Many whose work gravitates to more practically pressing issues have, nevertheless, often taken some time out for this less practical question, if only to endorse an anti-idealist methodological position. I sense, then, that the question is important to many of them, as it is to me.

A different way of opposing idealist political theory is to hold not that such theories must be mistaken, but that there is little value in determining what is correct or mistaken on such practically remote matters. Questions about the value of intellectual work in practical and nonpractical settings are difficult, and I turn to them in the book's final part. I mention the question of the value of ideal theory not to take a position here, but mainly to draw a bright circle around the distinction between the value issue and the correctness issue. This is the difference between, on one hand, denying that some line of inquiry is valuable or a good use of time or resources, and on the other hand, having substantial reasons or arguments that cast doubt on the arguments and conclusions of the work in question. Some will think that studying the correctness issue lacks value and is not worth the time, but in that case it is worth noting that, having chosen not to spend the time, they do not claim to have developed opposing arguments.

There is a different line of critique yet, which says not that idealistic theory is mistaken, nor that it is of no value, but that there is too much of it. Many authors have argued that the field of political philosophy is dominated by ideal theory, and that is their complaint—not ideal theory itself. It is hard to see how, for sure, to confirm or disprove that charge, though it is not clearly confirmed by scanning the issues of prominent journals in the last several decades. Rawls, who defends and does a certain kind of ideal theory (and coined the term), has been extraordinarily influential, though, of course, a large fraction of the flood of work that revolves significantly around his is highly critical, and partly on this very point. Of course, if one thinks ideal theory is worthless, then perhaps any is too much. In any case, work, such as G. A. Cohen's, this book, and most other work that defends ideal theory, is not taking any stand on whether the fraction of published political philosophy devoted to ideal theory is proper or not, any more than defending political philosophy or theory in general takes any stand on whether there is enough or too much of it compared to other activities.

Of course, even if ideal theory is not as dominant as sometimes claimed, there may yet be strong reasons for a larger fraction of political philosophy to be more directly relevant to political practice. Certainly, there ought to be plenty of such work, though how big a fraction would be big enough is, I would think, a hard question for anyone. Insofar as one believes that political events, now or at any time, so urgently call for practical attention that philosophers ought to focus predominantly, or far more than they do, on directly practical theoretical work, it is difficult to see why someone with that view should not also turn away from political philosophy and theory altogether in order to devote their time to doing some, or more, hands-on, non-scholarly work in the social and political world. Most of us could make a bigger and better practical difference in that way—the exceptions are rare. In spite of that, defenders of nonideal political theory and I agree that what *they* do is valuable, certainly justifiable. No one is against nonideal theory, but some seem to think nothing else is worthwhile—and it is a legitimate question. A further difficult question, notoriously, is what grounds such judgments, and how the urgent call of ubiquitous human victimization and suffering does not trump the value of a career spent doing nonideal theory (almost) as much as one spent doing ideal theory. I do not say there is no answer, but I am not aware of a compelling principle that draws the line precisely in that small gap—the place friendly only to nonideal scholarly academic political theory and philosophy. We know how hard the questions are about what could justify all the parts of our lives that are far less good for others than the things we might do instead. I attempt no theoretical defense (nor critique) of careers of philosophers or political theorists, or for our many colleagues in the various fields of a university whose work is not as directly helpful to the world as things they could easily do instead, much less of jewelry makers or realtors.[6] I wonder, simply, whether we might be boatmates. However, I also do not dismiss such questions, but take up the question of the value of unrealistic political theory in several ways in Part 5. For now, I conclude this brief treatment of the topic by expressing the hope that even readers who believe that my main theses are mistaken may find some of the arguments sufficiently challenging that our mutual engagement with these issues might seem to them a worthy, or justified, use of our time and talent (such as it is). The aim of these reflections is less a defense against critics of "ideal theory," and more an invitation to join what might not be recognized initially as an inquiry of mutual interest. At least in many cases, their critique appears to manifest their interest.

A smaller point about method: I normally hesitate to revert to formalism, for example, the use of such deviations from normal prose as single-letter variables and special characters like →. With some effort it is often possible to be just as precise and also more transparent to a broader readership with regular language. Not always, of course, and some important topics are fruitfully tackled with highly technical methods. Flipping through the book will show that there is a certain amount of formalism, but upon reading I hope it becomes clear that it is very basic and does not depend on any familiarity with formal logic or decision theory, or any other fully developed formal systems—something that varies greatly across disciplines such as philosophy and political science as well as their subfields. The aim is to be more easily and clearly understood than I could otherwise be, not less. While some respond to formalism as if it purports to be especially "rigorous," hardened and unbreakable, I make no such claim. In my view, the value of such "rigor" is that the brittleness of the arguments might be more obvious, allowing us to see more clearly when and where they will break, if they will. It is a more exposed method, if done well, than the use of elegant natural language, though that also has undeniable value by conveying context and significance of the ideas at hand. Also, in a less technical attempt to keep the arguments and claims understandable, certain terms that occur frequently, such as "Build" and "Comply," will be capitalized for easy visual scanning of the logical structure of the propositions in question.

It bears remarking that perhaps the most frequently used phrase throughout the book is "for the sake of argument." That can be frustrating to a reader, who will often wonder why the other cards are being kept close to the breast. But, of course, it is often a crucial step in making as precise as possible which question is under discussion and which questions are not. The remarkable frequency with which this phrase arises in the book suggests that, at least as I am approaching the topic, ways in which these issues are or might naturally be discussed are prone to conflate distinct questions at many points. If that is so, there will be value in pulling them apart. The other, perhaps unfortunate, side of this is that the reader is encouraged to keep track of how these repeated disambiguations may narrow the scope of what I am arguing for. On the upside from my point of view, this narrowed ambition might make it easier for the reader to be persuaded.

Acknowledgments

The book has about tripled in size from its initial conception. This is not mainly because it is wordy (I hope it is not), but because one issue led to another in ways I could not ignore. As some consolation, I have in several places briefly explained the topic of a chapter at its outset in order to alert readers who, given their own interests, may wish to skip those parts.

No chapter here is a verbatim reproduction of any of my published papers, but passages and ideas are drawn, with kind permission, from the following published pieces:

"Human Nature and the Limits (If Any) of Political Philosophy," in *Philosophy & Public Affairs*, 39, no. 3 (2011): 207–37.
"Utopophobia," *Philosophy & Public Affairs* (Spring 2014): 113–34.
"What's Circumstantial About Justice?" in special issue, *Social Philosophy and Policy*, 33, nos. 1 & 2, double issue (Winter 2016).
"Just and Juster," *Oxford Studies in Political Philosophy, Volume 2* (Oxford: Oxford University Press, 2016).

"G. A. Cohen's Critique of the Original Position," in *The Original Position*, ed. Timothy Hinton (Cambridge: Cambridge University Press 2016).
"Methodological Moralism in Political Philosophy," *Critical Review of International Social and Political Philosophy*, 20, no. 3 (2017): 365–379.
"Prime Justice," in *Political Utopias*, ed. Kevin Vallier and Michael Weber (Oxford: Oxford University Press 2017).

I have worked on this book for about ten years, which included four workshops on drafts in progress, and dozens of departmental colloquia, conference talks, visiting stints, public lectures, and formative conversations: I will not try to name all the hosts and interlocutors to whom I owe a debt of gratitude for the attention and interest, and all the questions, suggestions, criticism, and encouragement. I do want to thank the sponsors and commentators from the manuscript workshops: Workshop at the Philosophy Department in the Research School of the Social Sciences at Australian National University, July, 2014. Commentators: Christian Barry, Geoff Brennan, Cecile Fabre, Pablo Gilabert, Holly Lawford-Smith, Massimo Renzo, Nic Southwood, Laura Valentini, David Wiens. Workshop at Brown University, February, 2015, co-sponsored by the Philosophy Department and the Political Theory Project. Commentators: Jerry Gaus, Charles Larmore, Zofia Stemplowska (by video). Workshop at the Philosophy Department, University of Warwick, February, 2016: Dan Halliday, Fabienne Peter, Hwa Young Kim, Stephanie Collins, Tom Parr. Workshop at Goethe University Frankfurt, June, 2017, Co-Hosted by the Department of Philosophy and the Center for Advanced Studies, and "Justitia Amplificata." Commentators: Sara Amighetti, Stefano Bertea, Claudia Blöser, Jochen Bojanowski, Eva Buddeberg, Julian Culp, Rainer Forst, Alon Harel, Philipp Schink, Achim Vesper.

I am also grateful for a semester-long fellowship at Brown's Cogut Center for the Humanities in the Fall of 2014, and for a sabbatical leave from Brown in Fall 2017. Thanks to Chad Marxen and Kirun Sankaran for editing help with the draft; Matthew Adams for comments on a late draft; Leif Wenar for, in addition to encouragement, a probing exchange about the nature and point of political philosophy, to be continued; Nic Southwood for close engagement with my arguments throughout their development; Alison McQueen for helpful conversations and correspondence, especially about political realism.

For fifteen years I have had the privilege of sharing a weekly meal and conversation with Nomy Arpaly, often about our respective philosophical work in progress. The philosophical benefits for me have been great, but no greater than the laughs and encouragement along the way.

In 2009, Jerry Cohen had generously accepted the press's invitation to review the initial book proposal, which would have reached him the very day he died. The influence of his ground-breaking book, *Rescuing Justice and Equality*, will be apparent throughout, even if the line of argument here is rather different. I am grateful for having had the chance to talk with him about early versions of these ideas. But I'm grateful to Jerry most of all for the springboard of his egalitarian engagement with and encouragement of the fledgling criticisms of an undergraduate at Wisconsin.

I believe my urge to delve into these issues has stemmed, ultimately, from the patient methodological conversations that have arisen from time to time over many years in Brown's Political Philosophy Workshop. Philosophers and political theorists, both local and invited, have (among many other things) constructively scrutinized some of our deepest assumptions about the nature and value of normative theorizing about the political. I am fortunate to have the colleagues in political thought I do at Brown. Some are newer and I am just getting to know them (including Bonnie Honig, Juliet Hooker, and Melvin Rogers) but I have benefited for years from getting to engage with Corey Brettschneider, Stephen Bush, Mark Cladis, Alex Gourevitch, Paul Guyer, Nancy Khalek, Charles Larmore, Sharon Krause, Tal Lewis, and John Tomasi, as well as the students, postdocs, and visiting scholars who have regularly gathered around our table in the Lownes room for an intensive and interdisciplinary Thursday afternoon and evening.

At Princeton University Press I wish to thank Rob Tempio, Matt Rohal, and Kathleen Cioffi for their guidance and patience. And, finally, despite its best efforts this book has not consumed me. For this I'm especially grateful for all the loving adventures with my children, to whom I have dedicated this volume.

PART I

Looking Up to Justice

CHAPTER ONE

An Unrealistic Introduction

They were Utopians, which meant that they saw imperfection everywhere they looked.

—MICHAEL CHABON, *THE YIDDISH POLICEMEN'S UNION*

I BEGIN WITH SOME METHODOLOGICAL remarks and introduce a methodological project. The aim of this preface is to locate the book's motivating concerns in the context of traditional and contemporary political philosophy. (In a more impressionistic way, this is also one of the purposes of the diverse epigraphs at the head of each chapter.) Then, in the next chapter, I provide a substantive overview of many of the main issues and lines of argument in the book, which might help the reader to see in advance how the various parts are to fit together. In the remaining two chapters of Part 1, I confront the important underlying issues about "moralism" in political philosophy, and about the supposedly anti-idealistic implications of the "circumstances of justice" as understood especially in Hume and Rawls.

1. Being Realistic, and the Alternatives

Imperfection is everywhere, and it doesn't take a utopian to see that. Indeed, critics of "utopian" approaches to political philosophy are often emphatic about the robustness of human moral deficiency. In that realistic unromantic spirit, the guiding question of this book is whether people might also be robustly politically deficient (at least in principle—I do not take up the question whether we actually are or not). Political "realists" and others often say, in effect, "no." They reject the cogency of unrealistic standards for evaluating political arrangements, and that would settle, by a kind of conceptual fiat, that humans (in all their moral deficiency) do not robustly fall short politically.[1]

Standards, then, are either bent to fit—and thereby to condone?—our political proclivities whatever they might be (at least if they are robust), or perhaps standards for politics are eschewed altogether. Either way, the possibilities for critique of human political life are, with questionable reason, curtailed. My aim here is not to engage in a sweeping political critique drawing on high standards, but to resist this and related lines of argument that would foreclose it. The issues to be treated here are of more than academic interest. When I was a teenager in the 1970s my father, like many parents I suppose, would say, "You're an idealist; I'm a realist." Many people even outside academic debates have strong views and deep questions about what it would mean to put idealism and realism about politics in their proper places. Stated very broadly, that is my question.

I hasten to point out that the approach taken here is, in one fundamental sense, realistic—though it is too late to reclaim the term "realism" for this usage—in refusing to foreclose, prior to substantive investigation, the possibility that human societies might be prone (maybe even for deep human motivational reasons) to being significantly unjust, possibly even forever. Let us hope that is not true, and I don't say that it is. But the conception of political philosophy or theory that rules it out by assumption or definition will be scrutinized and rejected here, and the alternative approach that allows unrealistic standards will be developed and explored in several ways.

The argument to come is not a defense, nor is it a critique, of any particular conception of what justice requires. The guiding idea is rather, roughly stated, that an account that requires more than we ever expect to achieve is not thereby in the least flawed, even if it is not everything worth having. Whether anyone ought to set out for justice given pessimistic prospects is a separate matter; futility is plausibly a defect in a practical project.[2] A second theme, then, is that the connection between sound political philosophy and guidance for political practice has often been exaggerated, and not just in recent times.

In the later parts of the book, I consider the difficult question of what value there might be in understanding the nature of justice, including its having unrealistic aspects—or the value of exploring what unrealistic justice might require either in detail or in broad principle. That is a different issue, and I don't explore it in this work. Debates about the value of engaging in a certain inquiry bear little on the question of what is learned or not learned, be it valuable or not, in their pursuit. Whether or not such inquiries are valuable, as I will argue, in passing, that they are, is a wholly separate question from whether arguments encountered in such work, including arguments in this book, are successful.

There is a proverbial tension between the best and the good, and we are advised to avoid their becoming enemies, even perhaps by ignoring the best altogether. This is just one of the ways in which it has become customary for political philosophers to urge each other to keep their feet on the ground and eyes straight ahead—or, more accurately, slightly lowered. There is important work to be done right here and now—work in the social world, that is. And according to this eyes-lowered approach, the work we do as thinkers, as philosophers, ought to serve the most urgent practical tasks we see around us.

There are two parts to this view: our philosophical work ought (only?) to serve practical purposes, and then, additionally, it ought (only or mainly?) to serve the practical purposes presented to us here and now. This practicalist outlook is not universally shared, of course, and I am one of those who does not accept it. Rather than attempt to refute this thesis about how philosophers ought to spend their time, I will mostly ignore that question until Part 5. My principal objective is to defend some unfamiliar, if not novel, claims about the nature (not the content) of social justice.

We are told, by Machiavelli and others, that, in effect, political philosophy must not be utopian.[3] I am sure there is wisdom in this vague injunction, but there is also the danger of a chilling effect. Unless we are very clear about what kind of theorizing can appropriately be proscribed, there is the risk that a broader set of projects go unpursued, and for no good reason. Machiavelli says that theories of politics that describe things that have "never been seen or known to exist" could not be useful. He admits in the next breath, however, that there is "a great distance between how we live and how we ought to live." He admits, then, that it is one thing to ask what sort of thing we might write that will be "useful to anyone who understands,"[4] and quite another to ask how we ought to live. The two questions do not, even in Machiavelli, collapse into the useful, and so my project is, perhaps surprisingly, not at odds with his or those of various followers in that way.

Rousseau writes, in the Preface to *Emile*, " 'Propose what can be done,' they never stop repeating to me. It is as if I were told, 'Propose doing what is done.' "[5] Few writers believe that things are already, or are bound eventually to be, precisely as they ought to be, and so almost all normative political theory departs from "realism" in this strict sense. Any theory that implies criticism of actual institutions or behavior is not as realistic as it could be. For example, a normative framework that criticizes existing legal regulations on political advertising for being either too strict or too lax is not entirely maximally realistic. A theory that criticizes actual voters for being too selfish—or even too idealistic— departs from strict realism in exactly the same way. Since no one will insist on this extreme kind of realism in normative theory, we can safely give it a derogatory label: *complacent realism.*

On the other hand, there are surely ways in which normative political theory can be too morally idealized. It was Rousseau, again, who, in *The Social Contract*, influentially pledged to proceed by "taking men as they are, and laws as they might be." This sentiment is widely embraced even as its meaning is far from clear. When, for example, Rawls endorses the Rousseauian dictum, he interprets it as merely confining political philosophy within the laws of nature.[6] It is not made clear what those laws are, but they are held to allow, within those broad limits on what is "realistic," significant, even "utopian," extensions of our view of what is possible in human affairs. "Utopian," of course, is often (though not in Rawls) an epithet (its etymology suggests "no place at all") used to ridicule theories that are thought to violate some version of the

Rousseauian stricture—to be too unrealistic about people and their motivational nature. Rawls, whose concession to realism is no more than to limit his prescriptions to what is possible, however unlikely it might be, attempts to reclaim the term, speaking of his own "realistic utopianism."[7] I prefer to speak, less eloquently, of a noncomplacent and nonconcessive approach to social justice. A narrower constraint—to take people as they are, now, in their observed aims, conviction, and tendencies—is (if anyone were to recommend it) to set the bar indefensibly low for the investigation of principles of social justice. To charge a theory of justice with being "utopian" seems generally to imply that its standards are false because they are too unrealistic—still a vague charge, since there are various ways in which theories might fail to be sufficiently realistic. Utopophobia, we may say, is the unreasonable fear of the sin of utopianism, and it can lead to the marginalization of inquiries and insights without demonstrating any defect in them.

There are many cases where what we are required to do is conditioned by the fact that we do not live up to what is required of us in other areas. "Since you have stolen, you ought to apologize." "Since you will not put money away each month, you ought (prudentially) to set up an automated transfer." "Since we will not comply with socialist institutions in sufficient numbers, we ought not to build them." These are, indeed, requirements, but they are, in a certain way, not fundamental. They concede violations and ask what is required in that "concessive" context, as I shall call it. That is all I mean by a "concessive" principle or requirement: it is a requirement that is in place owing to our conceding certain violations of other requirements. Some requirements are in no way conditioned by violations in that way, such as the requirement (duly formulated) not to steal in the first place. That is nonconcessive. Much thought about social justice is in a concessive mode, taking people "as they are," or responding to the facts of human life, and so forth. There is nothing wrong with that, of course. But that is not fundamental in a certain way, since it may well be that those facts of human life themselves incorporate violations of requirements of morality or justice. There certainly are questions about what ought to be done conceding certain other violations. But there is also the nonconcessive kind of question: What ought I to do, morally, if I don't concede any moral violations on my part? So, in a formulation whose frequent appearance may tax the reader's patience, there is a fine concessive question about justice: Given the predictable violations by humans as we know them, including tendencies not to comply with certain things, what institutions ought we to build? But there is also the nonconcessive kind of question: What institutions ought we to build and comply with? The fact, if it is one, that we will not comply with those very institutions, opens up the concessive question, but is not responsive to the nonconcessive one.

While already familiar to Rousseau and Machiavelli, the debate about utopianism in moral and political philosophy continued in the late nineteenth century between, among others, the philosophers Henry Sidgwick and Herbert Spencer about the merits of Spencer's approach, in which individuals (and perhaps also social relations) were assumed, for certain philosophical purposes, to be morally perfect. For the most part, their dispute was about whether such a study would serve the pressing practical aim of determining what ought to be done under actual and decidedly nonideal conditions. Spencer argued in the affirmative, that the study of the ideal case was an essential step toward eventual understanding of real and more complicated moral conditions. This "first step" defense of highly idealized theory anticipates Rawls's suggestion that "ideal theory" is a crucial first step to systematically addressing nonideal theory. Rawls famously—perhaps notoriously—wrote:

> Obviously the problems of partial compliance theory are the pressing and urgent matters. These are the things that we are faced with in everyday life. The reason for beginning with ideal theory is that it provides, I believe, the only basis for the systematic grasp of these more pressing problems. . . . I shall assume that a deeper understanding can be gained in no other way, and that the nature and aims of a perfectly just society is the fundamental part of the theory of justice.[8]

Spencer used analogies from mathematics, mechanics, and astronomy to argue that understanding the real and imperfect cases would be impossible without first understanding idealized and pure cases of circles, straight lines, perfectly rigid levers, and so on. He wrote, "[T]he philosophical moralist . . . determines the properties of the straight man; describes how the straight man comports himself; shows in what relationship he stands to other straight men; shows how a community of straight men is constituted."[9] Spencer and Rawls make this *priority claim*: sound understanding of what is required in realistic nonideal conditions is severely constrained without a prior sound understanding of the requirements under conditions of full compliance. This has met with voluminous criticism. At least as I have stated it, the claim is not that there is no point in undertaking nonideal inquiry until ideal theory is understood, but it asserts more than I will argue for (in the book's last part), which is only (and yet this is disputed, as I have said) that both have significant value.

Sidgwick objected that not only is it beyond our grasp to ascertain what the content of moral rules would be in such a fantastical scenario,[10] but even if we could know that much, it is far from clear that such knowledge would be of any practical value with respect to the question of what we ought to do in the very different actual conditions we are bound to find ourselves in. Sidgwick frankly embraced the conservatism this entails, the implication that the appropriate form of society, as far as we can know, will then turn out to be "one varying but little from the actual, with its actually established code of moral rules and customary judgments concerning virtue and vice."[11] (Neither Rawls nor

Sidgwick is known for reckless flights of conjecture, but they could hardly be more different on this question.)

Neither Sidgwick nor Spencer made much effort either to ascertain the content of such moral rules, or to investigate (rather than declare) whether there would be valuable things of a less practical nature to learn from such a project. They were mostly focused on the question of the practical usefulness of proceeding in one way or the other. Only in passing did Spencer bother to mention his belief that the requirements applicable to ideal agents are *true*.[12] The question is of at least philosophical interest: whether the more realistic approach favored by Sidgwick and so many others deserves to be seen as the method by which to understand the *truth* about moral standards, including those of social justice. Famously, it would be comical to look for one's dropped car keys far from where they surely lie simply because the light is better there. What we cannot clearly see (supposing that were true of full justice) is not for that reason unreal.

As I say, the term "utopian" is sometimes, though not always, a term of abuse, and it will be here. In 1848 Marx and Engels introduced the term "utopian socialism" in *The Communist Manifesto* to chastise certain "unscientific" forms of socialist thought: roughly, those that (a) presented what are often called "blueprints" for the institutional structure of the highest form of socialism, but (b) supplied no basis in the predictable course of history for seeing how the envisaged arrangements might ever come about.[13] Certainly, hesitation about what we might call ungrounded blueprints has a lot to be said for it. That issue is more substantial than whether the oft-ridiculed extravagances of some utopian writers are indeed ridiculous, such as those of Fourier, who argued:

> When . . . the globe shall be duly organized, and have a population of three thousand millions, it will contain, commonly, thirty-seven millions of poets equal to Homer, thirty-seven millions of astronomers equal to Newton, thirty-seven millions of dramatists equal to Molière, and so on with all imaginable talents. (These, of course, are only proximate calculations.)[14]

Fourier is just one example of a utopian thinker, but a fecund one. In addition to his bizarre predictive calculations, we also get from him obsessively detailed blueprints for the ideal society, including floor plans, work schedules, and much else. The difficulty here is not their being out of reach—there is no patent impossibility in gathering eighteen hundred diverse people to live and work in a vast edifice, and so on, as he proposes. Nor is there a clear moral objection, since he does not propose to assemble them by force. What is troubling about his specificity is partly that we cannot ascertain enough from our profoundly dissimilar standpoint to know which highly specific arrangements would facilitate the fulfillment of plausible principles of justice and promotion of welfare. Very likely, the minute details need to be left to judgment that could be informed by the whole empirical context as well as by good principles (which would themselves plausibly be refined in the light of experience). A second concern about detailed utopian blueprints is that they might illegitimately bypass the moral necessity, or so it will often be thought, for arrangements to be determined in certain ways by those who will be subject to them. Granted, a blueprint could serve as one proposal to be entered into democratic deliberation, and this latter concern would be mitigated in that case, though the former would remain.

It might be argued that in light of those sources of indeterminacy there is really nothing at all to be said about what standards must be met by basic social structures. But the points made so far tend to block that possibility. For example, we have already conjectured that there is some requirement of democracy or responsiveness. Regardless of the form that requirement takes, it sets at least one standard. Also, we observed that such indeterminacy results from the wide variety of possible fact sets, which are hard to know in advance. That implies that given a single fact set, at least some requirements (or a much-narrowed range of requirements) would indeed be the applicable ones. This in turn suggests that there are principles according to which a fact set narrows the range of requirements. The actual variety of facts across societies and over time is not, on this ground, any obstacle to formulating the principles (fallibly, of course).

For my own part, as I say, I am not going so far as to offer any particular account of principles of justice, much less institutional specifics, since my point is higher order—methodological and metanormative. I also argue that while it is by no means guaranteed that sound principles of substantive social justice would turn out to be wildly unrealistic, it would not count against them if they did (see chapter 10: "Prime Justice"). I also grant that Marx and Engels might also have meant to criticize the very general idea of critical standards by which current arrangements might be evaluated. But even if so, they unfortunately do not offer any argument that such standards are flawed, or impossible to know, or that they have no value, in the way they do suggest some formidable arguments against ungrounded utopian blueprints. None of the above arguments for the limited, or negative value of detailed blueprints takes aim at *general principles of justice* on the ground that they are unrealistic. So far, then, an account including principles of full social justice, so long as it does not presume to fix too much institutional detail, and so long as it is not presented to activists, vanguards, or governments as a practical proposal, is free of the mentioned vices. For these reasons, when recent critics of "ideal theory" target authors who "build Utopias" (in theory, they mean), they risk stalking a straw philosopher. However unrealistic they might (or might not) be, conceptions of justice such as those of Cohen or Rawls do not presume to fix institutional details with any precision.[15] To say that they are building Utopias may misleadingly imply the kind of fictional world building, with blueprints and details, that has sometimes been seen in utopian writers from previous centuries. There is certainly "ideal theory" being done, in various senses, and there are things to scrutinize about such approaches, but "Utopia building" has been mostly absent from the scene of prominent political philosophy for many decades, perhaps a century.

The concern, often attributed to Marx and Engels, regarding the absence of a plausible causal or historical account of how the high standards might come to be met does not have any clear force on its own. It may be a serious problem in the context of an institutional blueprint that is urged as a practical proposal—a goal to set out for. Leaving aside the pitfall of excessive detail, it is indeed often reckless to set out for an attractive goal when there is no adequate understanding of what path might lead there[16] (though even here such a constraint can take overly fastidious forms), but it is important to stay mindful of the difference (introduced above) between principles and practical proposals.

Suppose we are hiking, and we spy a beautiful spot some miles off, down the slope, across the valley. It isn't just beautiful, it looks like a great place to stay, or even to live. Alas, it is not yet clear whether we can get there, so we might try to contain our excitement. Be realistic. Things are fine where we are, so we could just conclude that the new spot is not really worth considering. It is unrealistic in one way simply because it is not where we are, but this complacent realism has little appeal, as we have seen. If we admit that the new spot is beautiful, we might nevertheless come to conclude that it is impossible to get there. (As I proceed, let the scenery change from a pastoral landscape to the space of political alternatives.) If we cannot get there, then there is no sense in worrying too much about the different routes we could try. Alternatively, we might think that it is possible to get there, or might be for all we know, but, realistically, we *will not* get there because we are likely to make careless navigational errors, or eventually just to give up prematurely. This differs from our being unable, but it is still practically important. However, if we are not sure that it is beyond our abilities, then even if we are unlikely to get there, it could be worth thinking about how we might. This is not yet the same as recommending that we set out for it. That would be a different and later question. Perhaps the slim chances of success will give us sufficient reason to make other plans. But why jump to that conclusion? After all, the place is beautiful, and for all we can tell getting there is not beyond our abilities. In a way, this little story emphasizes hope, where the question about what role there might still be for hopeless (but not impossible) standards remains open. It suggests that we should, to some cautious extent, relax about the line between hopeful and hopeless standards in a spirit of hope. I accept this.[17]

AN UNREALISTIC INTRODUCTION   [11]

We are reminded here that something might be a desirable destination—it might even be one that differs from alternative, unacceptable destinations in being at least *acceptable* in certain respects, even if we ought not to set out for it. In the pastoral example, if the obstacle is a chasm that makes our progress impossible then the desirability of the destination is not action guiding. In the political cases I am concentrating on, however, where the obstacle is the fact that certain things will not be done even though they could be done, then the imperative to do those things and get to the destination is action guiding in an important sense—our tendency, however robust, not to set out and carry through is powerless as a refutation of the requirement (here, a requirement of prudence or rationality, perhaps) to do so.

Just a few years before Marx and Engels, Bentham listed the term "Utopian" in his *The Book of Fallacies* (with a fairly similar meaning):

> As to the epithet Utopian, the case to which it is rightly applied seems to be that to which, in the event of the adoption of the proposed plan, felicitous effects are represented as about to take place, no causes adequate to the production of such effects being to be found in it.[18]

I will follow these classic thinkers (thereby departing from Rawls's usage) in using "utopian" as an epithet, which refers to a vice, sin, or defect, and I follow them more or less in its definition as well: in my usage of the term, a social proposal has the vice of being utopian if, roughly, there is no evident basis for believing that efforts to stably achieve it would have any significant tendency to succeed. The argument of this book is *not* a defense of proposals that are utopian—unrealistic in the stated way. Oversimplifying a little for now, this is because the arguments here are not in defense of proposals at all, but of principles (or standards, or requirements—as you prefer) of justice. Irrealism (the property of being unrealistic) is a vice of proposals, but not a vice of principles, and so while this book is no defense of anything utopian in the narrow sense I adopt here, it is a defense of unrealistic principles of justice—not of any highly specific principles (much less of any practical proposals)—but as a counter to the charge that irrealism is a defect of such principles.

I stated that this oversimplifies matters somewhat for the following reason. It may seem that what I have called nonconcessive institutional principles must count as utopian *proposals* in the above sense.[19] In fact, however, they do not, since what they require are conditions such that, should the relevant set of agents all set out for them, they would indeed have a sufficient (not to say strong) tendency to succeed. Of course, such a prescription addressed to the complete set of members is not a proposal aimed at any subset of them, such as governments or activists.[20] *Their*—the subset's—setting out for it might, given the actual behavior of others, have an insufficient chance of success, and it would be inappropriate on that basis for it to be either proposed or required. But, formulating this carefully now: nonconcessive principles only issue requirements to agents or sets of agents that would tend to be successfully met if the agents were to try and not give up. I assume, for the sake of argument, that there is no requirement unless there is ability.[21] So nonconcessive requirements do not suffer from the vice of being utopian under the definition adopted here, a vice that only practical proposals can have. Insofar as they are unrealistic, the requirements I discuss are not proposals but principles. Insofar as they call for action, they are not unrealistic. To have a handy formulation, we might say that the sin of utopianism attaches to *unrealistically optimistic proposals*. In the case of principles, by contrast, there is no sin in being unrealistic, and so principles, as such, cannot possess the defect of being utopian. This might seem like mere semantics, but that would be unfair. The important and non-terminological point underlying this adopted usage is this: being unrealistic is not a defect in a principle of justice, though it would be in a proposal.

2. Human Nature

Kant was probably correct[22] that since (or at least partly because) we humans are flawed morally and in other ways—our timber is crooked—there will never be a fully just society.[23] Approximate justice would be a very good thing—approximately a great thing—but it is dangerous to assume that approximating a constitutional and institutional framework for a perfectly just society would approximate justice. Without the motives and behaviors for which the framework is designed, it might be a disaster.[24] What arrangements we should build or promote given that we will not be a just society (domestically or globally) will always be a pressing question, and a sound understanding of full justice might or might not be of any use at all for that purpose. If some such normative outlook is of no such use it might lose its grip on us, of course. We might begin to think the whole idea of social justice is a philosophically bankrupt vestige of, say, Christian ideas which claim that we humans are, through our own fault, and yet inevitably, moral failures. This might now seem to be an inhumane, otherworldly, impossibly straight imaginary line by which to measure social life. Such a test might seem inappropriate if we are sure to fail. We might wonder whether a more adequate view would show that we are not inevitably defective after all. One way of pursuing that project would take our bent, the human bent, to constrain the shape of moral standards. It would lash the moral standards for politics (if not for all agency) to the serpentine shape of real (not to say fixed or unchangeable) human proclivities. On that view, Kant erred in imagining some straight alien standards by which we appear to be crooked. By philosophical fiat, instead, our timber no longer counts as crooked. It does not, after all, deviate from supposedly appropriate evaluative standards, and is in that sense, straight—nondivergent—after all. In a helpful pun, I will argue that this Bent View of social justice—is indefensible.

The Bent View
Standards of justice are shaped in order to ensure that people could, at least in due course and without oppressive control, bring themselves to behave in ways such that justice is achieved.

I defend the Unbent View: there is no adequate argument that the content of justice ought to defer to our proclivities (now and as they might vary across time and context) as in the Bent View.

3. Justice and Basic Social Structure

Before turning to an overview of the book's arguments in the next chapter, I conclude this introduction with a few remarks about how I will understand the idea of social justice for present purposes. It may be helpful to briefly situate my approach to that idea with respect to important recent approaches of Rawls, Sen, and Cohen. My thesis in this book is, as I have emphasized, only indirectly about social justice itself. It is more directly methodological—about how we are to think or theorize about justice—how "realistic" we need or needn't be. Still, social justice is central to my concerns in that way. I will carry no brief for or against egalitarian, Rawlsian, liberal, free-market, global, etc. accounts of the content of social justice. This rough neutrality ought to avoid misleading readers into thinking any of my points are meant either to be supported by, or to lend support to, or to be refuted by, certain positions in these debates. That would distract from what I take my arguments really to be.

In some theories of social justice, it might be said that it is not the basic social structure but something else that is up for evaluation, such as whether the sum of utility is maximized, or certain individual outcomes are equalized, or people's holdings are owed to morally permissible acquisition and transfer, and so on. We might say, on the other hand, that such theories do not really evaluate the entire society as just or unjust, but only certain of its distributions or historical trajectories, though this semantic quibble hardly carries much weight against such approaches. Alternatively, such theories, or closely related ones, might evaluate a society itself as just or unjust according to whether it is institutionally arranged (perhaps dynamically) so as to facilitate or promote satisfaction of the preferred principle. At any rate, that is the form in which my assumption that justice is about the basic social structure will accommodate friends of those principles. The emphasis on basic structure is a distinctive feature of Rawls's approach, and this indirect role for principles applying to outcomes (especially the Difference Principle) also characterizes his view. Admittedly, this emphasis on social structure does not accommodate views according to which a society is itself just only insofar as some such principle—such as a principle of equally distributed wealth or opportunity—is actually met, regardless of anything else about social structure. Consequently, my approach is not entirely neutral as far as different normative theories of justice are concerned.

The focus on social structure as the subject of justice is more than a trivial simplifying device, since it fits with my treatment of social justice as a requirement over actions (in a plural fashion)—so long as the basic structure of a society ultimately just consists of certain patterns and orientations of action. In that respect, it is indeed a distinctive way of framing the issue, and so, as I say, not entirely neutral as between different normative approaches. Still, it is more a formal methodological feature than it is a normative commitment, even if it is not wholly non-normative. It does not side for or against any particular principles the promotion of which is the test of the basic structure, from the standpoint of social justice. The principles could be utilitarian, egalitarian, libertarian, or many others. Having said all this, I suspect that little of what I say will run afoul of this lack of complete generality in any important way.

I will assume that for a society to be just is for its basic structure to be the way it ought to be in certain respects. So, the "subject of justice" is the basic social structure, following Rawls. As understood here, the basic social structure is partly constituted by certain prevalent attitudes, motivations, and patterns of behavior even including many patterns of behavior not significantly associated with law or government.[25] It will not be necessary to have a precise account of what exactly constitutes the basic structure. Instead, I will take up questions of that kind as they arise.

G. A. Cohen lets the "subject of justice," that which is just or unjust by standards of social justice, include individual behavior, but strongly resists counting such behavior as part of the basic structure. So there are two questions: How capacious is the basic structure?[26] Is the subject of justice still something broader than the basic structure properly construed? I prefer to think of institutional structure in terms of patterns and motives of behavior rather than something else which somehow constrains all behavior. So when Cohen insists that certain aspects of behavior in the family or in the market are within the purview of standards of justice, it is tempting to think that would be enough to show they are part of the basic structure. But he resists.[27] So there is a question whether some things that are not properly regarded as basic structure—even letting the idea of basic structure expand beyond merely coercive institutions—are nevertheless part of the "subject of justice." That is indeed how Cohen sees it, for example.

We can avoid some of the difficult associated questions in the following way: there is some content (possibly highly disjunctive) included in the requirements of justice, which can be fully met regardless of what motives or intentions anyone has with respect to justice. Some of it can, plausibly, be met by the very existence of certain institutions, though it might not all be institutional, some of it being perhaps purely distributional. Then there is a further achievement, which can either be built into the idea of full justice, or conceived as something in addition to justice, namely a society's being well-ordered, in Rawls's sense, by a sound conception of justice. (We could let the characterization "well-ordered" apply even when the shared conception is either false, or, alternatively, true but not actually satisfied, but when the relevant common knowledge, compliance, and motivation are present. It need not be claimed that there is any value in well-orderedness in that case, but only in the case where the society is indeed just as well.)

Notice that there must at least be some part of a standard of justice that makes no reference to justice-oriented motivations of the kind named in well-orderedness. Call this *thin justice*. Otherwise, there would be no coherent content available *for* such motivations. There is, additionally, a plausible dimension of social justice consisting in its being well-ordered—where it is common knowledge that all accept and are motivated to promote the satisfaction of a shared and sound conception of thin justice. Without well-orderedness, on the basis of thin justice alone, there is nothing that constitutes (or much less manifests) *respect or proper regard* for people, their interests, and their rights. People may be getting what they are owed, but not because it is owed to them (this is not the same as a "publicity" requirement). So it is reasonable to say that thin justice together with well-orderedness represents a fuller achievement of justice, which I will call *thick justice*.

Now, Cohen's points, even if correct, do not show that thin justice reaches beyond the basic institutional structure. They would show only that thick justice does. But this is obvious in the very idea of well-orderedness—it is the point of well-orderedness. It is hard to see how it is a critique—as Cohen says it is—of Rawls. Rawls says the subject of justice is the basic social structure, but he also (and seminally) insists that a full kind of social justice goes beyond this to certain motives and understandings that are not comprehended by institutions themselves. The subject of justice here must mean the subject of thin justice, which is then a determinate content that one can assume enters into people's motives when the question of thick justice is taken up.

So I will assume, following Rawls, that the question of the subject of social justice, as discussed in this work, is the question of thin justice—the basic institutional structure of society. There is room for broader or narrower views of what even this includes, since the idea of the institutional is far from perfectly clear. Then, regardless of how that might be settled, it can be allowed that a fuller, thick kind of justice depends not only on thin justice but also well-orderedness—the common knowledge of acceptance and compliance with a conception (or family of conceptions, as Rawls, sensibly, would have it) of thin justice.

4. Charles Mills on Ideal Theory

In a seminal article, "Ideal Theory as Ideology,"[28] Charles Mills criticizes what he calls "ideal theory" in moral and political philosophy in strong terms. Putting aside several other kinds of idealization, he focuses on "ideal as model": the development of models of morally good people and a just society. Ideal theory, so understood, is argued to "ignore" female subordination, centuries of white supremacy, and increasingly inequitable class society.[29] "Perform an operation of Brechtian defamiliarization, estrangement, on your cognition," he suggests. "Wouldn't your spontaneous reaction be: *How in God's name could anybody think that this is the appropriate way to do ethics?*"[30]

As I have said, in this book I do not propose any particular theory of justice, and so I cannot be accused of engaging in ideal theory in that way. On the other hand, I am obviously defending an approach to thought about justice that fits under that somewhat vague rubric. I argue that social justice might be best understood as a certain social-structural element of a sweeping moral requirement in which not only institutions, but also individual behavior, are rightful. And I argue in chapter 4 that the idea of circumstances of justice does not entail that such idealized scenarios are beyond the very idea of justice. In this section I want to suggest that the sorts of enterprise that I defend are not, despite natural appearances, bound to be targets of Mills's critique.

While Mills obviously objects to something he describes as "ideal theory," it is important to notice that he speaks without hesitation of ideals whose acceptance and realization would be desirable. He writes,

> A nonideal approach is also superior to an ideal approach in being better able to realize the ideals, by virtue of realistically recognizing the obstacles to their acceptance and implementation. . . . Summing it all up, then, one could say epigrammatically that the best way to bring about the ideal is by recognizing the nonideal, and that by assuming the ideal or the near-ideal, one is only guaranteeing the perpetuation of the nonideal.[31]

Mills, then, does not eschew the place of "ideals" in proper normative theory. Mills is not, I think, criticizing the very enterprise of seeking philosophical understanding of the criteria for a fully or ideally just society. None of his arguments appear to take that enterprise as their target. It is also no part of Mills's purpose in that piece to raise objections to the content of the ideal theory of justice that is his central example of an objectionably "ideal" theory, that of Rawls. We get no such normative objections, though he may well harbor them.

Instead, Mills emphasizes all that is *missing* from Rawls: the absence of any serious discussion of the glaring injustices around race, gender, poverty, and class, their ineluctable marks on our social relations and our thought, and questions about corrective justice.

In this light, we see that much of the argument is devoted to criticizing the academic *hegemony* of ideal theory in Anglophone philosophy. Mills is not so much criticizing thinking about full justice, as he is criticizing what he takes to be the dominant method of attempting to understand what full justice requires in a way that is entirely cordoned off from, and silent about, the real injustices before our eyes and the bearing they must undeniably have on how to understand people, institutions, and social structure accurately and perceptively. Understood in this fashion, Mills's critique may be best seen as a critique of a method, employed in the field as part of a collective enterprise, and maybe also in the works of any single theorist, that neglects the study of real social injustice. Among the many passages in the essay that fit this pattern, as mounting a critique of the neglect of nonideal theory, we read, "What distinguishes ideal theory is the reliance on idealization *to the exclusion, or at least marginalization*, of the actual."[32] And there are others.[33]

The way that political philosophy is damaged by the neglect of the real world including its injustices, is, according to Mills, that the very concepts with which theorists build their normative theoretical structures float free, untested by any attempt to use them in understanding and acting in societies and with people as they actually are, as known by, for example, our best historical, empirical, and explanatory theories—lumping these together, let's call this "social theory." Mills calls for political philosophy that is more continuous with empirically and historically informed social theory. Part of the contribution that philosophy might make to that nexus of enterprises, he argues, would be the identification of the concepts that best map social reality, and the incorporation of these reality-forged concepts into normative moral and political thought.

Now, in recommending a "nonideal approach,"[34] there may be a danger of insisting on an overly strong primacy of nonideal theory, the mirror image of the much criticized Rawlsian thesis of the primacy of ideal theory. Social theory that is philosophically unsophisticated about morality and justice is in danger of adopting concepts that fit some intuitive or culturally current ideas about justice that cannot be philosophically sustained. There is no such thing as starting with the project of first understanding how things actually work, to the exclusion of all else. Which things would you want to know about? Just anything? Marx, whose work is often pointed to as an example of that primacy, was plainly driven to his analyses of capitalism, among other things, partly by his moral disgust with the practices of early industrial times. Would the concept of exploitation of labor ever have occurred to him were it not for the fact that it seemed to be unjust in its taking advantage of the workers? A social theory *will* be informed by normative assumptions and commitments whether the latter are philosophically well considered or not.

In any case, Mills's line of argument need not, it seems to me, be burdened with that strong (reversed) doctrine of primacy. Its emphasis is on the impoverishment of political philosophy that is not adequately conversant with the most observant and injustice-attuned social theory. So the point is not only that there should be nonideal theory alongside ideal theory. It is that theorizing about ideal justice cannot be done well without fruitful formative engagement with social theory. The reverse might also be true, as I have suggested, though that is not Mills's emphasis.

To summarize Mills's critique of ideal theory: the field of political philosophy has, for no good reason, fixated on trying to understand full justice. The problem is that by neglecting to take any close look at real injustices—historical and ongoing—there is a strong likelihood, or at least a grave danger, that the very concepts philosophers bring to political thought are naïve, or distorted, or ideological, since they have never had to confront the stark realities of real injustice properly understood. A better set of concepts is bound to arise if there is more nonideal theory, and more engagement with it. Then, once the concepts are no longer so deficient, there may indeed be value in trying to deploy them in understating the requirements of full social justice. If this last proposition is available to the Mills perspective, as I believe it is, then there is nothing in this book with which it is inconsistent.[35]

5. Justice as Ingredient or Recipe

Theories of the justice of the basic social structure have a rather unclear stance on whether certain outcomes of the just structure, as distinct from the structure itself, are better or worse than others with respect to justice. On one hand, outcomes can be said to be just if and only if they were legitimate outcomes of a just social structure—a "pure procedural," or in Nozick's term, "historical," way of counting as just. On the other hand, it is often held that some outcomes, such as certain distributions of wealth or opportunity, ought to be aimed at or promoted by a basic social structure if that structure is to count as just. But why? If there is no difference with respect to justice between one outcome and another, so long as either one is produced by the right kind of procedure, why should the procedure aim at some outcomes but not others? Maybe it is on account of some value other than justice, such as efficiency, but this is not always what is going on. In Rawls's theory, of course, the distribution of primary social goods ought to be as good for the worst-off class as any alternative arrangement, so long as the prior principles are also met. But the difference principle is not a principle of efficiency. It is a principle of justice. But then there must be a difference, as a matter of, justice, between its being met and its not being met. Whether it is met is not settled by showing that the basic structure is aimed at meeting it, since it is assumed to be fallible. This shows, I think, that the pure procedural account of the "justice" of any outcome of a just basic structure does not really provide a full account of that theory if there are also principles of justice the procedure should aim to satisfy. It is a weaker standard than the one that is met by a distribution's *both* being produced by a just social structure and its meeting the difference principle, and other principles at whose satisfaction it is to be aimed. Of course, Rawls's theory is just an example that will be widely familiar, and nothing in my argument in this book depends on accepting Rawls's conception of justice. I make this distinction in order to emphasize that while I will conceive of the justice *of a society* as being about the basic structure, I intend to allow for distributions or other outcomes that a social structure ought to aim at or promote, and that these, as well as the basic structure itself, must be granted, in a sense, to admit of justice or injustice.

Even if we limit social justice to the basic social structure in this way, it might still be understood to be either a moral standard in which justice is an *ingredient*, one of a number of values which apply to the basic social structure that ought morally to be met according to some proper balance, or a *comprehensive* standard for the basic social structure (not "comprehensive" in the sense of Rawls's distinction between comprehensive and political conceptions of justice),[36] in which all the applicable values are met according to their appropriate balance. Sen conceives of social justice as a dimension that morally ranks alternatives that are faced in contexts of social choice, and so he is apparently conceiving of justice comprehensively.[37] After all, social choices ought to take due account of all applicable values, not just some of them. Cohen rejects that way of conceiving of justice because he believes that some of the values that ought to be taken into account in social choice are plainly not relevant to justice properly conceived.[38] The point is important to Cohen, since it plays a role in his critique of Rawls.[39] For now it is enough to note this distinction, and I do not need to choose sides. The distinction will come up a number of times, and I will just try to keep the terms sufficiently clear.

6. Compared to Cohen

There is a strong affinity between my approach and that of Cohen in that, for example, we both argue that it is no defect in a conception of social justice if it is, in certain ways, unrealistic. Pointing to this common ground omits important differences, however, and stating some of the differences here will help to avoid misunderstanding. First, Cohen holds that the fundamental truths about justice are in no way dependent on facts. I take no stand on this issue. I argue that it would not have the normative significance that Cohen seems to hope for in any case.[40] I do emphasize how truths about justice must not be concessive to certain kinds of *bad facts*, a view that differs from Cohen's, even if there are traces of it in some of his arguments.[41]

Second, Cohen holds that principles of justice (and morality generally) may perfectly well require things that are beyond the abilities of any agents individually or collectively. He finds it entirely comprehensible that it may not be possible to achieve justice. He is not quite rejecting the widely held axiom that 'ought implies can,' but insisting that something might be unjust even if remedying it is impossible, and might on that ground not be something that *ought* to be done. He holds that there are normatively more fundamental truths than ought claims if the latter depend on our abilities, namely, things we ought to do *if we can*.[42] This is, to my mind, an important suggestion that is worthy of more investigation, but I do not commit myself to it here. Since I consider justice to only be free from certain kinds of bad facts rather than from all facts, I am not led, as Cohen is, to confront the question whether it is even free from facts about what agents could do. As I have said, I allow, then, for the sake of argument, that nothing is a requirement of social justice that relevant agents are unable to do. It is a central theme of my argument that this is less of a brake on highly idealistic content than it is often taken to be, especially since many things that are taken to be inabilities—such as what we often describe as what an agent cannot bring himself to do—are not inabilities at all.

Third, while they might easily be conflated, Cohen's important distinction between principles of justice and rules of regulation is different from mine between concessive and nonconcessive principles. (Here I am presupposing some familiarity with Cohen's distinction, though later it will be explained more fully.)[43] First, the structure of the difference between concessive and nonconcessive requirement has a direct application even within the domain of rules of regulation. Even if we ought to implement and comply with rule set R, there is also the question of what rules we should implement if we would not comply with R were we to implement it. That suffices to show that there are two distinctions here. This is because the question remains whether the structure of concessive vs. nonconcessive requirements applies also within the domain of what Cohen calls principles and values. Suppose there is a fully nonconcessive or ideal balance of all values relevant to the quality of a basic social structure, without yet specifying anything about what rules should be implemented. There is also a substantial question of what the best balance of values given some specified deviation from the ideal would be. It cannot be assumed that any remaining subset of those values is the best option, since their value may depend on the presence of things that will be missing.[44] So some things that are required by nonconcessive justice might be contrary to what is required in a concessive context. So, by introducing the concessive question, we are not slipping from the domain of principles and ideals into the domain of which rules of regulation to implement. The structure of concession can apply within each of those domains, making the two distinctions cross-cutting or orthogonal.

The central concern of the book is to respond more completely than has normally been done previously to two influential critiques of much political philosophy: anti-idealism and anti-moralism. Neither implies the other, so a settled view of one leaves the other yet to be settled. While I resist both of those positions, residues of both remain. As for anti-moralism, while I argue that the extant critiques of moralism are not persuasive, the normativity of judgments about social justice and injustice are, indeed, difficult to interpret as straightforwardly moral. My conclusions about this matter keep justice judgments tied to agential moral normativity, but without being instances of it. They are best seen as still moral, but only in a broader sense of the moral than the agential conception. As for anti-idealism, the view here is less, but still slightly, equivocal. There are serious problems involved when either trying to do without the idea of full justice, or when calibrating or relativizing the standard of full justice to realistic assumptions about individual moral deficiency. I find insufficient reasons to decide between calibrating justice to full moral compliance, and a variant that takes account of some moral deficiencies, namely those that would not themselves count a society as unjust (if they could be adequately distinguished in the necessary way). Either way, the idea of full justice would not shape itself to a realistic picture of human behavior, which can still be expected to be significantly non-compliant. There is no argument here that on the best account of justice its requirements will indeed be unrealistic in this way, but only that, short of substantive normative considerations there is no defensible conceptual or methodological precept, laid down in advance, that rules it out. This defense of what we might call political irrealism brings us to a further point that frames the book's argument in a very central way, namely that no one—certainly not me—can seriously dispute that political thought must, among other things, make and consider proposals about what is to be done given the best information about, among other things, how real people can be expected to behave and respond in real circumstances. There can be disagreement about which such assumptions are, to what degree, probable, but that is an entirely different matter. Proceeding on the basis of what are known to be false or improbable assumptions is obviously indefensible. There is no interesting divide in political theory about that. What it leaves open is whether what we have most reason to realistically expect of people also sets the outer limit of what social justice requires. Realism of that kind is an obvious constraint on practical proposals, but I argue—contrary to a widespread view—that it is an illegitimate constraint on what principles of justice might require. The arguments for this, and understanding its implications, must wait for the chapters to play out, but the distinction between so constraining practical proposals and so constraining principles of justice in this fashion ought to be kept in mind from the beginning.

7. Enoch on Multiple Agents

In a valuable discussion of several papers that appeared prior to this book, David Enoch grants that a requirement applying to a society or collectivity cannot be refuted by the fact that the society will not comply. Still, he points out, a requirement on, say, the state subsystem can be refuted by facts about the behavior of the society's members.[45] He adds that political philosophy importantly includes questions about requirements of that second kind even if it also includes the first.[46] These points are obviously correct. He argues, however, that these points, which he acknowledges that I accept,[47] undermine what he understands as my main line of argument, or rather, "a very natural and common understanding of [my] *point*" in several of my earlier papers.[48] This natural understanding, he says, would be that I argue that, "worries about feasibility cannot defeat a normative theory in political philosophy." But, of course they could, since a normative theory will often be concerned not only with the content of justice but also with questions about practical proposals when justice is not a realistic possibility.[49] What I argue for (in those papers and in this book) is the more specific proposition that, contrary to what might be supposed, one kind of infeasibility—the fact that the society would not comply with certain institutions even if they were implemented—cannot refute a theory according to which those institutions are required of that society by justice. For that reason, principles of social justice cannot be plausibly assimilated to practical proposals, though the latter are of unquestionable importance.[50]

I use the term "concessive theory" for questions regarding what institutions society ought to build or maintain, given that it will not comply with what justice requires. If we ask what the state, as a social subsystem, ought to do given that citizens or society will not comply with what justice requires, that is not, as Enoch notes, concessive in the same intrapersonal sense.[51] And surely there can be, in that intrapersonal sense, nonconcessive theory addressing what some agent other than society—perhaps the state—ought to do given what others will do. All this is compatible with my arguments that what justice requires of a society given that it will not comply with justice, would fall into concessive theory. Now this might be of little interest if it were thought that the question of social justice is nothing but the question of what the state should do given what others will do. But social justice does not seem to be simply what some part of society, the state or any other, ought to do given what others will do, as I will argue next.

Before turning to that, I should point out that the argument in chapter 10, "Prime Justice" is that full justice might be best conceived as the political portion (so to speak, simplifying here) of the case (satisfaction of what I call the Global Prime Requirement) in which each agent does as they should *given* how others will act. Since I do not posit a group agent that comprises "society," the only requirements on agents that I countenance are conditional on what (they and) other agents will do whenever this is relevant. So, at bottom, it is all a question of multiagent requirement in Enoch's sense after. Still, Enoch's critique raises the question not only about the group-agent form of the point, but also more generally about the interest or importance of requirements that apply to the society as a whole.

Enoch is surely right, in one sense, when he writes that, "Political philosophy is essentially about multiple agents."[52] Much of political philosophy will concern questions about how one agent or set of agents ought to act given how other agents will act. There is also a stronger possible thesis worth addressing, namely that questions about what an agent or set of agents ought to do, given how that very agent or set of agents will act, are of only the most marginal importance or interest in political philosophy. The *main* questions for political theory may seem to be (what we are calling) multi-agent questions: What ought the state to do given what the citizens will do? What ought certain activists to do given what other citizens will do? And so on. There is no dispute about whether questions of that form are highly important and in no way marginal. The question at hand is whether they are, more or less, *the* real subject of political philosophy.

To test that suggestion, consider the following thought experiment, focusing on the state as one agent operating in an environment where the citizens are the other agents: Can you devise a scenario in which the state acts exactly as it should given how the citizens will act, and yet this is patently not a just society? This is rather easy, I think. Suppose that a virulently racist citizenry would furiously and successfully resist fully equal civil rights, and these are genuinely, but not terribly, unequal at present. Plausibly, at least, the state ought not to press ahead with that agenda if there is virtually no chance of success (lower the chance as much as you need to in order to accept this assumption), and an overwhelming likelihood (again, set this where you need to) that it would lead to civil war, still with no hope of equal civil rights at the end. Indeed, we might add the supposition that in the imagined conditions the most likely outcome of such a civil war is destruction of even the modest degree of equality in the *status quo ante*. In this case, the state that retreats from the egalitarian agenda does as it should given what the citizens will do. But this is patently not a just society. The question of what the state should do is not the question of what social justice requires of this society.

We can try a similar thought experiment, focusing on citizens as agents (not counting the state as a citizen): Can we devise a scenario wherein the citizens do just what they should given what the state will do, but in which the society is nevertheless patently unjust?[53] Again, this seems easy. Suppose the society is structured by a racist constitution, and the state is virtually guaranteed to continue to entrench the racist nature of its structure, the citizenry being unfortunately powerless to change this. In that case, whatever the citizens ought to do, suppose they do it. This will nevertheless be an unjust society. The question of what the citizens should do given what the state will do is not the question of what social justice requires of that society.

The line of argument generalizes as follows: no account of what some agents ought to do given what others will do could capture the requirements of full social justice if, as will often be the case, the actions of those others, which are taken as given by that approach, already constitute social injustice. This is not meant to question the obvious importance of such multiperson requirements. Rather, the upshot, as I see it, is this: it would be an important mistake to infer from the fact, if it is one, that practical proposals concerning improving social justice must normally operate under the constraint that full justice will not be achieved, that this constrained practical domain is the true locus of the requirements of social justice.

Now, Enoch agrees that, "the fact that an aspirational theory may be hopeless, and that it may therefore not be the best guide to practical goal-setting, doesn't show that it's false."[54] If that is granted, it might nevertheless seem that the requirements of social justice must be of little interest or importance. I will address this question directly in chapter 17. For now, I ask the reader, have you now lost interest in the kinds of injustice posited in the two examples of deeply rooted racism just above? You might even ask this imagining yourself as part of the oppressed racial group in those examples. Is that fact of racism, even if is categorized as social injustice, not of any great importance unless there is, fortunately, something that some agents other than society as a whole could and ought to do to change it? I have not tried to disprove that possible view, but I doubt many will find it an attractive position.

CHAPTER TWO

Overview

But having the intention to write something useful to anyone who understands, it seems to me better to concentrate on what really happens rather than on theories or speculations. For many have imagined republics and principalities that have never been seen or known to exist. Because there is such a great distance between how we live and how we ought to live, anyone who sets aside what is done for what ought to be done learns more quickly what will ruin him rather than preserve him.

—NICCOLÓ MACHIAVELLI, *THE PRINCE*

A free society is indeed unrealistically and undefinably different from the existing ones.

—HERBERT MARCUSE, "REPRESSIVE TOLERANCE"

THIS OVERVIEW CHAPTER is meant to be self-contained. It leaves out much that is important in the argument, while it also contains occasional passages that are repeated elsewhere in the book. I will not attempt to cross-reference them all. It could be skipped without substantive loss, though it may be helpful to look over the project, as it were, in miniature before embarking on it in full scale.

1. Introduction

There is a common thought about utopian thinking: "Even if we could build a Utopia, I would not want to live there." Call this *Utopia as Dystopia*.[1] For purposes of this chapter, I want to bracket that important thought in two ways: first, let's not think about where we'd like to live, but about what would be truly and fully just. For simplicity, let's just posit for present purposes that a fully just society could be a fine place to live. Second, for reasons presented in the Introduction, let's not focus on blueprints for the design of institutions in a fully just society, but rather on principles of full social justice. It might be that the principles could be met by various different institutional arrangements, so they are not institutional blueprints. I am not even going to be concerned with any particular principles, since my points will not be concerned with whether justice is more of a left, or right, or utilitarian, or egalitarian, or rights-based kind of thing. My topic will be specifically about unrealistically high standards or principles of full social justice. By principles I mean such things as the following:

- All people ought to have equal rights under the law.
- Government ought to be democratically authorized.
- Economic institutions ought to aim at equal income for everyone . . . or at the greatest sum of aggregate wealth . . . or at maximizing individual liberty, and so forth.

I am not endorsing or criticizing any particular principles of justice. I am going to be defending the following simple claim:

My Claim (against Utopophobia)
It is no defect in a theory or conception of social justice if it sets such a high standard that there is little or no chance of its being met, by any society, ever. Such a theory could nevertheless be true.

You could call my argument a kind of defense of utopian political theory. However, and again as discussed in the Introduction, instead, as I prefer to use the term, a social proposal has the vice of being utopian if, roughly, there is no evident basis for believing that efforts to stably achieve it would have any significant tendency to succeed. The argument of this book is *not* a defense of proposals that are utopian—unrealistic in the stated way. Oversimplifying a little (see more in the Introduction), this is because the arguments here are a defense not of proposals (proffered knowing what we do about human tendencies) at all, but of certain kinds of principles (or standards, or requirements—as you prefer) of justice. Irrealism (the property of being unrealistic) is a vice of proposals but not a vice of principles, and so while this book is no defense of anything utopian in the narrow sense I adopt here, it is a defense of unrealistic principles of justice—not of any highly specific principles (much less of any practical proposals)—but as against the charge that irrealism is a defect of such principles.

2. Couldn't Justice Be Unlikely?

Here is a widely accepted principle in moral and political philosophy:

Ought implies can.

What it means is that if you are required to do something, then you are able to do it. The more intuitive way to put this is that you are not morally required to do anything you cannot do. No can, no ought. Ought implies can. I grant that not everyone accepts this, and I am going to accept it simply for the sake of argument. If it is correct, it is one way in which moral requirements must be realistic. Applied to our topic, I will grant that a theory of justice for a society can be refuted if its alleged requirements can be shown to be more than the society is able to do. The 'ought' of social justice implies 'can,' or so I will allow for the sake of argument.

Here is a little piece of reasoning that purports to make use of that principle:

> I've just studied a certain theory of justice, but its requirements are very idealistic. Knowing what we do about people and history, there is little or no chance of a society ever meeting those principles. But since ought implies can, those are false requirements of justice.

Now, this makes a clear mistake in assuming, without any argument, that if society will not meet some standard then it is not able to. Recall, I am granting that if it is indeed not able to meet a certain standard then it is a bogus requirement. But knowing that a society will not meet a standard says nothing at all about whether it is able to meet it. To see this, think about a simple example outside of the context of morality or politics:

Chicken Dance
I am not going to dance like a chicken during any lecture. I also want you to understand that dancing like a chicken is, for most people (and certainly for me) easy. I could do it, and I could easily do it. So from the fact that I will not do it, you cannot infer that I can't do it.

In the same way, think about the society that will not meet a certain standard of social justice. But it is certainly not refuted simply because the society will not meet it. For one thing, if anything a society will not do is thereby not required, this would prevent any society from ever counting as unjust. Ought does not imply will.

A bit more generally yet, moral requirements are pretty obviously not blocked by the fact that we probably, or even certainly, will not meet them.

Lying
Whatever the correct requirements are about when it is wrong to lie, probably, or perhaps certainly, none of us will, over our lives, meet the requirement fully: we will almost certainly tell some lies we ought not to tell. We do not complain that this makes the principles "impractical" or "unrealistic" in a way that is a defect.

The same goes for the moral requirements of social justice, whatever they might be: a society does not escape an alleged requirement of justice just because—probably, certainly, or in fact—it will not meet it. If this is right, then you cannot criticize a conception of social justice by showing that it is unrealistic in that way, namely that it will probably or even certainly never be met.

There may seem to be a more formidable version of the likelihood objection, one that my arguments so far do not touch. Suppose that a standard of justice is very high and probably or certainly will never be met, but in addition, suppose that it is grounded in the facts of human nature. You might be attracted to the following:

The Human Nature Constraint (to be rejected)
A normative political theory is defective and so false if it imposes standards or requirements that ignore human nature—that is, requirements that will not, owing to human nature and the motivational incapacities it entails, ever be satisfied.[2]

I deny this, for reasons I will give shortly. I will not be engaging in the dispute about what is or is not in human nature. Instead, I will argue against the constraint itself. To keep things simple I will grant for the sake of argument that it is in the nature of humans to be more selfish and partial than some idealistic theories would need them to be. I deny, however, that this refutes any such normative political theories.

First, consider whether requirements are blocked when the agent 'can't bring himself' to do it.

Messy Bill
Suppose Bill pleads that he is not required to refrain from dumping his trash in the yard because he is motivationally unable to bring himself to refrain. Assume that there is no special phobia, compulsion, or illness involved. He is simply deeply selfish and so cannot thoroughly will, or 'bring himself,' to comply. Refraining is something he could, in all other respects, easily do. Still, he will either not really try, or he will stop trying even if he might have succeeded.

It would be silly for Bill to suggest that, since he is lazy and selfish in this way, he is out from under any requirement to take his trash to the curb. So it turns out that even if 'ought implies can' not only does 'ought' not imply 'will' (as we saw) but, also,

Ought does not imply 'can will.'

That is just shorthand for saying, being so deeply motivated that you can't bring yourself to do something does not block or refute a moral requirement to do it. It would be requirement-blocking if this entailed that you are unable to do it, but it does not. Bill is able to take his garbage out, but he can't bring himself to do it.

Turn next to the second thing suggested by an appeal to human nature: suppose this deep motivational disinclination is not just Bill's, but is true of every human being, and even true of human beings as such. Would it then be requirement-blocking? I see no reason to think that it would. Here is why:

The Line behind Bill

Suppose people line up to get your moral opinion on their behavior. Bill is told his selfishness does not exempt him from the requirement to be less selfish. Behind Bill comes Nina with the same query. Again, we dispatch her, on the same grounds as Bill. Behind Nina is Kim, but, since each poses the same case, our judgment is the same. The line might contain all humans, but that fact adds nothing to any individual's case.

I take this to show the following rather significant thing: even if a large dose of selfishness or laziness is part of human nature (in either or both of the senses just discussed) this does not refute theories of justice that require people to be less selfish than that.

You might hesitate. Surely we want principles "for us," not for some very different beings. I agree. The requirement to not be a litterbug is for litterbugs, even really deep ones like Bill who can't bring themselves to comply. That is, the requirement applies to them in all their selfish and lazy glory. It is a standard by which their actions are wrong. A theory of social justice is not refuted by showing that people (even as such) deeply can't bring themselves to do what it purports to require. The principle might yet be right and the society, and maybe even any human society, wrong. I am not saying this is so. I have not explored the question of what justice might actually require. But what people can or can't bring themselves to do is not a constraint on a correct or sound theory of the content of social justice. The "human nature constraint" is false.

3. Prime Justice

I now want to make a case for the perhaps surprising claim that the content of full social justice is whatever the basic social structure should be, along with full moral compliance (non-wrongdoing) of all individuals and groups. The reason for this depends on a certain kind of primacy of the nonconcessive over the concessive. In morality generally there seem to be both "concessive" and "nonconcessive" requirements, in the following sense.

Professor Procrastinate[3]

Assume that he is morally required (for whatever reason) to accept an assignment to write a book review, and then to write it. Suppose he will not write it even if he accepts. Ought he to accept?

The requirement to do both is not concessive in any way to wrongdoing, but there are also concessive moral requirements. Is he required to accept, given (that is, conceding) that he will not comply? It does not follow, and arguably he is not. It would only make a bigger mess of things. Suppose in that case he ought not.

Here is an analogous point at the social level:

> Society is required by justice to Build and Comply (by assumption) with certain institutions. Suppose society will not comply even if it builds the institutions.

Again, the requirement to do both is not concessive in any way, but there are also concessive moral requirements. Is society required to build those institutions given (that is, conceding) that they won't comply? It does not follow, and arguably not. Suppose in that case society ought not.

In both cases, there is a certain primacy of the nonconcessive requirement: the Professor's requirement not to accept arises only if the nonconcessive requirement—to both accept and write—is violated by his not writing. It evaporates if that requirement is met. The reverse is not the case: the nonconcessive requirement to accept and write does not appear or disappear depending on whether he accepts or writes. Call this the *primacy* of the nonconcessive: concessive requirements are subordinate, arising only because of violations of nonconcessive requirements. In the limit, the fully nonconcessive requirement is for a person to act as they ought in light of all their other acts which are also all morally right. Call this the *individual prime requirement*, which, clearly, there will be numerous ways to meet.

There is not a requirement to do each of the things that would be part of a compliant set of actions, since the value of doing it might depend on which of the other things actually get done. (Putting this syntactically: the 'ought' does not distribute across the conjuncts.) Rather it is a requirement to do all of them. Then, if a person violates that prime requirement by not doing some of them, the question arises what concessive requirements come into force. The prime requirement stands, and it is violated, but then there are also concessive requirements. So, Professor Procrastinate ought to accept and write. If he will not write, then there is a concessive requirement to not accept. Suppose society ought to Build and Comply with certain institutions. If it will not comply, then there is (or might be) a concessive requirement not to build them.[4]

So much for primacy. Now notice that not only is society required to both Build and Comply. It is also, as we have mentioned, required of people that they behave morally in other ways. So there is what we might call an overarching *global prime requirement*, which requires the combination of basic social structure and behavior of individuals (and groups).

> It is required that [social structure is x, and Joe does y, and Ali does z, and so forth].

We saw that there is an individual prime requirement. Call this the global prime requirement, but let us limit ourselves to the domain of a single society (which could either include the whole globe or not). Along with all the ways people ought, together, to behave, there will also be the part of the global prime requirement that applies to the basic social structure—the justice part of the prime requirement. Call this *prime justice*.

There are now two parts to the topic of social justice. One is the principles for the basic social structure in a nonconcessive setting: prime justice. The other is principles for the basic structure in a concessive setting in which there are various kinds of violation of justice or morality. Obviously, the nonconcessive scenario of moral perfection is unlikely ever to be met, but we have seen that this does not refute the requirement. The question I want to consider is whether prime justice has a claim to be the content of full social justice, a stronger claim than any concessive requirement shaped by (fully expected) moral deficiency.

Consider these two accounts of the content of full social justice:

Concessive
Principles the basic structure should meet given the expected amount of individual moral deficiency.

Nonconcessive
Principles the basic structure should meet given full individual moral compliance.

There are two things to be said in favor of the nonconcessive conception, according to which the content of social justice is given by the principles that would go with general moral perfection.

a. Primacy
The nonconcessive approach, here as elsewhere, has a clear kind of primacy.

That is, (as we saw) the concessive requirements arise only from failure to meet the nonconcessive. The nonconcessive requirement is not contingent in this way: even if society is not just, or people are not morally good, that is all (together) still morally required. Second,

b. No privileged concessive scenario
Which of the infinitely many possible profiles of moral deficiency would be specially fit to set the concessive requirement of true social justice?

On the view (which I will resist) that justice is essentially concessive, and always relative to some specified concession, there is no single salient standard of social justice at all, just a field of concessive requirements. This indeterminacy is unmotivated, however, given the salience of one requirement, the prime requirement.

This may be too fast, however, and we will shortly consider a proposal for a salient kind of concession by which to calibrate principles of social justice, namely concession to expected moral violations which are not themselves (even in aggregate) defects in social or political justice.

Interestingly, it does not follow from the fact that full moral compliance is highly unrealistic that the standard of justice that goes with that scenario (the nonconcessive standard) would be unrealistic as well. One way to see this point is to consider some philosophical accounts of what social justice requires. Many people are familiar with Rawls, for example, so consider: Is there any point in the Rawlsian method where the content of the principles of justice is determined by some concession to expected levels of moral deficiency? I am not aware of any, and in any case, there is no general reason to think this must be the case for theories of justice. So, it is entirely conceivable that prime justice, whatever its content, is "robust" in this way—call that *robust prime justice.*

If justice should turn out to be robust in that way, it would be significant. What is required by justice in our real morally deficient conditions would not be second-rate. What is justice for the flawless might be realistic and appropriate justice for the flawed. It might not, but it might. If not, of course, there would still be concessive requirements suited to our specific conditions of moral deficiency. But there is no such special scenario that would give content to "full social justice," nothing with the special salience—the complete nonconcessive nature of—prime justice. This is a partial case for full justice being morally nonconcessive in a rather sweeping way.

4. Plural Requirement

The idea of prime justice brings us to a philosophical puzzle, but one that is important whether you are interested in prime justice or not. It is a puzzle for moral philosophy generally, but with clear importance here. The requirement of prime justice arises as part of a requirement that appears to obligate a bunch of agents, but not to obligate any of them individually. That is, prime justice arises as part of what I called the global prime requirement, and that ranges over all individuals, groups, as well as the social structure itself. It is a requirement on all of them at once. It is similar to a requirement on a single agent, like Professor Procrastinate, that ranges over several actions at once, such as accepting and writing. In both cases, we cannot assume that each part of the required combination is itself required. It might depend on whether the other part of the package will be present.

What's special about prime justice and the global prime requirement is that there is no agent that is under the overarching nonconcessive requirement. This is puzzling. Let me explain and pursue this in a very simple version:[5]

Slice and Patch Go Golfing
Suppose that unless a patient is cut and stitched he will worsen and die
(though not painfully). Surgery and stitching would save his life. If there
is surgery without stitching, the death will be agonizing. Ought Slice to
do the surgery? This depends, of course, on whether Patch (or someone)
will be stitching up the wound. Slice and Patch are each going golfing
whether the other attends to the patient or not. Does anyone act
wrongly?

Surely Slice should not cut; no one will stitch! Surely Patch should not stitch;
no one will have made an incision!
Which proposition ought to be discarded? They cannot all be true:

a. *Moral Failure*
   It is morally wrong if the patient is left to die.
b. *No Wrong without Obligation*
   If something is morally wrong, then there was an obligation on
   some agent to act or abstain other than as they did.
c. *No Violating Agent*
   There is no agent in this case who is morally required to act (or abstain) otherwise.

If we think that the patient is wronged by the combination of Slice's and
Patch's behavior, then we will apparently need to accept (and account for)
moral wrongs that are not committed by any agent. That is, moral requirements
that are not requirements on any agent. This is an important issue for the topic
of social justice. If it is a moral requirement, who is the required agent? It is not
guaranteed that there are requirements on each agent, since those might depend on what the others will do. It is far from guaranteed that the society itself
is an agent. So the requirement does not require any agent at all.
   It is important to see that this kind of moral standard is not just going
beyond a kind of individualism and itself applies to sets of individuals. That
much would be true if requirements still applied at least to some individual *or
collective agent*. What we are facing here are requirements that not only do not
apply to individuals but do not apply to any agent at all, individual or collective. I am introducing this only briefly, and there are various ways in which you
might try to explain Slice/Patch cases without this somewhat mysterious account of the moral. I myself think that none of them is successful, but I postpone that issue until later chapters.[6]
   In response to the puzzle of plural obligation, then, I propose to recognize
a non-agential form of moral requirement: "Plural Requirement." It is motivated by what I perceive to be the failure of attempts to capture cases of ostensibly plural obligation in a way that attaches obligations to agents. I am in-

clined to believe that no such account can succeed. A Plural Requirement, as I will call it, ranges over a conjunction of two or more propositions stating that a certain agent does a certain act, as in:

It is a Plural Requirement that [S does x and T does y].

This is not what I am calling an agential obligation, since it does not attach to any agent, and so is no agent's obligation or requirement. This is because the central puzzling cases are such that neither agent does have the obligation unless the other performs the specified act. It is also not simply an 'ought' as in 'it ought to be the case that.' That would have the advantage of there not needing to be an obligated agent, but it is weaker than the form of requirement I propose. It is, however, part of it, as we will see.

Let me make some terminological stipulations. I am christening a form of moral requirement that is not agential obligation, which always binds some agent. So we will have to use the terms "requirement" and "obligation" advisedly, and not interchangeably. There is a general category, requirement, that comprises Plural Requirement and agential obligation. When I am speaking of the particular version of requirement that is Plural Requirement, I will be explicit about that. With that rule in place, it should be safe to continue to say that even agential obligations require things of agents. Plural Requirements, I will say, require things of sets of agents in the way I will explain, but they do not obligate any agents, and their violation does not entail that any agent behaves wrongly.

I propose that to say that,

It is a Plural Requirement that (S does x, & T does y)

is to say that,

    i. If S does x, then T is obligated to do y, and,
    ii. If T does y, then S is obligated to do x, and,
    iii. It ought to be the case that (S does x, and T does y)

The two conditionals alone would not capture the idea we are after, since they would be satisfied when neither x nor y is performed. We are trying to capture cases where there is an intuition that those acts ought to be performed. Thus, we add the third condition, (iii). The occurrence of 'ought' in that condition is not yet defined, but just to be clear, it is neither agential obligation nor Plural Requirement. While it is important to alert readers to this non-agential understanding of the standards or requirements of social justice that I only present later in the book, I leave the matter here and more fully explain and defend the idea in chapter 12, "Plural Requirement."

For much of the book, I keep postponing the problem of agency until the chapters on Plural Requirement. When I finally lay out that non-agential idea, it is important but difficult to inquire whether it is suitable for the various

kinds of judgments about justice that I hope to be able to make, about requirements, etc., ties between justice and individual members, and so forth. I am
not at all sure that I can, but I will try. However, if this approach fails it is not
the fault of its idealism, or even of my "moralism." The problem, instead, is a
very general one for the idea that there are normative standards of social justice of any kind. I cannot emphasize this enough. Moreover, some who reject
my approach will nevertheless be happy with the idea that requirements of
justice can apply to a society, sometimes on the ground that a society is an
agent in its own right. I will explain why I find that unpersuasive, but my
broader argument is only simpler and stronger if that is so.

5. Against Practicalism

I am, so far, mostly not offering a case for thinking that nonconcessive theorizing is valuable, or important, or a good way to spend your time, or a good use
of tax dollars. I am mostly sticking to the question of *whether there are truths
there*. But let's also think about that, just for a moment. Consider an account
of social justice according to which society ought to Build and Comply with
institutions that meet certain principles. But suppose society will not comply
even if they were built. We have seen that we cannot conclude that they should
be built. In that case, there arises a concessive question: What to do then?

Now it may be that in the real world society would not comply with just
institutions. I grant that the nonconcessive theory is silent about what standards ought to be met by the basic social structure in that case. And this might
make it seem like a nonconcessive account of social justice is not of any practical interest. However, while there is some truth to this contention, it should not
be exaggerated. In the very same way, which is a limited way, *given* that Prof.
Procrastinate won't write, the requirement to Accept *and* Write is of no practical interest. That is not very damning. That conjunctive requirement itself,
even though he will not meet it, is perfectly practical: he can and should Accept
and Write. The same goes for social justice: even if we would not comply, the
conjunctive requirement to Build and Comply with certain institutions would
be perfectly practical: we can and we should Build and Comply. The theory
does not answer all practical questions, such as whether to Build if we will not
Comply, but that does not render the requirement nonpractical overall.

So the verdict on whether nonconcessive justice would be practical is
mixed. But what of it? You might ask: If it does not tell us what to do given how
we will actually behave, then what good is it? The challenge might seem to
assume a very general "practicalism" about intellectual work.

Practicalism: (to be rejected)
There is little or no value in studying or understanding anything unless
this has practical implications.

This is hard to square with what most people think about the value of achievements in many other fields. One category is, broadly, the arts. We do not think their value is exhausted by their practical value for producing other things of value. On the other hand, I am not satisfied to think that the value of understanding political justice is something akin to the aesthetic, so I put those cases aside. But practicalism is also hard to square with what many people think about achievements in other sciences. Here are two examples to think about:

> a. *Higher mathematics*
> Many of what are regarded as the great mathematical achievements (or problems still outstanding, like proving the Riemann Hypothesis) either don't have, or were not expected to have, any practical value. Practicalism would say they are a waste of time.
> b. *Cosmology*
> Coming to understand the so-called origins of the universe is hardly guaranteed to have any practical value (in itself, apart from incidental achievements that might). Suppose that it does not. Practicalism would say it is a waste of time.

The examples of math and cosmology suggest that practicalism is implausible. I admit, though, that this does not yet show us how to give an account of what kinds of intellectual work do have nonpractical value, and why. It just raises the stakes. Still, as long as you think practicalism is implausible (maybe because of math and cosmology), then it is not available as a critique of some part of political philosophy that lacks (in a certain limited way!) practical value.

There is a kind of value we may attribute to understanding justice, even though it may not point the way to accounts of the value of such things as higher math and cosmology. I now sketch an argument for this kind of value and reply to some objections.

Justice itself, I shall assume, is a great value, and I hope this first premise is common ground. Whether one prefers to speak only of some condition being much more just than another, or also accepts that there is such a thing as full justice, these would be conditions of great value. The thing that I am claiming to be of value here is not an abstract object such as a standard, a principle, or a concept, "justice," nor am I yet addressing the value of any knowledge or understanding, but rather the real condition of a social structure that is just or at least juster. That, I will assume, is valuable.

Some will think that justice is only a good thing if it is good for somebody, but I am not assuming that.[7] Consider a system of criminal law which applies an appropriate standard of proof to black defendants, but applies a higher standard to whites, acquitting them more easily. This may be unjust even if it hurts no one (although it probably also would). Justice might require even-handedness even if that is worse for whites and better for no one. We can leave that unsettled. My premise is that justice is a great value, not that this is so because it is good for people. But nor do I deny that it is.

A first premise, then, is,

1. Justice is a highly morally *valuable* human social condition, and its violation is *bad*.

The violation of justice is something more than its absence, since it is absent but not violated whenever it is inapplicable. Justice is also different from some other values in that even where a standard applies and is violated this is not always bad, except in the sense of less good. I assume it is part of the concept of justice that its violation is (at least) agent-neutrally bad, in some way that goes beyond its being less good. (It is similar to the concepts of illness or tragedy in this way.)

Next, a link between what is morally valuable in those ways, and appropriate attitudes:

2. What is morally valuable is morally *desirable*, and what is a moral violation is morally *lamentable*. That is, those attitudes are morally appropriate, and their lack is inappropriate.
3. Therefore, justice (where it applies) is morally desirable, and its violation is morally lamentable. (from 1 and 2)

Some might even hold that there is nothing more to the greatness of justice except facts about appropriate attitudes toward that condition—say, its desirability, or its absence being lamentable. Others might think the justice of a condition is explanatorily prior to any facts about attitudes, which can be responses to that justice or injustice, appropriate or inappropriate responses. Nothing here will hang on that issue, since both sides can (not to say that they must) agree with my next claim: that a certain concern for justice—tending to desire it and to lament its violation—is virtuous.

4. It is morally *virtuous* to have a *concern* for justice in that sense: to desire or wish for it and to lament its absence. A person who does not care about the justice or injustice of social conditions is thereby morally deficient, lacking that virtue. (from 2 and 3)

(4) really just clarifies or sharpens the point of (3) for our purposes. Next, I propose that

5. In order to have a concern for justice that is virtuous (or more virtuous) it must be *informed* by sound (or sounder) understanding of the nature of justice—what it is for a social condition to be just or juster.

Whether or not there is some worth in caring about social justice *de dicto*—that is, about so-called justice whatever it might be—(a question which is controversial), there is significant moral deficiency even in an agent with that concern, to the extent that their conception of justice is too rudimentary or mistaken or unsound.

It follows from those steps that

6. A sounder understanding of justice (whether or not that understanding is practically valuable) is a contributing constituent of having a concern for justice that is morally better or more virtuous. (from 4, 5)

Put another way, it is morally better to be duly concerned with justice and injustice in the world—with how just things were, are, and might be—and that depends on a sufficiently rich and sound concept of justice.

The value that is at stake here is not practical (even if there happens to be some practical value as well, which is disputable). The value of the understanding of justice that figures in this argument does not consist in the understanding's availability for the production of something else valuable. Rather, its value is that it is an essential constituent of a valuable condition of a person: their having an informed concern about justice. That is, it is a constituent without which the value would be absent—it contributes value in that sense. That is the outline of the informed concern account of the value of understanding justice even if it is not practical. A number of issues are raised by this approach, and I address some of them in turn.

It might give one pause to hear that there is supposedly some moral value in a tendency to be sad—in this case, to lament injustice. But after a moment of thought, denying that would be the more radical and implausible view. Plausibly, at least for many or most people, it is a moral defect in a person if they are not saddened (in many cases) by another's suffering, or by a person's being unfairly taken advantage of. In that same way, a morally good person will, as a constituent feature of their goodness, tend to be saddened by (the fact, not only the experience, of) social injustice. Now there are people whose suffering it would make me sad to know about even though it is not true that I have an interest in knowing how they are doing—most strangers. But the limited point for the moment is that their suffering is lamentable from my point of view even so, and entirely regardless of whether there is anything I can do about it. Should I be told about some stranger not that she suffers but that she is subject to great injustice (say she was lied to about something she very much cares about), if I am a good person I would tend to be saddened by that as well. It is lamentable in that sense.

6. Conclusion

To be convincing, the line of argument sketched in this overview would need more fleshing out at many points, and I attempt some of that, though hardly all, in the remainder of the book. I conclude merely by trying to state in a concise way the broad shape of the position that emerges. It is an argument to the effect that social justice is, broadly speaking, a moral standard, and that like moral standards generally it does not conform itself to human tendencies or proclivities. Any shaping of one by the other ought to go in the opposite direction, though we know it would never be complete. Let it be allowed that nothing is required by justice, any more than by morality, if the people ostensibly required are unable to do it. That is a minimal constraint of realisticness, and it has little in common with the tradition of "political realism." In any case, there is much that people can do that we have little reason to expect they ever will do, and this is as true of people collectively as it is of any single person. In both cases, moral and political, the requirement does not plausibly lapse in the face of actual, or expected, or even certain violation. The picture of social justice as (in several ways) nonconcessive emerges from seeing it as, broadly speaking, a moral standard. But that parallel treatment raises several philosophical problems, which fortunately also are of independent interest. One is how there could be both nonconcessive requirements (such as to Build and Comply) and closely related concessive requirements (such as to not Build), when it looks as though they cannot be jointly satisfied. Another is how a moral standard might apply to a set of individuals even if the set is not itself an agent, and even if it does not apply to each individual. And there are others. It remains to be seen, of course, whether accounts of these matters can be given, by me or by others, that are sufficiently satisfactory to vindicate the account of social justice as a nonconcessive Plural Requirement in the way I have laid out.

CHAPTER THREE

Anti-Anti-Moralism

[I]t is no argument against the theory here presented that actual foreign policy does not or cannot live up to it.

—HANS MORGENTHAU, "SIX PRINCIPLES OF POLITICAL REALISM"

1. Introduction

"Moralism" has recently come to be pitted against "realism" in political philosophy, although there are strands of this division throughout the Western tradition.[1] The following distinction might help in thinking about the vague idea of being "realistic" in political philosophy. Consider two propositions that are not very controversial:

Proposal Realism
Proposals for political action or change are worthless (as proposals) if they are not informed by and sensitive to the best available assessment of the relevant facts and probabilities, however depressing they might be (but also without irrational pessimism).

Nobody could plausibly deny Proposal Realism, and I doubt that anyone ever has. (Obviously, some thinkers have been wildly more optimistic than others, but that dispute about probabilities is entirely different.) So, if the question is whether to be realistic, we are all realists in that sense. Consider, next,

Principle Idealism
Appropriate normative standards for the evaluation of political arrangements are neither committed to nor refuted by facts about whether those standards will (or probably will) be met in practice.

Has anyone ever denied Principle Idealism? I do think many writers have said things in tension with this, often conflating likelihood with ability, often turning on the slippery term "feasibility." But they also might often be equivocating between proposals and principles. Once the question is put explicitly in terms of principles (or standards, or requirements) I cannot see how it could be denied.[2]

So basically everyone is a realist about proposals, and no one is a realist (in this sense) about principles. So if there is an interesting debate between realists and some opponents, it must lie elsewhere. A number of thinkers associated with the realist school of thought claim that it is, in some way, a mistake to evaluate political arrangements by moral standards.[3] I want to distinguish several versions of this idea, and consider to what extent these thinkers ground a case in favor of a distinctive method, "realism," as against "moralism" in political philosophy.[4]

The connotation of "political realism," surely not unintentional, is that realists are those who believe we should be realistic in political theory and practice. The opposing camp has been labeled, by the realists, as the party of "moralism" (the term possibly coined by Bernard Williams). *Merriam-Webster* proposes as synonyms for "moralism," "prudery, nice-nellyism, prudishness, puritanism." Reluctantly, I propose to align myself provisionally with so-called moralism in political philosophy. I have no proposal for substituting new terms, at least not a realistic one. So I will also stick with "realism" (though it will sometimes be useful to refer to "anti-moralism" which is one realist strand) and "political moralism." While political moralism is hardly bound to be unrealistic, it is true that the version as defended in this book is frankly opposed to the tyranny of the realistic in certain ways.[5] Elsewhere in this book I defend the possibility that justice might be idealistic—a moral requirement that will rarely or improbably be met. This is in opposition to one aspect of what is often called realism in political philosophy, but in this chapter I criticize a different aspect of realism, namely a family of views and arguments against the very idea—apart from any connection to idealism—that the evaluation of political practices and institutions is (primarily) a moral matter.

It will be useful for present purposes to have a rough formulation of what moralism in political philosophy is.

Political Moralism
Political standards such as justice and legitimacy are moral standards— and part of the broader domain of the moral (sometimes called "the right") that also includes standards of evaluation of individual actions and motives.

There is no hope of addressing every significant version of the skepticism about political moralism, and I grant at the start that many of them do not have precisely the above view precisely as their target. In many cases, however, their target is never made especially clear, and so it may be helpful to focus on a relatively clear target. I hope many of my points will have merit against a somewhat broader range of skeptics.

This chapter is called "Anti-Anti-Moralism," since that is the more qualified position I will defend here, rather than moralism itself. The reason is that there are difficult questions about the boundaries of the moral that I do not want to ignore, and they leave it less than clear in what sense political justice is properly a moral question after all. I have in mind the difficulties, introduced in chapter 2 (Overview) and pursued in detail later, about the puzzle of plural obligation. Importantly, however, these particular qualms about the moral domain are largely unrelated to the strand of realist thought that opposes "political moralism." I will put them aside until much later, in Part 4.

2. What Is the Moral?

The difficulty about the boundaries of the moral stems from the natural thought that nothing is morally required unless there is a required agent who thereby has a reason for action. The problem is that there are various cases that might seem to defy this criterion. Some of them are pressing for the topic of social justice. For example, Rawls famously says, and not jarringly, that justice is a "virtue of social institutions."[6] He continues the sentence, "as truth is of systems of thought," so virtue does not *mean* moral virtue here, but he adds, "laws and institutions no matter how efficient and well-arranged must be reformed or abolished if they are unjust." Isn't that a moral injunction? Indeed, he elsewhere confirms that he takes the question of justice to be a moral one.[7]

This is evidently incompatible with the agential conception of the moral, since Rawls does not indicate either that society itself is an agent that is thereby given reasons for action, or that the moral standard of justice is reducible to individual moral obligations, neither of which would be very plausible in any case. He, like so many, does repeatedly speak of the "requirements" of social justice, though he does not say clearly whether these are standards of action, and for what agent. The idea that it might be a virtue is suggestive, even though Rawls did not mean moral virtue. People do often seem to make virtue-like moral judgments that are not action-evaluating, such as, "Marcus ought to be more sympathetic." This is intended, often, as a moral judgment, or so we would normally suppose. Sometimes, of course, one means thereby to say that some actions are required, but not always.

Still, in cases such as that of Marcus, the moral evaluation of motives or character is necessarily limited to those of agents—only agents have them—even if there is no action thereby required of those agents. There is normally a close connection between the evaluations of their motives or character on the one hand, and moral standards applying to their actions on the other. This, then, may still be counted as "agential" moral evaluation for that reason, and in a way that the idea of a "virtue of social institutions" is not agential, unless society is conceived as an agent. There is controversy about whether a social structure could have the virtue of justice without individual agents sharing a certain ethos, but even that position does not presume to entirely relocate the question to the moral evaluation of individuals. The principles of justice—and this is clear in Rawls and many others—have no direct application to individuals. An individual is not a basic social structure, nor can any person be a fair system of social cooperation.[8]

The idea that justice is a moral standard of social institutions deviates, then, from an agential conception of the moral, which implies that anything that is a moral standard is a standard evaluating actions or motives of some agent. This agential conception is not committed to *moral individualism*, the idea that it must be individual agents who are thereby evaluated, since it can be left open whether there might be groups that are themselves agents.[9] But unless a society can be plausibly shown to be an agent the idea that justice is a moral virtue of social institutions is incompatible with the agential conception of the moral. Justice might be said to be a virtue, but not a virtue of any individual or collective moral agent. And, surely not just any collection of individuals counts as a moral agent or an agent at all, and so that way of avoiding the problem is not simple, a point we will look more closely at when we consider the idea of Plural Requirement. In any case, whatever it takes for a group to be an agent, it is not plausible that all societies or collectives that fall short of those criteria (perhaps such as coercively imposed dictatorships) thereby escape the judgment of justice.

The agential account, then, comprises both individual and collective versions (if any groups are agents), as well as deontic and nondeontic versions. The deontic, let us say, evaluates action, and so it involves agents, be they individual or collective. A nondeontic agential mode evaluates agents (via their motives or character, etc.), not necessarily actions. Even with all these varieties available, an agential account of the whole domain of the moral, or of the right, strains to capture the idea of social justice as a moral standard, since its requirements do not clearly bind any agent.

The agential conception of the moral might be recovered if we understand the injustice of social institutions to simply mean that people ought to reform or replace those institutions, or to create and uphold just institutions. This formulation displays agents who are said to have moral requirements, as the agential conception requires.[10] Or does it? The problem is that reforming and replacing institutions is not something that one individual can do. The intuitive idea seems to be that some *set* of agents ought each, and together, to perform certain coordinated actions that amount to changing the institutions, but this does not clearly place any individual under any obligations. To see why, suppose that none of the individuals will in fact do their part. That would not seem to be enough to cancel the intuitive requirement that they change the institutions, but it does seem to be enough—or could often be enough—to remove any single individual from the obligation to do anything toward institutional change, given that no one else will do their part anyway. So who is under an obligation to do what?

Now, there are several answers one might try, but I know of none that succeeds in finding a required agent in the relevant range of cases. I call this the puzzle of plural obligation, and consider it in detail in chapter 11. The simpler example of the puzzle, which has been introduced and which we will study later, is this: it may seem to be obligatory in the case of two doctors that one perform surgery and the other stitch up the wound. But there are easily constructed cases where it is clear that neither doctor thereby has an obligation, since, for example, the other will not, as a matter of fact, do her part. Much more on this later. The point for now is that moving from justice as a virtue of social institutions to a requirement on people to change the institutions if they are unjust might appear to be more deontic and agential, but this turns out not to be clear.

If the agential approach cannot account for social justice as a moral standard, is the problem with our intuitive idea of social justice, or is it with agentialism (as we call this conception) itself? There are, after all, several outliers—cases that many find to be intuitively moral, but which do not square with agentialism.

> *Social justice*: Many believe that a distribution of opportunities or goods can count as just or unjust, the most familiar being certain forms of egalitarianism.[11] A slightly different case might be the evaluation of institutional configurations, perhaps leaving the idea of distribution out of it.
>
> *Plural Requirement*: The case of the two doctors described above strikes many as a moral violation, even if there is no violation by either doctor, or by any collective agent.
>
> *Disjunctive requirement*: Another example of ostensibly non-agential moral judgment is, "One of you ought to help her!"

The point of these examples is to suggest that the agential conception of the moral is by no means obviously true to what we recognize as moral thought. On the other hand, if that criterion is false then it is still not clear, so far as the mere observations are concerned, *in virtue of what* the deviant examples *are* moral.

In light of this puzzle, which I confront head-on later, I am not here arguing that political justice is clearly a moral matter. Rather, my aim is to criticize several characteristically realist lines of argument for the view that political justice (or political normativity more generally) is not—or is not primarily—a moral matter. Even if (contrary to what I will argue later) these are not quite moral matters owing to their standards not entailing moral standards for any genuine agents, this is no vindication of any of the realist critiques of moralism that we will consider here. A non-agential standard of Plural Requirement resonates with one realist theme, that political normativity is not individual moral normativity. However, it does not lend any support to the realist idea that justice must not be an unrealistic standard. Those two concerns—moralism and realisticness—come apart.

I hope that these are the most worthy candidates to consider, but my arguments will not purport to cover all possible realist critiques of moralism. Other candidates would have to be considered one by one.

3. The Irrelevance of Platonism (and Its Denial)

Before turning to the varieties of anti-moralism, there is another issue that it will be helpful to address. It might seem as though highly idealistic (and so also moralist) theories of justice need to avail themselves of one or another more controversial metaphysical apparatus, sometimes loosely grouped together as "Platonist." Cohen, for one, is happy to avow Plato's extreme anti-relativism, as well as an idealistic luck-egalitarian view of social justice,[12] and it might seem as though he could not hold the latter without the former. In that vein, it might seem as though the Humean interpretation of justice through the "circumstances of justice," might tend to yield a tightly connected pair of positions: factually grounded, and normatively realistic. I look specifically at the supposed connection between realistic standards and circumstances of justice in chapter 4. In any case, I want briefly to argue that there is no such connection: Platonist theories and "naturalist" theories can be equally idealistic or realistic. Consider Cohen's position, which appears to have several elements.[13] First,

Moral Fundamentalism
There are fundamental (morally grounding but morally ungrounded) moral principles which *a fortiori* are not grounded in any nonmoral facts.

As for principles such as "Other things equal, it is wrong to hit people," insofar as they rest on facts such as that hitting people hurts them, Cohen argues, in effect, that this is only morally relevant owing to the principle, "other things equal, it is wrong to hurt people." And either there are no nonmoral facts in virtue of which that is true, or there are but their relevance depends on a deeper principle yet again which is not grounded in such facts. Is this metaphysically elaborate?

One important issue in metaethics is whether moral facts are "naturalistic," namely, either physical facts or grounded in (or supervening on) physical facts.

Naturalism (about justice)
All substantial (non-analytic) facts of justice or injustice are, or are grounded in, facts about the physical world of space and time. Call them "natural facts." All facts about justice are natural facts.

Moral fundamentalism might seem to be anti-naturalistic, but in fact it does not imply any particular position about "naturalism." It says nothing either way about physical facts, but only about moral and nonmoral facts. If some natural facts can *constitute* moral facts, then fundamentalism will be compatible with naturalism. That possibility is famously denied by G. E. Moore, who called it the "naturalistic fallacy," but his arguments remain controversial at best.[14]

The second element of Cohen's view, which I formulate in my own terms here, he calls,

Anti-relativism
What justice *fundamentally* is or requires does not necessarily vary with any changes in nonmoral facts (such as attitudes, history, social norms, or anything). Fundamental justice is therefore timeless as well. Of course, the fundamental principles might specify what is differentially required given certain facts, but those requirements are not fundamental.

Let us call this combination of positions that Cohen adopts,

Platonism about justice
Fundamentalism together with anti-relativism.

Cohen, as I have said, holds a highly idealistic theory of justice, namely "Luck Egalitarianism," and also a Platonic metaethics in the above sense, but it is doubtful that there is any necessary connection between these positions. Consider,

Luck Egalitarianism
Justice requires that there are no inequalities between the prospects of any pair of people that are owed to brute luck.

It is true that many accounts of the nature of justice are more realistic than luck-egalitarianism. For example, consider this view, comprising two alternative versions (a) and (b):

Optimal Rules (schema 1)
Justice requires that a society have whatever social rules of regulation would, given expected levels of compliance and other facts, maximize welfare (a) in aggregate, or (b) of the worst off.

It seems vastly more likely that some society might someday have those rules, should it try, than it is that (as Luck Egalitarianism requires) there might ever be only inequalities that are not owed to brute luck. However, this has nothing to do with metaphysics.

Both Luck Egalitarianism and Optimal Rules have the justice of any particular society depend on natural facts. For Luck Egalitarianism it depends on whether there are any inequalities that were not causally owed to responsibility-entailing choices in certain ways. For Optimal Rules it depends on expected levels of compliance with the various alternatives. If it is thought that Optimal Rules is somehow less metaphysically committed than Luck Egalitarianism, notice that Cohen will insist that Optimal Rules, as stated, is a putative principle of justice whose truth evidently does not depend on any nonmoral facts. In one sense it grounds justice in facts about welfare. Nevertheless, it is itself a moral principle that is not grounded in any such facts.

Now, some will wish to deny that Optimal Rules, or a suitably reformulated proposition, is a moral principle at all.[15] The relevant position might be understood by way of this principle about what justice is, not about what it requires:

Optimal Rules (schema 2)
For a society to be just *is for it to be such that* it has whatever social rules of regulation would, given expected levels of compliance and other facts, maximize welfare (a) in aggregate, or (b) of the worst off.

This, it might be argued, is a statement about what social justice is, not itself a moral or normative principle. Call it a *constitutive* principle. If so, it is not itself an example of a factually ungrounded moral principle, keeping alive the thought that it is metaphysically tame. It is still *some* kind of principle, of course, and one that entails a Luck Egalitarian moral standard of justice, and still a principle that is evidently not grounded in any nonmoral facts, so questions remain about how exactly this is metaphysically more spare, but I let that pass here. The important point is that this constitutive move is utterly independent of how high or idealistic the entailed standard is. Even if we allow that this constitutive move avoids certain troubling metaphysical commitments, a Luck Egalitarian constitutive principle would have those same advantages:

Luck Egalitarianism (constitutive)
For a society to be just *is for it to be such that* there are no inequalities between the prospects of any pair of people that are owed to brute luck.

That entails the highly idealistic Luck Egalitarian standard which is violated whenever there are inequalities owed to brute luck. As noted above, this is much less likely ever to be met than Optimal Rules—it is much more idealistic—even though no "Platonic" fact-free moral principles are (supposedly) involved.

There is a difficult issue here about whether Cohen's moral fundamentalism can be avoided by treating Optimal Rules or Luck Egalitarianism as "constitutive" principles and not moral ones. But whatever the correct answer, Optimal Rules and Luck Egalitarianism would be equally affected. The fact that Luck Egalitarianism is much more idealistic than Optimal Rules does not carry with it any special liability to moral fundamentalism. So even if moral fundamentalism is a metaphysically problematic position (a question that is not taken up here), that does not count especially against highly idealistic theories of justice. The case for or against moral fundamentalism is utterly independent of the cases for or against more or less realistic views of justice. *Highly idealistic standards do not carry any special metaphysical burden.*[16]

4. *Against the Primacy of Disagreement*

Politics, like the narrower topic of political justice, essentially involves conflict, a point to be emphasized (and tamed?) in the next chapter (chapter 4: "Circumstances and Justice"). One kind of conflict that is persistent is moral disagreement. As Jeremy Waldron observes, it is characteristic of the political condition that even as a society needs to find ways forward, the individuals and groups that make up the society will disagree even about what would count in favor of one social decision over another.[17] It is not only that many will press their own interests against the interests of others. Some will also have conflicting moral views. It might seem that politics should not be seen as falling under moral principles at all, since (a) no agreement is forthcoming about which moral principles are the correct and applicable ones, and (b) politics is at least partly about what is to be done in the face of moral disagreement. The problem with this argument is that (a) and (b) are no evident support for the claim that politics does not fall under moral principles (nor does Waldron suggest otherwise). That would follow if one supposed either that (c) politics only falls under moral principles if those principles are agreed to by the members, or (d) the question of what is to be done in the face of moral disagreement is not a moral question. Neither of those is initially very plausible, and so a compelling argument would be needed to establish them.

A separate point is important here, namely that the moral views that give rise to the conflict in question are themselves political views, at least on any recognizable understanding of a political view—for example, the view that abortion ought to be illegal, or that schools ought not to be funded by local property taxes. This is important since if they are both moral and political views, the moral is not somehow excluded from the political. It is sometimes said that the question of social justice, about which citizens disagree, is a topic for moral philosophy and not for political philosophy, with the latter only entering when this problem of moral disagreement arises. This is doubly wrong if the competing moral views are political views, and the political question of what is to be done in the case of disagreement is a moral question. And indeed, those are both plausible—not discredited by arbitrary definitions of "moral" and "political" that would falsify them. The problem of disagreement between political views arises only after there are conflicting first-order political views. Nothing about offering a first-order view of justice is incompatible with acknowledging that others will disagree and that something must, politically, be done about that. Nothing is clarified by counting only this latter question about disagreement as a genuine topic for political philosophy. Indeed, there is some danger in narrowing the concerns of political philosophy in this way, since it might encourage the assumption that people's contending and conflicting first-order views about social justice are brute, to be "taken as given" by normative philosophy, much as social choice theory does with individual preferences. If they were, then debates about justice in political forums must be premised on a delusion or a cynical pretense that the question of justice, about which each participant takes a view, is subject to rational and critical assessment and revision at all. Whether, for example, a society is unjust if some people are, through no fault of their own, excluded from access to minimally adequate health care depends on at least a partial conception of justice that is prior to the question of how legitimately to deal with disagreement about that matter.

Even apart from what gets counted as political, some assert a certain primacy of the questions about how society might be governed given fundamental moral disagreements about justice and morality. Charles Larmore writes,

> [P]olitical philosophy must begin, as Williams claimed, not with the question of social justice, but instead with the question of authority and legitimacy. The idea is not therefore that it should simply concern itself with both. On the contrary, the one question is prior to the other. For the conditions under which the state is justified in exercising its coercive power constrain what can count from a political point of view (as opposed to the more absolute standpoint of morality) as the ideal of social justice to be pursued: the morally best may not be politically justifiable.[18]

It is not clear what the primacy is meant to consist in. If it is a matter of where political philosophy "must begin," surely the circumstances of politics are posterior, logically speaking, to the moral and other disagreements that raise those political problems about how to govern. There is no question of what to do about disagreement except in contemplating views, which are not themselves necessarily about disagreement, but which are in conflict. There is that primacy of the first-order views, the ones that are in disagreement but are not about disagreement. Larmore and many others plausibly hold that being correct on those first-order matters is not enough to warrant your legitimately ruling, but that does nothing to place the question of legitimate rule in a position somehow prior to the other questions. It is a question—and evidently a moral one—about how they are to be politically handled. Since, as I have argued, questions in both categories can plainly be political (as well as moral), the question of legitimate rule does not get primacy by default after excluding the other questions altogether from the political. It is surely correct that in addition to (other) questions about social justice there are questions about what doctrines may justifiably (morally speaking, I presume) be pursued through the coercive measures of laws and states. Nothing in that position marginalizes the moral within the space of the many fine questions in political philosophy.

5. Varieties of Anti-Moralism

It is difficult to resist the very general idea that there are moral questions about what a society's basic social structure ought to be like. It is difficult to credit any skepticism about this. For one example, some societies institutionalize disadvantage on the basis of race, gender, sexuality, religion, in ways that render those societies morally defective. The resentment or outrage that seems appropriate in such cases (or substitute others; I hang nothing on particular moral judgments, as I say) is *moral* resentment or outrage, or so I assume. If there is some distinctive "political" form of outrage, resentment, or failure in such cases which is not a species of the moral, then this would need to be explained with some care. Calling it "political" does not in any obvious way exclude its being moral. So what grounds might there be for opposing "moralism" in political philosophy?

a.

One way of opposing an overly moralized approach to political standards would be to reject basing requirements of, for example, justice on what are taken to be plausible principles of individual morality. But I find this hard to understand. Here are some common schematic candidates for requirements of political justice:

- Members should have certain guaranteed basic rights and liberties (maybe equal, maybe not . . .).
- Certain goods or opportunities ought to be distributed in some certain way.
- The social structure itself ought to meet certain standards.

We notice right away that none of these has an analogue in "individual morality." An individual is not a society, and so, unlike a society, is not made up of agents who might have rights or liberties or between whom certain assets might be distributed. And not being a society, an individual cannot be required to instantiate any principles of social structure. This might seem to be a point in favor of the view that political requirements are not based on "pre-political" moral requirements. It can look like a category mistake. The problem, though, is that there is, again, no debate about this claim once it is interpreted in this way. There is no school of thought, no idealist or utopian outlook, that thinks there are moral requirements on individuals of the kind that are proposed as requirements of social justice. So this cannot be the locus of any significant debate.

b.

Some, in the tradition of Machiavelli, for example, investigate how rulers ought to rule *given* the moral defects of humans. But they often suppose that this kind of 'ought' must, for this reason, be other than moral. It is hard to see why. Whether or not Machiavelli was reasoning morally, there is no difficulty about there being paradigmatically moral questions of this kind. I am unaware of any argument by any author that there is no moral question about how to govern immoral people.[19] So the view (which, as it happens, I deny) that questions about politics take facts about individual moral vice as given is no reason for thinking the questions about politics are something other than moral.

c.

It would be possible to hold that there is a *sui generis* mode of practical normativity that is political but not moral. But if we survey the main things this might mean, the meaning and appeal of this idea is elusive. It is notoriously difficult to say clearly what the moral consists in, and I do not have a proposal. But if someone claims to have arguments that normative standards for appropriate politics are not moral standards, they owe us enough of an account of the nature of the moral for us to understand what it is that they mean.

d.

"Realist" writers have recently often denied only that political standards are moral in any way that is "*prior* to politics."[20] So maybe they mean to allow that they are moral after all. But then it remains unclear to me what they mean to claim—what precise kind of priority they have in mind. The intention in the idea that politics is not subject to any morality that is "prior to politics" might be to reject the idea that we can think soundly about the content of moral requirements prior to considering politics and justice. But everyone rejects that, roughly speaking. It is an epistemological issue, and it seems to me a fairly simple one. It is preposterous to hold that one could attain strong epistemic justification for moral views, even for those that would bear on politics, entirely before considering what they would imply in political contexts. That is not a serious contender in moral or political philosophy, and I take it that realists who reject the priority of morality to politics mean to reject moralism in political thought in some deeper way than this.[21]

e.

A different way of resisting some kind of primacy of the moral in political philosophy is an objection to the use of the kind of substantive normative convictions that are employed in nonpolitical moral reasoning. One objection to that might stem from the thought that political philosophy must step back and take a critical view of that whole enterprise, including what comes to count as a commonsense moral conviction under certain historical conditions. I am happy to grant that this is one important thing political philosophy can do. I am less sure that this undercuts in any thorough way the legitimacy of reasoning about politics through the use of morally substantial convictions. That is how interpersonal reasoning works: it starts with premises acceptable to one's interlocutor and explores whether its implications are also acceptable. There is no alternative—no way of arguing without the use of unargued premises. Nothing in this method commits us to the view that generally accepted moral views are likely to be even remotely close to the truth. Rather, it can be a way of scrutinizing them. There might also be things to learn from stepping back from them entirely—proceeding as if we did not really hold them—and asking how these came to be our views, or came to be prevalent, or prevalent in certain classes or times. Such causal inquiries can often loosen our attachment to our previous views if they seem to be manufactured or otherwise irrational. None of that would be a critique of the moral as a mode of political evaluation, but rather a critique of certain moral convictions. Some especially deep inquiry might lead some to lose any attachment to the moral at all, but it is hard to see what that would have *especially* to do with political philosophy. In any case, my approach in this work makes no appeal to any particular moral premises, and so not to any that happen to be widely plausible among my readers. My questions are not directly normative in that way. I proceed as though the question of social justice is, among other things, a moral one, and so it is worth canvassing, as I am doing presently, a number of lines of objection to thinking of the moral as central, in various ways, to political philosophy.

f.

Some who oppose moralism about politics have a complaint of one kind or another about moral thought itself. Certainly, philosophers have long debated whether moral thought can ever gain significant epistemological warrant or authority, and partly for reasons having to do with rationalization. Notoriously, moral views vary widely across history and culture. In addition, there are no instruments to detect the moral facts in the ways that are sometimes available for scientific facts. And so on. And, of course, this might all open the door to rationalization. E. H. Carr, a classic political realist, writes,

> "Ethical notions," as Mr. Bertrand Russell has remarked, "are very seldom a cause, but almost always an effect, a means of claiming universal

legislative authority for our own preferences, not, as we fondly imagine, the actual ground of those preferences." This is by far the most formidable attack which utopianism has to face; for here the very foundations of its belief are undermined by the realist critique.[22]

This grounds a kind of political realism in the general thesis that "ethical notions" are always rationalizations of preferences. No less a realist than Hans Morgenthau found such dismissiveness of moral standards to be dangerous or worse:

> Mr. Carr, philosophically so ill-equipped, has no transcendent point of view from which to survey the political scene and to appraise the phenomenon of power. . . . It is a dangerous thing to be a Machiavelli. It is a disastrous thing to be a Machiavelli without *virtù*.[23]

Carr's position in that passage is not quite moral nihilism, the view that nothing is right or wrong. The claim, so far, is only that humans will tend to form moral judgments that would justify or advance their preferences and interests. That is an empirical psychological claim, not a moral or philosophical one. In fact, Russell, whom Carr is quoting, was no nihilist, but a kind of utilitarian.[24] But this still distances Carr from taking moral judgment seriously, and so Morgenthau should not be placated.

Incidentally, nihilism, and perhaps even this less extreme debunking position, would appear as nonsense to all those (everyone?) whose moral views are supposedly formed to calm their minds. If they believed nothing was right or wrong or that no moral judgment is to be taken seriously, there would be no question of justification to trouble them or calm them. The psychological thesis that moral views are rationalizations seems forced to admit that people are not nihilists or debunkers. And unless such theorists exempt themselves from their sweeping psychological claim, they are not nihilists or debunkers either, or at least not in their heart of hearts.

A more important point for my purposes is this: the claim that someone's moral views or arguments are psychologically explained by trying to rationalize preferences is no argument at all against the resulting moral positions. Beliefs and arguments cannot be refuted by identifying their cause or even their motive—that commits the so-called genetic fallacy. And, pertinently, Carr's claim that moral views are caused by (and perhaps mean to rationalize) political structure (or, in Marx, by economic modes, to be discussed below) merely purports to identify their cause and motive. So, it is no argument at all against them. For this reason, the thesis of morality as rationalization is perfectly compatible with the "moralist" (or, in Carr, "utopian") view that political arrangements are subject to moral standards.

Carr endorsed Russell's thesis of individual psychological rationalization (mentioned above), but he also held that moral thought was a kind of superstructure, in a Marxian sense, resting on a more fundamental explanatory "base" consisting in social and political structures. Marx, of course, thought that even political structures were superstructural relative to the more fundamental explanatory level of the succession through history of what he called modes of production, and also that not just moral thought but thought or ideas generally were superstructural in this way. Nevertheless, Carr's general idea of base/superstructure is similar to, and clearly drawn from, Marx's.

Russell, or Carr, or Marx, could add to the causal explanatory theory a metaethical claim that there is nothing to morality except these causally situated phenomena—no such thing as true or sound moral views. They could embrace moral nihilism, so understood. Or they might embrace some kind of metaethical expressivism or other non-cognitivism, where moral judgments do not answer to attitude-independent moral facts.[25] But the important point here is that the diagnostic causal claims (rationalization and superstructure), which are disputable in themselves, would in any case be no support for such metaethical views. Like Russell, who accepted a form of utilitarianism, Carr or Marx could consistently hold moral views of their own (presumably they all thought that rape is wrong), or at least take the general position that some moral views are sound or true even if is difficult to get things right in the face of these social and psychological causal forces. A causal diagnosis of moral thought either at the individual (as I have said before) or the social level, however sweeping and plausible, simply does not engage any moral question, nor does it engage, much less damage, the view that political arrangements are properly subject to moral standards. It commits a genetic fallacy. Analogously, we know that arguments in criminal court are overwhelmingly self-serving, and often produced for that reason. This should alert us, but it does not somehow sidestep the pressing issue of whether the defendant's arguments can be answered. So, even if moralized views of political justice tend to be produced or even motivated by their functionality for the status quo or the ruling class (which is not to be easily conceded), the question remains in full force: Can the arguments for those views be answered? (Often, prudence fuels ingenuity, after all, as criminal defense attorneys can attest.) If the arguments are sound, then the arrangements are indeed justified, though all agree it is not easy to find those arguments.

What is often not properly appreciated about many critiques of the moral from a political point of view is that similar challenges face normativity of every kind, not just moral normativity. There are no instruments to detect the true principles of rational prudence (dear to many realists' hearts) or logical inference either, or any other normative standard. Granted, there is less cultural and historical disagreement about some of these than about morality. But consider the anti-moralist position. Either it eschews normative standards for the evaluation of politics altogether (in which case, we need this explained), or it accepts some (ostensibly pre- or non-moral) kind of distinctively political normativity.[26] But it is difficult to see how anyone's view of the substance of those alternative standards could dodge the slings and arrows that are cast toward moral normativity: after all, whatever kind of normativity this is supposed to be, there is surely pervasive disagreement about its content, no instrument to detect it, a psychological tendency to rationalize, and all the rest. If, instead of proposing a distinctive (but in the above way, vulnerable) normativity, political anti-moralism is meant to rest on a comprehensive normative skepticism, then the debate is one about moral epistemology, and the realists have not begun to engage the vast philosophical literature about the possibility of moral knowledge. But, more likely, realists do not mean to rest their case on sweeping epistemological skepticism about normativity in general.

g.

When realists say that politics is not subject to morality in any way that is "prior to politics" they often mean by "politics" actual political processes and events, rather than, say, political concepts or the very idea of politics. So one view is that moral standards for politics such as standards of social justice depend on outcomes and settlements (democratic or not) that arise in real historical time out of real historical agency. On that view, the idea of evaluating political arrangements by standards that are somehow prior to or independent of those historical developments is nonsense. We might call this the view that politics *produces* the relevant standards. It is still a vague position in several ways. For example, it might mean that the produced standards are genuinely valid, or it might mean that there are no valid moral standards for politics at all, but only the norms that predominate or are purveyed as a matter of descriptive social fact.

On the latter, debunking reading, the question whether politically pertinent morality is "prior to politics" is a distraction. The view is that there is no valid politically pertinent morality. It is a form of nihilism about such standards, whether or not it is nihilistic about individual morality as well. It is not the view that moral standards such as justice are wrongly sought outside of serious attention to political and historical developments. It is, rather, the view that they are chimerical in any case. We have considered the case of moral skepticism just above, and this would be one form. I mention it here in order to distinguish it clearly from the former view, on which certain historically produced norms are valid. However, this production view, in its non-debunking variation, is uncomfortably committed to some prior unproduced moral principle according to which political settlements get this moral authority (akin to the Euthyphro question about how God's commands might generate morality). So it does not generally avoid the positing of unproduced moral standards pertaining to politics. Still, it might satisfy some realist impulses by nevertheless letting substantive political standards themselves arise from actual historical agency. As we will see, this suggests one way to understand the position of Bernard Williams.

h.

First, however, contrast this with a rather different kind of claim that political morality is not prior to politics, namely the claim that the moral norms that apply in a political setting depend on the kind of practice that it is. Sangiovanni and Rossi both suggest that this captures a strand of realist thinking. On this "practice dependence" view, the valid moral standards for a constitutional democracy, say, might be substantively different from the valid standards for an international partnership owing to the very different kinds of practices these are. Sangiovanni has explored this view and counts Rawls as an exponent. Rawls famously denied that his principles of justice would make sense for practices other than (certain forms of) whole societies. And he later argued that, in fact, they are not the appropriate principles for the evaluation of a global practice involving multiple (or all) nations.[27] This kind of denial that the moral standards are "prior to politics" is not meant to claim that the standards are produced by actual political developments in real historical time. On this view, rather, the right standard for a given political practice is settled prior to and independent of what emerges or is decided out of any actual politics that take that form. The standards are not dependent on how the actual practices go. Rather they are dependent on what kind of practice is in question. For present purposes it might be helpful to call this the practice-relativity view, lest "dependence" suggest the very different view that evaluative political standards are products of historical political developments.

There is a point at which the two views—the production and the practice relativity versions—can agree, though they remain very different views. One kind of thing that can be produced by actual historical political developments is transition to wholly different forms of political practice. There were not always states, after all, and then only much later were there constitutional democracies. The practice-production and the practice-relativity versions of "practice dependence" can agree that the standards that are relevant change when politics produces a new form of practice. But on one view—the practice-production view—it is not because it is a new form of practice. The standards could have changed even if the practice had not, namely if the standing practice had produced certain settlements or other social facts. On the practice-relativity view the relevant standards in this example would change not because new standards had been produced in political practice, but because the standard that was already (prior to political-production) the appropriate standard for this as yet undeveloped practice kicked in, found application, when the practice actually emerged.

To see how antithetical the practice-relativity view is to at least some prominent versions of political realism, we need only point out that it can (and in several authors, it does)[28] maintain that there are general standards of inter-personal fairness that are triggered when certain kinds of practices emerge. The appropriateness of those standards for those practices is not historically produced on this view, but is, let us say, "transhistorical." The idea that fairness is an appropriate standard for many forms of political practice should they arise is the kind of thing that many realists make it their mission to deny. Suf-fice it to say that Sangiovanni is explicitly developing a deep commitment of Rawlsian philosophy, so often the bête noire of political realists. I am not sure whether there is a strand of realism that is captured by the practice-relativity view, but the more important question is whether that kind of realism would support a critique of modern liberal political philosophy of the kind realism is normally understood to propose.

A radical version of practice-relativity would be the claim that there are no moral standards for the evaluation of political arrangements other than whether they are good instances of their kind. If it is a monarchy then its actual arrangement might meet the standards appropriate to monarchy or it might not. If it does, there is no moral defect such as injustice or illegitimacy in those arrangements. If it is a constitutional democracy, then again it might meet or violate the different applicable standards.[29] This radical version is not entailed by the general idea of practice-relativity for the following reason. Even if moral standards of politics such as justice are always and only standards for some-thing's being a good instance of its kind, the form known as a *state* might also be a kind in the relevant way, as many have, in effect, argued. If so, the practice-relativity view must be open to the possibility that there are moral standards that are triggered by the state-like form of political practice itself. For example, this opens the possibility that states are always unjust unless they are consti-tutional democracies. Monarchies, then, even when they are a good instance of that kind, would always be unjust, being poor instances of a state.

i.

One could, of course, resist this last idea by being "minimalist" about the stan-dards that are triggered by mere statehood, an option worth exploring at greater length. Williams can be read that way, as I will explain. But it is impor-tant to distinguish between justice and legitimacy in thinking about that issue. By "legitimacy" I mean the moral permissibility of a law's or regime's coercive political enforcement. By "justice" here I mean the question whether a law or political regime is morally right whether or not its enforcement is permissi-ble.[30] Even if there is good reason to be relatively minimalist about legitimacy (a question I will not consider), that does not preclude there also being more demanding standards of justice. To see this point in action, let us lump what Williams calls the "critical theory" and "making sense" principles together and call this the "critical sense principle."[31] First, "The critical theory principle, [is] that the acceptance of a justification does not count if the acceptance itself is produced by the coercive power which is supposedly being justified."³² Second, for a legitimating account to "make sense" requires that it "goes beyond the assertion of power; and we can recognize such a thing because in the light of the historical and cultural circumstances, and so forth, it [makes sense] to us as a legitimation." This two-part constraint on legitimating accounts is relatively minimal in the sense that it is clearly understood by Williams not to declare generally against monarchy or to require liberal or constitutional democracy, and so on. But it might be only a standard of legitimacy—of what it takes for the coercive enforcement of political arrangements to be morally permissible or justified. This leaves the field open for less minimal standards of substantive political or social justice. Minimalism about justice is not implied by minimalism about legitimacy. There is no contradiction implied by, for example, holding that the outcome of a free and fair vote is, for that reason (and surely within limits) permissibly enforceable even though that outcome is itself an unjust law. That (rough and simple) standard of legitimacy is relatively minimalist, leaving unaddressed what further standards there might be for substantive political justice.

For now, focus on the question of legitimacy for simplicity. Here is a Williams-inspired and realism-friendly position: the critical sense principle is the only moral standard that is triggered by mere statehood. Liberal democracy, for example, is not a standard for all states as such. The critical sense principle, in turn, implies that all and only political arrangements that are justifiable in a way that makes critical sense in the given historical and cultural conditions are permissibly enforceable (legitimate). Before considering which approaches this really opposes, we should first bring to bear the realist idea I discussed above that moral standards for politics are historically produced (and not just triggered). Assume for now that the critical sense principle speaks of "acceptance" of a proffered justification in the descriptive psychological sense: the political subjects tend to accept it. So understood, this view is quite congenial to the realist idea that purported moral standards such as those requiring liberal democracy or rejecting monarchy have no validity except as products of actual political and cultural developments—except, that is, as convictions that political subjects might actually come to adopt. They are not, in that strong sense, prior to politics.

Even so, this view crucially incorporates the critical sense principle, which has an entirely different status. It is not put forward (in my construction, or by Williams) as something that owes its own validity to its being a widespread conviction at some historical time—to its making critical sense. It is offered as having a validity that is, in that sense, transhistorical. This is not an inconsistency, of course, even if it is unacceptable to some who hope to reject all transhistorical moral principles pertaining to politics. It is, rather, a kind of transhistorical moral minimalism: except for the critical sense principle itself, moral standards for political arrangements are produced by the contingent course of actual historical developments. Call this collection of precepts *Minimalist Moralism* about legitimacy.[33]

There is a reading of Rawls along these very lines that resonates with many interpretations of his mature body of work. In the end, I doubt that it can be a sound interpretation for reasons that pose a deep Rawlsian challenge to such a Williams-inspired view, and this gives the point more than exegetical interest. On this reading of Rawls, putting things roughly for brevity, the liberal principle of legitimacy is transhistorical, requiring justifications of political arrangements to all reasonable comprehensive points of view including many that are mistaken. In the modern Western historical context a political conception must be liberal and democratic to meet that principle, so this view would go, but liberal democracy has no transhistorical authority of its own. Its legitimacy is historically produced in the way laid out by Williams's (transhistorical) principle of legitimate justification. In other times, and pointedly even in other places at this time, the principle of justification can be satisfied by nondemocratic and illiberal political conceptions, such as, perhaps, in some contemporary Middle Eastern settings which lack the liberal and democratic philosophical traditions of thought and practice. I do not believe this is Rawls's view, but it has structural similarities, and so construed it would be remarkably similar to the Minimalist Moralism I provisionally attribute to Williams.

I doubt that Rawls would have accepted that what is just or legitimate could be wholly determined, in that way, by what most people contingently come to accept or resist without any further questions about whether their responses themselves meet certain standards. This departure may be precisely the "moralistic" Rawlsian move that Williams is opposing, but his position is unstable as we will see. For now, note that it is possible (and anyway, it is conceivable) that a large fraction of subjects could come to share some point of view which, while freely formed (the critical theory principle is met), is morally not just flawed but heinous. Suppose many come to take the view that children are available to their parents on terms much like slavery: they may be forced to work, and their education and well-being make no claims on the parents except insofar as they bear on the interests of the parents themselves. This is just an example, and others would do just as well.

Now, Williams's amoral conception of the relevant kind of acceptability would seem to say that the state must find some justification for its measures that are (as a descriptive matter) acceptable to this point of view—one that "makes sense" to these people. Notice that this is a moral "must" if I am right that the critical sense principle is a transhistorical, if minimal, moral principle of legitimacy. It is not simply the "must" of pragmatic necessity. We need to be careful to distinguish between the obvious fact that obstacles are obstacles and cannot be ignored, and the much less obvious claim (perhaps of Williams) that the legitimacy of a political order—its permissible enforceability—is nothing but its *de facto* acceptability to whatever freely formed points of view are extant, however morally bad they might be.

So far, I am just developing an interpretation of Williams, or at least an interesting Williams-inspired position. Briefly, now, consider the separate question whether such a position is to be believed. It is hard to see what basis there is for holding that such execrable moral convictions about children among the populace have that kind of moral weight as justification defeaters. This is a moral view in its own right, a jarring one. Even jarring views can be correct, of course, but we are given no reason to believe that this one is correct. If this objection from heinousness were sidestepped by understanding the whole view as a nonmoral conception of legitimacy, then it is no challenge to political moralism at all, but simply a change of subject. Political moralism is surely not committed to any particular view of what should be counted as legitimacy in some wholly nonmoral sense. But that kind of dodge is not what Williams is up to. If it were, there would be no rationale for his "critical theory principle." After all, manufactured consent is as good as freely formed consent if the question is nothing but where the obstacles to stable state rule might be found and how they might be effectively overcome. To disqualify the kinds of acceptance that are manufactured by propaganda from counting toward legitimacy is a moral argument.

So we see a distinctively Rawlsian objection to the amoral form of the minimal acceptability requirement suggested by Williams's writings. The other point to keep in mind, even if it is not a direct objection, is that whether the criterion of legitimacy is or is not adjusted in the direction of a moralized standard of "reasonableness," recall that such minimalism in a theory of legitimacy would not commit one to similar minimalism about standards of social justice. Rawls's more moralistic approach (though still far more minimal than traditional "comprehensive" liberal political philosophy) may be necessary to avoid a serious objection, namely that otherwise there are absurd implications for what would count as morally legitimate or illegitimate states. However, whether or not that critique is persuasive, the Williams-inspired minimalism as I have understood it here would still not be a wholesale rejection of moral standards applied to politics, or even of applicable moral standards that are prior to the products of politics. And yet there would be some resonance with the realist idea of letting moral standards for politics such as putative requirements of liberal rights or democracy arise as products of social history. It is a nuanced version of some recognizably realist ideas, even if it is hardly the rejection of moral standards of social justice (or legitimacy). If my argument against it is successful, then we have an argument against a sophisticated form of the realist objection to (any less minimalist) political moralism.

6. Conclusion

If the moral is about what we ought to do, then it is ironic that the resistance to seeing political philosophy in moral terms is partly motivated by the concern that this would divorce it too much from practice. Reality, such critics observe, tends to deviate so much from what is right. (As Machiavelli says, "there is such a great distance between how we live and how we ought to live.")[34] But it is a profound mistake to think that all sound philosophical reflection about ethics or politics should bear more or less directly or immediately on practical choices.[35] One reason is that when the time for action does come, one hopes (though it cannot be guaranteed) that there has been much time for long and hard thought about what to do and when. This is not a conservative view of political philosophy. We are more likely to understand what needs to be done and what to aim for if we foster a constant space for reflection, not just about what to do, but about what to think about such matters as social justice. If we do not, whatever action we do take may be more likely to be ill-considered. I am not arguing against action, of course. Call for as much action as you please, at whatever rate you please. My point is that however much action there ought to be, we ought to have had the space to think long and hard, without the pressure of impending practical decision.

So far, this, of course, is still what I will call a "practicalist" argument, one that takes a long view. I do not believe that philosophical reflection is subservient to practice even in that way. If I were in prison and without any way to communicate my views to the outside world, I doubt that the nature and content of social justice is a question that would somehow lose its interest or evident importance. I do not believe that we think about such things only in order to act. This raises important questions, and we will address them head-on in chapter 17, "Informed Concern."

CHAPTER FOUR

Circumstances and Justice

*When our social world is pervaded by duplicity and deceit we are tempted
to think that law and government are necessary only because of the
propensity of individuals to act unfairly. But, to the contrary, the
tendency is rather for background justice to be eroded even when
individuals act fairly: the overall result of separate and independent
transactions is away from and not toward background justice. We might
say: in this case the invisible hand guides things in the wrong direction.*

—JOHN RAWLS, *POLITICAL LIBERALISM*

Introduction

Justice is often said, and not wrongly, to be a solution to a problem. It is often
concluded that justice and even the political itself are not applicable to highly
favorable conditions of certain kinds, especially conditions in which people
are very good. Justice and the political, as concepts, are confined to the realm
of the nonideal. Reflections on standards for, say, basic social structure under
which people would be good and just have left the topics of justice and politics
behind. Even if that were all so, it might be that unrealistic standards nevertheless apply—their normative standing would not thereby be challenged.
However, in this chapter I argue for the deeper position that this familiar line
of thought is in any case mistaken.

David Hume influentially argued that humans would never have developed
the idea of justice at all if it were not for certain contingent but prevalent circumstances in human life, especially competition and disagreement. John
Rawls adapted Hume's idea under the name "circumstances of justice," arguing
that standards of justice only have application in conditions (mainly) of competition and disagreement. Both are adaptations of the momentous Hobbesian
analysis of the point and value of political relations as a solution to severe en-

demic problems of, again, competition and disagreement in human life. Considered together loosely, these ideas might seem to suggest that high idealistic standards of justice are simply confused, failing to understand that the very idea of justice is out of place except in the setting of widespread mutual suspicion, selfishness, stubbornness, and (barely, or not at all submerged) tendencies toward battle. Justice, properly conceived, cannot be idealistic, even if there is some admitted value in certain imaginary conditions that are beyond justice. If we look more closely, we will see that the three claims—Hume's, Rawls's, and Hobbes's—are distinct, being, respectively, about conditions of the *emergence* of ideas of justice, conditions of their *applicability*, and conditions of their *point* or value. Taking these distinctions seriously will allow us to see that this cluster of ideas is no challenge at all to idealism about justice, the idea that it is a moral requirement, applying to societies, that is unlikely ever or often to be met. Indeed, there is no basis in the idea of circumstances of justice for holding that a world of morally perfect agents is (while surely unrealistic) beyond justice.[1]

My broader thesis in this chapter is that there is a variety of conditions we would all regard as highly idealistic and unrealistic which are, nevertheless, not beyond justice. Nothing in a proper understanding of circumstances of justice precludes applicability of justice in any of the following conditions, or even in certain combinations of them. Justice might have application even where

- there is no need for social rules of justice.
- there are no social rules or other mechanisms of adjudication.
- there are no conflicting aims or interests.
- there are no differences of opinion or conviction.
- no one is morally deficient in the slightest.

My argument is not that justice could have application even if *none* of these things were the case, and that is evidently not true. But each of the above claims—taking each of the points as something compatible with the applicability of justice—I will argue, is true. I also argue for two further theses:

1. Mutual advantage might constrain what mechanisms of adjudication would arise, but it does not follow (and it is plausibly not true) that it constrains what arrangements might successfully specify justice.
2. Even if ideas of justice would only arise in the train of mutually advantageous social rules of adjudication, this does not support the conventionalist view of justice—that it is, in any way, a human creation.

A few preliminaries will be helpful in introducing what comes in the following sections. First, we are not concerned here with every kind of justice and injustice, such as deserved or undeserved punishment, or the various things that might be meant by an individual virtue of justice.[2] Rather, the kind of justice in question specifies appropriate resolutions to interpersonal conflicts of desires or beliefs, roughly speaking. It is too easily assumed that the needed resolutions must be provided by the threat of sanctions, or even specifically by government. Or seen from the other side, it is too easily assumed that in conditions where there is no need for government or sanctions, there is no applicability of this kind of justice at all. I hope to show that those assumptions are mistaken.

Second, the issue here is not merely semantic, but substantively moral. If someone proposes to use the word "justice" to refer only to conditions that include, say, states, laws, familiar moral deficiencies, and/or other elements that might be arbitrarily defined as essential to "the political," then the question whether moral perfection makes the idea of justice inapplicable is answered by definitional fiat, though implausibly to my mind. Nevertheless, I argue that there is a familiar form of behavioral need (as I will call it) for some or other mechanism of adjudication of interpersonal conflict that is not necessarily met simply by people being morally flawless. Furthermore, the need might conceivably (even if unrealistically) be met without any sanction-based rules or coercive government. If this is taken to show that justice as so understood is not essentially political, so be it. It is not especially interesting to claim that *political* justice depends on the presence of political elements, however "political" might be defined. Now, having said all this, my topic is not limited to the question about moral perfection. More generally, I emphasize that justice might apply to a variety of highly idealistic conditions, moral perfection among them.

Third, here as throughout the book, I will speak of the standard of justice without presupposing any particular account of what the standard requires. This neutral use of the concept of justice is the operative one when, for example, we ask what justice requires. "Justice," in that setting, does not refer to or assume any specific conception of the content of justice. It will be central to my argument to assume that the standard of justice (whatever it might require) is not identical with the standards embodied in social rules or conventions of any kind. This should be common ground. My point is not only that any actual set of rules might be unjust, but that the standard is at a higher level of abstraction. That is why adjudicatory social rules, conventions, or motives can embody the same standards—have the same standards as their content. Just as beliefs have propositions as their contents, rules and conventions of justice have standards as their contents. And just as a rule or a convention can embody a certain standard of justice, so can a person's motives, sentiments, or attitudes. When a person obeys a social rule or convention she abides by its standards. If she should come to develop motives to behave in the same ways that those rules or conventions dictated even where there are no such rules or conventions, she would still abide by the same standards, now internalized. They are now her own standards, those she possesses or accepts. So the standard of justice is not conceptually linked to social rules. That leaves open the possibility that the standard of justice is conceptually linked to mechanisms of justice of some kind, be they rules, conventions, or moral motives. The role of justice, one might conjecture, is nothing but to be the content of one or another such social mechanism. I will resist that way of thinking.

Fourth, I will speak of the applicability conditions of the standard of justice, which is worth explaining briefly. In all of these cases of mechanisms—rules, conventions, or moral motives—we can consider the embodied standard itself in order to ask under what conditions it would have application. All standards are bound to have necessary conditions of their applicability. Decorum is not a standard that applies to the evaluation of a financial decision. Efficiency is not a standard that applies to the evaluation of the state of someone's health. Justice is not a standard that applies to conditions in which there is nothing to put people's interests and opinions at odds, at the very least.[3] There is that much truth in the idea that there is no justice without a problem. But that is not as inimical to idealistic conceptions of justice as one might suppose.

2. Uncoupling Justice from the Need for Social Rules

It will be helpful to distinguish what I will call social rules from social conventions as follows, limiting ourselves to ones that serve to adjudicate conflicts between individuals. A social *rule* of adjudication not only specifies resolutions of conflicts but is also accompanied by social or official sanctions for noncompliance with the standard. We can regard a *convention* of adjudication as the case where such a standard is conformed to in practice, even without any threat or mechanism of punishment for noncompliance, but still followed conditionally on most others complying as well. We will distinguish both of those from the case in which the standard is complied with, but owing neither to any social rule nor to any convention as I have defined these, but owing rather entirely to individuals having or adopting these standards in their own *motives*.[4] I will call these—rules, conventions, and motives—the three mechanisms by which the behavioral need (about which more shortly) might be met.

Hume famously says, "if men pursu'd the publick interest naturally, and with a hearty affection, they wou'd never have dream'd of restraining each other by these rules"[5] This Humean point will eventually suit my purposes nicely, but first notice how it is grist for the mill of the critic of idealistically high standards of justice. Hume is arguing that the very idea of justice is owed, causally speaking, to real conditions of human life which, being far from ideal in certain ways, gave rise to a human need for and development of social rules of adjudication. For my purposes we can allow that Hume is right about this. The lesson many seem to have drawn is that whatever the standard of justice might require, it is, for this Humean reason, inseparable from—has no application outside of—those unfortunate conditions that explain its emergence in rules. The problem to which such rules provide a solution sets the conditions for the very applicability of the standard of justice. This is one of the claims I propose to challenge. The conditions necessary for the emergence of mechanisms of justice are not (at least not necessarily) conditions necessary for the applicability of justice. This will allow us to see at least one highly idealistic scenario that is not justice-inapt even though no rules are necessary there, namely a condition of widespread moral motives of justice.

We should consider first whether justice only applies when there is a human need for social rules of adjudication. In the first stage of the argument, I will argue that this is not so, since those needs might be met by conventions or by motives embodying similar standards. That is an important first result, but it would not yet challenge the suggestion that justice applies only when there is a human need for one or another of the adjudicatory mechanisms, even if only internalized motives of justice. I turn later to questioning the broad strategy of linking justice to a human need. (See the section on "Who Needs Justice?")

The suggestion to be scrutinized first is that the applicability of a standard of justice depends on the presence of conditions where there is a practical need for social rules embodying such a standard. This suggestion, which I will criticize, makes use of the following two ideas:

Need for justice: conditions under which a society will have the need for some social rules (or, considered later, other mechanisms) for adjudicating conflicts.

Applicability of justice: conditions under which the standard of justice has application.

In order to have all three in one place, I introduce a third class of conditions here and come back to it later:

Emergence of justice: conditions under which a mechanism of justice will emerge, evolve, or be developed.

The need for social rules (the rule-need) is derivative, we must assume, from a need for a certain organization of behavior (I will refer to it as the *behavioral need*). In particular, the rules would serve to bring about behavior that is more peaceful and productive, largely by avoiding uncertainty and battle. The details should not matter. We are to consider circumstances in which a collection of socially interacting people stands to benefit greatly from behavior that is organized in the right way. We are to suppose further that behavior would never come to be suitably organized if not for the emergence of some social rules for adjudicating disputes and conflicts. In that derivative way, the people have a great need for such social rules, in order to meet the need for such behavior.

To say that the behavior, and derivatively the rules, are "needed" is plainly to claim that it would be in people's interest. We might wonder, which people's interest? I want to flag this issue and return to it (see section on "Who Needs Justice?"), but we can proceed for now on the simple assumption that to say that the behavior and rules are needed in the relevant sense is to say that having them would be to everyone's mutual advantage, adding, if you like, that the relevant interests that are mutually served are dire or urgent ones as opposed to refinements of the good life.

There are ways in which the needed organization of behavior could, in principle, be produced without social rules, and we will consider two such ways. If it were possible to arrive at a social convention in which the needed organization of behavior was present, each individual's behavior being conditional on the expectation of the others', but without threats of sanction, no social rules would be needed—rules being defined for our purposes as including sanctions. Maybe they were needed in the past as a precursor, or maybe not, but either way, they are not needed once there is such a convention. Maybe rules are needed because no such convention will, in fact, arise, but what is needed is either rules, or a convention, or some way of producing the behavior.

All sides agree that justice has application in the case where the organized behavior is needed and social rules are present. The question, as I have said, is whether that is the only case in which it applies. But once we consider the case of a convention, there is evidently as much application of the idea of justice there as in the case of enforced rules. The content of the standards is, we can suppose, unchanged and the need they are serving is also precisely the same: the suitable organization of behavior along the conflict-resolving lines we described. So, as a first step, in the specific sanction-entailing sense of "rules," there is a condition in which the standard of justice applies even though there is no need for social rules: when there is the behavioral need plus a convention.

By distinguishing, in that way, the standard from the particular mechanism of social rules, it is easy to see that there is also a second way in which the behavioral need could in principle be met without the presence of social rules. Imagine, in a Humean spirit if you like, some long peaceful period of life under such conventions of justice. It is conceivable that people will become attached to the motive of compliance with these norms, praising it in others and taking pride in their own. (We might even regard them as becoming, in that Humean way, moral motives.) Predictions are not what matters here; just suppose this happens. Alternatively, and more generally, suppose that people come (maybe by this convention-induced mechanism, or some other functional explanation, or in some entirely different way) to be motivated to behave in just the same way as under that convention, except now the motive to comply with that same standard is not contingent on its being conventional to do so. Suppose the motive to so act has its force for each agent regardless of whether others are expected to behave similarly, though suppose they all do. The norms are now, as we might say, internalized. For simplicity, call these *coordinate motives of justice* in the case where there are no social rules or conventions of justice, even if there might have been in the past. Coordinate motives of justice would meet the need for suitably organized behavior, since the behavior produced by the rules and conventions is the very same behavior (modulo the motives) that is produced by these coordinate motives. So we see that there could be conditions where neither rules nor conventions are needed, because there are coordinate motives to meet the behavioral need.[6]

If the standard of justice, having been granted to have application where no rules or conventions of adjudication were needed, applies here too then we will have decoupled the conditions of the applicability from the conditions in which rules or conventions of adjudication are needed. And, indeed, I see no way it could be denied even on the broadly Humean approach. Even if the standard of justice gets its content in a certain way from the standards embodied in the mechanisms of adjudication that arise from certain human needs, internalized motives of adjudication are one such mechanism. Justice, then, could apply even in conditions where there is no need for social rules or conventions because there is the alternative mechanism of just people. Not only does this let justice apply independently of the need for rules, it applies in what anyone would recognize as a highly idealistic, and maybe very unlikely condition—the condition in which motives of justice are sufficient to produce the needed behavior even with social rules or conventions (as defined).

The idea that such a mechanism might arise, but only at a later historical period than the mechanisms of rules and conventions is important in Marx, as when he contrasts merely "political emancipation" with the "human emancipation" in which "the actual, individual man has taken back into himself the abstract citizen," a social function previously farmed out to political institutions in which one is seen as merely an "egoistic independent individual."[7] Marx and others sympathetic to this picture might conceive of that achievement as beyond politics, law, and the state. I will argue only that it is not beyond justice. The late stages of Marxian theory, if I am right, fall under the general theory of justice as a domain of inquiry, not outside it.

As we saw earlier, Hume says, "if men pursu'd the publick interest naturally, and with a hearty affection, they wou'd never have dream'd of restraining each other by these rules."[8] This passage, which is followed by many other authors, is double edged. On one edge, it says that if people's interests, understanding, and motives were never competing or conflicting in any way in the first place we would have no need for behavior to be organized by standards of justice, and (what is different) justice would fail to apply. I grant that. But on the other edge it also, inadvertently I suppose, shows us that sometimes where justice does apply, because something in people's conditions puts them at odds, there might still be no need for social rules of adjudication (by which people "restrain each other," as Hume says), or even conventions, and this is because there might be internalized standards of justice by which men pursue "the publick interest" if not "naturally," then still "with a hearty affection." Hume says that there would be no need for restraint by rules in that case. Whether or not you agree that we can find the point in Hume, while there would be no need in that case for sanction-backed social rules, the hearty affection for the public good would itself be a needed, and happily present, mechanism. The public interest is, presumably, some appropriate arrangement that, among other things, resolves conflicts and disputes of aims and beliefs. Those conflicts do not disappear just because all parties are motivated to deal with them in some specified way, and so justice plainly applies. The motive of justice will have (perhaps inherited from rules) content that coordinates behavior in order to adjudicate the admitted conflicts among people's other interests. The point is that justice cannot be denied application in that fortuitous case, since it is just a third mechanism, embodying the same standard as might be embodied by rules or conventions, which tends to meet the need for certain kinds of organized behavior. Of course, justice, like any standard, has application only in certain conditions, as I have mentioned. If people had no attitudes that put them at odds in the first place—no self-favoring desires or headstrong beliefs that rules or conventions or motives of justice might restrain—then justice would not even apply. But those conditions of application are compatible with a highly idealistic world of people who have no need for rules or conventions of justice, because they are just in their coordinate motives.

Government, roughly the promulgation and coercive enforcement of laws, is obviously one salient form that social rules, in my sense, might take. So, if the presence of convention or coordinate motives of justice can meet the behavioral need, government would not be needed to serve that role. There is a traditional interest in the question whether morally perfect people would still need government, to which I return below.[9] For now, notice that no position is taken on that question by noting that there is a conceivable arrangement of motives that would make government unnecessary. I will argue below that moral perfection does not ensure such an arrangement, in which case government might yet be necessary.

It might seem that if there are no rules or conventions then there will be no source to specify which of several competing interpretations of the norms is (already, or by fiat) correct or authoritative. There must be some agent or source with the final, fully specifying, say. There are two things to notice about this issue. The first is that whatever indeterminacy there might be prior to the introduction of that authoritative source, indeterminacy can just as well arise again in the interpretation of the source itself (a court, written law, or whatever). Second, even if some such source is needed, that is compatible with the mechanism by which the behavioral need is met being nothing more than moral motives. That is, no sanctions, and no conditionality of the motives on similar behavior by others is shown to be necessary. So, the question of whether for some reason there needs to be such a source of specification and coordination outside of the motives themselves is not especially pertinent to our question whether justice might apply and even be satisfied even without rules or conventions.

3. Multiple Realizability and Specification

Prior to any mechanism, there might be no particular behaviors that count as unjust, since there are multiple, and indeed infinitely many, coordinate patterns of behavior any of which would be eligible as a pattern that specifies the content of justice. We might call patterns of which this is true *eligible patterns*. We sometimes say that it is arbitrary which specification is adopted. Certainly, when considering the enormous number and complexity of rules of property in a modern state, it is probable that there would be lots of alternative patterns that would be just. If some particular change would plausibly make a certain arrangement less just, it will often be possible to devise a second change elsewhere in the system that countervails the first from the standpoint of justice. And that procedure could probably be repeated a large number of times, generating a new just system with each iteration. If so, there might be a wide variety of systems of property that are equally eligible from the standpoint of justice—equally suited to specify which behaviors count as just and unjust. We can speak, then, of the *multiple realizability* of justice, and also of a *prespecification* phase in the development of just arrangements. It is important not to exaggerate the multiplicity. Not just any pattern would count as a specification of justice. (Consider, for example, the initial changes to a just system but without the countervailing changes just discussed.) Still, there is multiplicity and it is in some ways vast.

If none of the eligible patterns has been selected by the emergence of eligible social rules or other mechanisms, does nothing count as just or unjust? We should allow for the possibility that some acts would be forbidden by each and every member of a set of eligible patterns.[10] Whatever is in that overlapping set is the portion of the content of justice that is, as I will call it, naturally determinate. Still, there is bound to be much that is not common in that way. We can grant for the sake of argument that social rules or conventions of justice are necessary in order to give fuller specification to justice, selecting among morally eligible patterns.

An arrangement that is selected by the rules at one time can remain selected whether the rules themselves persist or not. Think of a law that selects left-side driving. If convention or even internalized motives come to conform to that standard, left-side driving might remain selected even if the law were to expire or be repealed. The same point applies to social rules or conventions of adjudication. They do not need to persist in order for their power of selection to persist.

Similarly, once some mechanism has done the specifying, then not even a mechanism of internalized motives is required in order for justice of behavior to be specified. Imagine such motives weakening over time. At least for some period this will count as a falling into injustice. The standard of behavior applies whether any mechanism is in place or not, even if some mechanism must previously have been in place to accomplish the specification. The behavioral standard's applicability is not ultimately owing to any positive rule or norm or practice's being currently in place or being needed. Plausibly, if all mechanisms have lapsed for too long, the specification lapses as well and there is a new need for one or another mechanism of justice. As we noticed, there might still be some requirements of justice if, as seems likely, there is some overlapping content of all eligible mechanisms, the naturally determinate portion of the standard of justice.

If not just any stable order of behavior is sufficient to count compliant behavior as just, we ought to ask which patterns are justice-apt in that sense and which are not. That is a hard question, and I return to it (without answering it) in the next section. However, acknowledging the question is enough to suggest the unavoidability of appealing to a higher-order standard by which whole systems (basic social structures?) are to be judged, so that only some are eligible as just (understood as justice-specifying) arrangements. Call this higher-order standard the *standard for just arrangements*. It is higher-order because it is the arrangements themselves that embody standards of just behavior.

There is the need, then, to appeal both to (a) a standard for just arrangements, those that would, by specification from the eligible candidates, render certain behaviors just and unjust, as well as (b) standards of justice that are specified by the emergence of one of the eligible arrangements. The higher-order standard's status cannot coherently itself be a matter of artifice or invention, even if the specification of some particular arrangement is. Rather, it ranges over possibilities of human artifice—the mechanisms of adjudication that could conceivably be devised—and counts some of them as mechanisms of justice, other ones not.

One might hope to avoid appealing to any such standard of just arrangements (perhaps if one is hoping to stay broadly conventionalist about all standards of justice) simply by appeal to the question of which arrangements have any chance of actually emerging. Suppose only arrangements that would benefit everyone would tend to emerge. That would select some arrangements out of the set of all conceivable possibilities. And mutual advantage has a promising ring to it. I turn in the next section to criticizing this familiar approach.

Conflict or disagreement alone may not themselves be enough to count any behaviors as unjust prior to the selection of any of the eligible arrangements of adjudication; standards of justice of behavior would not apply. But either conflict or disagreement is enough to give meaning to the possibility of a system of adjudication, and prior to the emergence of any such system some of the possible systems are disqualified by a higher-order standard of justice. Those conditions are ones in which, as Rawls says, "questions of justice arise."[11] The standard of justice is doing some work already. We might express it this way: the conditions of the applicability of justice come in two kinds: (a) conditions in which non-artificial standards of justice-eligible arrangements apply, categorizing some possible arrangements as systems of adjudication that would successfully specify which behaviors are just, and (b) conditions in which one of the eligible arrangements has been somehow selected in practice, and so now certain behaviors are just and others unjust (or ones that were not already naturally determinate). And, not to be forgotten: the specification might well persist, even if all mechanisms come to disappear, leaving certain behaviors to count as just or unjust even there, at least for a time.

Since, to some extent, the content of justice gets specified by whichever mechanism arises, it might seem as though there is no independent basis upon which someone might criticize prevailing mechanisms. But it is always open to people to question whether the mechanism that has arisen is truly in the eligible set of arrangements—arrangements which, should they arise, not only specify resolutions, but also count as genuine norms of justice. That is a substantive moral question, not a sociological one.

4. Who Needs Justice?

We noticed that there is this question: Which arrangements of adjudication are the justice-apt ones? Suppose the arrangements of behavior for purposes of adjudication that are to be counted as genuinely justice-determining are whichever ones are likely to emerge in real human social conditions, in response to a profound human need for such a thing. Central to this strategy is the suggestion that in certain conditions there *comes to be a need* for rules or some other mechanism of justice. What kind of need is referred to? It might mean that there are conditions in which the standard of justice applies, and that it will not be met unless there is some such mechanism. A mechanism is *needed if* there is to be justice. Or maybe that plus the claim that it is necessary—in the sense of being morally required—to have justice. However, this is not the proposal I want to consider, since it does not yet link justice to human needs in any way.

A second thing it might mean to say that there comes to be a need for some mechanism of justice is that there are certain human needs, understood as especially important and basic interests, that will only be satisfied if there is some mechanism of justice—some mechanism to specify and help produce behaviors that thereby count as just. This is saying importantly more than, as in the first interpretation of its being needed, that mechanisms are needed if justice, which ought to obtain, is going to obtain. It now makes essential reference to fundamental human needs that would be met. On this approach, the content of justice is eventually to be understood by first understanding justice's function, so defined, as meeting a certain human need. I believe such a linkage between justice and human need is often thought to have the advantage of forestalling flights of fancy, keeping justice down to earth. The thought might be that mechanisms embodying high idealistic standards are patently not something humans would ever need. In any case, I want to cast doubt on the need-grounding approach in general, which would then undermine any alleged moderating pressure it is claimed to exert on the standard of justice.

When it is said that people come urgently to need some mechanism of adjudication, we ought to ask: Which people? When people are at odds, it is hardly guaranteed that everyone would benefit from the emergence of mechanisms of adjudication. Some might be better off without rules or other mechanisms of justice, retaining their advantages even while absorbing some costs of widespread dispute and conflict. They might win the battles and weather the storms.

Of course, there might be some method of adjudication that is better for all, including the most powerful, than the status quo. That idea, of justice being mutually beneficial, is part of the Humean strategy that aims to show that justice is "artificial"—that is, invented by people to serve certain purposes. This is a claim about how rules of justice come about, plus a philosophical view about how the standard itself can be rooted in that functional causal history of certain social rules. The causal story invokes the idea of Pareto efficiency, and it is easy to let that suggest something normatively valuable in the causal process. That is, to give one specific such story, suppose that a method of adjudication would arise if and only if it were Pareto optimal, that is both (a) Pareto superior (better for some, worse for none) to the status quo, and also (b) such that there is no alternative to it that is better for anyone.[12] This might seem to be a salient case for the following reason: first, if people are initially at odds, then there will normally be some benefits for at least some people in having mechanisms of adjudication. However, since different methods might benefit different people, some methods might, in effect, be blocked by those with an interest in doing so. We might notice next that if any mechanism is Pareto superior to the status quo and there is no alternative that is better for anyone then no one would have an interest in blocking it. For that reason, we might focus on this particular set of solutions—call them the mutually advantageous ones—when we ask what is likely to emerge. And then it might seem to be an auspicious side-benefit of this attention to likelihood that it has led us to a normatively attractive set of cases, those that are good for everyone.

The charms of mutual advantage can be deceptive. If something is to everyone's advantage in that way, then no one is in a position to complain. But the loveliness of that possibility too easily draws the spotlight away from what might be the plainer and yet still potent value of some alternatives that would not benefit everyone. The dubious claim is not that it would be great if there were a solution that is to everyone's advantage. Rather it is the suggestion that nothing but mutual advantage is good enough. Suppose that no mechanism would emerge unless it were to everyone's advantage. That is no support for the idea that mutual advantage is a necessary condition of justice—that is, of an arrangement's being an eligible candidate to specify just and unjust behaviors. Even if no other arrangements will tend to actually emerge, this is no reason to doubt that there are some which, *if they were to emerge*, would fully and plausibly specify which behaviors are just and which unjust. Their being justice-apt, so-categorized by the standard of just arrangements discussed above, is simply different from their being emergence-apt, so to speak.

We could, of course, yet ask whether mutual advantage happens also to be suited for this moral question. It would be a kind of coincidence if it were. But in fact it is not so suited. The reason, to put it perhaps a little cryptically, is that pointing out that some arrangement is not in everyone's interest plainly has no bearing on whether it would be required by justice.[13] However, I will not argue for this last claim, and I do not believe that any of my other arguments in this chapter depend on this verdict.

5. Does Justice Apply Only in Nonideal Conditions?

The conditions for the applicability of justice seem to include certain things in two main categories: competing interests and conflicting judgments among people who must find a way forward together. Cases of either kind can put people at odds, and questions of a just resolution arise.[14] Since a cause in either category is sufficient for questions of justice to arise, neither of them is necessary.

Conflicts of both kinds will also often be present, of course. If there were no conflicting fundamental aims or desires, there might yet be conflicts in practice owing to failures of understanding. It might be that you and I both desire that a bridge be built over the river, and yet we might disagree irreconcilably about how this can be accomplished. This could put us at odds going forward, and the question arises about a just settlement of such a conflict. The source of conflict is a cognitive limitation (broadly speaking), and not competing desires. It is sufficient, and so fundamentally competing aims or desires are not necessary, for matters of justice to arise.

Likewise, suppose there were no cognitive limitations of the right kind to trigger questions of justice. Indeed, suppose people did not disagree about any matters of fact or doctrine. Still, of course, if there could be competing interests and desires, the question can arise about what would be a just adjudication. Earlier we considered whether the standard could apply even if there had not yet ever been any justice-specifying social rules or conventions. All that is needed for now is that, at least if there are or have been such specifying mechanisms, the applicability of justice can be triggered by competing interests or aims alone, even if there were (bizarrely) no disagreements of other kinds. And vice versa.

The conditions in these two categories—competition and disagreement—are sometimes treated as if they are each necessary conditions of applicability. If that were so, then justice would only apply if conditions of both kinds were present, and so things were, in that way, especially nonideal. I have argued that this is a mistake, but we might conjecture that there is often the following explanation for making it: one might think that justice ought to be defined so that it is, in some way, responsive to the normal conditions of human life. Rawls, whose treatment of these issues is at least as influential as Hume's, famously says, "The circumstances of justice may be described as the *normal conditions* under which human cooperation is both possible and necessary."[15] Normal human life surely does include conditions of both kinds, and these are the conditions which, in normal life, "set the stage for questions of justice."[16] None of this, however, is any basis for concluding that either or both of them is necessary for such questions to apply. In our normal conditions, questions of justice apply not because both or any particular one of these—competition and disagreement—is the case, but because at least one or the other of them is.

6. Is Moral Deficiency a Circumstance of Justice?

Suppose there were no conflicting aims and no cognitive failure. Things are sounding pretty good so far. However, there might yet be (as of course there always would be) some degree of individual moral deficiency. We know that moral deficiency is not necessary for the applicability of justice since we have seen that either competing interests or certain cognitive disagreement are sufficient.

We should not skip over this point too quickly, since I believe many have been inclined to assume that justice has no application in conditions where people are morally perfect—morally perfect, that is, in other ways, leaving the virtue of justice out of it, since the question is whether justice has any application here. That is a mistake, at least so long as there could be disagreement or competing interests even without moral defect. It might seem that morally flawless people would not have conflicting interests or desires, but this is very hard to believe. Consider several people each of whom has a parent painfully and prematurely dying of a condition that can only be fully cured by the one available dose of medicine. The claim in question is that there is no occasion for rules or even motives of justice so long as no one is morally deficient. But, if justice is temporarily put aside, it is hard to discern any moral deficiency merely in the profound desire of each party to save her parent's life even at the cost of another person's life. Since any population's members would find themselves confronted with many such scenarios, questions of justice would seem to arise even if no one were (in that pre-justice context) morally deficient.[17] Morally excessive selfishness does seem possible there, as in a person who cares not at all for the suffering of others and only for himself, but that sort of extreme selfishness would not be necessary in order for the issue of justice to arise.

Hobbes, whose account of the need for coercively backed political authority is a clear precursor of Hume's account of circumstances of justice, saw the need for adjudicatory mechanisms even in the absence of vice. He argues that before there are any rules with sanctions, if a contract is made, "upon any reasonable suspision, it is Voyd." The violation of contracts in those conditions is not owed to any vice. If and when there are, instead, credibly threatened sanctions, "that feare is no more reasonable."[18] Hobbes, of course, doubted that such assurance could be present without the threat of force, and we do not need to deny that psychological conjecture, which Hume plainly rejected, here. We can simply note the agreement between Hobbes and Hume that it is not essentially owing to any moral defect that the need for coercively enforced social rules emerges. Even morally perfect people might need government, or other social rules, although this depends on whether conventions or coordinate moral motives are available to meet the behavioral need instead.

It is important to distinguish two points in this context:

a. People who are morally perfect apart from the question of justice may (indeed, certainly will) yet have conflicting aims and beliefs, leading to a need for some mechanism of justice, coordinate motives being one such mechanism.
b. Even people who are just, as well as morally good in other ways, might not lexically prioritize justice, so there might well remain a need for coercive social rules in order to meet the behavioral need.

It might seem as though this threatens my claim that coordinate motives of justice could meet the behavioral need. But it does not. That would be a conceivable motivational solution even if it is not one entailed by moral perfection including perfect compliance with the due demands of justice. Even morally perfect people, even if they are just according to a shared specification of justice, might yet need social rules or even government. However, even though moral perfection does not guarantee it, there is a possible arrangement of moral motives in which they meet the behavioral need even without government or other sanctions.

Moral fault comes in for mention in Rawls's treatment of circumstances of justice, but only as an aside. He points out that while moral fault can sometimes lead to deep disagreements, it is not an essential ingredient:

> Some of these defects [of knowledge, thought, and judgment] spring
> from moral faults, from selfishness and negligence; but to a large de-

gree, they [DE: those cognitive defects] are simply part of men's natural situation. As a consequence individuals not only have different plans of life but there exists a diversity of philosophical and religious belief, and of political and social doctrines.[19]

This normal cognitive imperfection is the source of conflict that comes, in Rawls's later work, to be called "the burdens of judgment."[20] There is no reason to disagree with Rawls here: this source of conflict does not depend on any moral defects.

It is important not to misunderstand Rawls when he also writes,

In an association of saints agreeing on a common ideal, if such a community could exist, disputes about justice would not occur. Each would work selflessly for one end as determined by their common religion, and reference to this end (assuming it to be clearly defined) would settle every question of right. But a human society is characterized by the circumstances of justice.[21]

Grant that justice has no application in that case. But the condition envisaged there is not that of moral perfection, but (in addition or instead) a set of agents whose overriding motives are all perfectly common and determinate. That goes beyond conditions of the applicability of justice, but there is no reason, as I have argued, to think that such a scenario is entailed by individual moral flawlessness.

Moral deficiency is not a necessary condition for the applicability of justice, but consider the view that moral deficiency belongs on the list of conditions, along with competing interests and disagreement, *sufficient* to trigger questions of justice. It is hard to see how moral defect itself might put people at odds independently of competing aims and interests, or of conflicting judgments and beliefs. In particular, an immoral degree of selfishness only gives rise to conflict because people's aims differ. In normal conditions, it is true, conflicts of interest come to a head and need resolution often only because one person or the other is, morally speaking, insufficiently concerned with the interests of others. Moral defect plays an exacerbating role. But conflicts of interest would raise questions of justice whether or not they were intensified by moral defect. A parallel point applies to the fact that sometimes people's conflicting beliefs or convictions depend on one of them being morally deficient in some way. Again, that moral point might intensify matters but the moral defect itself does not trigger questions of justice unless it gives rise to the disagreement. Moral defect by itself is not a source of conflict but only a potential intensifier. It is not sufficient for the applicability of justice.

Moreover, even if moral deficiency were a third category of individually sufficient conditions that can trigger the applicability of justice, it would not be a necessary condition, since either of the others would be sufficient. For these over-determining reasons, then, justice cannot be denied applicability to some imagined scenario on the ground that moral defect has disappeared or been assumed away. For example, whatever the interest of doing so might be, there would be no conceptual mistake in theorizing about what would be just or unjust under otherwise morally flawless conditions, or to ask whether moral flawlessness is in some way part of what justice requires, and so on. There is no reason, including no reason stemming from the idea of circumstances of justice, to think that that kind of highly idealistic condition is outside the scope of justice's application. This conclusion is important when I come to discuss what I will call prime justice in chapter 10.

7. Conclusion

Even though justice is, in a certain way, a standard applicable to conditions of conflict or disagreement, this is hardly support for the idea that it is not a high standard—even so high as to be unlikely ever to be met. It is also no support for the idea that justice takes human moral defect for granted, even though institutional proposals obviously must. We will see in the next chapters that justice (again unlike institutional proposals) is not shaped by what is likely in human affairs, or by what humans (even if this is a matter of their nature) can or cannot bring themselves to do.

Unbending Justice

CHAPTER FIVE

Utopophobia

[W]hat if my reason for thinking that the intention cannot be carried out is my belief that I lack the willpower to see it through? That had better only count as a reason for thinking that I will not see it through, not that I cannot.

—RICHARD HOLTON, *WILLING, WANTING, WAITING*

Introduction to Part II

Before beginning the work of the present chapter, it will be helpful to sketch the course of argument over the three upcoming chapters of Part 2. (I have divided each of these long chapters into two parts, A and B, at what seems a natural dividing point.) In the chapters that make up this second part, we will assess the limits of the idea that what social justice requires of us is bounded in certain ways by the motivational nature of the people it would bind. I will argue that on the best account of the relationship between justice and motives, justice could yet (though it need not) be a standard for basic social structure that is beyond and better than what has been or will ever be seen.

The main line of inquiry will revolve around the relationships between requirement, ability, and motivational incapacity of various kinds. Together the three chapters are meant as a response to the influential view (in several forms) that normative political philosophy takes human motives and dispositions— allowing for new ones that can be reasonably predicted under changed institutions and history, as parameters—as constraints within which the real work of political philosophy takes place. Evaluation of those motives and dispositions is not a matter for political philosophy, on that view, and a standard of just or proper basic social structure is defective if it could not be achieved and sustained by motives and behavior that can be realistically expected.

The core of my line of argument will be as follows: this demand of motivational plausibility is obviously correct for the project of proposing to build or maintain practices and institutions. Institutional proposals purport to be appropriate in light of the best information about how they would operate in practice. However, when the question is what basic social structures would count as just, expectable individual motives and behavior cannot plausibly be put outside the inquiry as given (if partly malleable) constraints, but fall within the content of what justice demands. A society may count as unjust even if its institutions are precisely the ones it is right to have given the expected individual dispositions under available alternative arrangements. Those dispositions may, in principle—the question here is not an empirical one—limit the available alternatives to basic social structures that are patently unjust, such as forms of apartheid, dictatorship, or other forms of oppression. Since that is conceivable, justice is not plausibly constrained by whatever we expect of people's motives and behavior, even though practical institutional proposals certainly are. When theorists seem to believe otherwise, it is possible that they are not sufficiently distinguishing the question of what would be a just social structure from the question of what ought institutionally to be done given what we expect from people under the available alternatives. Some, of course, may deny that there is any difference between these questions, but the arguments of these chapters are meant to make that position appear deeply implausible. In some respects, the arguments in the book are responding to certain kinds of "realism" in political philosophy, and that is plausibly so here. But the view that political philosophy is constrained by expectable human motives is advanced also by Rawls, who is in other respects a central target of realists' critique.[1] So the central issue under consideration in Part 2 is one that is especially deeply rooted, even if not everyone would accept it.

My discussion of the connections between certain kinds of motives on one hand, and ability and requirement on the other, draws on the work of others and is not meant to advance those discussions in any general way, but only to make several points available for our question in political philosophy: Do moral standards of political order, or specifically of the basic social structure, bend to fit characteristic human motives in light of which people cannot bring themselves to be, for example, very impartial, benevolent, conscientious, or just? We do not have to reject the widespread view that, "An ethic for human beings must take them as they are, or as they have some chance of becoming."[2] An ethic for any kind of agent must not require what agents are unable to do, or so I will grant for the sake of argument. None of that decides the main question here, which is whether people count as being unable to do whatever they cannot, in various respects, bring themselves to do.

PART A

1. Principles and Probability

I begin this chapter narrowly with a focus on the question of likelihood, or probability: Is a requirement of justice refuted if its achievement is sufficiently unlikely? This is not because there is a set of authors who explicitly impose a likelihood constraint on theorizing about justice. Rather, there is a heterogeneous antipathy in much traditional and contemporary political philosophy for accounts of justice according to which it is nothing we have ever seen or ever expect to see.[3] Recently, this point of view also plays a role in the burgeoning literature about the idea of political feasibility,[4] and in the so-called ideal/nonideal theory debate about social justice, as well as in the recent philosophical work around the idea we have discussed of "political realism."[5] I conjecture that a tempting idea underlying some of this antipathy is that a sound standard of social justice must be something it would be appropriate to set as a practical social goal given our best assessment of, among other things, how people will behave. Since the likelihood of success is, we must grant, a criterion of appropriate practical goals, the likelihood of achieving justice would emerge, on this view, as a constraint on a sound conception of the content of justice. But then, put the other way around, if I am right that likelihood is no such constraint on principles of justice, then it is a mistake to suppose that a sound standard of justice must be an appropriate practical goal in light of expectations about behavior. This is a recurring theme in this book, of course.

There is less temptation, for some reason, in moral philosophy than there is in political philosophy to withdraw a principle on the ground that it is too unlikely to be satisfied. Consider the principle, "You should not lie except in exceptional circumstances E." Fill in the exceptions as you understand them. Still, on any plausible way of specifying the exceptions, this requirement is not realistic. There is probably no agent who will live up to it. But this does not tempt us to withdraw the requirement. 'Ought' might entail 'can,' but it does not entail 'reasonably likely,' as I have argued. It is an important puzzle why someone would think normative principles about politics should be withdrawn on grounds of improbability when there is no similar constraint in nonpolitical moral contexts.[6] As we have seen, this does not mean that there is no place for a concessive layer of normative political theory: a domain of inquiry into what we ought politically to do given that we will, probably or certainly, not live up to our requirements of justice. Given that certain sound moral principles of politics are not likely to be met, we can go on to ask what should be done then. If voters will be lazy and selfish and so justice will not be achieved, then what should they do politically in light of that fact? This is no less a moral question than what justice itself requires of us. Also, importantly, there is apparently no general reason to believe that the standard we arrive at on this concessive question will have any greater likelihood of being met than the nonconcessive standard.

Consider a theory that holds individuals and institutions to standards that it is within their ability to meet, but which there is good reason to believe they will never meet. So far, I contend, the theory has no defect. It might be a false theory if it claimed that the standards would someday be met, but it does not say that. And we can suppose that it would be false if the standards were impossible to meet, but, by assumption, they are not. Many things that are within people's abilities will never be done. The imagined theory simply constructs an account of how a society should and could arrange itself even while acknowledging that this will not happen.

So, for example, suppose this theory posits a conception of democracy in which citizens are publicly and privately highly virtuous (but not more than people are capable of), and institutions are designed accordingly, so that in the imagined world laws are just, rights are protected, the vulnerable are cared for, minorities are embraced and respected, and so forth. In an obvious sense, realizing this may not be realistic. But by saying that we do not mean only that it is more than people actually do; that complacent realism, as we saw in chapter 1, is a worthless constraint. Nor do we mean that the standard of civic virtue used by the theory is impossible for people to live up to. People could behave this well—that is by assumption; they just don't and won't. Their failures are avoidable and wrong, but they are also entirely to be expected as a matter of fact in the scenario I have sketched. So far, as I have said, there is no discernible defect in the theory. For all we have said, the standards to which it holds people and institutions might be sound and true. The fact that people will not live up to them even though they could is, in that case, a defect of people, not of the theory. We might call this kind of theory a version of hopeless aspirational theory. The name "hopeless" might suggest that I aim to criticize this kind of theory, but in fact I want to defend it. I keep the sad name in order to avoid any suggestion that my point is that maybe the standards will, after all, be met.[7] The possibilities for unanticipated moral achievement in the future are suggested by history to be vast, and highly idealistic political thought might find some justification there, a question I will discuss in chapter 13. But I am insisting on a different but compatible point. I want to defend political theory that presses certain standards even if they will not be met, and even if we were to know this for sure.

For this reason, it could be misleading to continue to refer to such standards as "aspirational," an idea that might be linked closely to hope. For some, the term connotes some non-negligible probability of success, and then it would be misleading for my purposes. On the other hand, these nonconcessive standards, by stipulation, can be met by the agent. Perhaps that is a ground for some hope, if not expectation. Nonconcessive standards might never be completely hopeless in that sense.[8] When there is a requirement that an agent will not meet, raising further questions about relatively concessive requirements, in that case, the first requirement remains in place. So we cannot say simply that it is not practical. None of that is contradicted by the further considerations about relatively concessive requirements. All told, then, I think there is nothing strictly wrong with calling nonconcessive requirements "aspirational." Still, I will henceforth use the more neutral and sterile term "nonconcessive," in order not to tempt certain confusions about principles versus proposals that it is a central part of my aim to clarify. We can and should meet nonconcessive standards, but if we will not (or probably not) meet them, they are often inappropriate guides to the steps we should take or the institutions we should build in light of our unfortunate, certain or probable, failure to meet them.

2. The Ability/Probability Distinction

It is quite clear, then, that improbability of being satisfied is no defect in a principle or requirement. However, is this still so clear in the case of utter improbability—that is, zero probability? Wouldn't it count against a theory of justice if it were not only unlikely to be met, but there were no chance at all? The reasoning for this worry might go like this: if there is no chance, then it is impossible, but the impossible is never required.

It is easy to confuse standards that certainly—that is, with probability of or arbitrarily close to 1—will not be met, with standards that are impossible to meet. It is worth dwelling on the distinction between those two things in a general way for a moment. If something simply will not happen—if there is no chance of it happening—we are tempted to describe it as impossible. It is sometimes said that "impossible" just means "zero probability," but that view is subject to difficulties, at least where our interest is in what it is possible or impossible for an agent to do.[9] Consider this case: What is the chance that I will dance like a chicken while giving a lecture? It is very, very close to zero, trust me. (You might think I have my price. Maybe, but I can assure you that, if I do, it is so high that there is minimal probability that anyone would offer it just to see me dance like a chicken.) So should we accept that this is nearly impossible to do? To say that an action is "nearly impossible to do" suggests at least that it is extremely difficult, but that would be a *non sequitur*. It does not get more difficult as it gets less likely. Dancing like a chicken during a lecture is easy; I just very much do not want to do it. This shows, I think, that it would be misleading to call an action with zero probability impossible, unless it were added that, in the intended sense of "impossible," this does not mean that it is at all difficult.[10]

To say that a certain action by a certain agent is impossible can mean either of two quite different things, then: first, it sometimes means that the agent cannot do it—that she is unable to do it. We could mark this use of "impossible," which I am in no position to linguistically forbid, by saying that it is impossible *for her to do*. Second, it sometimes means that there is no chance that she will do it, that the (objective) probability of her doing it is zero. This might be marked by saying that it is impossible *that she will do it*. In short, calling an action impossible is sometimes a claim about ability, but sometimes a claim, instead, about probability. Missing probability does not entail missing ability. Of course, sometimes the explanation for low probability of an action will be inability, but that is not guaranteed, to say the least.

What I have said suggests that even zero probability that an action will be performed does not entail inability. My argument for that was that zero probability does not entail even difficulty much less inability. Add to this the unexceptional premise that, if some action is easy for an agent, then it is within the agent's ability. It follows that an action's having even zero probability does not entail that it is beyond the agent's ability (or even that it is difficult). This argument does not depend on denying that there might be some other useful sense of 'impossible' that is entailed by zero probability, as I suggest above that we mark with the phrase 'impossible that she will do it.' That kind of impossibility, which is about probability rather than ability, would not engage with the assumption that 'ought implies can'—that unless something is within an agent's ability it is not morally required of her. In any case, nothing in my argument ultimately depends on a view about the zero probability case, since that is not the form in which idealistic political theories are criticized for being too unlikely. And it is clear that some cases of very low likelihood simply reflect agents' ordinary motives and choices, not obstacles of any kind.

The ability/probability distinction matters a lot for political philosophy. We might not believe in moral standards or requirements that are beyond agents' abilities, but this is not yet any reason for rejecting standards that will certainly (or almost certainly) not be met. It is an important question, and one that has not often been directly confronted, what reason there might be to want normative political theory to limit its inquiries to standards that are not only possible, not only not too difficult, but also not too unlikely to be met in practice. There is, I have argued, no good reason for such a limitation.[11]

3. The Limited Relevance of Human Nature

A requirement, then, is not blocked or refuted just by its being improbable (even maximally so) that it will be met. Of course, inability is often one category of cases of an act's being improbable,[12] but low or zero probability does not entail inability. So I turn next to ways in which requirements of justice are sometimes held to be beyond people's ability, the requirements being blocked or refuted on that ground. In particular, I focus in this section on the idea that requirements of justice are refuted if they are beyond what people can (any of them, or in sufficient numbers) bring themselves to do. There are two aspects to this question: First, focusing on a single individual, if she can't bring herself to do a certain thing does it follow that she is unable to do it, blocking the requirement on that ground? I argue that it does not. Second, even if I am right that it does not, suppose that not only this one agent, but human agents in general, or in sufficiently great numbers, can't now or in any foreseeable historical setting bring themselves to do it. Suppose it is, in that sense, requiring what is against human motivational nature. Does that fact about humans in general block the putative requirement of social justice? I argue that it does not.

Here, then, is what I believe is a common position that I will argue against:

The Human Nature Constraint
A normative political theory is defective and so false if it imposes standards or requirements that ignore human nature in requiring things that will not, owing to human nature and the motivational incapacities it entails, ever be satisfied.

Again, I am allowing that there are no requirements without abilities to do the required things. There are other aspects of human nature that render certain things impossible for people to do (such as flying), of course, and I am not criticizing the correspondingly different version of a human nature constraint that would apply to those. I focus on the version I have stated in which motivational incapacities are taken, at least if they are part of human nature, to be requirement-blocking. I will have much more to say about which motivational structures are properly regarded in which way.

Many authors take this constraint for granted, and some endorse it explicitly. We find the idea in Rawls, who writes, without elaborating, "However attractive a conception of justice might be on other grounds, it is seriously defective if the principles of moral psychology are such that it fails to engender in human beings the requisite desire to act upon it."[13] Elizabeth Anderson writes in passing that, "we need to tailor our principles to the motivational and cognitive capacities of human beings."[14] The most searching recent defense of this idea is, I believe, Thomas Nagel's reflection on what he regards as "the problem of utopianism." He writes that, "A political ideal, however attractive it may be to contemplate, is utopian if reasonable individuals cannot be motivated to live by it." Of course, the conception of a reasonable individual could turn out to give all the moral weight to, say, impartial ideals, and to give little or no weight to any resistant motives however common they might be. But Nagel finds that approach to be profoundly counterintuitive:

> One might [say] that a political theory should concern itself exclusively with what is right, for if it can be shown that a certain form of social organization is the right one, that should be all the reason anyone needs

to want it to be realized. But this seems excessively high-minded, and it ignores the relevance of what is motivationally reasonable to what is right. If real people find it psychologically very difficult or even impossible to live as the theory requires, or to adopt the relevant institutions, that should carry some weight against the ideal. [15]

Nagel sees the other side of this question, and acknowledges that, "It is not clear how one can allow supposed psychological facts about natural human resistance to impartiality to determine the conditions of moral justification, without being guilty of capitulation to simple human *badness*." He sees some force in the view that, "A political system that is completely tied down to individual motives may fail to embody any ideal at all." His aim is to reconcile, to "balance,"[16] a human nature constraint in some form with this warning about amorally capitulating to moral failings. The linchpin of his account is to accommodate only "reasonable" resistant motives, not just whatever motives people might characteristically have. We will consider that suggestion in the next chapter.

The idea that principles must stay within the bounds of human motivational limits, then, is familiar. Equally familiar and traditional is a certain way of responding to such charges. For an example that I will use throughout my argument, Marxist and other socialist and egalitarian political theories have long been burdened with the charge that humans, in their nature, are not and never will be like that—say, egalitarian and public-spirited in certain profound ways. The response to this charge has often been to accept the human nature constraint on political theorizing but deny that human nature is really as the critics charge. For example, it is often said that while humans as we have observed them up to this point in history might be more partial and selfish than socialist theory would require, that would not show that our nature is such that this will continue.[17]

Nagel acknowledges some leeway of this kind, but insists on a suitably adjusted human nature constraint nonetheless. Even though people's motivations can be deeply transformed, and partly by moral thought itself, there are probably limits. And, "What is right must be possible, even if our understanding of what is possible can be partly transformed by arguments about what is right." The term "possible" is worth pausing on. Recall that it is easily granted that what is required ("right" in that sense) must be within the agent's ability, possible for them. But Nagel means more than this here. He is defending the view that what is required must not be beyond what we are calling the agents' motivational capacities. That does not obviously follow from the need for it to be within their ability to do, since, as I will argue at some length, people can be *unable to bring themselves* do so something (have that motivational incapacity, so to speak) even in cases where they are *able to do* that very thing. So, intro-

ducing some helpful names, the *ability condition*—that there is no requirement without ability—does not entail a *motivational capacity condition*—that
there is no requirement on an agent without their being able to bring themselves to do it. Nagel's concern is motivational limits, not other constraints on
what is possible for agents. His view, then, appears to be that, as we might
summarize it, ought implies can will—can bring oneself—at least eventually.

We have begun to speak of human nature, but it is important to emphasize
our focus. First, as I say, we are only concerned here with arguments that appeal in certain ways to supposed essentially human motivational capacities and
incapacities—human nature only in that respect. Second, even in that limited
arena I will not be engaging in the dispute about what is or is not within
human motivational nature. Rather, I will argue against the human nature
constraint itself. To keep things simple I will grant for the sake of argument
that it is in the nature of humans to be more selfish and partial than socialist
or egalitarian or some other idealistic theories would need them to be, with
corresponding assumptions for other theories of justice. I deny, however, that
this refutes any such normative political theories. Far from taking a stand on
the content of human nature, it would be open to me to deny that there is such
a thing as human nature at all. But I will grant it for the sake of argument.
Some have suggested that philosophical criticism is often in one or the other
of two categories: "Oh yeah?" or "So what?"[18] When a political theory is alleged
to violate the bounds of human nature, many have responded with "Oh yeah?"
My response, by contrast, is "So what?"

The appeal to human nature suggests something more than merely making claims about how people *will* act or are likely to act. The suggestion seems
to be that, in addition, forces or laws are at work. And that may put us in mind
of constraints and inability. But consider the weaker claim first, that people
(simply) *won't* act as the theory requires—people are not generally like that—
never mind any claims about what is essential or law-like.[19] In addition to the
example of socialist or egalitarian theory, it might be held against a theory that
requires significant civic virtue, for example, or one that requires honest dealing in commerce, that people will never do that. It is hard to see how this is
an objection to the proposed principle. It would not be surprising, I think, if
people will never be generally very good, or if societies will never be very just.
But that very thought requires reference to a standard not met. And, of course,
to say (supposing that one can show it) that a standard will not be met can
count against people's behavior rather than against the standard. Of course,
it may be that the thought embodied in such a complaint is that if people
won't do it then maybe this is because they can't. Then, if people can't do it
they are not required, and the theory that says they are required is thereby
refuted. But then the "can't" is in need of more support, something more than
a very robust "won't."

4. Can't Bring Oneself

It is necessary to pause to note two important points to keep in mind. First, for present purposes, when we ask ourselves whether a person can do something we should not be assuming that causal determinism prevents it. If every event, including every action, is necessitated by causal antecedents and this shows that nothing is ever morally required other than (if the idea of requirement still makes sense) what we actually do, then the issue about justice and human nature is not of any further interest. This would not be the view that requirements of justice must stay within the bounds of human nature, but the far stronger and stranger view that they must stay within the bounds of what people and societies actually do. I will be assuming then that whether or not determinism is true, people can often do other than what they actually do. For example, you can close this book and put it down right now, and it is also true that you can instead continue to read, even though you will only do one of those, at most. And when someone who *will not* meet you for dinner says that they *cannot*, this is often not true. (I return to the question of how 'can' might be understood for our purposes below in the section "The Success Conditional.")

Often, the suggestion in appeals to human nature, and the one I will concentrate on, is that the reason people won't behave in some way is that they are not motivationally made up that way. That is, because of their motivational natures, they are unable to get themselves to do so. Consider Plato's theory of justice, part of which requires parents to permanently surrender their infants to community care and upbringing.[20] This might be requiring something contrary to human nature in the following respect: many parents, however persuaded they might be by the conception of justice, might find themselves unable to bring themselves to do it. Or consider a theory that requires people to devote their time and skills impartially to the common good rather than to personal benefit. Even people who accept the conception of justice would, perhaps, still find themselves unable to bring themselves to comply. This motivational incapacity might be in the very nature of human beings. So suppose that it is—that there is something about what it is to be human that guarantees such motives at least with significant frequency.

Second, we have spoken of 'won't do' cases, which are not requirement-blocking, and 'can't do' cases, which we will grant are requirement-blocking. To have a similar convenient formulation, I will call (and have already been calling) cases where a person can't bring herself to do what she (otherwise) can do, 'can't will' cases. We often say, "I couldn't bring myself to do it." My thesis is that the uses of that phraseology that will concern us do not entail inability of any kind. The inability-connoting term 'couldn't' is technically unwarranted, but I have no interest in policing ordinary language. For my purposes in this book, I let the term 'incapacity' pair with the ordinary occurrence of 'can't' in these cases:

Motivational Incapacity
To say that a person can't bring herself to φ, which will be interchangeable with saying she can't will to do it, or that she has a motivational incapacity of that kind, is to say that even if she were to set out to φ—initiate a volitional process toward φ-ing—motives of her own would lead to her discontinuing that process prematurely, i.e., without having fully tried. (I refine this slightly below.)

One can try and give up, which is not fully trying. *Fully trying*, let us say, is trying without giving up unless one's failure so far supports the reasonable belief that further trying would be futile. Despite the strong suggestion of the vernacular phrase 'cannot bring myself,' or my compact phrase, 'can't will,' I do not mean that 'bringing oneself' is any kind of mental act or event which one might or might not be capable of, something that one can or cannot do. It is a common phrase, which sometimes misleadingly connotes some kind of inability.[21] So, to bring these points together, to say that S cannot bring herself to do a certain thing is to say that even were she to set out to do it, she would either not 'really' try at all, or prematurely give up. My claim is that while some instances of this phenomenon do entail that that agent is unable to do a certain thing, many of them do not. Again, I do not mean to police ordinary language. There is no denying that we sometimes say things such as, "I can't" in cases where, apart from our own motivational structures, there is no obstacle at all to our doing the action. We might say this when we are in the grip of fear, or revulsion, or a contrary temptation, for example. But, as Holton says in this chapter's epigraph, it would be hasty to let this way of talking convince us that these are genuine inabilities to do those actions. If 'ought' implies 'can' we would hastily be committing ourselves to the moral position that there is no requirement to do them. As Frankfurt observes, sometimes interfering motives "prevent [an agent] from performing an action that he had thought he wanted to perform, . . . only by virtue of the fact that he does not really want to perform it."[22] I will look more closely at the conditional analysis of ability and argue that in its most plausible form, it does not support a conclusion of 'can't do' from a premise of 'can't will.' For now, I ask the reader to at least hold that question open.

My aim is not to decide precisely where the line falls, as important as that question is. The purpose of this discussion is to support my claim that many cases that might be used in political philosophy to show that a society is unable to do something, and so to conclude that it is not so required, are erroneous. Many of them are, at best, cases of "can't bring oneself" which are fully compatible with the ability to do them.

PART B

6. The Success Conditional

We are led to consider what counts as ability by the need to answer a certain line of objection to my claim that 'can't will' does not entail 'can't do.' After explaining how this need arises, I propose to understand the objector as suggesting a familiar, but contested, understanding of ability—a so-called conditional analysis. Rather than rebut that approach to ability, I will allow it at least for the sake of argument but argue that the objection will still not succeed.[23]

Why might someone believe that if a person can't bring herself to do something this entails that she is unable to do it? One reason would rest on understanding of what ability amounts to. The argument goes like this: where a person can't bring herself to do something, *she will tend to fail to do it even if she tries*. It might be that many people try to be, say, more beneficent (or civically engaged, or tolerant of other cultures, etc.) than they manage, in the end, to be. But, this argument continues, if a person would tend to fail even if she tried to do something, then this should count as inability to do it, which would then (as I am granting) block the requirement. In effect, then, a version of what is often called the *conditional analysis* of ability is introduced by the objector I am considering. So, I want both to explain how a conditional analysis of ability has much to be said for it, making this a charitable interpretation of a salient objection to my argument, and then without accepting or rejecting that as the proper analysis also argue that it will not deliver the intended refutation of unrealistic theories.

This conditional account of ability understands it in terms of a subjunctive (often called 'counterfactual,' though it needn't be counter to the facts) conditional, which I will call a *success conditional*: roughly, if the agent were to try then she would tend to succeed. The general conditional analysis of ability goes like this:

> Agent S is able to do act φ if, and only if, were S oriented in a certain way toward φ-ing, S would succeed in φ-ing.[24]

This is rough for now, and will need to be refined. The objection to my position that I am considering adopts a version of this approach, where the kind of orientation to the action is *trying* to do it. The view I argue against says, in effect, that even if a person tries to do a certain action she might fail to do it owing to her own contrary motivations. Such an agent, even if she were to try to φ, would not succeed in φ-ing, precisely because her contrary motives will lead her to leave off before completion. Any plausibility I find in that idea—and I do find some—relies on the observation that it is a kind of *attempt that will fail*, along with the thought that this situation, somehow worked out, is constitutive of inability. Without that success-conditional idea (which may or may not be ultimately defensible) in the background, I fail to see why the objection would be tempting.[25]

Beyond rebutting the objector who appeals to the conditional analysis, my only support for the claim that 'can't will' does not entail 'can't do' would rest on intuitive cases in which a person is obligated to do something that they can't bring themselves to do, combined with the assumption that 'ought implies can.'[26] If someone rejects that latter principle, then I am offering nothing further against them. There should be no surprise in this. The core of my argument is that the idea that 'can't will' entails 'can't do' is seriously challenged by cases in which a person is morally required to do something even though she cannot bring herself to do it. I focus especially on the challenge arising from motivational deficiencies that are themselves morally problematic. If those cases of requirement are granted, then one can save the entailment between 'can't will' and 'can't do' only by giving up 'ought implies can.' Having clarified the polemical situation around the success-conditional understanding of ability, it should be clear that I adopt the broad success-conditional approach for purposes of argument. The question, then, is which of several versions of it is more defensible, to which I now turn.[27]

I propose to strengthen the objector's position in two further ways. First, suppose that the conditional is only put forward as stating a necessary condition for ability, leaving aside whether it is both necessary and sufficient as in the general schema above. We focus, then, on such a partial analysis of ability (stated explicitly below). Second, assume that it is not success that is necessary for ability, but only some *tendency* to success. J. L. Austin[28] observes that a person might be able to make a certain golf putt even though he tries and misses, which violates the success conditional. He proposes that, "a human ability or power or capacity is inherently liable not to produce success, on occasion." Grant that failing to sink one putt does not show that he has no ability to do such a thing. But, of course, the suggestion was never that he had what we might call a perfect, or infallible ability to sink short putts. To accommodate this point, we will assume that being able to do something comes in degrees. We will, for other purposes, often want also to have available a non-scalar, binary notion of an ability. For certain purposes, you have it or you don't. Before lending our truck or our skis, we want to know whether Larry can drive a stick shift, or whether Mona can ski. Surely, context will determine how high the probability of success must be (and relative to which set of possibilities) in order to warrant a threshold answer of "yes." The experienced golfer can sink 2-foot putts, yes, but not a 5-year-old first-timer, who will get lucky now and then. I will not pursue the details of how these thresholds might be determined by context, but the conditional analysis with the scalar element faces no particular difficulty in these cases as far as I can see.[29]

This gives us the following partial conditional analysis of ability, meant to apply at least to cases where no 'clinical' motives such as phobias or compulsions (further explained in the next chapter) are present:

S can φ *only if* were S to try (and persevere), S would tend to φ.

I will call the conditional that comes after "only if" the *trying conditional*. The whole statement says that it is a necessary condition of being able to do something that were one to try one would tend to succeed. I want to postpone the question whether this is also sufficient for being able, for the following reason: the conditional analysis arises as a sympathetic interpretation of the objector who claims that 'can't will' is a case of 'can't do.' I read them as assuming that if a person would try but not succeed then they are unable. That has the objector supposing that the trying conditional is a necessary condition of being able. I grant this much for now, and return below to the question whether it is also sufficient.

To anticipate the course of argument to come: having granted for the sake of argument that the trying conditional is necessary for ability, I will argue that 'can't will' is not always a case where trying would not succeed, but often a case where one does not fully try, even though doing so would succeed. In those cases the ability conditional is, contrary to the suggestion of the hypothetical objector, still true after all, and so nothing yet has been offered to show that 'can't will' is a case of 'can't do.' I will then consider the response that it is a case of inability in some special cases, and I explain and grant this as well. However, that would show only that the trying conditional is not *sufficient* for ability. I will describe a rough family of motives that I call 'clinical' and allow for the sake of argument (only) that their interference with trying may be disabling, even if trying would tend to succeed. I argue that settling that does not matter for my central claims in political philosophy, where the appeals to what people can't bring themselves to do are not appeals to motives in that clinical set, but to more garden-variety motives that often lead people not to try or not to follow through.

Let's look more closely before turning to the question whether this analysis will support the objector's hope to show that 'can't will' entails 'can't do.' There are well-known complications to such a view that are thought to be called for in order to avoid certain counterexamples stemming from what are often called 'fink' cases in conditional analyses of dispositions generally. A glass may be fragile even if, were it to be dropped, some agent would leap in to catch it before it hits the floor. It is not, then, such that if dropped it would tend to break, but it is nevertheless fragile. Thus, it is suggested, fragility is not a tendency to break if dropped. A standard revision is to refer to dispositions of the glass, where, unlike tendencies, these are not changed by the systematic presence of a quick-catching agent.

It might seem as though some similar fix is required for any simple conditional analysis of what a person is able to do. For the following reasons, I doubt that this is so, and that the lesson applies, at best, only to the different project of analyzing what it is for an agent (not to be able, but) to *have* an ability to φ. Sometimes a person has an ability even if she is not typically able to demonstrate or exercise it.

So, consider this first, even though it is not what we are proposing to analyze here. It seems as though S might, at time 1, have the ability to play a certain song on the piano even if it is not true that (as a simple conditional analysis of having an ability would hold), were she to try she would tend to succeed. Suppose that her little brother has the uncanny ability to notice when she is trying, and when she does try he will close the lid on the keyboard, preventing her from playing. Intuitively, she still has the ability to play, so the conditional analysis is wrong to imply otherwise. However, we are not, in this chapter, explicating the having of an ability, but rather the idea of *being able* to do something. This should not be thought to be a scholastic distinction. In her unfortunate sibling environment, despite her having a certain ability (granting it for the sake of argument), she is *not able to perform the song*, because he keeps stopping her. It is a fine, everyday distinction: we have some abilities that circumstances might systematically prevent us from successfully exercising.

Nor should the "finkish" (as he would be called in the literature on this topic[30]) brother be thought a silly and only marginally interesting imaginary case. Consider not a pianist but a parliamentarian. She has the ability, honed over years of experience, to make laws. But, rather like our pianist's brother, except that now it is their job, finkish members of opposing parties constantly jump in just as she tries to do it. She has a certain impressive ability which most people do not have, and this is not subject to whether her efforts are systematically opposed—or at least let us allow it. But she is, under the circumstances I have described, unable to make any laws. A conditional analysis in terms of her tendency to succeed should she try gives the right answer if that is the question, even if it is not the right analysis of her having the impressive ability just acknowledged. Similarly, some people have the ability to kick soccer goals, but they may not be able to succeed when they try, owing to finkish opponents.

It may be that in cases like legislating and soccer one does not even *have* the relevant ability properly understood if one will not tend to overcome opposition, since the opposition is part of the practice. But I am arguing that even if they do have the ability, suitably formulated, they might yet be unable in all actual cases to make a law or a goal. The objection in question assumes, after all, that they do have a certain ability even if there are finks, and so I can here allow that for the sake of argument. So I will stick with an analysis of "S is able to φ" in terms of a counterfactual conditional such as: "Were she to try and persist she would tend to succeed." Whether trying is the appropriate thing to place in the antecedent is a separate issue, which I consider in the following section. Unless otherwise noted, my subsequent usage of the term "ability" is meant to denote an agent's being able, not her having the ability in the fink-independent sense we have considered.

The conditional analysis of ability is similar to conditional analyses of free action and free agency, where the underlying question is whether, and if so when and how, agents are responsible for their actions in a way that supports the appropriateness of attitudes of praise and blame, or practices of sanction or reward. Causal determinism is often held to be incompatible with responsibility of that kind, making it metaphysically impossible that anyone act other than as they actually do. Notice that the conditional might, even so, be met: had they (contrary to the causal necessities) tried, they would have succeeded (consult logically possible, albeit causally impossible, worlds, for example). If all our actions are necessitated in that way, then it is argued that we are not morally responsible for acting as we do, or for not acting otherwise. This would be an objection to a conditional analysis of freedom or responsibility. But this is not our question. Our issue arises only if it is taken for granted that sometimes agents are morally required to do certain things, since it purports to carve out a special exception for cases of 'can't will.' Our question is whether such a special exception would be warranted. The present use, by the imagined objector to unrealistic theories, of a conditional analysis of ability is not put forward as an account of how actions or agents can be free and yet causally determined. It is meant only as an account of how agents who are often able to act, and are often required to act in certain ways, are sometimes unable to comply with a requirement—such as contributing more to the common good— owing to certain motives that make them unable to bring themselves to undertake the action—such as self-interest, partiality to loved ones, or stronger desires to do other things, or just to rest.

It might still be objected that conditional accounts even of only ability implausibly allow that one is able to φ (never mind freedom or responsibility) even when it is metaphysically impossible that the agent do φ, since even if determinism is true it might be true that were they to try they would tend to succeed. However, in reply, and as I said earlier, even if causal determinism is true and metaphysically necessitates each action given all the previous facts, I take it for granted, and as a constraint on our theories of these things, that people are able to do many things they do not do, such as putting cream in their coffee.[31]

7. Can't Try?

I turn next to a different line of objection to a certain class of conditional analyses of when a person is able to do something. A number of objections to conditional analyses center around the question, 'but can she try?' That is, it is objected that even though, if she were to try she would tend (almost certainly) to succeed (the *success conditional*), still, if she is unable to try, then, contrary to the conditional analysis, she is unable to do the act. Since we are putting aside clinical cases, the question is about the force of this objection in non-clinical cases. Lehrer gives a famous example in which he can't bring himself to eat some red candies, since he has a "pathological" (Lehrer's term) aversion possibly tied to images of drops of blood. Such pathological cases are not germane for my purposes, as I explain in the following section, since they are not the kinds of motives that are at issue between advocates and opponents of psychologically unrealistic theories of social justice. In any case, there is not much pressure from the candy example to concede that he obviously cannot even try to eat the candy. Why not say that mere trying is easy, even if he will not try, and even if were he to try failure is extremely likely?[32]

I grant that it may be natural to describe many non-pathological (non-clinical) cases as 'can't try,' in cases where we would say the agent can't bring himself to do the action. But in many of these cases we would not conclude that the agent 'can't do' the action, as my example of Messy Bill (introduced in chapter 2, and discussed again in chapter 6 below) is meant to show. So, that kind of 'can't try,' if we allow the expression, does not entail can't do—at least not in a way that blocks requirements.

A further point against the 'can't try' objection to conditional analyses is that trying may not be the kind of thing that agents are able or unable to do, because in the case of succeeding, trying is not, at least on some views, a separate action. In that case, the idea that someone 'can't try' might have to be seen as loose talk. One reason is that every action, in order to succeed, must be tried. If trying were an action, then for it to succeed it would itself have to be tried. And so on for that trying, resulting in an infinite regress of tryings for any action.[33] We can avoid this problem by understanding trying to do something as exactly like doing that thing, minus the success.[34] Where there is not success, then one has not φ'd (such as hitting the target), but has, successfully as it were, done another thing (such as throwing the dart, in the general direction of the target) in an effort to φ. In this story, throwing is not some distinctive kind of action called[35] 'trying,' and there is no such thing. Accordingly, we can speak of undertaking to φ, endeavoring to φ, taking action (of the φ kind), doing what can be done to φ, and trying to φ interchangeably.

However, the idea of trying, it must be admitted, is notoriously unclear. On some uses of the idea, a person might (in some rudimentary sense) set out to φ, but never get as far as 'really trying.' Call that 'downstream trying'—downstream from setting out to φ. It might be that certain systematic tendencies of the agent not to get all the way to downstream trying strike us as refuting the agent's being able to φ, since it will not be true that given that she sets out to do it she will tend to do it. There is some systematic interruption on her way to φ-ing, which intervenes before she downstream-tries. The fact that, *should she* downstream-try, she would tend to succeed is not enough to show that she is able to φ. Does this refute the conditional analysis in terms of trying?

At most it refutes a version that makes use of downstream trying as the attitude (using the term loosely) appearing in the antecedent of the conditional. But it is, it seems to me, a permissible use of the word to speak of a person who sets out to, say, perform a piano piece as having thereby begun the attempt. (If "deciding" to do it is different, somehow still upstream from any trying, then do not let that count as setting out in the previous sentence.) If the curtain rises, and the performer, who practiced, dressed, and came to the hall, never appears, having receded to the bar next door, we should not be so sure that she did not try to perform the piece publicly. She may very possibly (depending on the details) have either tried and failed, or tried to a certain extent but given up prematurely. So, the analysis in terms of trying can be taken to refer to the initiation of a volitional process aimed at φ-ing. Importantly, if something gets in the way of her even trying in that sense—call it "initial trying," that is no interruption of her will, and so no kind of inability to φ.

In any case, the suggestion that some people might be "unable" to downstream-try ought to be questioned. Suppose the performer knows perfectly well how to play the piece, her anxiety does not incapacitate her fingers or concentration, but just before showtime she retreats to the bar in fear. Given the fear, she will not downstream-try to play, but there is not yet the modal element that is needed for this to count as an *inability* to downstream try. She will not try; what is it here that shows that, in addition, she cannot try? Surely in some cases one would be unable, such as if one collapses, or one has a panic attack. The issues here anticipate those canvassed later, of which cases of "cannot bring oneself to φ" (rather than try, which is the issue here) are disabling. Some cases are disabling, but some are not, and this goes for downstream-trying as much as for acting itself. The idea that trying might be too hard can even seem like a conceptual mistake: succeeding is where the concept of difficulty seems to apply. The concept of degree of difficulty up to and including inability may be one that takes trying as given, and then notes certain connections—or not—to succeeding. That would still admittedly allow for the possibility that one might be unable to try insofar as one tries to try. Maybe such a thing makes sense, maybe not, though the risk of Ryle's regress must be borne in mind.[36]

We can now make reasonably precise just why 'can't do' is not entailed by 'can't will.'[37] We can analyze 'can't will' cases as follows:

> *S can't will (can't bring herself) to* φ if and only if, even if S believed that trying and persevering would, if carried through, be likely to succeed,
>> i. were S to *decide* to φ, then she would not tend [i.e., be sufficiently likely] initially to *try* to φ,

or,

ii. were S to initially *try* to φ, then she would not tend [i.e. be sufficiently likely] to *persevere* (to fully try).

Sometimes a person refrains from trying, or stops trying, because she comes
to believe her efforts are futile. This is not part of the phenomenon I am trying to capture, which involves, rather, motives that lead one not to try or not
to persevere even should such an effort seem to the agent likely, if carried
through, to succeed. So that is built into the schema. We will consider again,
in the next chapter, Messy Bill, who can't bring himself to properly dispose of
his trash. Even if he decides to do so, he will either not begin trying or will not
carry through with the attempt. But this is not because he doubts that he
could really get the trash to the curb even if he (however improbably) per-
sisted. We are assuming there are no further obstacles of that kind to his
succeeding.

It may be that some talented people can't bring themselves to work as hard
or as well without the incentive of unequally handsome pay. (I discuss such
possibilities in chapter 7: "Justice Unbent.") Again, their not trying or not persevering is not owed to their thinking that their efforts, fully carried through,
would still not succeed. The whole point of the example is that they will not try
or not persevere even though there is no such further obstacle.

8. Clinical Motives

As promised, I now briefly introduce the idea of clinical motives and explain
its place in the overall argument. There is important variety among cases in
which people can't bring themselves to act in certain ways. Some cases are
"clinical" such as addictions, phobias, and compulsions. There is no need to
define a precise class here, and so I am happy to leave the interpretation of
"such as" to a sympathetic reader. The rough class can be defined as motives
that are commonly understood as chronic or temporary psychological disorders of the kind that call for medical care. That institutional part of the definition is obviously not relevant to whether they count as disabling, but that is
not its point. Rather, the definition groups a rough set of motivational conditions in order to not inquire further into whether they are disabling or not. I
will put these cases aside for now and allow that, for all I say, it might be that
some such cases are indeed requirement-blocking. In effect, then, my substantial claim is that other motives are not requirement-blocking even if they lead
an agent either not to try or not to persist. As I have said, I will not separately
treat all other motives, but concentrate on (what I grant (*only*) for the sake of
argument to be) characteristic and essential human selfishness and partiality.
That emphasis gets at what are often the main kinds of motives at issue in
critiques of "psychologically unrealistic" motives in political philosophy. More

broadly, our treatment of those cases can probably be generalized to some other motives as well, though I don't explore that here.

To conclude, I have argued that even if it is true that a person who would not succeed at some aim even if she tried lacks the ability to achieve that aim, this fails to show that people who can't bring themselves to do it cannot do it. While that may be so in some special cases, it is not true in the central cases of motives of strong self-interest or partiality. In the next chapter, we will turn to several ways in which some interfering motives that are not disabling might nevertheless be morally mitigating on other grounds—that is, requirement-blocking, or at least partly excusing. Again, these cases are best seen as granted for the sake of argument, since the point for my purposes will be that none of that would allow the target view—the Bent View's critique of psychologically unrealistic political theory—to be defended.

CHAPTER SIX

Mitigating Motives

So an initially attractive moral ideal is blocked by a recalcitrant human nature. Does this reveal the sinful inadequacy of human beings or the utopian inadequacy of communism?

—THOMAS NAGEL, *EQUALITY AND PARTIALITY*

PART A

1. Selfishness Is Not Requirement-Blocking, and Typicality Adds Nothing

Before looking at supposedly characteristic and essential human selfishness, we should look at the selfishness of a single person. Consider a plausible moral requirement to refrain from dumping your household garbage by the side of the road. It would be silly for Messy Bill to propose this as requirement-blocking.[1] Of course, we needn't say that he is misspeaking if he says, "Sorry, I can't." That might not be an improper use of language even if it is not literally true. But notice that if we had let 'can't will' genuinely count as 'can't do' then the 'ought' implies 'can' principle would yield the answer that the requirement is blocked here. This is very counter-intuitive, and there was no sufficiently weighty reason to proceed in that way. His selfishness, even if it is strong, does not plausibly render him unable to comply, and so it is not exculpating in that way. Some other motives, such as a strong partiality toward his family members, if those motives led him to litter, would raise further questions in virtue of their less objectionable moral content, but I put that issue aside for the moment and return to it in the next chapter.[2] If Bill's selfishness does not block that requirement, the reason is that it simply does not block any requirements. If he is too selfish to comply with certain social principles, then, again, this is no challenge to those principles or the associated theory of justice at all. I allow, for the sake of argument, that some requirements are refuted by their being too burdensome or demanding, or some such thing, and I will return to the question whether this is itself a concession to human motivational incapacities (hint: no). For now, I take the case of Bill to refute what I will call the *unqualified view* that every case of 'can't will' is requirement-blocking. The point of the example of Bill is mainly that it is obvious that his motives are not requirement-blocking. If that is granted, it does not matter for my purposes whether it is also granted that he is able to comply. But I am assuming that one main basis for an objector to think that he is not required is the thought that he is unable to comply, so I will argue against that.

We are directly discussing ability, but with an eye to implications for obligation. On some views, which are worth mentioning briefly, a person does not have an obligation to do an action unless it would not be pointless or worse to *plan* on fulfilling it.[3] On that view, people who can't bring themselves to φ will not be required to φ, since it admittedly would not make sense for them to plan as though they will φ. But that general view is highly implausible. It implies that for any agent at t1 who knows or reasonably believes that at t2 she will not φ is not required to φ. Because surely, knowing that she will not φ it would (normally) be senseless to plan as if she will. Naturally, the view also implies, implausibly, that Messy Bill, who is lazy but otherwise motivationally intact, is not required (at least not when he first considers the matter)[4] to take the trash to the curb. This would be exculpating on a massive and implausible scale.

Now, even if a case of 'can't will' is not requirement-blocking in an individual case, what if it is typical of humans, or even of humans *as such*? I see no reason to say anything other than that,

Typicality Adds Nothing
If S's being unable to will φ is not requirement-blocking then this is still the case if many or all humans are (even essentially) like S in this respect.

Suppose people line up to get your moral opinion on their behavior. Bill is told his selfishness does not exempt him from the requirement to be less selfish. Behind Bill comes Nina with the same query. Again, we dispatch her, on the same grounds as Bill. Behind Nina is Kim, but, since each poses the same case, our judgment is the same. The line might contain all humans, but that fact adds nothing to any individual's case. I take this to show that even if the reason people will not comply with certain institutional arrangements is because there is a motivational incapacity (meaning only that agents cannot bring themselves to do so) that is part of human nature, this is not requirement-blocking and so does not refute the theory of justice. The requirement of justice, which we might suppose is to Build and Comply with those institutions, would not be refuted. I take this to show the following rather significant thing: even if a large dose of selfishness is part of human nature this does not refute theories of justice that require people to be less selfish than that. (We will sharpen the issue by looking at what I will call a Carens market in the next chapter.)

Define an *interfering motive* (a notion we have already been using in a loose way) as,

- a motive that would tend to win out against desires to perform a certain action, so that the agent does not ultimately perform the action,
- even when the agent would, for all she knows, tend to successfully perform the action should she undertake to do it.

Must requirements of social justice shape themselves to fit (at least) characteristic human motives that tend to interfere in this way with compliance with more extensive (putative) requirements? A certain kind of realistic approach to justice would say yes, as we have seen.[5] I will argue that, with qualifications, the answer is no.

There is no point in my trying to deny that it is a proper use of ordinary language to say that Bill, being so unconcerned with cleanliness, "can't" keep his yard clean. We might also, without misspeaking, lament the "tons" of garbage he leaves there. The broad correctness of these utterances is not much help in determining how many pounds there are in a ton, or what it is to be able to do something. There is a fair amount of variability in people's instincts about when it sounds right to say that a person is or is not able to do something. We even say things like, "I'm busy with several assignments already, so I'm afraid I can't accept this one," when we do not intend for a moment to indicate that we are genuinely unable (and so, incidentally, free from any supposed requirements to do it). I will not try to analyze that use of "can't," or the earlier use of "ton." Maybe they are both just colorful exaggerations. For my purposes, the best account of ability might turn out to imply that certain common and unexceptionable utterances about "can" or "able" are not literally true. Our question is not that, but whether we should think that certain 'can't will' cases are disabilities of a kind that block moral requirement, and this is not primarily about what it might be natural to say in ordinary linguistic contexts.[6]

My argument that the Bent View (see chapter 1: "Introduction"), the view that the moral requirements of justice bend to fit the shape of characteristic motives of human agents, is not morally plausible stays within the domain of moral reasoning. It is not a view about the nature of practical reason, and takes no stand on whether practical reasons depend on motives in certain ways. For example, I believe what I say is consistent with, but not committed to, Bernard Williams's influential, broadly Humean view that practical reasons require a grounding in the agent's attitudes, though I mean to take no stand either way.[7] I also am not suggesting that what is morally right and wrong is independent of psychology in every way. The wrongness of sexually using children is undoubtedly tied to certain specifics of the psychology of children and their development, among other things. And moral requirements (leave aside practical reasons) might only have application to agents with certain cognitive and emotional prerequisites.[8] And so on. None of those ways in which reasons or requirements may depend on motives or other attitudes would bear very helpfully on the question whether the content of social justice bends to fit our particular motives or proclivities (allowing for their own plasticity, however extensive that might be, under varying institutions) whatever they might be. Even Williams does not consult the facts of human psychology in order to determine whether morality is fundamentally impartial—it's a separate question. The content of justice is also presumably impartial in some way or at some level, though my aim is not to determine its shape or content. The point is that justice, like morality, bears on whether our basic structure, which in certain ways encompasses motives and practices, is rightful. Neither justice nor morality simply ratifies them whatever they are.

2. Mitigation as Justification or Excuse

I will call an action or omission "justified" to mean that it is not morally wrong. When a person acts wrongly this often reflects some immorality in the person, even if it is only fleeting. But not always. If a person cannot bring himself to tell the police about a robbery that he witnessed, the explanation need not be that he is lazy, or selfish, or callous about the victim's interests. It might simply be that he is irrationally anxious about talking to the police. If so, he is less blameworthy than if his silence was due simply to a general disregard for other people's interests. His failure to report it is, to this extent, excusable. That does not make it right or justified, and he might be the first to insist on this: he might wish very much that he was a little braver so that he would have done the right thing. If reporting it were not even the right thing, then this would be hard to explain. It might not be entirely clear what wrongness amounts to if it is pulled apart from blameworthiness in this way. However, it does seem substantial and illuminating to say that wrongness entails (and maybe grounds) blameworthiness unless the agent has an excuse. This, at any rate, is a rough account of a standard distinction between moral justification and excuse.[9] I will allow this distinction, but my argument rests nothing on whether it is ultimately correct. Even if there can be excuse without justification, many widespread human motives that are commonly held to constrain the legitimate requirements of social justice fail to show that shortfalls from high idealistic standards would be even excused, much less justified.

I will grant for the sake of argument that interfering motives can sometimes be justifying or excusing (together, call this "mitigating"). I will lay out two categories that arise even within motives that are neither clinical nor disabling: first, some interfering motives are what I will call "weighty," insofar as they reflect morally sound priorities and views. These can fully justify acts which would, in many other familiar conditions, be wrong. Second, some interfering motives are what I will call "severe," and these are (to varying degrees) excusing. I also want to grant that while severe motives might be mitigating, much characteristic human selfishness and partiality is not motivationally that severe, and add that, in any case, severity normally only excuses rather than justifies (according to plausible views), and so the content of the requirements of justice is not affected.

Since I am granting for the sake of argument that certain motives are mitigating (excusing and/or justifying), there is no burden on me to argue this is indeed correct. My argumentative burden is to show that these categories of mitigation leave uncovered a lot of the (supposed) human bent that is often held, wrongly I am arguing, to give social justice its shape. However robust or characteristic these unmitigated motives might be, justice is unbent by them. In that case, injustice itself may be as characteristic of our natures as any of the motives to which advocates of the Bent View appeal. That is not ruled out, though it is no part of the project here to consider whether it is actually so.

3. Weighty Motives

Deference to eminently human motives that are resistant to moral considerations, including requirements of social justice, comes in two importantly different varieties: qualified and unqualified. On the unqualified approach, the motives to which standards of justice ought, supposedly, to defer are owed this deference simply because they are the motives that are or would be present under realistic institutions. The motives do not need to qualify in any way in virtue of their content. On the qualified approach, by contrast, only some motives are, in virtue of their content, owed such deference—call them the *weighty* ones. The "unqualified view" says that cases of 'can't will' are requirement-blocking without the resistant motive needing to meet any standards of qualification. The "qualified view" says that some cases of 'can't will' are requirement-blocking, those where the resistant motive is weighty in virtue of its content. So far, I have been arguing against unqualified accounts, those that propose to defer to motives regardless of their content. I now turn to qualified accounts.[10]

Before considering which motives might be weighty in this requirement-blocking way, we should get clear about whether that qualified approach counts as deferring to any facts about humans and their natures at all. It might appear not. The focus on weighty motives is very different from a focus on common or typical motives. The mere fact that the motive is common or even characteristic of humans does nothing to recommend it morally, as I have argued.[11] So it might seem that this very different qualified approach has abandoned, as I am recommending, any reliance on facts about actual humans and their natures, relying instead on moral arguments about the quality of certain *possible* motives.

On the other hand, the qualified view might seem to give a place to facts about humans or their motivational nature in the following way. It might hold that standards of justice, while they should not defer to unqualified motives but only to weighty ones, should defer only to weighty motives that are also *actual*. That is, unless the weighty motives are expected to be actually present (and more or less widespread) now or in relevant possible futures, they are to be ignored. This "actual weighty motives" version appears to have standards of justice defer to some facts about human motivational nature. However, I believe that is misleading: the view cannot avoid holding that justice would have been further shaped by certain possible but non-actual motivational facts *had they been actual*. The moral standard itself is not in any discernible way limited to those weighty motives that are actual after all. Despite appearances, there is no difference between:

> *Actual only:*
> Actual motive x constrains justice. Motives y and z do not, but they would were they actual (because they are weighty).

> *Actual or not:*
> Motives x, y, and z constrain justice whether they are actual or not (because they are weighty).

In both cases, the principle of justice addresses actual and non-actual motives alike, even if no one has discerned all of what it has to say. Certainly, any actual policies or institutions ought to be designed in light of the facts as they are, whether or not those facts are good news. But how policies and institutions ought to be designed is grounded partly in the content of principles of justice, which are not themselves proposals for any particular institutions. Such a principle must evidently provide guidance over the wide array of possible motivational scenarios. The scenario that is actual will engage with the relevant portion of the principle of justice to generate institutional guidance.

But some will still resist this. So suppose, as some might insist, that a principle of justice addresses only actual scenarios. In that case, it would fail to ground or explain the institutional guidance it offers, since it would lack any generality. This is not G. A. Cohen's point that there must be a fact-free principle that says, in effect, "IF those are the facts then do this."[12] That would still be the very kind of principle I am charging with inadequate generality, so my point is not about fact sensitivity in that way. Rather it is about *extra-factual generality*. A principle is not grounding or explanatory if it only addresses actual factual scenarios. It must also (at least) address counterfactual scenarios.

A similar point applies, perhaps more obviously, to moral requirements generally. We are under moral requirements—call them latent—to do certain things should certain circumstances arise. If you see money protruding precariously from someone's purse, you should warn them. Morality already covers that circumstance whether or not it ever arises. If you insist that there is no obligation unless and until the case actually arises, what accounts for the sudden occurrence of the obligation when the case does arise if not some standing moral principle linking you, the circumstances, and the act of warning? If that seems mysterious, it is no more mysterious than the suggestion that the moral fact pops into existence unwarranted by any standing moral considerations.[13]

Once the view is put into that morally "qualified" form, nothing I say in this chapter is meant to raise any challenge to such a view. (Nagel's position might be of this unproblematic kind.) In any case, and here is what has been at stake, it makes all the difference whether the requirements of justice are said to be constrained by what people are motivationally like (which I have denied), or whether they are constrained by consideration of what motives would be reasonable or weighty. The latter does not constrain the principles of justice by what people are like at all, and so it avoids the objections I have advanced against views that do. On the view that putative requirements can be blocked when there are resistant motives that are, owing to their content, morally weighty in the right way, requirements are not thereby bent to fit people's actual motivational nature at all.

We can now consider a couple of examples. What are some such weighty motives that might interfere with some putative requirements arising within a theory of social justice?[14] One cluster of weighty motives would include motives to honor any moral duties that simply outweigh the demands of social justice.[15] For example, suppose you cannot bring yourself to divulge the secrets of your psychiatric patients even if doing so is necessary in some way for the advancement of social justice (suppose that, when assembled on a large scale, this is valuable sociological information that could inform the design of social institutions). But of course you might have a moral duty of some weight not to divulge it. The resistant motive, if sufficiently weighty, is a response to a consideration that is requirement-blocking—fully justifying of the refusal to divulge. Remember, it is not the fact that anyone has the motive that blocks the requirement. Rather, the requirements of justice have limits, and they do not reach all the way to divulging confidential patient information at least if the stakes for justice are not high.

A somewhat different kind of case arises where an agent has, let us suppose, a morally authorized prerogative to choose as she wishes within a certain range, but where the range is carved out by its distinctive moral value rather than merely by the claims of the agent not to be subject to excessive demands in a purely quantitative sense. I have in mind prerogatives (if there are such) to favor the interests of one's close friend or partner over the interests of others. The explanation of the blocked requirement to, say, sacrifice the friend's interests for another is not anything about excessive burden on the agent, but is rather grounded in a certain (weighty) moral significance of close relationships.

4. Severe and Merely Insistent Motives

Here we fill out the menu of mitigating motives. Moving beyond the clinical or literally disabling motives, and also beyond morally weighty motives, we find motives that may be mitigating in virtue of being simply motivationally insistent. A special subset of such insistent motives are those that are, in the way I will explain, *severe*. While it is not plausible to regard interfering motives as generally ability-blocking, since they are, as Frankfurt says,[16] facts about what we ourselves want to do, they do often appear to mitigate an agent's blameworthiness. They do not mitigate by being reasonable or weighty in their content; often they are not. Rather, their presence can lead an agent away from the right action, but in a way that reflects poorly, morally speaking, on the agent. To have a convenient name, I will refer to these interfering motives as "insistent." This is meant to capture their sheer motivational force, so to speak. There is a range of insistence of this kind, and motives that are especially severe in a certain way might well cross the line from excusing to justifying, as I will explain. Severe motives are a subset of the insistent motives. I will concentrate on cases where the motive is not morally weighty in its content, in order to see whether it is nevertheless capable of blocking requirements with which it conflicts, or at least excusing their violation to some extent. Also, I begin with cases where the motive is not in itself morally objectionable, turning to that case afterward.

Consider a few examples that make this kind of mitigation plausible: shyness, temptation, and fear. Suppose that you tend to be embarrassed when meeting someone new, and this leads you sometimes to avoid doing so. There are two ways in which this could be extreme. One is a case in which you are so averse that you will not meet new people even when you have a real need to do so, such as applying for a job, or changing doctors. There may be cases like this in which we should regard you as unable to meet new people, the kinds of cases we put aside earlier as clinical. Suppose this is not like that. Still, it might be that while you are able to meet people, you tend to be flooded with anxiety and distress when you do. This is different from being unable to accomplish it, since it is about the suffering that comes with accomplishing it. Just to have a handy name, call this a "severe" interfering motive. I will come back to that case shortly, but focus now on a case of shyness that is neither clinical nor severe. This is a person who finds it difficult to bring himself to meet new people, though he manages often to do it, and it does not result in any great distress. Call this a merely "insistent" motive. It is reasonable and usual to say that a person who does not meet a new person when they apparently ought to do so is partly excused from the full measure of blameworthiness if the explanation is some interfering insistent motive such as significant shyness. As we saw earlier (see the section above: "Mitigation as Justification or Excuse"), this is different from concluding that there was no requirement after all in that case. The shy person has failed to do the right thing, but she faced a kind of challenge or difficulty which makes the failure less blameworthy than it otherwise would be. A less shy person who also fails to meet the new person has no such excuse. The underlying idea is that the person who would have met the new person but for her shyness has an appropriate concern for the morally significant reasons in favor of meeting the person. The less shy person (unless there is some other excuse) lacks that underlying good will. The merely insistent motive can be excusing, but not justifying—requirement-blocking. The distinction will be important when we turn to politically salient cases, since the central question will be whether certain motives block ostensible requirements of justice. Merely insistent motives, while they might excuse, do not block requirements, and justice is not bent to accommodate them in any way.

There is an important qualification: if the insistent motive is morally objectionable in its own right, such as a racist or sadistic inclination, then it does not intuitively seem to be even excusing. Such motives might still put difficulties in the agent's way, but since they are morally bad features of the agent, they seem powerless to mitigate the blameworthiness. "I'm sorry I didn't meet your friend, but I'm very shy," is plausibly partly excusing, whereas, "I'm sorry, but your friend is black, and I really hate meeting people from that contemptible race," is not.

We can return, now, to what I called the severe case of insistent motives, the case in which performing the action results in great pain or distress for the agent. The pain and distress must themselves be given some moral weight. A person ought not to have to endure them except for a good reason. What this suggests is that severe cases of that kind do have the potential to be requirement-blocking, and not merely excusing. Some acts that would otherwise be required do not have enough at stake to ground reason on balance for such an agent to endure the pain and distress that would be involved. This is not just extenuating or excusing, since there is no error by the agent at all in this case. While that pain and distress might not block a requirement to act where a great deal is at stake, such as some number of lives, it might plausibly block any putative requirement where the stakes are low. Suppose the moral reason to meet the new person is that your friend would be pleased if you did, and has asked you to. If meeting the person would be sufficiently painful, it is not wrong in any way for you not to meet the person. Your failure to do so does not exercise or manifest any morally inadequate concern for the morally relevant matters, since they are plausibly morally outweighed in this case.

I have argued that while some clinical motives (as I have called them) might be justifying because they are disabling, other motives that are not clinical might yet be disabling, some resistant motives might be justifying because they are morally weighty in their content, and some insistent motives are in none of those categories. These might nevertheless still be justifying in light of the severe psychological effects of resisting them. Where there are no such effects, then insistent motives that are not disabling or morally weighty are not justifying. If the motives are not themselves morally objectionable, they might yet be partially excusing, although that is importantly different. In any case, they do not bend the standard of justice to their shape. In the next chapter, we follow up some matters that arise from this position, and begin to indicate its meaning in specific politically salient cases in which many people cannot bring themselves to do what justice nevertheless—or so I am arguing—requires.

The aim in considering the mitigating force of various kinds of motives has been merely to record what seem to be views that are sensible on reflection. It is hoped that they are not very controversial, and then are available for our use in political contexts. As a brief check on that, it may help to try out our verdicts so far in a nonpolitical context.

The Glass Bridge
There is a glass bridge, or balcony, over a part of the Grand Canyon—the Skywalk. This horseshoe-shaped glass-bottomed structure extends out from the edge of the canyon at a point that is 4,000 feet above the Colorado River. For many people walking on the bridge is a challenge. The interfering motives can take different forms, and these differentially affect a person's justification or blameworthiness in morally substantial cases.

Some people might literally get too dizzy or weak in the knees to successfully ambulate, and that is clearly a case of inability to walk on the bridge. Others, though they are able to walk, are so frightened or anxious that if they do walk they will suffer greatly—maybe cry or have nightmares later. Others yet again will not suffer in those ways, but still need to work especially hard to (as we might put it) muster the will—their motives are insistent but not severe. Now suppose that Mari is out on the bridge, about to fall, and can be saved only if Jin walks out and lends her a hand—no more is needed, but only Jin could get there in time. Now, is Mari about to fall down on the bridge thereby injuring her head, or is she about to fall off the bridge to a painful death? If Jin's reluctance to walk out would cause her great suffering, and the head injury would be sufficiently minor or moderate, this interfering motive may be severe enough to permit Jin not to go. If not, if the motives of reluctance are insistent but not severe in those ways, it is merely a case in which Jin would very much rather not go, but at least if Mari's injury would be significant, this does not permit Jin to let her fall. On the other hand, Jin's blameworthiness is surely less than it would be if she refrained even without any such fear. That would manifest a greater moral deficiency than if she has an insistent fear as a partial excuse, even if it is the morally wrong choice either way. Next, suppose that Jin's failure to overcome her fear and help Mari is explained by her reasonable reluctance to leave her own child alone and in fear or danger. This might be justifying, owing to its moral weight. Finally, suppose that Jin's failure is explained by an insistent motive but one that she would have overcome if not for the fact that Mari is black. It is implausible to think that the insistent motive is even partly excusing in that case. Let us see how these distinctions play out in the case of interfering motives and ostensible requirements of social justice.

PART B

5. Examples from Theories of Justice

Now, where in this scheme of mitigating and non-mitigating motives should we place various interfering motives that may be thought to refute some theories of what social justice requires? We are not looking for a comprehensive theory of all this, but aim only to consider several cases in light of the distinctions we have drawn between motives that are justifying, excusing, or neither. Before looking at a few illustrative interfering motives, we can make an illustrative short list of things that might be required according to certain theories of justice—standards with which the motives we will go on to consider might seem to interfere.

We want to consider accounts of social justice (or parts of such accounts) that purport to require actions and practices which, as Bent theorists point out, are very unlikely ever to occur given the prevalence and persistence of certain familiar human motives. So, some specified motive is held to preclude satisfaction of a specified (supposed) requirement, and this is taken to refute the requirement. That form of argument against theories of justice can be shown to be indefensible if any (and especially if many) of the intended requirement/ motive pairs leave the individual requirement unimpugned by the motive. I am not seeking some narrow unanticipated counterexamples to the Bent View. I want to argue, in light of the distinctions we have made, that the very motives that are typically appealed to by that view do not, with any plausibility, defeat the kinds of requirements they are alleged to defeat.

We should assemble, then, lists of the kinds of motives and the kinds of requirements the Bent View is best understood as having in mind. Here are some requirements to consider, principles which some thinkers of the Bent persuasion will doubt that human nature can live up to:

Unpaid effort
Some accounts of social justice require people to exert themselves, at work or in private life, in socially productive ways even where extra work or effort is not met with extra pay or reward. One example is the first clause from the famous socialist slogan, "From each according to his abilities." More is required, other things equal, from a person with more relevant ability.

Fair dealing
A lot of thinking about social justice acknowledges that it consists in or depends on a good amount of reciprocity in the real practices of civic and institutional norms, rules, and practices. For example, there will normally need to be high levels of compliance with norms of non-cheating, nonexploitation, nondiscrimination, and so on.

Surrender of wealth or status to the worse off
Some theories of justice require that the better-off receive less than they might, in order to channel those benefits to those worse off. Even a libertarian theory of justice, in which the law may not require such transfers, can accept a theory of justice whose requirements include, as part of the basic social structure, practices of significant private charity, aid, or philanthropy. Some non-libertarian theories, of course, allow or require this differential promotion of the worst-off to be pursued through law and policy.

Honest public discourse
This might be valued in a broad way including much of what counts as expression on matters of public or political concern, or it might be limited to a subset such as statements issuing from certain offices on certain matters, and subject to various exceptions. Any such view will suffice for our purposes.

Honest commerce
Many would accept that a society is unjust if the realm of commerce is pervaded by lies, deception, false promises, reneging, and so forth. The question is not whether these behaviors are morally wrong, since in a context in which they are pervasive, they might be permissible defensive strategies. But many will hold that that, too, would be an unjust society.[17] Some might only think that commercial dishonesty is a matter of social justice if it occurs in certain parts of the system, or on some special subset of commerce. Let any of those examples serve here.

In the example cases, there are (at least often) multiple dimensions to these requirements of justice, including, for example: private behavior, compliance by law, and political support for such laws or institutions. The Bent View might challenge the realism of a theory of justice along any of these dimensions. Turn next to a short illustrative list of motives that might characterize the human bent. As I have said, it is not my claim that they do, but something I allow for the sake of argument. When someone holds that standards of justice ought not to require more of people than we have robust reason to expect in light of certain deep and pervasive human motives, they might mean such motives as:

- Wealth
- Relative status
- Self-interest
- Implicit bias
- Association
- Leisure
- Love
- Fear

We can now bring the preceding discussion of mitigating motives to bear. No appeal to motives such as these will properly cast any doubt on requirements of justice unless the further case is made that, in the intended cases and contexts, the presence of these motives either *disables* agents from complying, or the motives are aimed at matters whose own moral *weight* casts doubt on the alleged requirement, or where the motive is so *severe* that avoiding the pain or distress in resisting the motive fully justifies noncompliance. And, barring any of these, there is the further inquiry into whether the motives might be *excusing* even if they are not requirement-blocking.

It is also important that such motives are normally not in the clinical category, motives which we are granting may be requirement-blocking. No doubt, some people violate such requirements from motives that belong in the "clinical" category along with severe phobias, addictions, compulsions, and so on. But much discrimination, to take one example, is not plausibly in that "clinical" category. Even many genuine bigots are intuitively in control of their bigoted behavior in a way that agoraphobes, heroin addicts, and anorexics intuitively are not. And the clinical category is designed expressly to capture, in order to put to the side, such extreme cases where full-blown agency, or some such thing, is reasonably in doubt.[18] I believe the same can be said for the general run of violations of the other requirements.

"Implicit bias" may raise special questions, insofar as it can be argued to operate outside of many of the intentional and conscious processes that characterize other forms of discriminatory behavior. Does justice bend to condone implicit bias, on the grounds that it is outside of any agential control and that requirements depend on abilities? This strikes me as implausible, but that is no argument. I leave open, for now, the following difficult question: suppose a person is morally bad in her motives, and this leads her to act in ways that escape her agential control. Supposing, for simplicity, that she has done what she can to improve her motives, but without success: Does she violate any requirements, or if she does, is she at least partly excused?[19] I will leave this question open, allowing that implicit bias might be at least excusing, if not also justifying. But that is just one item on the list of motives championed by the Bent view, and the others get no benefit from this.

So, are the motives listed above, as they interfere with the sorts of requirements listed just before that, typically or even commonly either disabling, weighty, or severe in ways that we have allowed would mitigate by either blocking requirements or excusing violation? There is no such thing as an exhaustive treatment of the infinite range of cases. So we can hope for only limited conclusions. At the very least, it may be progress simply to frame the question in terms of which motives, however widespread, are nevertheless not disabling, justifying, or excusing along the lines I have sketched. Two examples ought to illustrate the point, each one pertinent to a normatively very different conception of social justice.

First, a common tenet of many liberal conceptions of justice requires some version of entrenched practices of hiring, school admission, and eligibility for many other social goods without invidious regard to applicants' race, gender, sexuality, religion, or certain other categories. Call this feature of social justice *nondiscrimination*. At the same time, many will argue that this is a standard that humans, as we know them to be now and expect them to be in any plausible future, cannot bring themselves to conform to. Grant, then, (only) for the sake of argument, that people are unlikely to conform in anything approaching a complete way to such a principle of nondiscrimination. If the standard of justice itself is bent to fit this aspect of humans' crooked shape, then a social world with these expectable levels of invidious discrimination might nevertheless count as fully just. This is implausible on its face, and so the Bent View would have no appeal if the bending argument were not supplemented by the additional claims that the motives in question are not only widespread and persistent but that they are also either disabling, morally weighty, or psychologically severe in the ways we have been discussing. Is the allegedly widespread and robust human tendency to invidious discrimination plausibly in any of these requirement-blocking categories? The question is not whether these motives sometimes fall into one or another of these categories. The question is whether the motives that are held to account for a significant shortfall from the principle of nondiscrimination predominantly do so. We will not engage in an empirical investigation of the question. It should suffice to point out that it is implausible or at least far from obvious and that this is what would need to be true for the requirements of justice to be mitigated by the ubiquity of such motivations.

6. Human Nature versus a Socialist Theory of Justice

For a second example of motives whose claims to be mitigating are challenged by the discussion so far, it will be helpful to look closely at an illustrative socialist interpretation of justice. Consider a specific theory of justice that requires a strong kind of impartiality or selflessness. Joseph Carens[20] has invented a fascinating and (in a way) utopian social arrangement. His guiding question is how distributive equality might be compatible with both efficiency and individual freedom. He does not assess these desiderata, alone or together, as principles of justice, although it will be useful for our purposes to think of them in that way. I will simplify things for my own purposes here, but there are essentially three parts to Carens's reconciliation of those three desiderata:

    a. The underlying *distributive principle* is equality of income, along with principles about individual freedom.

    b. *Institutionally*, there is taxation or another means of redistributing income that is earned in the familiar market manner, so that income is equal (per household/per individual . . . it doesn't matter here).

    c. Finally, there is a *behavioral* requirement: citizens are required to devote themselves to maximizing their pre-tax income, even knowing that it will be redistributed equally.

Carens's interest in this kind of market concerns certain advantages possessed by markets, and showing how these might be retained in an egalitarian system. Call the theory that society ought to implement and comply with the Carens market the *Pre-Tax Max* theory of justice. Carens characterizes the theory as "utopian" to signal that he does not believe it to be relevant to actual policy in any existing society.[21] He does argue, however, that there is reason to believe that with proper socialization over time (and what conception of normatively desirable social structure would not depend on socialization to some extent?) people might well develop the motivational and behavioral characters needed for the reconciliation of equality, efficiency, and freedom.

Suppose, however, that people, in virtue of human nature, would not be able to bring themselves to comply. Suppose people cannot, even with the most propitious socialization, bring themselves to devote their energies to the common good in this way. Would that be requirement-blocking, thus refuting the *Pre-Tax Max* theory of justice? For reasons we have seen it would not. It would need to be shown further—what it would seem difficult to show—that such motives are bound to be clinical, or disabling, weighty, or severe, as we have defined those criteria above.

Now, it is important to acknowledge that any institutional proposal that ignores the facts about how people will actually tend to behave is worthless, and this gives rise to an important point about the relation between institutions and principles. It might seem as though the Carens market is an institutional proposal, and if it were then it would be worthless for this reason. However, the Carens market is not proposed by Carens for actual implementation under anything like actual or foreseeable circumstances. It is not, then, an institutional proposal.

But if the Carens market is not an institutional proposal, what is it? It does not look like a fundamental principle of justice, a status held, perhaps, by the egalitarian principle of distribution. It is institutional, but not a proposal. In order to understand its status better, it will be helpful, first, to recall the idea of a concessive requirement. As I have briefly argued (chapter 1) and as we will see more thoroughly (chapter 8: "Concessive Requirement"), a requirement on a society to Build and Comply with certain institutions does not entail a requirement to Build them even if the compliance will be missing. In the case of the Carens market, given the fact that people will not (say, because they can't bring themselves to) work to maximize their pre-tax income without the incentive of unequal reward, then we ought not to build these institutions, as Carens would agree. Our question is whether this constitutes an objection to Carens's principle, which is that society ought to *Build and Comply* with those institutions, and for reasons that are by now familiar, it is not.

We can now return to our earlier question: If the Carens market is not an institutional proposal, what is it? It will help to distinguish three things.

Fundamental Political Principles
Abstract principles, often without much institutional content, such as a distributive pattern (equality, priority, sufficiency, etc.), or historical principles (free transfer, legislative proceduralism, etc.), combinations of these, and so on.

At the more institutional end of the spectrum:

Institutional Proposals
These propose the implementation of rules and arrangements such as election and legislation procedure, economic rules and regulations, laws of property, marriage, employment, and much else.

Distinct from either fundamental principles or institutional proposals is what I shall call,

Institutional Principles
An institutional principle describes institutional arrangements as part of a broader prescription or proposal, even if the described arrangement is not itself proposed or prescribed. In the form that matters for our purposes, an institution might be described as one that ought to be

instituted and complied with, even if, because it will not be complied with, it ought not to be instituted. Thus, it is not an institutional proposal.

The Carens market is a case of an institutional principle. It is institutional but it is not a proposal to build the institutions—after all, they would not be complied with. In general, then, my claim is that institutional principles, which tell us to build-and-comply, are unlike institutional proposals in that they are *not refuted by any facts about whether people will build or comply with them.*

Anderson, in apparent amplification of her claim[22] that "we need to tailor our *principles* to the motivational and cognitive capacities of human beings,"[23] adds that, "Just institutions must be designed to block, work around, or cancel out our motivational and cognitive deficiencies, to harness our nonmoral motives to moral ends, to make up for each other's limitations by pooling our knowledge and wills." The claim about institutions as they figure in proposals is obviously correct, but it is apparently a mistake, though hardly one limited to her, to suppose that it entails the claim about principles.[24] It is a common mistake to think that principle is linked to ideal modes of theorizing, and that the alternative to ideal theory is a focus on institutions. An important lesson here is that nonconcessive requirements are no less "institutional" than concessive requirements. It is not as if ideal or nonconcessive standards are only about principles and not about institutions. Those are cross-cutting distinctions. If someone is especially interested in institutions that is not yet any special dispensation for concessive (or in that sense "nonideal") theory over nonconcessive theory.

There remains the question whether a theory such as the Pre–Tax Max theory of Carens depends on motivations that violate the constraints of the circumstances of justice, a question which is not at all settled by the supposition that they will never, in fact, be overcome. "Limited altruism," the condition in which agents have interests or aims that can conflict with those of others, is a "circumstance of justice" in the sense of being a sufficient condition for justice having application (as argued earlier in chapter 4, "Circumstances and Justice"). As we saw earlier, it is not a necessary condition, but in any case, the motivations required to meet the Pre–Tax Max theory hardly overcome limited altruism. People are assumed to work as productively under the egalitarian tax scheme as they would under a less egalitarian one, but each can still be assumed to have an interest in having more rather than less of the scarce social goods. The change in motivations is relatively modest, as compared with (what is hard even to comprehend) overcoming limited altruism, even if we might doubt that it will ever come about. A theory does not move beyond the circumstances of justice merely by depending on motivational structures that are, owing to human nature, never going to come about.

7. Hopeless Theory (Defended)

Having explained in some detail the roles we should allow and deny to appeals to human motives, we can now step back to consider the picture that is emerging—the possibility that requirements of justice are, in a way, psychologically unrealistic. A theory including such requirements would be, in a way, hopeless. A hopeless theory can be dangerous under some conditions, of course. The soundness of the standards might lead some to take actions in their pursuit, and this might be bad. Actions in pursuit of what will never be achieved can be wasteful or even disastrous. A theory that counsels action in pursuit of high standards that are not sufficiently likely to be achieved, where the costs of failing are very high, often deserves to be chastised as utopian.

On the other hand, some people might be led by unrealistically high standards to improve themselves or their institutions, even though not all the way (full achievement is hopeless after all, by hypothesis). This might be fine, and even a good thing. However, admittedly, some things that would be good in a context of other good things can be very bad on their own. An important category of example involves institutions that should be a certain way, conjoined with people living up to their institutional duties: but, on the other hand, institutions which would only make things worse, or at least bad, if people did not live up to them. The world is not always brought closer to the ideal by having the institutions called for in the ideal even while citizens are far from living up to them. Indeed, those institutions may only make things worse. Ideals of society often have this sort of holistic character, and so hopeless realistic normative theories pose the danger of piecemeal "improvements" that are likely only to do more damage, a point to be explored in more detail later.[25] Granting these dangers, they nevertheless reveal no defect in the hopeless theory, which might be perfectly correct. What to do in such a case is an important question, but it is important to see how separate that is from the question of what the truth (or the best theory) is about justice. The same can be said for theories of authority, legitimacy, and so on.

It might seem that a theory is not moral or normative unless it counsels action of some kind. A hopeless theory, in the present sense, might seem not to counsel any action, and so not to be normative. First, however, a theory can be normative in one sense by being evaluative, whether or not evaluation itself counsels action. "Society would be just if only it were like this" might be true whether or not there is anything it makes sense to do in light of this fact. And if the kind of value in question is not aesthetic, or epistemic, or instrumental, it might best be thought of as moral. Still, this point would not yet show it to be practical in any way, and that is a separate complaint: hopeless theory might be merely evaluative but without any practical import. But, second, the sort of hopeless realistic theory in question does prescribe action in a certain way after all. It counsels society to behave differently, and in ways that it could. It is not rendered practically idle, any more than a putative requirement of individual morality is, just because the requirement will not be met. Bad behavior does not strip the practicality from requirements to behave better.

This brings us naturally to the idea of a hopeful (by which I mean simply non-hopeless) realistic normative political theory. This is one that applies appropriate standards that are not only possible for people and institutions to meet (that is, within their abilities), but which it is also reasonable to believe they might meet. It is hard to resist the sense that a hopeful theory is a better kind of theory. Still, I think this is an important mistake. There is no defect in a hopeless normative theory, and so none that hopeful theories avoid to their advantage. Things are better in one way, of course, if the best theory turns out to be hopeful rather than hopeless: it is unfortunate if people and societies will not live up to sound requirements, and fortunate if they will. But this consideration is patently no support for a less hopeless theory. That would be to believe in different, more easily satisfied moral standards for the reason that they are more likely to be satisfied. This is not moral or normative reasoning at all, it seems to me. The likelihood that a person will not behave in a certain (entirely possible) way simply does not bear on whether they morally should. It is not a fact that has that kind of moral significance.

One way in which a normative political theory might expect too much is by demanding something that is possible but yet more than can reasonably be demanded. Utilitarianism is often accused of requiring that we sacrifice our own pursuits and wealth almost endlessly, making the promotion of the total amount of well-being our dominant project. Some say this places demands that agents often lack reason, on balance, to heed.[26] Many people believe that this would be a defect in the theory even if the demands were entirely possible to meet. To have a handy name for them, let us call theories whose purported requirements involve more strain or sacrifice than is genuinely required *harsh*. By definition, then, harsh theories are false. They assert standards that are not genuine standards because they demand too much of agents. For the sake of argument, then, I will grant that at some level of required hardship, the theory purporting to require it has the fatal defect of harshness. On the other hand, I have so far not said anything about where the line between harsh and non-harsh theories might lie. I introduce the idea here to point out that a theory might be hopeless without being harsh. As we have said, a hopeless normative standard is one that there is reason to think will never be met, but the explanation might be only that people are unlikely to do what they should do. A standard might be improbable without even being harsh, much less impossible. It may seem that this theoretical stricture against harshness is precisely an accommodation to the way people motivationally happen to be, but I will argue that this is not so below in chapter 7.[27]

There is a place for non-hopeless theory, but it is not privileged in the way that is often assumed. Non-hopeless theory is what we want when we wish to know what we should do, in practice, *given* what people and institutions are actually likely to do and taking those facts as given. This is obviously an important inquiry. We do, after all, have to act one way or another. Acting as if people or institutions will behave in some better way might sometimes be a way of improving them, but even in that case, action is to be guided by what we think the probabilities are. In other words, an action plan that has false premises about how people or institutions are likely to act is a bad action plan and sometimes dangerous. We need to concede these facts in practice, but not in all of our moral conclusions. In addition to nonconcessive theory, then, we also need concessive normative theory. The view I am arguing against holds that hopeless theory is misguided and based on a mistake about moral thinking. The stance I defend here is inclusive: hopeless theory and concessive theorizing are both perfectly legitimate—there are moral truths and insights of both kinds, and neither enterprise is based on some kind of mistake.

8. Ideal Theory

I have been arguing that there is no successful argument against political theorizing in which important normative achievements such as justice, authority, and legitimacy are held to depend on conditions that are probably or even certainly never going to happen. Some might call this a defense of "ideal theory," but that term often means other things. Here are two things that are often at issue when the concept of ideal theory is in play: full compliance and complete and universal moral virtue. Neither is a realistic assumption, and so each is a kind of idealization. It operates under assumptions that are known to be false, and does so for certain specified reasons. Full compliance theory, familiar from Rawls,[28] is theory that chooses between principles of (in his case) justice on the hypothetical assumption that those principles would be fully complied with by the people in the society. The second kind of ideal theory takes people not as they are but as they morally ought to be. That is, it operates on the assumption that they are morally good. This is not the same thing as assuming full compliance, since morality might not require compliance with the norms of social justice. In fact it might even prohibit it in some cases, as when obligations to a loved one outweigh the requirements to comply with a certain rule or norm. In both cases, the normative theory takes its conclusions to be conditional on assumptions that it grants to be false. This might sound immediately damning, but in any case I am not arguing for that conditional type of view—justice as what would be required if people were morally good—here, as I will explain. My concern is simply to distinguish what I call nonconcessive theory from ideal theory of that kind.

Several authors understand the category of ideal theory as making intentionally false assumptions.[29] The conclusions, then, are conditional on those counterfactual assumptions. As O'Neill points out, such "idealizations" are not always meant to be positing ideals. It would be an idealization in the general sense to assume that people are rational maximizers of their own utility. It would be an idealization of the more robust and controversial kind to add that this would be a good trait for people to have. In both cases, the assumptions are granted to be false with respect to how people actually are. There might be various reasons for operating on false assumptions. They might be simpler than the truth while yet approximating it in some way. Or, it may be that the question the author is after is one that is essentially about something more ideal than the real world, such as, "What should society be like if people were good?"

Consider, though, a theory of social justice that frankly admits that justice will probably never be achieved even though it is still morally required. The theory is not assuming that people will comply (it does not "set aside" their noncompliance[30]), or that they have certain simplified motives, or that they are morally good. It simply says that society is morally required to be a certain way, a way that perhaps it never will be owing to facts about people. It refuses to let certain facts change the content of the theory's conclusions. But that is not the same as assuming anything false about the facts. The difference is between saying that we should have certain institutions *if* people are good (the requirement being conditional on their being good), and saying it is required that people be good *and* have certain institutions (the requirement not being conditional on their being good). The theory is not conditional on any such assumption. It does not say: if people were better, this is what would be required. It says that this is what is required, and the requirement includes within its scope people being better than they will be. As a result it does not pull its punches when those conditions are not met: it judges society to be unjust partly owing to those underlying deficiencies. The conditional approach, by contrast, would fail to have application. This unconditional approach fully applies.

There is a sense in which what I call nonconcessive theory ignores certain facts. Perhaps we know that people will not inform themselves about politics as well as they ought to. Theories might make normative assertions whose truth is not conditional on an assumption either way about how well people will inform themselves. It might say, for example, that justice requires various things including thoroughly self-informing citizens. It "ignores" what we know about poor citizen behavior, but only in the sense that it declines to adjust its normative conclusions to accommodate those facts as compatible with justice. The important point, though, is that it does not assume that the facts are different. If it did that then its conclusions would be conditional on those fictional assumptions, and so false. Again, there might be good reasons to theorize in that conditional way among other ways, but that is not what nonconcessive theory does. Like concessive theory, it applies normative conclusions (such as, for example, "this society is unjust") to society as it actually is. For example, while concessive theory might ask what we should do given that people will not be well-informed, nonconcessive theory might say that a society is not just unless people are well-informed.

9. Would Perfect People Need Politics?

Here is another obvious issue about which facts to concede and which not to concede. If a normative theory refuses, say, to concede any facts that represent moral failings (along with the other facts it might ignore), then it will be assuming away a lot of crime, for example. Not all crime, since not everything that is illegal is immoral. Still, if we assume complete and universal moral virtue then what would become of law?[31] The objection is that whereas we might have thought we were investigating a position in political philosophy, politics itself is being assumed away from the beginning. We can make a few points briefly. Would theorizing for the case of moral flawlessness (either in the conditional or unconditional modes described above) lead, absurdly, to a political philosophy with no place (or an implausibly small place) for laws, police, judges, and juries? Would it be assuming away politics itself? If so, that may sound like fatal defect in a political philosophy.

But is it? A lot of work is being done in this objection by a definition. A theory's subject matter is asserted to lie outside of politics unless, and this is by definition, it grants a substantial role to laws, police, criminal courts, and so on. Consider a theory that gave compelling arguments for the conclusion that a society could not be characterized by political justice, or authority, or legitimacy in conditions if there was a substantial role for laws, police, and courts. On the definition of politics in question, this would not be political philosophy. But that is only because politics has been defined out from under it. Fine, let that not count as political philosophy. This would leave entirely intact its claim to have the correct theory of justice, authority and legitimacy. If the charge of utopianism is to be a criticism then it must mean more than this. (This is a point it will be helpful to recall several times throughout the book.)[32]

I have not seriously considered whether morally flawless people would need laws, courts, police, or other hallmarks of normal political conditions. I have mainly questioned why that question is supposed to matter. The point is not that political theory positively ought to assume moral perfection. It will pay at this point to remind ourselves of the polemical situation. A political theory gives an account of justice, authority, legitimacy or some other central normative political value, and is confronted by an objection on grounds of realism: we all know, it is said, people will never act in the ways this theory says that justice, or authority, or legitimacy are said to depend upon their behaving. I have argued that it is an adequate reply to point out that the theory never said they would. It only said that there would not be justice or authority or legitimacy (either fully, or to some stated degree) unless they did. So far we have not even specified whether the behavior in question would be morally good, much less morally perfect. So there is no pressure implied here for the theory to rest things on moral perfection. As it happens, in chapter 10 I will explain some reasons for thinking that justice has its home in a context of full moral compliance, but that is yet to come. Skepticism about that is not, as it were, admissible here.

CHAPTER SEVEN

Justice Unbent

Through a misinterpretation of what, insofar as it is true, "'ought' implies 'can'" means, some philosophers have (unwittingly or otherwise) demonstrated that human beings are not by nature unjust. I don't think that can be shown a priori.

—G. A. COHEN, *RESCUING*

PART A

1. Introduction

A society's failure to be just is, I will assume, a species of wrong. In that case, some important issues carry over from our consideration of how individual motives can be morally mitigating, which was, of course, the point of considering them in the previous chapter. In the case of political justification, the question is pointed: When, if ever, do certain motivational facts exonerate a society from the charge of injustice? If certain putative standards of justice are such that there is a justification for not meeting them, then they are not requirements, and it is not a case of wrong at all. In that case we should not call it unjust. Idealistic theories of social justice might be attacked in this way, held to be falsified by a close attention to characteristic human motives which are, it would be argued, sufficient to justify (not merely to excuse) the predictable shortfall from those allegedly high standards. Even where motives are not justifying in that way ought we to allow that they might yet be excusing of the society? That is, might a society be excused to some degree for its admitted injustice in light of certain motivational obstacles faced by its members?

These are among the questions for this chapter, along with a number of issues that remain from the position defended in these three chapters of Part 2 considered together. I will argue for and explore the thesis that individual motives are not collectively mitigating (justifying or excusing) unless they are individually mitigating. If the individual members are not justified or excused by certain motives then a society is neither exonerated from the charge of injustice, nor is it thereby rendered less blameworthy (more excused).

When a theory requires a highly unlikely or hopeless degree of widespread political participation it is natural to think that something here is impossible, or at least too difficult. As I argued in chapter 5, this might just be a confusion between missing probability and missing ability. However, a separate source for the slide from very low probability to impossibility or difficulty is the quite reasonable thought that it might well be impossible or very difficult to *get* people to participate to the specified degree. Even if they could all do it, and do it without undue difficulty, it does not follow that anyone could get them to do it. I could easily dance like a chicken while giving a lecture, but you could never get me to (at a price you can afford). My dancing is easy—your getting me to dance is impossible.[1] To consider this more closely, return to a theory requiring widespread political participation. It might not require anyone to get people to do anything. Instead, it directly requires the people to participate. There are no requirements here that are impossible or too difficult to fulfill. The point about "getting" can be made first without the extra complexity of a collective. The school requires your adolescent child to be present by 9 o'clock every morning. When you hear this as a parent your reaction might be that this is impossible. You know from experience that your son will preen endlessly in front of the mirror in the morning, which will often make him late, and he will do this *no matter what you do*. You simply cannot get him to be at school on time every day. However, in fact, the school is not requiring anything that is beyond anyone's abilities, because it is not requiring anything of you at all. It is requiring your son to be at school on time, which he could certainly do, even if it is clear that he won't.

The same structure is present in many cases of actions that are required on a mass scale. Assume that it is possible but difficult to refrain from nepotism in hiring choices. Consider a theory that requires everyone to refrain from nepotism in government hiring. It is impossible, or at least supremely difficult, to get everyone to comply with this rule. If something is impossible for the agent to do then it is not required. But that only shows that it is not required for anyone to *get* all people to refrain from nepotism. It is clear from the beginning that what one agent (including the state or government) ought to do can indeed be affected by what *other agents* will or will not do.[2] That is no challenge to a theory if it does not require anyone to get everyone to refrain from nepotism, and what it requires, rather, is everyone together to refrain from nepotism. Drawing on the conditional analysis of ability we explored in chapter 5, if everyone tried to refrain from intentionally hiring family members everyone would succeed. There is no action required by the theory that is difficult, much less impossible.

Another point, for now, about oughts and groups concerns two different issues about whether oughts applied to a group also apply to the individuals. One case is where the action is, as I will call it, essentially collective. An example would be a group singing a G chord. This is not the kind of thing an individual can do since the chord is made up of three distinct tones.[3] For that stark reason, we cannot infer from a group's obligation to sing the chord (suppose the ensemble has contracted to do so) that any of the individuals ought to sing the chord. Oughts on a group (to do φ) do not directly distribute into oughts on members (to do φ), at least when the group action in question is essentially collective. But, of course, often a member could nevertheless do her part, which would be something other than φ, and so there is a question whether the obligation on the group entails obligations on members to do their parts. This is still not always a possible action if others are not doing their parts, as in the case of "Add the clapboard to the house's frame." But there remain many cases without that holistic aspect, such as refraining from nepotism, voting, keeping agreements, and obeying many laws. These ways of doing one's part will not always be obligatory in the case where others are not playing their part, but the present point is only that these acts would not be impossible and so there is not that basis for denying the obligation. Later in the book, we will look in more depth at how requirements of social justice might apply to groups as such (see chaps. 11 and 12, "The Puzzle of Plural Obligation" and "Plural Requirement"). We can think separately about the conditional requirements that are part of Plural Requirement: the requirement on each to do a certain thing so long as others do their part. Where those conditional statements are not met, since they are requirements, this is unjustified, and society may count as unjust as a result of enough and the right kinds of such individual failures. The complication comes in where few or none will do their part even if others were to do so, since then the conditional requirements have no application. But that is the further topic to be taken up by the account of Plural Requirement.

2. Ability and Excuse in Individuals and Collectives

It is important to be clear about the relations between excuse and justification on the individual level on one hand and on the social level on the other. Social justice is a moral standard for societies and, strictly speaking, not for individuals. An individual cannot be characterized by any distribution of social goods or any institutional arrangement, and these are among the sorts of things that are assessed by standards of social justice. Requirements of social justice morally require things of societies as such. Still, obviously, whether a society meets standards of justice will depend at least partly on how the society's members act.[4]

There is an ambiguity in saying that individuals are required by social justice to act or refrain in certain ways. On one meaning, this is to say that a society's justice depends on how individuals act. To say that it requires certain actions in this sense is not to assert that the absence of those actions is any injustice, but only that they are necessary conditions for the existence of social justice. On another meaning, it is to say that individuals are morally required by standards of social justice to act in certain ways. That is not settled by facts of the first kind. Individuals may, indeed, be under certain moral requirements to promote or comply with standards of social justice (even though standards of social justice do not apply directly to them, but to societies), but that is not a question I will be considering in any detail. I have, however, been assuming, quite blandly I hope, that for any plausible standard of social justice, some morally bad individual behaviors, if sufficiently widespread, would entail that society fails to meet standards of social justice. This leaves open what moral requirements on individuals, if any, stem in some way from standards of social justice. It is a recurring theme in the book that the requirements of justice, while moral, apply to sets or groups of individual agents whether or not they are a group *agent* in their own right, and that such a requirement over a group does not logically entail obligations on the individuals. The idea is that (at least often) no individual is required to do her part if the others will not do theirs even when her own part alone lacks any evident moral value. And yet, in that case, there is a moral failure of a kind by that group of agents. (See chapter 12: "Plural Requirement.")

I have assumed (see the section "Being Realistic and the Alternatives" in chapter 1: "An Unrealistic Introduction") that societies as such are not required to do anything they cannot do. The idea of ability, or what an agent can or could do, is familiar in the case of individual agents, but less so for collective agents such as societies themselves. Since the requirements we are primarily concerned with are requirements of social justice, the question arises whether in some way there is an ability constraint—a collective version of 'ought implies can.' If there is, we can anticipate attempts to use this against unrealistic accounts of justice, claiming that, at least in familiar circumstances, society is *unable* to meet such requirements. To address this, I propose to allow for the sake of argument that there is a certain connection between group requirement, group ability, and individual members' ability. Allow, as a first approximation (which will be superseded but not rejected in chapter 12: "Plural Requirement):[5]

> *The Ability Bridge Principle*: Meeting some standard is within a society's (or any collective's) abilities only if all individual behaviors that would be necessary if society (or the collective) is to meet that standard are within those individuals' abilities.[6]

So, a moral requirement of social justice would indeed be blocked, let us allow, if individuals could not behave in the necessary ways, because in that case society is unable to meet the standard. The principle that 'ought' implies 'can,' in this sense, I take to apply at the collective level.

Of course, if individuals will not behave in the necessary ways, society will not meet the standard. Even if people won't do something, that does not imply that they can't. Moreover, as I have argued (chapter 5) even if people can't will the act—can't bring themselves to do it—that doesn't imply that people can't do it. So, while society can't do something if its members can't do what would be necessary, showing that people can't bring themselves to do something is not enough to show that they are unable to do that thing, and its relevance for refuting standards of justice is blunted in that way.

The ability bridge principle supplies the needed bridge between individual and collective ability, with its implications for requirements at the collective level. I turn next more generally to justifications and excuses at the individual and collective levels. The question of morally justified or excused individual behavior is important for the following reason. The following principle is, I think, plausible and not tendentious in the present context. That is, it is not asserting anything that begs the question against those who think a theory's irrealism will mitigate the wrong or blame of a society that fails to meet it:

The Mitigating Motive Bridge Principle
Widespread interfering individual motives mitigate a charge of social injustice (justifying or excusing at the social level) *only if* those motives are individually mitigating.

One part of this is that if the individual behaviors are not justified or excused, then the social condition is not justified or excused. Now, if society fails to meet a standard of justice because of excusable individual failures, then perhaps society's failure is excused—perhaps the individual excusability is sufficient for the collective excuse. I take no stand on this question, since it is no challenge to my main thesis, which is that requirements of social justice are not refuted by motivational incapacities even if they happen to be owing to human nature, unless those are of a requirement-blocking kind at the individual level.[7] Even if individual excusable failures were to render the social failure excusable, the moral *requirement* of social justice would stand unchallenged. Nevertheless, more needs to be said about the possibility that individual excusability entails social excusability even if not social justification, and I turn to that suggestion below.[8] It is also important to emphasize that many familiar individual motivational incapacities are not even excusing, much less justifying. Much of the behavior whose alleged ubiquity in human life is held against high standards of social justice is simply selfish, or bigoted, or otherwise powerless to excuse failures to act as social justice would require whether or not they are owed to human nature. By the mitigating motive bridge principle stated above, the social failure would not be excused either.

We can briefly bring these distinctions among interfering motives to bear on an example that, on some accounts, would raise questions of justice. What about people's motivational incapacity—supposing there was one—to work as productively under the egalitarian tax system as they would under one that allowed the more able and talented to have more post-tax money? Is this morally like the person who could not bring himself to walk on a glass bridge even to save a person's life? In the bridge case the motivational structure probably strikes us as at least an excusing condition, at least if it is not bound up with morally poor attitudes such as bigotry, and may be justifying if the agent would pay a sufficiently high psychic price for acting. It is entirely different, though, from the doctor who cannot bring himself to work an extra eight hours a week in order to help the extra dozen patients, even though he would have worked that long and more if only he were paid more—and more than others. It might be tempting even to deny that this is a motivational incapacity at all rather than just an unwillingness to do as (suppose) justice requires. But for my purposes, I am willing to let my opponent—the advocate of the Bent View—have that charitable description of the case. Let the doctor's case be a motivational incapacity. Even if that is granted, it is far from clear that it has excusing power (much less requirement-blocking power), since it is far from clear that it does not reflect poorly on the moral quality of the agent's motivations in justice-destroying ways. As I argued, sometimes motivational incapacities are not even excusing, much less justifying, since they reflect a morally deficient structure of concerns. And, again, they would not become excusing, much less justifying, simply by being widespread or even natural. This question about the excusing power of such motivational incapacities is a question that is illegitimately silenced by supposing, with the Bent View, that justice takes motivational incapacities as given, and shapes itself around them.

The view defended here is not essentially a kind of moral rigorism. It all depends on what grounds might be supplied for less strenuous moral requirements or standards of blameworthiness (to reflect the issue about excuse) on individuals and societies. My argument is meant to show that, not only would there be no support for that in mere statistical facts about how people do or might act, but that even appeals to natural motivational incapacity would not be decisive. The question would be whether or not those incapacities are, for all their naturalness, forms of morally deficient will or concern. Vicious, complacent, or selfish concerns are not somehow morally sanitized if they should happen to be characteristic of humans. However, if the forms of behavior and motivation in question are not only common but morally weighty in the right way, then, as I have argued, the standard of social justice may follow to that extent. I stop short of declaring on the question of what, whether, or how this does in fact affect what justice requires.

3. Incentive-Induced Abilities

In the remainder of this chapter I take up a series of questions that arise from the line of argument in this and the previous chapter, namely that principles of justice are not bent to fit even robust motivational properties of human agents except in the special cases where these are disabling, insistent, or morally outweighing. I begin with the suggestion, due to Samuel Scheffler, that in some cases incentivizing certain behavior may actually be necessary to enable—rather than merely induce—that behavior. [9]

What people can bring themselves to do is, often, relative to an environment of threats and incentives. In many cases, what look like motivational incapacities can be overcome by structuring those threats and incentives. It should not be assumed that this entails morally defective or unjust motivations absent those inducements, since there are many counterexamples to that. In a subset of cases that require inducement, only oppressive threats and incentives would be effective—such as the effort to get someone to confess or to incriminate another. (I do not assume that coercion, which law normally involves, is always oppressive and wrong, only that some cases are.) Even where the initial motivations are themselves morally deficient (such as weakness of will or willing vice), obviously not just any inducement, however oppressive, would be permitted. Often, that would only substitute one injustice for another. Nor, however, does the fact that the oppressive threat or inducement should be forgone somehow erase the injustice of the behavior that will result in that case. Just because we shouldn't amputate the hands of thieves in order to eradicate theft (supposing it would) does not mean that theft itself is permissible or that a society rife with it just. Similarly, just because we should not incarcerate or "reeducate" people who perpetuate bigotry (supposing that would work) does not mean that the resulting high levels of bigotry are compatible with a just society.[10]

When a doctor can't bring herself to work longer hours without the inducement of extra pay, the arguments offered above would suggest that it is not plausible to conclude that she is unable to work the extra hours. There is no case there, yet, against a moral requirement (for whatever reason) to work the extra hours—no 'can't' that blocks the 'ought.' There are cases, however, where abilities themselves seem, at least more plausibly, to depend on external inducements of various kinds. The question is important in moral psychology in general, but it has a special salience in political philosophy. In our time, one of the enduring debates in political philosophy is whether a market-based economic system is a capitulation to morally dubious, and possibly justice-tainting, individual selfishness and partiality. If some acts are truly outside of even a morally good agent's abilities, and not only beyond their motivational capacities, unless certain incentives are present, there would be a strong case for rejecting any moral requirement either on those individuals or on societies themselves that people perform those actions even without the incentives. The ability bridge principle allows that society is unable if individuals are unable to do their part (see section 2 above). In this section, I will argue that there plausibly are such cases, but that they are of only the most limited significance for the question of what social justice requires.

Before looking at political contexts, consider the case of a musician who can only play her best when the incentives or other motivating circumstances that are involved in an important public performance are present. Here it may be that without those inducements there is literally an inability to play well,[11] and it does not reflect a weak desire to do so. Even full trying without giving up will, in some cases, tend to fail. That is not normally the case, however, with the doctor's trying to stay at work for nine hours a day.

Consider cases where the ability's susceptibility to incentives reflects morally objectionable attitudes of the agent's. If it is disabling then it is requirement-blocking, but this might seem troubling. Maybe a violinist can only perform his very best if doing so would humiliate his rival. Now suppose that performing at a high level would provide much-needed comfort to someone whose suffering is this violinist's responsibility. He ought to do it if he can, and it grates to think he evades this requirement by having a malicious motive that renders him unable to do it when his rival is not present to be humiliated. Some might wish to see this as a case where he ought even though he can't, but I will hold onto 'ought implies can.' If he can't do it, then even if we conclude from this that he is not required to do it, we can perfectly well morally disapprove of his bad will. (So, maybe he ought to *be* such that he can; but that is not an obligation to do anything.) And, of course, there is no difficulty about our judging that he ought to do it if he can. Such a malicious motive should not get him entirely off the hook morally. On the other hand, there is no strong pressure to give up on our commitment to 'ought implies can,' in this case. We can allow that some abilities are incentive-induced, and grant that in cases where the incentive and ability are missing there is no requirement. Requirements depend on abilities, even if they are incentive-induced abilities.

Requirements of social justice then are constrained by such cases. The creative aspects of many lines of work might fall into this category. A putative requirement to innovate and create social value every bit as imaginatively even without any prospect of greater wealth or recognition or competitive success might be refuted in such cases by the fact that some agents are literally unable to do so. In some cases, of course, a person might simply decide not to try very hard if there will not be those rewards, which is not a case of inability, but that is not the only case. Even those who are willing to try very hard might be unable to produce the same level of performance in the absence of certain inducements. Consider a teacher who is unable to fully engage his students if he is dispirited by his low pay or poor professional treatment. It isn't that he decides not to try, but rather that his talent for exciting teaching cannot be called forth in these psychological conditions. Or consider an aspiring entrepreneur who is thinking hard about what goods or services, previously unimagined, might set the commercial world on fire. We do not need to suppose that he has decided not to try his best in order to explain how he might only be able to come upon the brilliant innovation if he foresees certain kinds of rewards such as public esteem, or an economically comfortable life, or even *more* esteem or pay than people working in certain other occupations.

So there may be some incentive-induced abilities, and in those cases where the incentive is absent there is a requirement-blocking inability. Granting this is no serious concession for my purposes. There is no plausibility to the idea that the following actions are impossible in that way in the absence of such inducements as extra money, status, or competitive success: voting for (as distinct from complying with) one tax scheme rather than another; working more hours per week; working as hard at a lower salary as at a higher; being honest in commercial transactions; staying informed about public affairs; and so on. These might be things that people will not do, and maybe cannot bring themselves to do. But, unlike some cases of insight or performance, these are not things that they literally could not do without inducements such as extra pay or status, even if they tried and persevered. There is no inability here that would block requirements.

Cohen argues[12] that even in cases where, for Schefflerian reasons, certain things are beyond our abilities to change without incentives, they might be condemned as unjust. It is not that the agent ought to do certain things even if she can't. He takes no stand on that.[13] Rather, a condition might be unjust, on his view, (because it is inequality owed to morally arbitrary, or luck-derived, circumstances) even if there is nothing that anyone can do about it. Despite the fact that this leads him to say that motivational features of human nature do not bear on justice in ways it is sometimes held to do, it should be clear that my point here is entirely different from his. The point here is that whether or not something we cannot change could be unjust, many motivational features attributed (rightly or not) to human nature do not rise to the level of Schefflerian incentive-starved inabilities, even if some do. So there is no case for exempting those motives from demands of justice even if justice does not (contrary to Cohen) ever require the impossible.

4. Profound and Less Profound Partiality

Might certain attachments such as those to family, friends, and lovers sometimes be literally disabling, even if many are not? Many will respond that such intense motivational attachments are socially constructed and variable under possible social arrangements. That might be so, but suppose that it is not. Intuitively, some cases might be thought of as sufficiently like the paradigm clinical cases of addiction, phobia, and compulsion, with the exception that they are much more common. Typicality, however, as I have argued, does not bear on whether a given motive is or is not requirement-blocking. The question is whether such attachments are sometimes literally disabling in each person subject to them. If it were, rather than disabling, a case of severe or non-severe insistent motives, then my treatment of those cases has already been offered. The new question is whether such attachments are ever disabling, such that even were the person to try, and not give up so long as success appeared in reach, she would still not succeed in performing the action. The answer seems to be that there are indeed at least some such cases. An example, horrible to contemplate, might be a parent who, even if he somehow did not cease the effort, would weaken, tremble, sob, or collapse, and so tend to fail in trying to kill or harm his own child—say, in order to prevent an overwhelming number of other tragic deaths. Of course, it will be hard to know in any given case whether there was a giving up or not rather than perseverance with failure, but it seems fairly clear that the latter is possible. Let us, at least, allow it for the sake of argument. More importantly for our purposes, how common is this, and what kinds and degrees of attachment does it take to produce such a case? This is not the place to attempt to settle such a complex and partly empirical matter. Instead, it will serve my purposes again to grant, for the sake of argument, that such cases are not extremely rare, so long as we pause to reflect carefully on the limits of what we are allowing.

Let it be granted for the sake of argument that there are some historically and institutionally robust and widespread human motives of partiality for (let us call them) loved ones, which are so psychologically powerful that an agent is no more able to act contrary to them than are agents who collapse from fear or are under the influence of the clinical versions of such disorders as the more extreme versions of such conditions as addiction, phobia, and compulsion. We do not need to characterize such profound partiality as a disorder (endemic, we are imagining, to human nature) in order to grant that its significance as a requirement blocker is akin to those disorders. Call this the case of robust and widespread *profound partiality*, and grant that it is requirement-blocking.

The reason we can grant this claim of robust and widespread profound human partiality without much loss to the overall thrust of my argument is that even if it is true, it will not encompass any large fraction of the kinds of motives appealed to by the Bent View in its most familiar forms. The harrowing prospect of surrendering one's infant to the communal nursery, for example, which might sometimes be a case of profound and disabling partiality, has little bearing on the prospect of refraining from favoritism in such decisions as hiring, paying, and grading. Both raise questions of partiality, but the motives in the latter case are not plausibly assimilated to the disabling kinds even if the former cases might be.[14] The profundity of separating oneself irreparably from one's child, parent, or lover has no analogy in the difficulties involved in dealing with others fairly and honestly, working hard even without extra reward, supporting institutions that help others more than oneself, staying informed, or the many other kinds of unlikely (or so we grant) behavior which the Bent View would delete from the requirements of justice. So we can bracket the question whether justice requires the most wrenching decisions without conceding anything about the broad swaths of less profound partiality.

5. Are Prerogatives a Concession to Human Nature?

From time to time, visionary thinkers have argued that the best social arrangements would see children raised not by parents but in some alternative manner. Plato, Charles Fourier, and the pioneers of the Kibbutzim are among the familiar examples.[15] Reasons for these proposals and practices have varied, sometimes stemming from moral criticisms of traditional family structures, sometimes from hopes that children might be more effectively raised and educated if the task were deliberately designed as a social one. Of course, it is difficult for many people to imagine such arrangements without horror, since it is often assumed that people have ineluctable needs and passions for the kind of intimate and pervasive community of the (idealized) traditional family. It may be impossible to know whether the familiar human passions that pass between many offspring and parents might eventually transform if enough other features of the social world were different. The traditional arrangement of spousal relations (a fluid tradition, of course) is another frequent target of writers who try to set their sights as high as possible for the organization of human social relations. The critique of traditional marriage is no longer an exotic theme by now, but the more expansive ideas of "free love" still strike some readers in the present era as naïve about human nature in various ways.

Suppose that it would be supremely difficult, in any possible future, for many parents to surrender their infant children to be raised by the community. In reality, perhaps people could be socialized so that fewer parents felt this way, and those who did, felt it less intensely. Or perhaps not. I will not try to resolve this, and I accept for the sake of argument that human nature would resist such socialization and many parents would always be unable to bring themselves to give up their children. Few accept that justice would require that children be raised by the state, and it may seem as though this is a concession to human nature: humans cannot bring themselves to surrender their children and so, for that reason, justice does not require it. This would be a concession to human nature of precisely the kind I am opposing. Such motives may be mitigating in other ways, as we have seen. First, there might be moral value in those relationships that would be missing from these forms of communal child raising, and which underwrites some significant moral weight for motivations in that direction. Second, whether or not that is so, people might be so constituted that being separated from parents or offspring in the proposed ways might cause enough pain and distress to morally outweigh whatever other considerations might count in favor of the separation, quite apart from whether there is anything to be said morally in favor of those strong emotions.

Third, even if not so severe, such motives might be partly excusing. This is familiar by now. The question for this section is whether the requirements of morality and justice themselves bend to accommodate the fact that agents have commitments and projects that are important to them and which often conflict with what morality might seem otherwise to require—that is, at least before the agent's own concerns are factored in. Requirements can seem, intuitively, to be absurdly demanding unless agents' own aims are accommodated to some extent. In order to act so as to maximize pre-tax income, for example, a person would have to forgo any projects that did not (directly or indirectly) contribute to that goal. Maybe reading bedtime stories to one's kids increases one's own productivity, but if not, it would have to be skipped when more productive activities were available. Spending a long evening over a fancy meal, or buying a nice bicycle with money that could be used to take more professional development courses would be morally wrong. Isn't it absurd to require maximizing pre-tax income if that means never reading to your children at night, or never going out to dinner with your partner, or never buying a nice bicycle?[16] Similar concerns have been pressed against highly demanding moral theories generally, and many believe that it is plausible to accept, in effect, a moral prerogative to pursue certain of one's own ends to some extent even when this is not the optimal way to contribute to the agent-neutral good.[17] There are various concerns an agent might have that might seem to have a claim on the agent even when they conflict with some more impartial or social good, including one's own aims, one's own valuable aims, the welfare of loved ones, local duties in the context of a family or neighborhood, and others.

We allow, then, as said in chapter 5, that 'ought' implies 'not unreasonably demanding': theories that are, as I have called them, harsh, are false. The boundaries can be left indeterminate for our purposes. The question I want to consider is whether this would be a concession to human nature, or at least to the brute fact that (supposing it is so) there will tend to be widespread motives of this kind. More specifically, is this to be granted on the grounds that humans (by their natures) will be unable to bring themselves to conform to such a demanding requirement? An instructive example, again, is Carens, who conjectures that people might well be able to bring themselves to (as I would put it) conform to his requirements if society has moved along a path in which they have been properly socialized to understand and care about their duties to others in this way.[18] So, when he grants that the original duty is too demanding it is no concession to human nature. He says, "The kind of work that a person finds most meaningful and important may not always be the work that contributes most to the productive output of society. A principle that gives absolute priority to society's demands is too demanding."[19] In other words, whether or not all people, or even any people, will especially value work that is not socially optimal, any who do are permitted to pursue that work to some extent even at some cost to the common good.

What moral basis one might give for this moral judgment is a complex and difficult question. What matters here is that there is no indication that the reasoning must proceed from observations about what humans can or cannot get themselves to do. Indeed, if the argument for a less demanding duty were to proceed from the observed motivational incapacities of humans, it would be a deeply troubling argument, having the following *brute bending* form:

The Argument from Partiality
This tendency to partiality is what people are motivationally like, as a matter of human nature. *Therefore*, requirements to be otherwise are specious and false.

If that is a good form of argument, then the following is a good form of argument:

The Argument from Cruelty
People tend to a certain degree of cruelty, and this is part of what they are motivationally like as a matter of human nature. (Suppose this is so.) Therefore, requirements to be otherwise are specious and false.

That, of course, is an absurd argument even apart from whether the empirical premise about cruelty is true. The *form* of argument is bad, and so no prerogative in favor of partiality can be inferred from the fact, if it is one, that humans are naturally partial or selfish.

I conclude that if the partiality of the parent is morally allowed when he refuses to deliver the infant to Plato's or Fourier's nursery, then this is not because it is a characteristic feature of human motivation. It must be for some other reason. Perhaps it is because the theory of justice that purports to require it is flawed in other ways that undermine this aspect of it. Or maybe there is a deep moral case that can be made for the proposition that *whether or not people are typically partial in this way*, it would be permissible for them to be so. That, manifestly, is not a principle that depends on whether people are, in fact, like that.

Samuel Scheffler has one of the most developed views about personal prerogatives, but they are not a concession to human nature on his view as I understand it. Rather, he argues that it is a pervasive feature of agency that the agent takes certain relationship-based and project-based considerations to be reasons. Agents could, of course, be either right or wrong about this, but Scheffler thinks we have no reason not to credit this pervasive appearance, and so he goes on to trace the implications of there being reasons of this kind.[20] No morally grounding argument for there being such reasons is offered (a feature I am not here criticizing), and instead the argument appeals to a presumption in favor of the way things robustly seem to valuing agents. Scheffler's case for prerogatives, then, is not an appeal to the "brute bending" form of argument.

He does not say that requirements of justice ought to be shaped to accommodate whatever motives humans or agents, characteristically or in all likely futures, tend to have. As far as my argument here is concerned, Scheffler's view about prerogatives is not Bent, and could be accepted.

6. Excused Injustice, a Safe Harbor?

Some amount of social injustice might be owing to individual behavior that stems from morally unexceptionable but still interfering motives, rendering that behavior if not justified, then excused. Might that render the social injustice itself excusable? While the requirements of justice might remain unrealistically high, the standard for social blameworthiness might be dramatically eased.[21] The attention of realistically minded theorists of justice might understandably be drawn to this standard of social blamelessness.

First, in one way this would be no threat to my larger aim in this book, since it lets stand the high idealistic requirements of justice. However, there are several points to make in reply to this suggestion. Remember that I have not granted that individual mitigation would imply social mitigation (I assert only the converse). Nor have I argued against it, but there is the following reason to be wary. There is an important class of cases in which something seems to be wrong with a collection of individual actions, and yet there is nothing morally wrong with any of the individual acts. In the case I briefly introduced in chapter 1 and will explore more deeply later, there is the illustrative case of two doctors, Slice and Patch, and the patient who urgently needs their care. If Slice wouldn't cut even if Patch would stitch, and also Patch wouldn't stitch even if Slice were to cut, then it is impossible to believe that either of them is acting wrongly by, respectively, not cutting and not stitching. There would be an obvious solution to that case if the team were itself an agent, but cases are easily constructed where that is not plausible. I consider this family of cases in chapter 12: "Plural Requirement."

If society is itself a moral agent, then the move from individual excuse to collective excuse loses any rationale. The question must then be whether the motives of the collective agent itself are excusing. For, it is hard to see how anything could count as an agent unless it does have motives of its own, among other things (such as beliefs, and so forth). And if it does, the account of excusing motives applies directly. However, I believe that a collective need not have whatever kind of organizational features that true collective agency would require in order to be subject to evaluation as just or unjust.[22] So, I believe, we should not assume that societies subject to evaluation as just or unjust are agents in their own right. But if a society is not an agent, then we are no longer in charted waters when asking whether its injustice might be excusable, since the idea of excusable wrongdoing is an idea from the domain of moral evaluation of actions and agents.

One reason for thinking that if the injustice-constituting individual wrongs are excused then the injustice is excused might be the thought that, in parallel fashion, if the individual behavior is justified then there is no injustice at the social level. But I will reject this latter link, and argue that there is an essentially collective form of moral violation which does not depend on any individual moral violation or deficiency. This is the idea of Plural Requirement, which I have so far only introduced briefly. If I am right that individual justification does not translate into social justification there is, at least, less reason than otherwise to think that individual excuse translates into social excuse. But so far this just leaves the question open.

Since social injustice does not depend on individual moral violation, the significant question may not be about whether the underlying behavior is excused—it could only be excused if it were wrong. The better question might be whether social injustice should count as excused, or something like it, if the underlying behavior (wrong or not) stems from morally unobjectionable motives and dispositions. Slice and Patch may be longstanding jerks, even though neither is wrong to refrain from operating given that the other would refrain in any case. In that case the collective violation, a violation of Plural Requirement, is resting not on wrongs but still on morally bad motives.

There is some temptation to locate the sense of injustice, or a collective violation, in the morally bad motives themselves. I will argue later that there is still a kind of infraction, or so it seems to many, that this would not capture, namely the apparently wrongful death of the patient. Even so, granted, we might be tempted to say that a society can be unjust (and something similar for other collective failures of the Plural Requirement kind) in virtue of the individuals' dispositions themselves, rather than behavior, but I think this is imprecise. I believe that in at least many standard references to social injustice, and as partly constitutive of that injustice, there are parties who would be right to be aggrieved, the ones who are thereby wronged—the victims of the injustice so to speak. However, I do not believe anyone is wronged merely by the wrongful or unjust attitudes of others. Those attitudes are morally bad features of the person whether or not anyone is wronged. It is certainly a significant question whether a society or a person is disposed to unjust behaviors. We might, if we wish, even speak of an unjust society in that sense, as we would of an unjust person in a similar sense. But there is also a different question, whether anyone is right to be aggrieved by the basic social structure. This is different, since two social structures are not different, and so no one is differentially aggrieved, owing only to motives and dispositions if they are in no way manifested in behavior. We could, if necessary, speak of two senses in which a society is unjust: say, distinguishing between dispositional and manifest injustice. But there does not appear to be sufficient reason to multiply senses in that way, since nothing important appears to be lost by simply distinguishing between a society (or a person) being *disposed* to injustice and its being *unjust*. I will adopt this latter way of describing the cases.

So, suppose there can be social injustice without individual wrongdoing, but that social injustice does not consist merely in motives or dispositions. Still, we might want to mark the difference between cases of social injustice according to whether they do or do not rest on morally objectionable motives. One possible view would be that the injustice is excused only if it does not arise from morally deficient individual motives. There are, I argue, such cases ("Good Motives Slice and Patch"). Notice, however, that we are not thereby moving from excused individual behavior to excused social injustice. The individual behavior in question need not even be wrong, in which case there is nothing to excuse. Rather, we would be letting the excusability of social injustice depend not on whether the underlying individual actions are excused, but on whether they stem from morally deficient motives or not. Where they do not, the wrong that is injustice (manifested, not just motivational) remains (even without any agential wrong) but, in a counterpart to the agential case, there is a sort of blame that is not appropriate even if it would be in the case of deficient motives. This would not be an exact counterpart to the structure of excuse and blame for individual agents, but it would capture a significant distinction in the possible grounds of social injustice, where it either does or does not rest on morally objectionable individual dispositions.

Now much social injustice, both intuitively and according to the Plural Requirement model, will rest on morally objectionable individual motives. It would be not only unjust, but, in that way, inexcusable. But some injustice might rest on behaviors that are neither wrong nor manifestations of morally bad motives. These can usefully be marked by calling such cases excusable social injustice. Here, then, is the halfway house. It might be argued that even if I am right that a set of behaviors might be required by justice even if this is contrary to characteristic human motives (see discussion of ability and 'can't will'), the motives from which injustice predictably results may often be morally unobjectionable. Such social injustice, which we might call excusable, does not reflect poorly on the members of society themselves. This does, indeed, mark a significant distinction between cases of social injustice. But it should not be thought that the "realistic" impulse that first hoped to bend requirements of justice to the shape of characteristic human dispositions has accomplished anything very similar by these other means. It no more follows from a human motive's typicality that it is morally unobjectionable than it follows that it is requirement-blocking. For that reason, we are given no reason to think that the range of excusable social injustice enlarges as we take account of characteristic human motives not to collectively do as justice requires. Acknowledging the excusable category of social injustice—that which does not entail any wrong or morally objectionable attitudes by any agents—does not somehow give a greater normative role to human nature and its associated motivational incapacities than we are prepared to give it in the determination of the requirements of justice themselves.

7. Rawlsian Realism Resisted

Recent advocates of "realism," and opponents of "ideal theory," often take the Rawlsian approach to justice as their central opponent. Somewhat against type, then, there are places where Rawls says things that lean toward insisting that the theory of justice be, let us say, realistic. If the great ideal-theorist Rawls and the realists agree on these points (which I suspect they do), the question arises whether there is any serious space left for contesting them. But I think there is, and I want to look at just a small part of this topic here. My interest is not primarily exegetical. I want to know what reason there is to believe this. But Rawls wrote so systematically that we might hope to find argument in his own text for the claims in question. As I will explain, I do not find it.

There is a feature of Rawls's theory of justice that might be at odds with the view taken here.[23] By conceiving of the principles of justice as the outcome of an imaginary contract Rawls finds an elegant way to account for the conviction that the claims made on individuals by the standards of justice should not be too demanding. In particular, if the parties to the original position were to know of motivational incapacities that are part of human nature (and so ones that would not be overcome in any institutional setting) they could not honestly commit, as parties to a contract, to comply with demands that conflicted with these known incapacities. If, for example, the demands of a conception of justice such as Pre–Tax Max were beyond human motivational capacities, then the parties would not commit themselves to it. On Rawls's theory, that means that it does not give us the correct principles of justice. This insistence on attention to strains of commitment seems unavoidable when the grounding idea is a contract or a commitment, so it is a deep feature of that whole family of approaches. And yet it is questionable as a way of identifying the requirements of justice.

Surely, society should not implement institutions that people will not be able to bring themselves to comply with (assuming their value depends on that compliance). The question is whether that is a constraint on the content of justice, as the contract methodology implies. The rules and institutions that should be constructed given what is known about everyone's likely compliance are hardly guaranteed to be rules and institutions that qualify a society as just. Suppose, for example, that it is part of human nature that people who recognize their own superior talents will tend to resent and envy less talented people who are, owing to the operation of social institutions, as well off as they are. This resentment, suppose, would undermine the levels of allegiance and compliance on which the operation of those institutions would depend. Rawls would have doubted that this is so, I think, but his theory of justice has a distinctive response to such hypothetical conditions nevertheless. If it were so, then the parties should (other things being equal) reject principles that do not tend to apportion the distribution of social goods according to levels of talent and ability. Not only should society so apportion things under the circumstances, on Rawls's approach, but this, according to the Rawlsian theory, would constitute the content of full social justice. It is this last point that is the crucial and, I believe, damaging one. The implausibility does not lie in the suggestion that in such unfortunate conditions there might be important reasons to accommodate those untoward but ineluctable motivational constraints.[24] But what institutions a society should implement given such practical constraints can hardly be thought to deliver the content of the idea of social justice. I am not relying on G. A. Cohen's sweeping argument that Rawls goes wrong by letting justice depend on any facts whatever. Whether or not that is correct, it is doubtful that the content of social justice is sensitive in this way to motivational features of people even if they are morally untoward. Rawls's doctrine of strains of commitment in his contractual framework would silence concerns about whether some motivational structures—however much they might be part of our natures—might be justice-tainting rather than justice-shaping.[25]

In a brief passage that is important for our purposes, Rawls writes,

> Let us agree that a political conception must be practicable, fall under the art of the possible. This contrasts with a moral conception that is not political: a moral conception may condemn the world and human nature as too corrupt to be moved by its precepts and ideals.[26]

Rawls is apparently not making the point that requirements depend on abilities, or 'ought implies can.' The constraint he is imposing here is more restrictive than that, namely, that a political conception must not include precepts and ideals that people would not, perhaps owing to human nature or other deep explanations, be moved by. We might call this a constraint of "motivational feasibility." We have looked at Nagel's development of a similar position, but Rawls here links this constraint to his distinctive idea of a "political conception" of justice. The suggestion seems to be that there is something about a political conception in particular such that it must be constrained by motivational feasibility. As we have granted all along (see the section "Being Realistic, and the Alternatives" in chapter 1: "An Unrealistic Introduction"), it is a desideratum of practical proposals for rules of regulation that they be suited to the environment of motives and other facts that are expected to obtain, otherwise they are quixotic or worse. No similar constraint applies, or so I have been arguing, if the task is not that practical one but rather the more philosophical one of determining what constitutes social justice.

The motivational feasibility constraint Rawls proposes, then, would make perfect sense if a political conception were a practical proposal taking all expected motives and other facts as given. However, that is not in the nature of a political conception as Rawls develops that idea. Perhaps the most striking departure from that fact-bound social regulation approach is Rawls's famous stipulation that the principles in his political conception of justice are to be identified subject to the factually false assumption that citizens will fully comply with the rules of the institutions in the society that meets the principles. This does not sound like the same method proposed in our quoted passage, namely, taking what we know about human motives as a constraint on a political conception, so as to guarantee that it is "practicable."

There are two other aspects of Rawls's idea of a "political conception of justice" that we should consider here. First, its content must be acceptable to all reasonable comprehensive conceptions. This, it is crucial to note, is not a practical or pragmatic constraint. It is an implication of a moral principle, what Rawls calls the liberal principle of legitimacy. That principle does not bid us to consult the actual comprehensive doctrines that will have a causal role in what kind of acceptance and compliance is likely to eventuate from promulgation of a certain conception of justice. Such a pragmatic concern would be mandatory for a genuine practical proposal, as I have said. The liberal principle of legitimacy's focus on only the reasonable comprehensive views (and probably not only on the ones that are likely to exist[27]) decisively shows that its point is not meant to be that it is required by practical considerations such as feasibility.

The other aspect of a political conception, in Rawls's view, is quite distinct from the reasonable acceptability aspect. It is that such a conception must be capable of serving as a public conception of justice. This may look more practically motivated, but that is not entirely clear. If it were, then the requirement would be that it can serve as a public conception of justice in the environment of comprehensive views that we expect it actually to face were it to be promulgated. But that is not how Rawls seems to intend this constraint. Instead, the requirement is only that it must be capable of serving as a public conception of justice in a society in which, "unreasonable comprehensive doctrines (these, we assume, always exist) do not gain enough currency to undermine society's essential justice."[28] My point is not that such a society is unrealistic—a rather vague attribution in any case. Rather, it is that Rawls is not constraining his theory of justice by the demand that it be capable of serving as a public conception of justice in any actual or probable society, but only for a society, however probable or improbable it might be, in which its essential justice is secured by the predominance of reasonable comprehensive views. This shows that the content of the political conception is not to be constrained in the way it should be if it were an actual practical proposal. There, of course, one has to contend with reasonable and unreasonable views alike in whatever proportion presents itself.

Since Rawls does not develop his idea of a political conception of justice in the ways that he would if it were to be a kind of actual practical proposal, it remains puzzling why he should think it obvious (if this is what the passage is taken to show) that a political conception must be "practicable," a conception that real people as we know or expect them to be could be "moved by." If it is not a practical proposal but a normative standard which might or might not actually attract compliance, then what basis is there for this strong practicability constraint, which goes well beyond the more easily granted stipulation that requirements must be within the abilities of those who are required? Why must a political conception of justice limit its precepts to ones that people can be expected to be moved to comply with?

It may be that Rawls does not mean that it must be practicable in any strongly predictive sense, but only that it be such that it would be practicable in a society that is largely made up of adherents of reasonable views, along with the assumption that this is not overly unrealistic even if it is not judged highly likely. My own reading, which I will not defend in any further depth, is that Rawls is only imposing a weak constraint of motivational feasibility, one that is not beholden to the environment of motives we either observe or expect, but only to the limits of the "laws of nature." The constraint is only what is "possible given the laws and tendencies of society." Those are plausible, and far broader than what we observe or expect: "the limits of the possible are not given by the actual."[29] If this is an application of 'ought implies can,' then that much I have granted from the beginning. But much hangs on which motivational phenomena count as inability.

What kind of motivational feasibility constraint results? There is one that is still apparently, or at least possibly, more restrictive than what I am defending. Rawls can be read as insisting that principles of justice and the resulting institutional rules be such that not only would people tend to succeed *if* they were to be so motivated (roughly the account I've defended), but also it must not be a "law of nature" that they will not have such motives. But since, as I have argued, neither Rawls nor I are making a practical proposal given all the facts as we know and expect them to be, I fail to see any rationale for that stricter constraint. And there is this problem with it: if it were (as it might be) a law of human nature that there is a certain statistical tendency to cruelty or bigotry even under otherwise just conditions, then the very content of social justice would be bent to fit our crooked shape. This is a deeply implausible implication of a view which is ambivalent, to the point of questionable coherence, between the project of making practical proposals for society in light of all the facts on the one hand, and the project of identifying a standard for the evaluation of society, letting chips concerning motivational feasibility fall where they may, on the other hand.

We might consider the view (even apart from Rawls) that social justice is a question that arises when we take individual proclivities, along with their tendencies to be shaped by changing times and institutions, as given empirical parameters. Critical evaluation of those individual proclivities is a matter for part of moral philosophy, but not for a theory of justice. So, then, a society is not to be considered unjust on the grounds that people are morally deficient. One quick point: it is no support for this idea that circumstances of justice assume people being at odds, since being at odds does not depend on moral deficiency. Another quick point: it cannot be assumed in this context that the theory of justice is not a branch of moral philosophy (and Rawls himself holds, many times, that it is).

So a possible view about justice that arises is this: ways in which empirical human proclivities fall short of appropriate moral standards cannot bear on whether their society counts as unjust, since social justice—a political standard—takes people's moral deficiencies as given. This is a version of what I have been calling the Bent View of justice. To test this, imagine a society in which most people are self-consciously and virulently racist, except that they broadly accept the institutions that are most appropriate under those motivational conditions. But institutions can only do so much, and across the races there is in this society massive de facto segregation, widely divergent prospects for health and success, members of the targeted race regularly ignored by others when they are not insulted, and so on. You might say that if the institutions are chosen properly then they will change people over time. Grant it for the sake of argument. In the society I sketch they are not changed yet. Now, the idea that there is no ground on which to count this society, in its basic social structure, as unjust is an exotic one, I think, and would need substantial defense of some kind, something more than jarring terminological fiat. If you simply *call* the despicable motives and behavior "institutional" then the theoretical gambit I am criticizing—that justice takes individual motives and behavior as given and calls for appropriate institutions in light of them— is abandoned.

Notice that Rawls does not, in the recent passage, say that human moral deficiencies do not bear on justice. He is not here contrasting thinking about justice with thinking about some other topic like individual morality, but rather he contrasts "a political conception" with "a moral conception." This allows for the possibility of a conception *of justice* that is moral but not political. And to reject that possibility would be a great stretch, I think—to deny that a view that "condemn(s) the world and human nature as too corrupt to be moved by its precepts and ideals" is a view about injustice. All he says is that this would not count as a political conception, and this on the ground that it does not stay within the bounds of the "practicable." (It may be that for his present purposes this is all that "political" vs. "moral but not political" means.)

What puzzles me is this: however we might categorize it in the space of the political and the nonpolitical, the following issue emerges unscathed—no argumentative ordnance has even been directed at it:

What principles must a basic social structure meet in order not to count
as unjust, or (if we are disallowed that word) wrong?

Rawls says that an answer to this would be a moral conception that is not a
political conception. The idea that such a conception is not "political" would,
I think, be to abuse language, but nothing hangs on that. (As I read the passage, Rawls is not guilty and means the technical sense, but the slide would
be subtle.) Whether or not it is political in that sense, it would still be a conception of *what counts a basic social structure as rightful*, while not prejudg-
ing whether such a conception would be motivationally feasible (which would
surely bear on whether we should set out for it). After all, people's motivational tendencies (now and as they would adapt to changes) might themselves
be such that what is rightful socially would not move people in the ways
needed to achieve or sustain it. How could that possibility be ruled out? Rawls
does not rule it out.

There is a different project from that moral but not "political" one, as I have
said, one that simply investigates what it calls "political justice," namely, whatever is (in some sense) the best conception compatible with whatever motivational tendencies humans actually have (over time and change, etc.). There is
no denying that this is also a possible project, and even an important one, inquiring into what institutions we should build given what we actually expect
of people. But, as I have argued,

a. given its capitulation to whatever motivational tendencies it might
find and expect, it is implausible to treat the fruition of such a project,
whatever it might be, as justice,

and,

b. so far as this dialectic has played out here (a brief treatment to be
sure), not a single point has been raised suggesting any deficiency in a
moral-not-political conception of justice: a moral inquiry into the
standards of rightful basic social structure.

Rawls does not only prefer the other project, the one relative to expected motives. He also says that this one is defective. But aside from some possible but
implausible definitional claims about what counts as political, so far I am not
aware of any *argument* that it is defective. Grant that its results might not be
capable of serving in the role of a public conception of justice. That may show
only that these are two different inquiries, two different questions to ask about
justice: (a) What must be true of a society for its basic structure to be just or
rightful? (b) What must be true of a conception of justice for it to serve a certain public causal and normative role?

A final thought. If, as I think, no defect has been demonstrated in the project around (a), then there is no guarantee that a society that lives up to the best

public conception of justice will meet the appropriate standards for a rightful basic structure, since ineluctable motivational proclivities may have ruled the latter out for that public role. We still ought, probably, to coordinate around the best public conception, but we should not carelessly think that our society is somehow thereby just.

PART III

Beyond Concessive
Justice

CHAPTER EIGHT

Concessive Requirement

To know with despair that the political act is inevitably evil, and to act
nevertheless, is moral courage. To choose among several expedient actions
the least evil one is moral judgment.

—HANS MORGENTHAU, *SCIENTIFICMAN VS. POWER POLITICS*

There may be transition cases where enslavement is better than current
practice. For example, suppose that city-states that previously have not
taken prisoners of war but have always put captives to death agree by
treaty to hold prisoners as slaves instead. . . . The arrangement seems
defensible as an advance on established institutions, if slaves are not
treated too severely.

—JOHN RAWLS, *A THEORY OF JUSTICE*

1. Introduction

Here is a line of reasoning that I mean to resist in this chapter: what justice
requires in realistic conditions may conflict with what would be required
along with morally better people, and so only these realistic ones, and not
those others, are genuine requirements. Thus, on that view, there are no genuine requirements of justice higher than those designed for the levels of virtue
or vice we have most reason to expect. In this chapter I will argue that even
though there is a part of the broad topic of justice that speaks to our morally
flawed condition, that does not rule out the possibility of a higher aspect of
justice, with genuine requirements (not only some standards of optional perfection, for example), which count our actual and expectable realistic conditions as unjust even if there is little chance that this will be overcome.

The structure of my suggestion can be seen in any number of moral contexts. In one of the epigraphs for this chapter we see an eminently sensible

limited defense of slavery from John Rawls. Plausibly, war prisoners ought to be enslaved rather than killed. Still, it goes without saying (now) that prisoners ought to be neither enslaved nor killed, and that was true even when it was unrealistic. That first requirement coexists with the second, higher requirement whose satisfaction happened to be unlikely at that historical time. In another example, Alan Dershowitz writes in this spirit, "I am generally against torture as a normative matter. . . . I pose the issue as follows: if torture . . . would in fact be used in an actual ticking bomb mass terrorism case, would it be normatively better or worse to have such torture regulated by some kind of warrant, with accountability, record-keeping, standards, and limitations?" Perhaps it ought to be done only with a warrant. As Dershowitz emphasizes, that would not cancel the prior moral requirement not to torture with or without a warrant.[1]

That form of reasoning is at the very center of my line of argument in this book, and familiar by now: there are moral standards even in the space of moral violation. If so, then, contrary to a certain kind of (overly) realistic view, our requirement not to build certain idealistic institutions because we would not sufficiently comply with them does not preclude there being a superordinate requirement that we build them and comply with them.

To emphasize the question's importance for political philosophy, suppose you wanted to maintain that some society is required to Build and Comply with certain institutions. In the case of highly idealistic requirements with that structure—maybe highly egalitarian, or highly libertarian, or whatever—it will often be the case that if they were built they would not be complied with. In that case, it may be obvious that we ought not to build them (either that we are required not to, or at least that we are not required to do so). Would that refute the initial requirement to Build and Comply? One such argument might go like this:

> It sounds lovely, your view about our building and complying with those institutions. But to think that is required by justice is a serious and dangerous mistake. This is because it would be a disaster to build them, for the simple reason that (as we both know) people would not comply. So building them is, at the very least, not required and probably not even permissible. But if building them is not required, then you must be wrong to think that building *and* complying is required. There is no such requirement, and so no such requirement that we violate if we wisely and justly decide not to build those institutions. The institutions required by justice must be, at the very least, institutions that will receive sufficient compliance to serve their valuable purpose. For these reasons, you are fundamentally wrong about what justice requires.

This objection, anti-utopian in spirit, hopes to press the importance of a certain kind of feasibility for even the most fundamental principles of social justice. In this chapter I will argue that this anti-utopian line of argument is indefensible.

CONCESSIVE REQUIREMENT [151]

Put simply, it wrongly suggests that if we are not required to Build certain institutions, then building them is no part of what we are required to do. That objection consists of a claim about the logic of requirement, and so we will engage it in those terms. To establish that the claim is a mistake it must be shown that there is no incompatibility between, on one hand, our not being required to Build the institutions, and on the other hand, our being required to Build and Comply with them. If those are compatible then the objection fails.

This can be a clarifying point: it may be that we should not Build the institutions because we would not Comply, but that leaves untouched the claim that we ought to both Build and Comply. The latter claim stands for a kind of idealistic requirement of justice—idealistic in that it stands firm even when confronted with the implausibility of its ever being met. I often avail myself of this point throughout the book. However, it must be admitted that this can feel like a logical trick of some kind. For example, and this puzzle is at the core of this chapter: How can it be both that we are required to Build and Comply, but also that we are not required to Build (because required not to, for example)? Building and Complying, which is required, obviously includes Building. How could that not be required? And yet something sounds quite wrong about saying that we ought to Build even though we will not Comply—what is the point of doing that? However, there is another route around the objection. Many philosophers insist that if we ought to Build and Comply with the institutions then it is a logical mistake, even in the case where we will not Comply, to say that we ought not to Build them. Of course, they grant that we ought not to Build without Complying. Many even grant that, *conditional* (in some way, more below) on our not Complying, we ought not to Build. But they insist that we ought to Build.

So we can see that there are two main families of response to cases like this: this second one is, at least on its surface, more consonant with the broad lines of argument in this book. It denies that the (morally dubious) fact that we will not Comply even if we Build—this fact about our crooked timber—has the right kind of moral significance to override the profoundly intuitive logical claim that if we ought to Build and Comply then we ought to Build. We ought to do it along with complying. And on this view, none of that gives way in the face of the fact that we, wrongly, will not actually Comply even if we Build.

The other, first, main approach, described just prior, is to take seriously a very natural way of speaking in such cases. Surely, we will say, if we are not going to Comply with the institutions then we should not Build them. After all, it could produce an unnecessary disaster to Build them in that case. True, this view grants, we ought to both Build and Comply, but (and contrary to a sort of logical illusion) this does not imply that we ought to Build. That depends on whether we will actually Comply. This position is nicely known as "actualism": what we ought to do (with respect to certain acts) can depend on what we will *actually* do (with respect to other acts). This contrasts with the other approach, known as "possibilism," which just denies that. It might be put as saying that what we ought to do does not depend on what we will actually do, but only on what is *possible* for us to do. But, most perspicuously, let us focus simply on the view that actualism is mistaken. I will speak of actualism and non-actualism.

I will often follow common patterns of language by saying that if we will not Comply then we ought not to Build, which is, taken literally, the actualist position. We can call those, and related statements, *actualist formulations*. The point of this chapter is to explain that I do not mean, by so speaking, to be siding with actualism. So, I will say that even if we ought not to build certain institutions, it could yet be that we ought to Build and Comply with those institutions. I will say, later, in the context of the fallacy of approximation (chapter 14) that even though you should take all of three pills, if you will not take the third one, you should not take the other two. These are superficially actualism-friendly, but I will assume that they remain perfectly legitimate ways of speaking whether actualism is true or not.

So, my aim in this chapter is to explain more fully why I am not willing to commit myself for or against actualism: the choice is too difficult and, it seems to me, underdetermined by the state of our understanding so far. I will also explain how my broader purposes in the book do not require that I do so in any case, despite some considerations (about what I will call *concessive requirement*) that may seem to suggest that I must. Readers who are not troubled by (or otherwise interested in) objections to the simpler actualist formulation of the cases—the one assuming that in the case where we will not comply we ought not to build—may wish to pass over this chapter.

It should not be thought that puzzles like this are complications that we are dragged into by thinking of social justice, as I am doing, in moral terms, or by countenancing the possibility that justice is, in certain ways, unrealistic. The issues would apparently arise for any interpretation of the idea that there is such a thing as social justice and injustice at all. If there is, then that must apparently be a requirement of some kind, a ground for ought-statements, on the society or its members collectively. That appears to be all it takes to generate these issues. The earlier arguments in chapter 3 criticizing anti-moralism about the political need not be accepted for purposes of the points in this chapter.

2. *The Procrastination Puzzle*

As it happens, a set of issues in this vicinity is voluminously discussed by moral philosophers, and the leading example to illustrate the puzzles that arise is not about a society and its requirements, but about a lazy academic:

> *Professor Procrastinate*[2] is, let us suppose, morally required to accept a certain assignment to write a book review for a journal. Maybe he

promised, or maybe there is some other reason for this requirement. However, as it happens, even though he is perfectly able to do it, he is the sort who will procrastinate and, in fact, he will not (or very probably will not) write it even if he accepts. If he accepts without writing it this is quite bad, for both the journal and the mistreated author of the book. Ought Professor Procrastinate to accept the assignment?

The case is realistic, alas. Moreover, it has a structure that will be similar in countless contexts having nothing to do with professors, book reviews, or procrastination. In order to lay out the puzzle in a general way, we will want to see the logical form of the claims we will consider. To facilitate that, I will use some simple variables and connectives, though I will also regularly keep us in touch with their natural language meanings. I will use the capital letter O to mean that the agent in question *ought*, or equivalently here, is *required* to do what follows the O. 'Ought' is not always used as equivalent to 'required' but it will be here. I will not use it, for example, to mean 'it ought to be the case that.' Rather, I will assume that we know what agent is at issue in context, and O means that this agent ought, is required, to do the specified thing.[3] Saying that an act by an agent is required will be the same as saying that not doing it would be wrong. It does not, for example, mean that there is a requirement that has been issued by anyone. While some moral requirements probably arise in that way, I assume that not all do. The moral requirement on me not to trip the person walking by does not arise from his or anyone's requiring me—say by authoritatively commanding me—not to do so. Finally, I will use "&" to mean "and" and "~" to mean "not." O(A&B) means that the agent in question is required—ought—to do actions A and B. In several key examples I will capitalize the words (as in "Accept," "Write," and soon "Build," "Comply") to make it easier to follow the narrative on the page. (I will, as economically as possible, proceed in a way that does not presuppose any prior familiarity with other treatments, much less with logical notation or issues in deontic logic.)

3. Beyond Actualism vs. Possibilism

Intuitively, it is tempting to say the following three things are all true in some cases, such as the Professor Procrastinate case: the agent is required to do A and B; the agent will not do B; and the agent is required not to do A without B:

1. The conjunctive requirement:
   O(A&B)
2. No follow through:
   ~B
3. The forbidden pair:
   O~(A&~B)

I will call any such cases "Procrastinate cases." Throughout, unless otherwise specified, we will assume the acts in question are within the agent's abilities—they can do it, even if they won't.

We can now restate the puzzle, making use of this slightly formalized and more general way of seeing it. As natural as it seems to say that all three features hold in the Procrastinate example, that is puzzling once we ask whether he ought to do A (in his case, that is, Accept the assignment). We know, by assumption, that A without B (where B is Writing the review) is wrong, and we are assuming ~B—he does not follow through and Write the review. Suppose we try saying that he ought to do A. How could it be right or even required to do A in that case—to Accept even though he will not Write? That will only make a big mess. On the other hand suppose we try saying that A is not required (because not permitted). But then how could it be that he is required to perform the combination of A and B, but not required to do A, plus required to do B? In cases where (as we will assume) none of the named acts is outside the agent's ability, the following is an attractive principle (hereafter, I will use "x → y" to mean "if x then y"): again, using the letters to stand for any two acts by the same agent:

Distributivity[4]
O(A&B) → O(A) & O(B)

That is, if the agent is required to do A and B, then that agent is required to do A and required to do B, distributing the requirement across the conjuncts. It is the attractiveness of that principle that makes it puzzling how the professor could fail to be required to do A. So is Professor Procrastinate required to Accept after all, even though he will not Write? Or is Distributivity, surprisingly, false?

We can now easily see how these issues have direct application to political philosophy, or the part of it that investigates the nature and content of requirements of social justice. To exhibit this applicability I will simplify in one important—and not at all innocent—way. I will proceed as if the society or social unit whose requirements are in question is an agent that can be subject to requirements. I postpone an important difficulty about this, namely that units that are naturally thought to be socially just or unjust are collectivities, and not always plausibly regarded as agents in their own right, even though of course they are made up of individual agents. The question, to be postponed, is what kind or sense of requirement, if any, can such a non-agential entity be subject to? I will propose an answer in chapters 11 and 12. For now, however, I ask the reader to suppose for simplicity that the relevant collectivity can be an agent and subject to requirements.

Supposing that is so, and referring to relevant units just for simplicity as "societies" (allowing that the relevant "society" might be the globe, or some other non-national collective entity), it is natural to suppose that they can satisfy or violate requirements of justice. For example, in addition to whatever individual moral wrongs are involved in slavery (and they are many), a society in which institutions of slavery are legally supported and enforced is manifestly (to us, now, if not to everyone always) deeply unjust. That is, or so I will assume, equivalent to saying that there is a requirement of justice applying to those societies and requiring that they not include institutions of slavery.

If a society can be subject to requirements, then it is not surprising that some cases will appear to present us with the procrastination puzzle. (They need not have anything to do with procrastination, any more than "prisoners' dilemmas" must have anything to do with prisoners.) To see this, suppose that full social justice requires of societies that they Build and Comply with certain institutions. Let the institutions be whatever idealistic institutions you would like to consider: highly egalitarian in certain ways, or highly protective of individual property rights, and so forth. Despite being required to Build and Comply, the required society may not in fact Comply even if they Build. The analogy with Professor Procrastinate is close: just as he will not Write even if he Accepts, the society in question will not Comply even if they Build. So there arises the same question since all three conditions on Procrastinate cases can be met, if we just mechanically substitute "Build" for "A," and "Comply" for "B" in our general explication of the structure of Procrastinate cases:

1. The conjunctive requirement:
    O(Build & Comply)
2. No follow-through:
    ~Comply
3. The forbidden pair:
    O~(Build & ~Comply)

This general and schematic example will be the main one I will use in order to explore several issues and controversies about ideal or unrealistic normative political standards of justice. In particular, it will help to clarify several matters concerning ways in which what individuals and societies are actually like— what they will or will not do under various conditions—might be held to refute certain alleged standards. Justice, it might be thought, includes no meaningful requirements that do not offer us guidance in actual political practice in light of our best knowledge about what we are like, what we will do, and what would happen under the various alternatives. So, Building and Complying is certainly one highly relevant form of case, but it stands in for any cases where it might be held that the fact that we *will not* do something shows that our doing it is no part of what justice requires. We will see an argument to this effect shortly.

If procrastination cases can arise when the question is about requirements of social justice, then the general direction of my arguments suggests that I should want to deny that facts about our compliance or noncompliance bear on whether we ought to Build and Comply. However, if we ought to Build and Comply notwithstanding the (assumed) fact that we will not Comply, there remains the problematic implication from Distributivity that we ought to Build even though we will not Comply (because a requirement to Build and Comply implies a requirement to Build). That is as jarring as the suggestion that Professor Procrastinate, even though he will not Write the review, ought to Accept the assignment.

So the dispute about Professor Procrastinate is pertinent here. Here is one more overview of the dilemma that seems to face us: Jackson and Pargetter, who introduced the vivid Procrastinate example, argued that it is so clear that he ought not (and so not-ought) to Accept, that this is strong reason to reject the Distributivity principle itself. Others have agreed that he indeed ought not to Accept, but argued that this does not violate Distributivity because the oughts or requirements are, in one way or another, at different "levels," or relative to different contexts and so not in danger of contradicting each other. But this all remains subject to dispute. As for rejecting Distributivity outright, many argue that doing so is intuitively even more implausible than allowing that he ought to Accept (and that we ought to Build). It is not as if he ought to Accept AND fail to Write, after all, they point out. The claim is that he ought to Accept *and ought go on to Write.* True, we stipulate that he will not go on to Write, but that hardly shows that he is not required to do so. So, even in the case where he will not Write, he ought to Accept (*and ought to Write!*). Distributivity is too firm a principle to dismiss without higher stakes than this, many argue. As for the introduction of levels or other sources of a plurality of oughts or requirements, it is objected that this diverts attention from the fundamental issue which must be staged at a single level or a single sense of ought or requirement, namely the final, central, or "deliberative" level at which an agent must consider the question what she ought, all things considered, to do.[5]

I proceed next to explain how my commitments for the broader argument of the book are less than a commitment for or against actualism, even though I will, as I say, employ actualist formulations.

4. Lesser Needs (A)

I will want to hold that justice might require certain things even if they are unrealistic, in the sense that people will never (or even 'can't will' to)[6] meet them. In many cases of such idealistic standards, what is unrealistic to expect, in particular, is people's complying with the social structure picked out by the standard of justice. We are focusing, then, on cases where it is granted that people will not (at least in sufficient numbers) comply even if the institutions were in other respects to be realized. I want to hold, as I have said, that justice could nevertheless require those very institutions along with compliance. That is the conjunctive requirement in question: to Build and Comply with certain institutions.

Lesser Need 1

The following are compatible: O(Build & Comply), and ~Comply. I will rely on the proposition that a requirement on a society to Build and Comply with certain institutions—such a conjunctive requirement—is not refuted by the fact that we will not Comply with them. This proposition is one case of the more general position I defended in Part 2 of the book, that, except in special cases, what we are required to do is not limited to things we will do, or will tend to do, or have certain motivations to do.

The challenge I want to respond to arises only for certain cases of O(A&B). There is no reason, for example, to doubt that O(repay a debt & be at work on time) could obtain even if I will not be at work on time. But Building and Complying are special, and so is the Procrastinate case of Accepting and Writing. These are cases where it is also true that it would be wrong to do the first thing without following through: Build but not Comply, or Accept but not Write. So we will be concentrating on cases where, to put it formally: O~(A&~B). (This will be recognized as one of the defining features of the procrastination puzzle specified above, the forbidden pair.) That is, it is required not to do both A and not B. I will call these *follow-through cases*, and call the second conjunct, the one that will not obtain, the follow-through conjunct. We might put the position I will rely on this way, a way that is salient for both the justice and Professor Procrastinate examples:

Follow-through
In follow-through cases, the conjunctive requirement stands even if the follow-through conjunct will not obtain.

We will shortly see a challenge to this that I will rebut. The point just now is that this is a weaker and less disputable claim than what is involved in the actualist formulations I will go on to use. Those formulations proceed as if the requirement to Build lapses in the case where we will not Comply. As plausible as that can seem, it leads to the previously described difficulties I wish to avoid. So, I will avoid relying on the controversial position that we ought not to Build in that case.

A requirement to Build and Comply, recall, is serving as an example of an idealistic requirement of justice, one that might be criticized on the ground that it is unrealistic: because we will not Comply even if we were to Build, we would never meet the requirement. Here is the objection we saw above, which might be brought even against the weaker position I am taking:

Objection:
Since (by assumption) we ought not to Build without Complying, and since we will not Comply, we ought not Build. Therefore, because of Distributivity, we are not required (or even permitted) to Build and Comply. The conjunctive requirement is false.

This view, in effect, denies that there are any genuine Procrastinate cases: the three conditions are never all true. To lay out the objection more carefully, consider a basic social structure and its institutional systems which, however inspiring, are such that, even were we to build them,

    i. We will not Comply.[7] (assumption)

Also, it might be held,

    ii. If we will not Comply, then we ought not to Build. (assumption)

Then it would appear to follow that,

    iii. We ought not to Build. (from (i) and (ii) by modus ponens)

It follows simply from this that,

    iv. It is not the case that we ought to Build. (assuming only that "ought not" entails "not ought")

Or, put more idiomatically and equivalently for our purposes, it is *not required* that we do so. But then, this objection continues,

    v. It is not the case that we ought to Build & Comply. (by (iv), and Distributivity)

That is, it is not the case that we are required to Build and Comply. So, on the basis of this argument, in the case where we will not Comply, the conjunctive requirement, stating that we ought to Build and Comply, is denied. That requirement, admittedly "unrealistic" in one way since we are stipulating that it will not be met, is held to be refuted by attention to our actual behavior. In this way, as I have said, the objection resonates with objections to overly idealized requirements of justice.

To rebut this objection, I will argue that it suffices if any of several lines of argument is correct, remaining noncommittal myself as between them. First, though, notice that the dialectical situation is slightly different from familiar debates about Professor Procrastinate and similar cases. Those cases ask the reader to grant that a certain case is one in which the conjunction of two actions is required, such as Accept and Write, or Build and Comply. By contrast, I want to consider someone who *rejects, and argues against* the alleged conjunctive requirement in certain kinds of cases. Our objector accepts distributivity and denies that Procrastinate ought to Accept under the circumstances. This would be awkward if it must be admitted that he ought to Accept and Write, but this objector, for reasons I have laid out, denies that conjunctive requirement. The issues are much the same either way of course. In effect, the Professor Procrastinate case just shows that some (*contra* Jackson and Pargetter) will think that the conjunctive requirement is incompatible with the claim that we ought not to Accept assignments that we will not Write. Those writers will often stick to the former, the conjunctive requirement, denying the latter, the rejection of the requirement to Accept. We see here that one could, instead, still hold that the two claims are incompatible, but do the reverse: stick to the claim that we ought not to Accept under the circumstances, but deny the conjunctive requirement. That is the position I need to refute for the first of my two purposes.

One possible reply to the objection is to suggest that claim (ii), that we are not required to Build institutions if we will not Comply with them, is stated more strongly than is plausible. That way of formulating the general idea of a conditional requirement, in terms of a simple if/then conditional of the kind that would support the step to (iii), a "material conditional," leads to serious problems. For example, there seems to be something roughly right in saying that, even though you ought not to kill Lu,

If you will kill Lu then you ought to kill her gently.[8]

Taken at face value that is absurd, since presumably if you ought to kill her gently then you ought to kill her. That maneuver is called "factual detachment." It allows us to pull the consequent of the conditional statement out to stand on its own as required when the antecedent is true.[9] Of course, this is often fine with if/then statements, a simple application of modus ponens: "If he will stop at the bar then he will be late for dinner" supports the move from "He will stop at the bar" to "He will be late for dinner." But the gentle murder objection suggests that conditional *requirement statements* may not really have that same if/then logical structure notwithstanding the similar English syntax, despite the fact that we often phrase them that way.

Since that if/then formulation about gentle murder may misrepresent the real logical form of what is going on also in our institution example, namely,

If we will not Comply, then we ought not to Build,

we should not be so sure that this is really the logical form we are dealing with. If it were the right form it would get us from our wrongful noncompliance to a requirement, and so a permission, not to Build, but, as we have seen from the gentle murder problem, we should be skeptical about that.

There is a quite different proposition which, while much easier to accept, may be all that is meant when it is said in ordinary language that if we will not Comply we ought not to Build, namely,

vi. *Forbidden Pair:* We ought not to Build those institutions without Complying.

If we focus on the right set of institutions, then this premise will be accepted on all sides, just as all accept that Procrastinate ought not to Accept without Writing. However, unlike (ii), (vi) does not threaten the conjunctive requirement (to Build and Comply), and so the objection to that—the objection we are responding to—founders if (vi) is substituted.

There is some temptation to reason from (vi) as follows: since we ought not to Build without Complying, and since we will not Comply, we ought not to Build, and so we ought not to Build and Comply. But (vi) does not warrant the view that we ought not to Build, nor, therefore, the view that we ought not to Build and Comply. This is because the Forbidden Pair premise is compatible with insisting that we ought indeed to Build, *and also* ought to Comply. That combination is held to be required, even though another combination—Build and not-Comply—is forbidden. So, one way to defeat the objection to the conjunctive requirement that we are considering is to reject (ii) and hold that the most that must be granted is (vi), the forbidden pair premise. On this approach, we can allow that we ought to Build (because we ought to do so and Comply). It will suffice for my purposes to point out that we are required not to Build without Complying. If, as might also be true, we ought to Build, then the conjunctive requirement is not threatened.[10]

One aspect of this approach is less than satisfying, at least to many. It leaves the very natural sounding statement (ii) "If we will not Comply then we ought not to Build" hanging, dismissed, as if there is no relevant conditional proposition in the vicinity. That may seem implausible. Now some philosophers propose to account for the naturalness of conditional talk in these cases in the following way, still without being forced to say that we ought not to Build, and so in a way that is still congenial for my purposes: what is required is a conditional itself. That is, in cases like this, they say,

vii. It is required of us that if we do not Comply we do not Build.

The requirement ranges over the whole if/then statement, thus: O(not-Comply → not-Build). It is commonly called a "wide-scope" conditional obligation, since it does not state (in "narrow-scope" fashion) that either Building or Complying (or their negations) is required. Only the conditional itself is required. It is not itself a conditional statement, but has one embedded in it—inside the scope of the ought-operator. We are said to be required (unconditionally in the relevant sense) to, as some put it, make the conditional true, and so a conditional proposition does show up in the analysis. This may help account for the naturalness of speaking about such cases in ways that involve conditionals. It may be that we speak loosely when we say that if we won't Comply we ought not to Build, but that we English speakers do so only because there is no smooth way in English (at least) to state the wide-scope conditional requirement. Statement (vii) above, for example, is a bit of a mouthful for ordinary language. But, it might be held, that is how we should be understood.

There are difficulties about this approach, even though it also has its defenders.[11] What matters here is not whether it is ultimately defensible, but only that it is one of the positions which would be good enough for my purposes. It is a natural view to hold along with the non-actualist position that, even in the case where we will not Comply we ought to Build (along with Complying). It does not warrant the move to a requirement not to Build, and so it leaves the conjunctive requirement unthreatened.

Suppose, then, that we resisted, in that wide-scope way, the argument that we ought not to Build—we reject actualism on these grounds. That, as I say, would save the conjunctive obligation and suit my purposes. If you are happy to reject actualism, then you are granting me all I need here, pending the discussion of my second Lesser Need below. Some, however, will insist that in such a case we obviously ought not to Build. And they have much ordinary language on their side, as we have seen. I want to allow that this actualist position might be correct, so I need to show how it also does not threaten the conjunctive requirement to Build and Comply.

As we have seen, it is a logical puzzle how I could be required to Build and Comply even when I am—as actualism holds—required not to Build (and so not required to Build). That is the principle we are calling Distributivity. If Distributivity could be shown not to apply in such cases, this objection would obviously be blocked. But on what grounds may such a plausible logical rule be abandoned? Here is one possible ground: if Distributivity were to apply in this case then we *ought to Build even though we will not Comply*. And Professor Procrastinate *ought to Accept even though he will not Write*. If those are implausible, Distributivity bears the blame. This, of course, is hardly decisive, since Distributivity may be found more plausible—more implausible to abandon—than the supposedly obvious view that we are not required to Build, and Procrastinate is not required to Accept in the cases where we and he, respectively, would not follow through. But it is awkward for non-actualism.

There remains a possible threat from an actualist position in which, in a new twist, Distributivity is insisted upon rather than rejected, and this brings us to the objection that we began with. If we ought not to Build, and Distributivity is correct, it would not be the case that we ought to Build and Comply. However, there is a further way to resist that threat, namely to argue that the ought or requirement about Building, and the ought or requirement about Building and Complying are heterogeneous in their contextual meaning. Before turning to that *heterogeneous oughts* idea, we can now briefly state more precisely, at the risk of being slightly repetitive, the alternatives just canvassed.

The first is to resist, along with non-actualism, any temptation to conclude that we ought not to Build,

A. *No Dependence*: the requirement to Build does not, in the way alleged by actualism, hang on whether we will Comply. Many take this view to be preferable to denying Distributivity or, as discussed further below, recognizing multiple levels or contexts of requirement. This position accepts O(Build) and so does not threaten the conjunctive requirement. The sense that some conditional is relevant might be explained, if necessary, in the wide-scope fashion. One price this non-actualist approach pays is that it must say, "we ought to Build even though we will not Comply," which is jarring since all agree that we ought not to Build without Complying.

If that option is rejected, as it will be by some such as actualists, it would suffice to,

> B. *Deny Distributivity:* it may be right, as actualism holds, that O~(Build) in that case, and so also ~O(Build), but distributivity does not hold. Therefore, it can still be the case that we ought, nevertheless, to Build and Comply. This position allows the conjunctive requirement, O(Build & Comply) even if O~(Build), and so would suffice for my aim of maintaining the conjunctive requirement. Of course, the price that is paid is rejecting the highly intuitive principle of distributivity.

Turning now to the third approach, if it is insisted that we ought not to Build, but one hopes to retain distributivity, there is the possibility of introducing,

> C. *Heterogeneous Oughts:* grant that we ought not to Build, but argue that there are oughts or requirements which are logically at different levels or indexed to different contexts from nonconcessive requirements. A concessive requirement not to Build is compatible with a nonconcessive requirement to Build and Comply. As this description suggests, there are at least two versions: I will call them levels and contexts, about which more shortly. Distributivity can unproblematically be granted within any single level or context.

Several authors have defended a levels-version of heterogeneous oughts.[12] Roughly, the view is that there is what we might call a nonconcessive level of requirement, call it level 1. It is helpful to imagine the 'ought' as subscripted, as in O_1(Accept & Write). On this view there are also what we might call concessive levels of requirement, requirements that apply specifically in and relative to a violation of a higher level requirement. So while Professor Procrastinate O_1(Accept and Write), since he will violate that by not Writing, he O_2(not-Accept). O_1 and O_2 are heterogeneous. So distributivity can be allowed within any level. So the conjunctive requirement, being at level 1, does entail O_1(Accept). But that is compatible with O_2(not-Accept), the latter being relative to and conceding the violation of the level 1 requirement.

A similar approach is to hold that conditional obligation statements such as "If we will not Comply then we ought not to Build," can be interpreted as relativizing that occurrence of 'ought' to the set of possible worlds in which we do not Comply.[13] If we again think of that relativization as attaching a sub-script to the 'ought' it is clear how it will not logically engage with the unsub-scripted ought in the statement "We ought to Build and Comply." That way Distributivity can again be accepted, but only within a given ought context. This is much like the levels view, except that this approach makes no use of the fact that some oughts are relativized to contexts of *concession*. No reference is made to the context being one of violation of any requirements, unlike the levels view.[14]

Roughly, then, the conjunctive requirement is saved if either (A) we ought to Build even though we won't Comply, or (B) we ought not to Build, but this is compatible with a requirement to Build and Comply since Distributivity is false, or (C) we ought not to Build, and Distributivity is correct, but this requirement is at a different level from, and so does not contradict, the requirement to Build that arises by Distributivity from the conjunctive requirement. Any objector to my maintaining the conjunctive requirement must then think that we ought not to Build, and accept Distributivity, and reject any levels or contextual approach that would avoid the alleged contradiction. I will leave the polemical situation here rather than pursuing the objector further. My position is insulated from controversy at least to this extent: there are ways to adhere to either actualism or non-actualism in familiar forms while granting me all I need.

Lesser Need 2

My second lesser need is this: of the prohibited options, some are more se-verely wrong than others. In the actualist formulations I will use, something stronger than this seems to be implied: in the situation where we will not Comply, we ought not to Build, in which case we are obviously not required to Build. It might seem that I need this. The reason is that I will want to say, or at least grant, that in such cases there may be a requirement to do some-thing other than Build, something incompatible with Building, perhaps building some other institutions, call that Build-2. But if we ought to Build-2, then, assuming there cannot be conflicting requirements, it must not be the case that we ought to Build. So it may seem that I need to say, with actualism, that when we will not Comply, we are not required to Build, landing me in controversy.

However, my needs steer shy of the controversy. All I need to say about Build-2 is that,

(Build-2 & Comply) is less severely wrong than
(Build & not-Comply) i.e., the forbidden pair

If that can be agreed to without taking a position about whether this means there is a *requirement* not to Build, then I have avoided the controversy about that. This is a possible reading of the Morgenthau quote (and perhaps even of the Rawls passage) that opens this chapter: the political act may be "evil," but choosing the least evil is an exercise of good, if tragic, moral judgment.

The idea of degrees of severity is fairly clear. It is hard to resist the idea that there is a moral reason to, for example, steal only part of a person's money rather than all of it. The thief who pauses to decide between those two acts of stealing makes the morally better choice, whereas the other choice would have been morally more wrong. Think of the example from Rawls, where soldiers will either enslave prisoners or put them to death. Rawls sensibly says that enslavement is "better," and "defensible." Or think of a kidnapper who will either bind and gag the prisoner, or instead allow them some movement in a confined space. It is tempting, and is not jarring to ordinary language, to say that the kidnapper ought to give the person the space even though he also ought not to confine the person at all. But it may be that such cases can be adequately handled even without positing such a requirement. One way to make sense of such a position would be to hold that as between two wrongs, one might be more wrong than another in the sense that there is more moral reason to do the other, even though there is no ought or requirement to do the less wrong thing.[15] I think this is somewhat strained, even if coherent. It separates moral reasons from oughts/requirements in a way that many would find troubling. But if it is an adequate position, it would suffice for my purposes. Some further structure might be added by holding, where X and Y are each wrong, X is more wrong if and only if $(X \text{ or } Y) \to O(Y)$.[16] So the "more wrong" claim does not entail a (non-embedded) ought claim. This allows "wronger" (so to speak) without ought. By embedding the ought in a conditional statement, it does not generate any requirement that would conflict with the conjunctive requirement.

If more severe wrongness cannot be accounted for without the ought or requirement that actualism posits but non-actualism denies, then I would be comfortable committing myself to the actualist side of the dispute, on grounds that this is a more serious defect in the non-actualist view than anything actualism has to swallow. If, however, that relative severity can be accounted for it does not matter for my purposes whether it is in terms of requirement or not. Either way, there is enough structure to ground our speaking, in the superficially actualist formulations, about what, rather than Building, we ought to do if we would not comply. (We can speak similarly about what you ought to do about the other two pills if you will not take the third.) Here, finally, is what permits my speaking of,

Concessive requirement
In some cases where one will violate a requirement of morality or justice to do some action A, morality or justice is not indifferent between the other alternatives. It is more severely wrong to do C than to do B. In an "actualist formulation" we can say that in that case one ought to do B

rather than C, or even, speaking loosely or in a contextually framed way, simply that one ought to (is required to) do B.

I will speak often of concessive requirements in the remainder of the book, though mainly I am doing so for the sake of argument rather than needing these to be requirements for my own purposes. The most frequent example will be a concessive requirement not to Build, where this stems from the fact that a society would not Comply in any case. The suggestion that this—not-Build— is a requirement may be thought, for reasons explained above, to refute the claim that we are required to Build & Comply. The arguments of this chapter are meant to explain that I am not committed to the actualist position, but that my actualist formulations can easily be translated into weaker claims that will suffice for my arguments.

There is an important point about the meeting of concessive requirements, namely that this can be an admirable response to genuine moral consider- ations. This might be missed since by assumption the agent or society is al- ready assumed to be violating a requirement and choosing between wrongful options. But that does not show that nothing the agent or society does in that context has moral value.

It is said that during World War II, Erwin Rommel burned the order from Hitler to execute the war prisoners in his control. And suppose this was for moral reasons.[17] Does this warrant admiration or anything like it, even as he prosecuted a profoundly unjust war in other ways? Suppose Rommel's role in that war, including holding the prisoners at all, is egregiously wrong even if he stayed within norms of *jus in bello* (though this is philosophically controver- sial).[18] Still, suppose that his sparing the prisoners was no whim but a consci- entious view that killing them would be wrong whether or not the rest of his role was permissible—and in that suppose, plausibly, that he was correct. Sup- pose, as might well have been the case, that by insubordinately burning the order he put not only his command but even his freedom or his life in danger. His motivation for the dispensation was in that case a sound moral judgment, which coexisted alongside badly flawed moral judgments or at least actions. Praise is too strong a concept, perhaps, for simply refraining from some great evil, but something like it is more suitable to cases where the right thing is done even in the face of great risks or costs to the agent. He ought not to have held or executed them, but given that he would at least hold them, it would have been more wrong to execute them than not to have done so. Lives were saved, rightly and for the morally right reasons, by Rommel's choice. That does not exculpate him for any of his other actions, not even his holding them pris- oner. Not every choice that is part of a bad cluster of choices is itself a bad choice, and some can be good.

Turning to social justice: suppose that justice requires a guaranteed social minimum. Since the point can be made for various conceptions of justice consider either a social minimum of, roughly, material well-being, or alternatively a social minimum of immunity from certain kinds of interference with individual choices—let it even be market choices. Either way, next suppose a certain society is not going to provide that required minimum. Even so, it may face the choice between guaranteeing something closer to it or guaranteeing nothing of the sort. If, in choosing between those two options (even though there is also the third, just option) society overcomes, for reasons of justice, costs and risks in order to guarantee something closer to what is required, this may be admirable.[19]

If social justice requires things that people will never do, then it is important to understand the normative space we will be living in. It would be a space of injustice, but also a space in which hard decisions might need to be made when faced with more or less severely unjust alternatives. Self-interest, partiality, and laziness will be in play still, and insofar as a society overcomes any of them for moral reasons in order to do the less severely unjust thing this is morally valuable and will tend to be worthy of a focused attitude of admiration or something like it.

5. A Technical Debate

Actualism is sometimes held to be morally heinous, but the case for this is very weak, and rests on extracting something that actualism would "have to say," and evincing our shock at saying it. However, that is no way to show that what they would have to say is not true and reasonable to believe when the philosophical context is filled in rather than treated as irrelevant. Ralph Wedgwood writes,

> Imagine a wicked paedophile, who has just abducted a 10-year-old girl and imprisoned her in his secret cellar. Suppose that it is still *possible*—though unfortunately quite unlikely—that the paedophile will repent of his evil plans, and return the girl unharmed to her parents. Surely, if anything is clear about this case, it is clear that it is not true that the paedophile ought to rape the girl. But (shockingly, as it seems to me) actualists like Jackson and Pargetter may well disagree . . . [*DE: three dots in original*] Suppose that it is also true in this case that if the paedophile did not rape the girl, he would torture her to death, whereas if he did rape her, he would not subject her to any additional torture, and would not kill her. So, presumably, the paedophile's conduct would be at least somewhat better if he raped her than if he didn't. Hence actualists must say that the paedophile *ought* to rape the girl. This seems to me a *reductio ad absurdum* of the actualist view.[20]

The possibilist view, by contrast, is that he ought not to rape her even though in that case he will torture and kill her. That does not sound like an entirely comfortable position either; possibilists cannot accept that he ought to do the less horrible of the two if he will do one or the other. They do not have to say, "He ought to rape her." But they do have to say some rather shocking things in other cases. Imagine a despicable doctor (Dr. Slatch, let's call him, who embodies in one person a similar case to the two doctors, Slice and Patch) who ought to do a bit of surgery and then, to avoid the patient's painfully bleeding to death, stitch the patient up. But suppose that even if he does the surgery (on which the patient's life does not depend) he will not stitch it up—he is always tired after surgery and would rather head home. No one else is around who can do the stitching. "Possibilism" has to say this: the doctor in this case ought to do the surgery even though he will not stitch, even though this will cause the patient to bleed to death. They must say this on the basis of their view that it follows logically from the fact that he ought to do the surgery and the stitching. My point is not about that logical claim, but only that the possibilist, like the actualist, can be charged with "having to say" horrible things.

However, the charge is not fair in either case. In truth, neither view has horrible moral implications, however skittish one might be of its linguistic consequences. Both sides agree that the criminal ought neither to rape nor murder, and that the surgeon ought to both operate and stitch. Both will fall short of this requirement, and each is grievously wrong on that ground. All sides also agree that raping is morally less seriously wrong than torturing plus killing. And they agree as well that operating without stitching is more seriously wrong than doing both (which would not be wrong at all). What they disagree about is, in a certain sense, a technicality—namely, whether it is true, even if potentially awkward, to say that "He ought to rape her" or "He ought to make the cut." The fact that it would be bizarre to say, without also giving the fuller explanation, "He ought to rape her," is a distraction. No one, I repeat, thinks that if he rapes her he does not thereby do something grievously wrong, and also that raping only is less morally wrong than torturing and murdering. What is at stake between actualism and possibilism is, in this way, not morally substantial, even if the puzzle it raises about deontic logic is a difficult one.

6. Nested Concessive Requirements

The relation of the concessive to the nonconcessive has both an absolute and a relative aspect. An absolutely nonconcessive requirement is one that does not arise as an implication (in the ways laid out by the alternative versions of Actualism) of the agent's violating some other requirement. For example, a society's obligation to Build & Comply with certain idealistic institutions might very well not depend in any way on society's doing something else wrong. But a requirement can be nonconcessive relative to another (relatively concessive) requirement without being absolutely nonconcessive. For example, suppose once again that society ought, nonconcessively, to Build &

Comply, and since it won't Comply it (concessively) ought not to Build. Now suppose that society will violate this concessive requirement by Building, even though it will not Comply. In light of that fact, there might very well be pressing respects in which it ought to Prepare for the fallout of this poor decision, maybe by passing certain laws and regulations which otherwise would have no rationale. The requirement to Prepare is concessive relative to the requirement not to Build, so that latter requirement is nonconcessive relative to the requirement to Prepare. But the requirement to Build is not absolutely nonconcessive; it is concessive relative to the requirement to Build and Comply. That, by contrast, might be absolutely nonconcessive. In this way we may speak of concessive requirements being "nested." (We will revisit this point at several points later in the book.)[21]

Some institutions might have no point except in a concessive theory, one that asks what we should do in light of the fact that we will not be doing all we can and should do. Suppose (what is not actually obvious, I think) that if we did all we should do there would be no point in having institutions of punishment. But, given the fact that we will not do all we should do, we need institutions of punishment. Now we must ask what they ought to be like. At this point, however, we face the nonconcessive/concessive distinction again. One question would be what institutions of punishment we should have if, except for the exceptions we already conceded, we do all (else) we should do. That is, beginning from a concession, we proceed nonconcessively under that constraint. For example, prison staff should presumably abide by certain fair and decent standards, and the prisoners ought to behave as directed. In fact, suppose the guards will not live up to those standards. Now we need a second level of concessive theory, and this highlights the fact that we would thereby be departing from a second level of nonconcessive (and maybe hopelessly so) theory about what is required of prison guards, a nonconcessive level of theory that is taking place under a previous level that is concessive. A piece of normative political theory might legitimately concede nothing, and then it would be purely nonconcessive—addressed to a genuine if limited range of moral questions. It might, however, concede some things and not others, a mixed case of concessive and nonconcessive. Or it might concede everything—or almost everything.

There is a limit. It is not clear that it makes any sense for a theory to concede all the facts about what we will do, since that would leave nothing to be normative about, so to speak. This brings us back to the absurdity of what, in chapter 1, "An Unrealistic Introduction," I called complacent realism. Even if we knew all the facts, including what everyone will do, unless every alternative is beyond people's abilities all normative theory must be partly (relatively) nonconcessive, purporting to recommend or require some things even if they will not be done. That there are important theoretical truths of a hopeless nonconcessive kind, then, should be beyond dispute. Once that structural point is clear, there is, I think, no good objection—or at least none of the kind we have canvassed—to hopeless nonconcessive theory of all degrees, including the limiting case of normative political theory that requires much and concedes nothing. I will return to that category of political theory in chapter 10: "Prime Justice."

Appendix: Oughts Going Forward

That completes the argument for this chapter, but this is an appropriate point to make some distinctions and stipulations about how the idea of 'ought' will be used in the remainder of the book. Eventually we will be using a non-agential mode of evaluation, which I call Plural Requirement. I cannot lay it out here, leaving that to chapter 12. All I can do is admit that there is now a further question whether the points in this chapter that have been made on the model of agential moral requirement can be sustained in a suitable translation into the mode of Plural Requirement. While a full discussion of plural requirement comes only later, this is a good place to make some points about ought-statements. This also introduces some important features of the idea of plural requirement, and serves more generally to explain the several ideas of ought, requirement, and obligation that will occur in other parts of the argument as well.

Philosophers have, for various purposes, defined different kinds of ought-statements and given them various names. To minimize confusion it will be helpful for me to lay out several related notions as I use them in this book, and briefly explain their similarities to and differences from several ideas of 'ought' in the literature. My interest is not in facts about language, nor do I assume that common ways of speaking are bound to be philosophically defensible. So in laying out the kinds of "oughts" or ought-statements that I refer to throughout the book I mean to be endorsing various contents of those statements, and certain distinctions between them, as legitimate: as contents of possible true or correct judgments or statements. I will also only attempt as much precision in these distinctions as it seems to me that I need for purposes of my arguments.

I allow that there is what I will call a purely evaluative 'ought,' which implies nothing about what any agent or plurality of agents is to do or is to be like. There is what I will call a "judgmental" ought which states what an agent is to be like rather than what she is to do. There is an ought which states what an agent is to do, which I will call "deontic." I group the judgmental and deontic oughts together as "agential." I also, and more originally, argue that there is a defensible idea of plural ought or plural requirement which is a kind of hybrid. It applies not to any agent itself, but to pluralities of agents as such. So it is not agential in either the judgmental or deontic manner. It might then seem to be what I have called purely evaluative, but that goes too far. There could certainly be purely evaluative statements about a plurality's set of acts, as in "It's too bad they didn't exit more calmly." But plural requirement, as I explain, incorporates certain conditional deontic requirements, as in "if she is going, then you ought to go." So plural requirement is partly evaluative, and partly conditionally deontic, though the subject of a plural (unconditional) requirement is not an agent but a set of agents. The conditional deontic requirements it entails are (in their consequents) requirements on genuine individual agents in the plurality, and so the plural requirement and its deontic elements do not apply to the same subject. For a plurality of agents to be plural required, then, is not for it (or any agent) to be subject to a deontic requirement, not even a conditional one. But plural requirement analytically incorporates conditional deontic requirements, unlike purely evaluative oughts.

It may be useful to bring these distinctions into engagement with a few views about "oughts" in the work of others. Wedgwood uses the term "the practical ought" for the concept I call "deontic."[22] While I want to deny that Plural Requirement requires or gives reason to any agent, and so is not "deontic," in light of its entailed conditional requirements it would risk confusion to say that it is in no way "practical."

Many philosophers admit a non-agential notion of 'ought.' In one example, Bernard Williams considers someone making an aesthetic comment about St. Peter's: "This place ought to be a railway station."[23] Wedgwood, again, speaks of what I call the purely evaluative ought, contrasting it with "the practical ought." Terminologically he follows Sidgwick[24] in calling this the "political ought." Sidgwick has in mind judgments such as "that the laws and constitution of my country 'ought to be' other than they are."[25] Wedgwood makes the point that Sidgwick's "political ought" is not essentially political as his own examples attest, but concerns only general desirability. Oddly, I think, Wedgwood chooses to continue using the term "the political ought" to refer to that nonpolitical ideal. I think this risks confusion, and 'purely evaluative' seems better. As I am arguing, there may be an 'ought' that is more closely related to the political, namely the ought of Plural Requirement, though political pluralities are just one special case of pluralities. Interestingly for our purposes, Mark Brown speaks, in passing, of a possible "utopian" use of 'ought,' which could mean that it would have been better if a certain thing had been possible.[26] For example, "Even if I go by bus I ought to let Sue know, though that's impossible." I must say that I do not recognize this as something that might naturally be said, but maybe there are better examples. He writes, "Utopian oughts, if we may call them that, no doubt play an important role in our normative reasoning, perhaps by providing ideals which can serve as a moral compass to help us navigate through the all too often disorienting moral terrain in which we find ourselves. But I suggest they do not express implacable current obligations for whose non-fulfillment we can be blamed even when they are unfulfillable."[27] This is different, then, from the purely evaluative ought, which does not imply that the condition being evaluated is impossible. Brown's "utopian ought" does not correspond to any of the varieties of requirement or 'ought' that I make use of in this book.

Wiens speaks of "axiological" oughts, which correspond to our purely evaluative oughts. And his "deontic" oughts are the same as ours. I prefer Wiens's "deontic" label to Wedgwood's "practical" for that class of oughts, because my plural oughts, while not deontic (as explained above) are not wholly nonpractical, unless conditional duties—some of which figure in plural requirement— are not practical. Perhaps we could just as well say that while plural requirement is not directly agential, deontic, or practical, it is indirectly all three of those things by way of its entailed conditional deontic requirements. But I will not use the term "practical ought."

A word on my use of "agential" vs. "non-agential": Vranas[28] defines a useful notion of agential obligations in which they do not necessarily require that the agent under the obligation be the agent that brings about what he calls the "satisfaction proposition." They are not obligations to do a certain thing, but to make something be the case. I might have an obligation that you receive directions to my party, but that does not entail that I have an obligation to be the one who delivers them. That would be an obligation with a more specific content. For my purposes, it will not be important to distinguish between these, and so "agential" obligation will be an obligation on an agent to do a certain thing.

I distinguish between requirements and obligations, so that the latter are the deontic subset of requirements. There are non-deontic (but sometimes still agential) requirements if there are requirements to be certain ways (for example, tolerant, or motivationally disposed to help in certain cases). Plural requirement, too, warrants the status of requirement, or so I submit, even without being deontic (and so not an obligation) by being a violable moral standard.

As I have said, unlike non-deontic requirements on agents to have certain motives and dispositions, plural requirement is not agential, since pluralities under such requirements are not (always) agents. But while many philosophers recognize non-agential oughts, as I have also said, they often have in mind cases that are not evidently instances of moral requirement in any plausible sense (such as Williams's railway station example). But we have seen what are plausibly moral requirements on agents to have certain motives or dispositions, so moral requirements need not be deontic. Plural requirement, then, is offered as another example of non-deontic moral requirement, but one that is also not (directly) agential. "The doctors ought to have done the surgery" states a plural requirement, as does "The voters ought to throw the bum out."

Sometimes a requirement is predicated of a political state formulated as if it were a singular agent, and perhaps some are agents. But plural requirement allows us to make sense of such statements even as applied to states which fall short of whatever group agency depends on. However, the state is under the plural requirement in its aspect as a plurality of agents, and not as an agent in its own right. A state that is an agent in its own right, if any, could be subject to requirements that are simply agential and deontic in the more familiar way.

CHAPTER NINE

Bad Facts

A constitution providing for the greatest human freedom according to
laws . . . is at least a necessary idea, which one must make the ground . . .
of all the laws; . . . and in it we must initially abstract from the present
obstacles. . . . For nothing is more harmful or less worthy of a philosopher
than the vulgar appeal to allegedly contrary experience, . . . frustrating all
good intentions by using crude concepts in place of ideas, just because
these concepts were drawn from experience.

—IMMANUEL KANT, *CRITIQUE OF PURE REASON*

1. Introduction

We are sinners, even if not for the metaphysically exotic ("original sin") reasons Christianity has accepted this. Even allowing for differing views of the boundaries of right action, and even if people often, or even usually, behave well morally speaking, people also act wrongly as a matter of course, falling short of due standards of honesty, generosity, compassion, and fairness. The moral requirements stand pat even in the face of (in order to define) routine violation—moral requirements are, we might say, ideal rather than realistic in that way. Saying so does not invoke anything as metaphysically fancy as a Platonist conception of the ontology of moral standards. It is simply another way of saying that a behavior being widespread is not enough to make it morally unobjectionable. As we have been exploring, what is politically rightful, by alleged contrast, is often thought (as we have observed several times[1]) to take its very subject matter from the "crooked timber of humanity,"[2] as if from the political point of view its bent shape is beyond judgment and in some way straight. As I have been indicating, I doubt, and hope to cast doubt upon, the idea that the central questions in political philosophy might somehow escape the idealizing, unbending features of morality itself.

[173]

In a version of this bent approach, social justice is often thought to be a matter of conformity to principles, where the principles have this status partly on the basis of how conformity with them would, in light of the facts, work out in practice. I want to consider a challenge of the following kind for theories of justice that take this general form. Among the facts that will affect how principles would work out in practice are many bad facts—facts about moral deficiencies. Is the content of social justice, even perfect or full social justice, shaped so as to accommodate or take account of these causally important moral deficiencies, or does it somehow put them aside? On one hand, principles of justice that ignore the morally unfortunate facts might seem to be quixotic, abstract, pointless (put aside as puzzling why few objectors say this about morality itself). On the other hand, justice is a standard, not a strategy. As such, it might instead be essentially above and independent of the unfortunate facts. Justice, it might be thought, evaluates the facts, an office it could not perform if it began by incorporating them. A moral standard that is already shaped by conceding morally unfortunate facts and putting them beyond reproach, it might naturally be thought, is contaminated. I will call this the problem of bad facts.

In this chapter, I begin by considering the sweeping rejection, stemming from G. A. Cohen, of incorporating any facts at all—good, bad, or indifferent—into fundamental principles of justice. I argue that his point, while not philosophically unimportant, does not have substantial normative significance. His arguments do, however, give us the merest glimpse of the normatively significant problem of bad facts. The close look at Cohen's arguments has the purpose of setting up and distinguishing that importantly different point about the insulation of principles of justice from facts, or some of them: the bad ones. I close this chapter by addressing a natural worry, that the effort to keep bad facts in their place is circular: bad facts about injustice cannot be identified and quarantined prior to the identification of the principles, in which case they have already functioned as ingredients, contaminating or not.

Looking ahead slightly, the following chapter (chapter 10, "Prime Justice") looks closely at the suggestion that requirements of justice are not contaminated when the bad facts that are incorporated are not themselves shortfalls from justice, but only shortfalls in individual morality. A common response, in effect, to the problem of bad facts is to distinguish between moral and political bad facts. Even granting that social justice cannot coherently incorporate injustice—bad political facts—it can and must, according to this common view, incorporate the crooked timber of humanity—bad moral facts. Part 4 grapples with the culprit problem, first arguing that it is a deep difficulty in moral thought and not an errant implication of the present idealistic approach to justice. In the next section, I develop an explicit account of "Plural Requirement" and explore some implications, and tie it back to the idea—hard to do without but hard to explain—that a society can be under a kind of moral requirement, say justice, in its own right.

Cohen vs. Facts

On Cohen's view, Rawls's employment of the original position (OP) rests on the erroneous assumption that the fundamental principles of justice are fact-dependent. Moreover, he argues, it leads the content of the principles chosen there to be distorted by categories of nonmoral fact that themselves have nothing to do with justice. I will refer to these critiques as Cohen's critique of "fact-dependent foundations," and his critique of "justice as regulation" respectively. I then turn, more sympathetically, to a third form of sensitivity to facts suggested but not developed by Cohen, namely the role that the OP method must give to morally bad facts in particular. I begin with Cohen's argument against fact-dependent foundations for justice.

Cohen argues that fact-independent principles are morally more basic than fact-dependent ones, because they explain them. His central target, Rawls, argues that principles of social justice are "constructed"[3] partly through engagement with nonmoral facts. The question that guides the Rawlsian approach is how things would work out in practice, in certain ways, if the basic social structure met certain principles rather than others. The parties who are selecting the principles in the hypothesized choice situation will bring to bear their general knowledge of such nonmoral facts as characteristic human motives and concerns, cognitive abilities, patterns of moral development, predictable strains from keeping certain commitments, not to mention the whole universe of facts about how nature itself operates.[4] The derivation of the fundamental principles of social justice in the OP renders those principles dependent on, and explained partly by, the nonmoral facts about people and nature that lead the parties to select them.

If Rawls is right that the two principles of "justice as fairness" are grounded wholly or partly in the nonmoral facts about the "conditions of our life as we know it,"[5] there must be, Cohen argues, a deeper principle that explains the particular moral relevance of those facts. To get to the fundamental principle or principles, we must unearth them by scraping away the facts whose relevance is grounded by something deeper. Suppose a Rawlsian were to acquiesce in the demand for further unearthing. She then reports on her findings:

The Unearthed Rawlsian Principle[6]
The fundamental principle of social justice is this: institutions ought to meet principles (which are in this way less fundamental), whatever they are, that would be chosen in the OP, with its sensitivity to the facts whatever they might be.

This principle is now independent of any of the facts the OP brings to bear, just as the wrongness of hurting, which explains the wrongness of hitting, is independent of the fact that hitting hurts.

Obviously, a key question is whether or not the unearthed Rawlsian principle, excavated in response to Cohen's challenge, would necessitate any revision of the content of Rawls's two principles of justice. On the face of it, it seems that their content should remain exactly the same. And indeed, Cohen acknowledges this.[7] Moreover, the unearthed principle would ground the whole OP methodology itself, unchanged. It merely adds the fact that, in a certain sense, the famous two principles, which depend on facts, are not fundamental because they are explained by a deeper principle—the unearthed Rawlsian principle—which does not depend on the facts. This is normatively (though not in every way) uninformative, and it leaves in place, even as it explains, the grounding or supporting relation between the facts and the principles Rawls had alleged. The unearthing move to the fact-independent principle is so simple that it does not appear to make any substantial difference in Rawls's theory at all.[8] What damage does this point of Cohen's do to a Rawlsian approach?

Cohen still has a complaint here—let us call it a *formal complaint*—because it is a complaint about how Rawls formulates the theory, not about its normative substance. (In that sense, we could also call it "metaethical.") The formal or metaethical complaint of Cohen's is structurally similar to the point (or a point, as I see it) of the famous Euthyphro problem:[9] if "It is wrong to murder" depends on the fact that God forbids murder, there is a deeper principle that does not depend on that fact about God, namely: "It is wrong to disobey God's will, whatever His will might require." On a divine command view of the grounds of moral requirements, this principle is more fundamental than "It is wrong to murder," because it explains the force of that prohibition. Similar points can be made for any view according to which moral principles stem from the outcome of a certain specified agency or procedure of any kind. Such views ascribe a certain moral authority to the agency or procedure. It looks to be a deeper (maybe fundamental, maybe not) normative truth that they have that authority to begin with. And that deeper normative force or authority does not stem from or depend on what those agencies or procedures do or say at all.[10] The structure of Cohen's point, then, has an ancient resonance in a broadly Platonic cast of thought.[11]

I take Cohen to be arguing that Rawls is committed to denying that moral principles are ultimately grounded in fundamental fact-independent principles. So Cohen takes Rawls to be committed to a faulty (because fact-bound) metaethics. However, there is a way of interpreting Rawls that would avoid any metaethical tussle with Cohen. It is one hinted at when Rawls says, "There is no necessity to invoke theological or metaphysical doctrines to support [these] principles." This is importantly not the same as asserting the metaphysical view that *there is no deeper grounding principle* for the relevance ascribed to the facts in the OP method. Rawls says, instead, and more characteristically, that the metaphysics (and here, metaethics) is beside the point if we are interested in the content and justification of the principles of social justice. Whether because God says so, or because there is a quasi-Platonic fact-free principle to the following effect, Rawls may still assert: the principles of justice are justified by their appeal to the parties in the OP in light of the facts of human life. Nothing about what would be just is added by pointing to the unearthed fact-independent principle (whether God-given, Platonic, or otherwise) that says, simply, that those are the principles of justice, justified by the OP argument which appeals to those very facts. To say, as Rawls does, (and as Cohen makes much of) that principles of justice are to be justified "by the conditions of our life as we know it or not at all,"[12] is not to deny that there might be deeper philosophical support for this very view in some further principle, such as the unearthed Rawlsian principle. Contrary to what Cohen argues, the OP method, in which principles are justified by facts, is not committed to denying that there is some fact-free basis for any such moral relevance of the facts in a deeper normative principle.

Turn next to Cohen's substantive objection to the way the OP grounds justice in facts. Cohen here denies that the facts of human life rightfully play any role in determining the content of justice, and we will consider his arguments shortly, but this second, substantive claim of Cohen's is neither implied by, nor does it imply, the unearthing point about fact-free fundamental principles. We should have names for two separate issues about the relation of facts to principles. Cohen's unearthing strategy uncovers principles that do not *rest on facts*. This leaves entirely open whether those principles *operate on facts*. To say that principles operate on facts is to say that their normative implications vary in accordance with relevant variations in the facts. Consider, again, the unearthed Rawlsian principle. It says that the content of justice is given by principles chosen in the OP in light of the nonmoral facts of human life and nature whatever they might be. As we have seen, this principle does not rest on any facts, such as those of human nature. Rather, the principle purports to ground the moral significance of those facts. But, in that way, the principle does operate on certain nonmoral facts. It gives them, or explains their having, a certain moral significance. The principle's normative implications vary depending on facts about "the conditions of our life."

Cohen's substantive objection is that the OP method, by letting principles of justice operate on the conditions of human life, mixes questions of justice with other considerations, as if one were choosing rules of social regulation to be implemented rather than (the real project at hand) trying to ascertain the true (or—if you find that somehow metaphysically ambitious—the most plausible, sound, or most conviction-worthy) principles of justice. The OP method wrongly assimilates principles of justice to rules of social regulation.

The explicit distinction between rules of social regulation and principles of social justice is, as far as I know, original to Cohen and it is powerful.[13] A precise account of rules of regulation is not needed in order to see the distinction Cohen is after.[14] It rests on the observation that when we make choices, there are often reasons in place that count for or against certain alternatives. Rules of social regulation are things we choose or adopt, and we do so for certain practical reasons. Among the reasons to consider are reasons of justice. Once

adopted, rules of regulation bear on how certain things are to be done, sometimes in the form of laws, sometimes as less formal norms. Being normative in
that way, they are easily confused with principles of justice. But we do not
choose principles of justice. Rather, principles of justice are among the considerations we consult in our choice of rules of regulation, a point that would
evaporate if those were the same thing.

To engage the Rawlsian interlocutor, here is one interpretation of Cohen's
line of thought:

1. The OP, with its regulatory reasoning (so to speak), requires that the
   choice of principles by the parties be made in light of (maybe among
   other things) whatever might affect people's interests—effects stemming from the adoption of one or another set of rules.
2. Not just anything about how the adoption of certain rules would affect
   individual interests in relevant ways is a consideration of justice.
3. Therefore, the OP's regulatory approach lets the choice of principles
   be determined by non-justice considerations, and so does not reliably
   identify justice.

Notice that even what Cohen casts as regulatory reasoning is itself a morally defined enterprise. The question of what rules of regulation we should
have in our society is partly a moral question. For example, in answering this
"regulatory" question presumably no one's interests should count more heavily
than anyone else's, and this is for moral reasons. So the OP might seem to
emerge as a good method for answering this moral question: Which rules of
regulation should we have for our society? It is hard to deny that such values
as efficiency and stability should appropriately influence the parties' choices.
What remains disputable, then, is whether Cohen has strong arguments showing that these values are not considerations that bear on justice. What we are
looking for is an argument that justice is the sort of thing that should be *balanced against* such things as stability and efficiency rather than *being the appropriate balance*. The latter is what constructivism, with its regulatory reasoning, would hold.

Cohen's argument for this lies mainly in his discussion of a number of problems of social policy or regulation, including the structure of tax rate schedules,
the problem of differential care (roughly, "moral hazard"), and issues around
publicity and stability.[15] As one of his examples, Cohen argues that step-wise
tax brackets are bound to be less than perfectly just, and yet they must be ir-
resistible to a constructivist theory of justice for reasons of administrability.
This puts daylight between the OP method and considerations of justice. How
could the person whose property or income is greater than another person's by
the single dollar that kicks him into the higher tax rate owe, *as a matter of
justice*, much more tax—not just a little more—than that other person, and yet
owe exactly the same as significantly richer rate-mates? Of course, it might be

impractical to spend vast sums of public money to implement a highly refined tax schedule—say, one for each dollar amount of income—and in that case it ought not to be done. The rates are not designed to track justice alone, since other things matter too. Cohen argues that the parties to the OP would not insist on an extremely fine-grained tax schedule if it would be vastly more expensive than a moderately fine-grained schedule. This is because the parties to the OP will be sensitive to how those extra resources might be used to benefit them in other ways. He takes this to show that a constructivist method must be prepared to trade greater justice off against gains with respect to other values such as efficiency.

Things are complicated by the fact that Rawls's view seems to be that tax rates are not directly matters upon which justice takes a position. For him, a given tax rate is just in the purely procedural sense if it is the product of a just basic structure where legislators duly aim to maintain the structure's justice by conforming it to the basic principles. Cohen might reply that Rawls's OP argument forces him to deny that there is anything unjust about, say, taxing the poor at a higher rate than the rich, if that should turn out to be the most sensible policy all things considered—where "things" can vary widely. Such perverse arrangements might be just on that view, he appears to argue. But the Rawlsian view does not quite say that. It says that there would be nothing unjust about doing that *so long as* that scheme is part of a basic social structure that meets the difference principle and the other principles. Rawls could argue that no such tax system is remotely likely to meet that proviso, thus explaining the absurdity in the suggestion that it "might" be just. But some will agree with Cohen that this does not accommodate the deep intuition that some tax rates are unjust, even if there are other good reasons for adopting them, irrespective of their downstream effects on distribution.

The case of what Cohen calls "differential care," similar to what is often called "moral hazard," is a second example he uses to support his view that Rawls's constructivist method in the OP incorporates values that have nothing to do with justice. Rehearsing his argument will bring us up to the threshold of the alternative approach I want to highlight, focusing not on all facts but on bad facts, though he does not clearly step over, or even mark the difference. Cohen sketches an example, which I slightly simplify here (these are my words, not his):

Suppose that there are two possible schemes S1 and S2 for publicly compensating homeowners should storms damage their property. Under S1 everyone gets fully compensated for any damage. However, some people might rely on this program and reduce the amount of care they take to prevent storm damage. When compensation is provided, this would seem to be unfair to homeowners who had, at their own expense, taken greater care and minimized their property damage. To reduce that kind of unfairness, we might prefer scheme S2, which requires anyone who claims benefits to bear the first $200 of repairs themselves. This provides people with an incentive not to skimp in their preparations in hopes of being bailed out later, thus reducing the unfairness produced by compensation under S1. Of course, the "deductible" in S2 is crude in that it is not scaled to each homeowner's incentives which will vary for any number of reasons. Therefore, there might remain homeowners who will still have prudential reason to do little or nothing even though the first $200 will be their own responsibility, calculating that their preventive costs would be considerably more than their expected compensation (the amount in excess of $200 multiplied by the probability of its occurring, say). Finally, suppose that while we could, at great expense, determine just how conscientiously each homeowner prepared her house for storms, and thereby tailor compensation so as to avoid such free riding, this scheme, S3, would be very expensive.[16]

To recap: S1 compensates for damages with no deductible, S2 compensates but with a $200 deductible to discourage skimping, and S3 expensively compensates each, partly according to how thoroughly she prepared. Cohen argues that, (a) if there are free riders, S3 would be the most just, but (b) the OP approach to justice, with its reliance on regulatory reasoning, would, if S3 is expensive enough, select S2. The Rawlsian method, then, really trades off justice against non-justice values such as efficiency rather than bringing various considerations into a balance that constitutes justice. To count against a policy the fact that it would be very expensive is to give weight to a consideration—total expense—that is not an ingredient of justice at all, but a different value altogether. Justice might be prohibitively expensive, after all. The OP method's reliance on regulatory reasoning evidently selects for less expensive options other things equal, and it thereby disqualifies itself as a reliable method for determining the content of justice.[17]

An explanation for his avoidance of the term "moral hazard" is that strictly speaking, the familiar problem of moral hazard is not about "differential care"—some exercising less care than others—at all, but about some or all—maybe even equally, and so not differentially—reducing their care in response to the policy, still with the clear implication that their doing so is a "moral" wrong as the name implies. In any case, we can see that Cohen wishes to focus on the case of *differentially* reduced care, and without the assumption that it is morally wrong. His point, as we have seen, is that even if no one is morally misbehaving, a policy that leads to such differentially reduced care will be unfair to those who reduce their care less or not at all, even though it might be the appropriate policy in light of the costs of fairer policies. So, despite a certain similarity between Cohen's concern and the issue known as "moral hazard," Cohen explicitly avoids resting his argument on the moral badness of any of the acts in question.

Now, how is this case an illustration of how Rawlsian theory incorporates non-justice considerations? If we keep in mind his insistence that the case need not involve any of the homeowners acting wrongly, the basis for Cohen's conviction that non-justice considerations are "transparently" present in the choice of S2 (the deductible) over S1 is not clear. Of course, if we already adhered to the luck-egalitarian conception of justice that Cohen endorses,[18] then S2 can be seen as a response, and only a partial remedy, to the injustice of some people doing worse than others through no fault of their own. But Cohen means the argument here to stand independently of luck egalitarianism, and so it is not clear how it should go. Consider the choice by Rawlsian choosers of S2 over the imagined expensive scheme S3, which tailors compensation precisely to each homeowner's level of prophylactic care. It would be enough for Cohen's purposes if this choice clearly rested on non-justice considerations. Indeed, it is clear that the great expense of S3 could be enough to dissuade the parties from opting for its fine-grained compensation rules. S2, while cruder, accomplishes some of what S3 aims for, but at much less cost. That appeal to economic efficiency, Cohen claims, is not a consideration of justice. Unfortunately, Cohen does not explicitly argue that economic efficiency is not a consideration of justice. It may be that he assumes that it must not be because it does not involve any comparison between how some people fare or are treated compared to other people. Thus, the OP is not suited to explicate the content of justice. A possible reply on behalf of Rawls is that Cohen has not claimed or argued that justice contains only such comparative aspects. The OP's sensitivity to some non-comparative considerations such as efficiency is compatible with its also being sensitive to some comparative ones, which we may grant would be a desideratum of a sound conception of justice. And indeed, Rawls argues that the parties would be led to avoid social arrangements that are too unequal in certain ways, especially as this might corrode the fair value of the political liberties. However, the question is whether justice involves *nothing but* comparative considerations. The Rawlsian (or other constructivist) can fairly ask who has a legitimate complaint against policies that implement the cruder S2, with the resources saved by declining S3 used to benefit (suppose) everyone? Cohen agrees that there may be no legitimate complaint, but only because appropriate social policy ought sometimes to compromise justice for the sake of other values. But if nobody has a legitimate complaint, the Rawlsian is not under strong pressure to concede that injustice is being chosen for the sake of other values. A kind of inequality (the kind, whether we regard it as an injustice or not, defined by luck-egalitarianism) is countenanced for the sake of a kind of efficiency, but this is done in order to ensure that no one has a legitimate complaint. Like Cohen's very different view, that is also a creditable interpretation of the idea of social justice, obviously one at the heart of Rawlsian thought.[19]

2. Bad Facts

We have seen two ways in which Cohen criticizes the OP method for bowing to facts. The first was his formal objection that Rawls fails to recognize that facts are only morally relevant owing to principles that determine their relevance. The second was his substantive argument that some of the considerations Rawls appeals to are not considerations of justice. In his treatment of the case of differential care, we glimpse a third kind of complaint about reliance on facts, but one that Cohen does not clearly demarcate as different from the other two. Repeatedly, as I will illustrate, Cohen rhetorically leverages the *moral deficiency* represented by some of the facts to which constructivism bends its results. We may call this a complaint about constructivism's reliance on bad facts.[20] In discussing the differential care case discussed above, Cohen observes that,

> The root cause . . . that induces a compromise with justice in the 'exploiter' variant of the differential care phenomenon is a certain human *moral infirmity*: Constructivists are, therefore, in the questionable position that they must defer to facts of human moral infirmity in the determination of what fundamental (nonrectificatory) justice is.[21]

He acknowledges that under full compliance with the principles of justice, which Rawls assumes to be in place, there might not be any exploitation, but only innocent differential care. Even if there is no exploitation, there might be reasonable fear of exploitation, which Cohen says is enough for his purposes. And yet he continues to suppose that "moral infirmity" might well be part of the differential care profile: "It would be transparently wrong to say that the facts about moral weaknesses and so on make S2 just (without qualification), as opposed to more worthy of selection."[22]

It might have seemed from the very beginning that Cohen objected to the OP's sensitivity to bad facts. He complained, in his argument against the Difference Principle's attention to incentives, that if talented citizens decide to withhold socially productive labor unless they are paid more than others, the OP will lead to the conclusion that justice requires paying them more even though such a demand seems to put them outside of the publicly shared sense of justice. To that extent, they look bad. But Cohen never quite embraced this route. Even in the earliest setting in the Tanner Lectures, he did not complain that justice is being bent to accommodate bad behavior, but complained, more obliquely, only that in that case the talented would not count as in "justificatory community" with the other citizens—quite a different point.[23] And true to form, in the much later treatment of differential care in *Rescuing*, he refers only glancingly to the inadequacy of "moral weaknesses *and so on*" (emphasis added) to qualify the OP's results as just. He does not make clear whether the OP is disqualified partly by the fact that its results are bent to make the best out of *morally* bad situations—adjusting not only to facts as such, or to justice-neutral facts, but to bad facts.[24]

Even if Cohen never offered that line of criticism in full voice, or even if he would not embrace it on reflection, it poses an important challenge to the OP method. If a certain predictable moral deficiency in some or all people—maybe indefensible selfishness or partiality, or maybe a certain ineluctable level of bigotry—leads the OP to reject certain arrangements as infeasible or unreasonably expensive, it may strain credulity to accept that justice is being reliably tracked by the OP method. Even on the deeply Rawlsian and more broadly contractualist association of justice with some person's legitimate complaint, this would seem to countenance injustice. The victims of institutionalized bigotry, however infeasible it may be to socially engineer that away, have a legitimate complaint if the accommodation to it is worse for them than alternatives without the bigotry. That is, suppose one disagreed with Cohen's view that feasibility or expense are values foreign to justice, holding that they are among the values that ought properly to be balanced in the constitution of justice, as the OP method holds. Nevertheless, when an arrangement is rejected because it would be too expensive, but where the expense stems from moral deficiencies people would have under the hypothesized conditions, there is, arguably, an untoward capitulation to vice that seems foreign to the idea of full social justice. That would be a third of three lines of objection to letting justice be sensitive to facts: to facts as such, to justice-neutral facts, and to morally bad facts.

3. Constructivism and Compliance

In order to see the issues clearly I propose to focus now on theories that are, in the following sense, constructivist, and conjecture that the lessons will be of broader significance. Let a *constructivist theory of justice* be one according to which the principles for the justice of a society are whichever principles would be chosen by suitably situated hypothetical choosers as a rule that would, in light of the facts, promote the choosers' (theoretically specified) interests.[25] If the constructivist theory is a theory only of justice, and not of moral right generally, call it a "partial constructivism," with a "complete constructivism" being one that offers a single and unitary constructivist account of moral right.

Any plausible version would have to avoid letting the results be determined by the power of some of the hypothetical choosers to tailor principles to benefit themselves at the expense of others. We would have no reason to accept that as an account of moral principles at all. Rawls famously puts the choosers behind a veil of ignorance so that they are not able to know which of the people living under the principles they are. This prevents them from self-dealing in certain obvious ways. There may be other ways to accomplish a similar purpose, and I will not say much about the merits of imposing a veil of ignorance, except to highlight the following fact: this is a restriction on what the choosers are assumed to know. Certain facts are hidden from them: the facts about their own identity. So when it is said that in constructivism the choosers select principles with an eye to their interests *in light of the facts*, veil of ignorance versions pointedly do not mean all of the facts. It is up to the theorist to decide which facts are to be known if this thought experiment is to be a plausible guide to genuine morally significant principles. (Of course, some constructivist theories do without the veil of ignorance and impose a kind of impartiality in other ways. Scanlon's theory of moral rightness is an example, as developed in *What We Owe to Each Other*.)

There is another way in which constructivist theories characteristically deny knowledge of all the facts to the choosers. When the hypothetical choosers are evaluating alternative principles with an eye to the promotion of their (theoretically specified) interests, they will need to do this in light of the facts that bear on how the principles will work out. Among those facts will be the level of compliance with the chosen principles themselves. Commonly, however, a constructivist theory installs in the choosers a false belief about levels of compliance. Even though compliance will, realistically, be far from full, the choosers are stipulated to assume that there will be more or less full compliance. To be clear, I am not raising an objection, but only noting that "the facts" that the choosers are to choose in light of are carefully selected by the theorist. Indeed, the choosers are sometimes, as in this case, given beliefs that are blatantly contrary to the facts. Constructivism, in its classic formulations, does not insist that the choosers know the truth, much less the whole truth. If there are good theoretical reasons for it, it may be supposed that they are ignorant of certain truths (such as those about their identity), and to believe certain falsehoods (such as that compliance will be more or less full).

We saw a decent reason for the veil of ignorance, but why should the choosers falsely assume that the chosen principles will be generally complied with?[26] We are seeking principles which, if complied with, would suit the choosers' interests (suitably constrained by the choice situation). If the parties were to choose some principles because a certain predictable low level of compliance would work out nicely, while full compliance would not work out nicely, justice as explicated by the principles would be divorced from the choosers' interests, contrary to the constructivist enterprise. What would suit the choosers' interests in that case would be *injustice*, by the theory's own lights, and it would have been injustice that they have opted for (because that is what suits their interests) by choosing certain principles of justice, which will attract poor compliance, to serve as rules of regulation. The content of justice will have been shaped by the brute fact of injustice in the world so as to accommodate that injustice. The selected principles would be the advantageous ones for the choosers only because many people will be unjust. The problem I am identifying is not that the chosen principles condone the noncompliance in that case—they do not; it is *non*compliance with the principles of justice, after all. The problem is that in that case the fact of injustice is given inappropriate influence over what counts as justice. In this way the principles of justice would be tainted or contaminated by capitulation to (even if not condoning of) injustice.

For these reasons I accept that in a constructivist theory the principles are to be chosen under the unrealistic assumption that they will be complied with. I take this to be an instance of insulating the content of justice from bad facts. If justice is a moral standard of any kind, noncompliance is (other things equal) morally bad in that way.[27] If justice were shaped by the sad fact of non-compliance, then it would be shaped by bad facts. I contend that the bad facts of noncompliance should not be allowed to affect the standard of justice.

Now, as I have emphasized throughout the book, we should not build or maintain institutions whose only value would depend on levels of compliance that we know are not going to occur. There is normally no value in having institutions that will not work given all the facts. So, how could the principles of justice, which would seem to tell us what institutions we should build, be properly insulated from any of the facts, good and bad alike? The answer, I believe, is that principles of justice do not tell us what institutions we ought to build. What institutions we ought to build depends on, among other things, whether and to what degree we live in a just world. The institutions we should build if we are in an unjust world, for example one in which compliance with just institutions is not in the cards, might be very different from those we should build otherwise, and we should hardly build our institutions under some willful pretense about how justly people will behave.

If principles of justice do not tell us what institutions to build, do they tell us to do anything? Recall, the distinction (from chapter 8: "Concessive Requirement") between concessive and nonconcessive requirements. The question of what institutions to build is often a question about certain concessive requirements. The reason is that practical proposals are justified (or not) in light of all the facts as we understand them, and among the facts we know is that there will not be full compliance (even perhaps by us ourselves) with any institutional arrangement. So, justice might say to Build and Comply with certain institutions. But it would not follow that it says to Build those institutions. That would depend on compliance, which as it happens will be lacking. So justice does not say to build those institutions. It says to Build and Comply with certain institutions, and, as I have argued, those institutions are to be specified without allowing the bad facts of noncompliance to bear on the question.[28]

4. More Bad Facts

I have argued that the content of principles of justice ought not to be shaped by the bad facts about noncompliance with *those* principles. So far, my position is orthodox among constructivist theorists. In the next chapter, I want to consider whether this argument can be extended to say that justice should not be shaped by bad facts about noncompliance with *any* genuine moral standards at all. It is a bad fact that people will not (considered collectively) comply very fully with the principles of justice, whatever they are.[29] But this is not the only bad fact. People are also morally deficient in lots of ways that have nothing much to do with social justice. Since those are not cases of noncompliance with justice itself, there is not quite the same rationale—the one about contamination—for insulating the selection of principles of justice from these other morally bad facts. The standard of social justice would only be contaminated by taking social injustice for granted, or so it might seem. In the next chapter, I will sympathetically consider the view that even though institutions and social rules must obviously be tailored to the facts whatever they are, the superior account of social justice does not tailor the principles to facts about moral noncompliance.

5. The Circularity Objection

Can bad facts of the relevant kind be identified at such an early and abstract stage of a theory of justice? After all, the facts we wish to exclude are facts that constitute defects from the standpoint of social justice.[30] It may seem that my proposal is to do things in the following order, and that it would be an incoherent kind of bootstrapping:

 a. Identify the justice-violating facts.
 b. Give constructivist choosers knowledge of all the facts except the justice-violating ones (plus assume full compliance, and impose a veil . . .).
 c. Then identify the content of justice by determining what principles the choosers, with knowledge of that filtered set of facts, would choose.

The circularity objection says that step (a) is impossible until step (c) has already been completed. But since (c) is conceived as taking place in light of (a) having already been completed, the methodology is incoherent.

However, the objection seems to depend on a bad argument. There are two points to consider in turn. The first is that even if none of the content of justice could be known prior to carrying out the constructivist reasoning in light of the relevant facts, that would only show that it would be impossible to *know* which of the facts are the relevantly bad ones. It would not touch the claim that some of them *are* bad ones, and are, for that reason, facts upon which justice does not genuinely depend.

The second point is that some of the content of justice surely can be known even before carrying out any of the constructivist reasoning. We might know at least some of the content of what justice requires even without (and so before) knowing which are the relevant facts upon which its content depends. If so, this could be helpful in deciding what the principles of justice are, since it might plausibly rule out certain possibilities. Indeed, this might be the more common order in which such kinds of knowledge are acquired. We probably know of many types of injustice before we know in virtue of what they count as unjust. You do not have to be a philosopher to know that the institution of slavery and some other kinds of exploitation and oppression are unjust. I do not mean that this has always been obvious; that is not so. Rather, when people come to know it, they need not also know in virtue of what slavery counts as unjust, which is a further more philosophical question. These considerations suggest that these epistemological concerns about a bootstrapping constructivism are not damaging. Since some of what is just and unjust might be independently known, bootstrapping theories (those exhibiting the structure above) probably do not entail a radical epistemological skepticism about justice. And even if they did, that would not rule out the possibility that some bootstrapping theory is nevertheless the truth about justice. And it would not rule out that this very general point could itself be known, even if (as seems very unlikely in any case) nothing about what is just could be known. In sum, the proposition that principles of justice are not grounded in certain kinds of facts does not imply anything about whether the set of facts could be known prior to the principles or vice versa. It is not, in that way, an epistemological claim at all.

In the next chapter I further illuminate the implications of the problem of bad facts, arguing tentatively that the standard that has the best claim to being real or true justice may be whatever would be the appropriate standard for a basic social structure on the (highly unrealistic) supposition that all the members comply fully with all requirements of morality. We will see that such requirements are not hypothetical, merely conditional on such unlikely circumstances, but apply to us as things actually are. Finally, whether this would be a wildly unrealistic conception of justice turns out to be less obvious than it might appear.

CHAPTER TEN

Prime Justice

[I]f he keeps within the limits that separate scientific prevision from fanciful Utopian conjecture, the form of society to which his practical conclusions relate will be one varying but little from the actual, with its actually established code of moral rules and customary judgments concerning virtue and vice.

—HENRY SIDGWICK, *THE METHODS OF ETHICS*

1. Introduction

Justice, sometimes, is a way in which things can be right even though things have gone wrong. It is just, and in that way right, for the thief to compensate the victim, or maybe even to be punished. Or, when neighbors selfishly compete to divert scarce stream water for themselves it would be just for the water to be apportioned impartially in some way. Without erasing the wrongs involved these solutions are right. This aspect of justice, that it can be a virtue in a context of vice, is sufficiently striking that, at least in the case of social justice, it is sometimes thought to be of its essence. I think this is a mistake, partly for reasons already presented in chapter 4: "Circumstances and Justice." Recognizing the mistake leads us, as I will explain, to the unfamiliar idea of justice for morally flawless people. In turn, we will see that this initially frivolous-sounding topic illuminates something important about the structure of moral normativity more generally, namely, the primacy of nonconcessive standards—standards of right that are not occasioned by wrong.

Let me begin with a rough definition of some terms I will be using. By "prime justice," I will mean a certain part of what I will call the *global prime requirement*. This is the requirement according to which all agents (individual or collective) behave as they morally ought to given that all others also do so. Presumably, or so I will assume, there will be a component part of this prime requirement that concerns a society's basic social structure, the social justice part of the morally flawless scenario. So, there is evidently this question: What ought a basic social structure to be like, on the assumption that nothing else is going morally wrong? I do not mean what it ought it to be like in descriptive detail,[1] but what standards or principles ought it to meet? It is entirely possible for two societies that are in many ways unlike each other both to meet the same principles of justice. Call this social-structural part of the global prime requirement *prime justice*, for reasons to be explained. I will not propose an answer to that question, but I want to reflect on its status in our thinking about social justice. I will ask whether there is any good alternative to this ostensibly wildly unrealistic standard for the title, simply, of full social justice. If not, then it may be that justice is wildly unrealistic. I will try to show, however, that even though meeting the global prime requirement is indeed highly unlikely, justice, even prime justice, might not be similarly unrealistic at all. Still, there is an alternative, coming in two flavors, which I will call *specific prime justice*, contrasted now with *global prime justice*. In the end I conclude in favor of global prime justice as the preferred account of fundamental and relevantly nonconcessive social justice.

It may be that none of my main points depends on conceiving of social justice as a standard for something called the basic social structure (following Rawls), but I frame it that way here, as throughout the book, just to fix ideas. Even framed in this fashion, as I noted earlier,[2] there is no need to limit the basic structure to legal or governmental structures, rather than having it include a much broader range of structured social norms of certain kinds. But even that more capacious use of "basic social structure" will not be essential for my purposes here, but merely convenient.

PART A

2. *The Conditional/Concessive Dilemma*

As I have said, it is a guiding hypothesis of this book that social justice is a moral matter, even though I do not treat this approach as obvious or unproblematic. Here, then, I appeal once more, as a place to start, to some points about individual moral requirement in order to see how far we can understand social justice in a closely related way. There is what I ought, as a matter of moral requirement, to do. That means what I ought to do given the facts, or (the choice will not matter here) my best judgment about them. But some of those very facts will be moral violations by me, which raises a difficulty. It is not that those bad facts do not bear on what I ought to do—all of the facts bear on that.[3] But it does mean that any moral requirements of mine that are as they are because of my moral violations are, in an obvious way, not my fundamental or primary requirements. They are *concessive* to violations of some morally prior requirements and in that way they are not fundamental.

In search of my nonconcessive moral requirements we can observe that there is a *conditional* requirement that is not concessive, one that specifies what I ought to do IF I do nothing (else) wrong. But that does not generate any unconditional requirement in the realistic case where I do other things wrong. So far, there appears to be a dilemma: concessiveness is avoided but only at the cost of conditionality. So there is still the further thing to look for: unconditional, nonconcessive requirements. As we have seen in discussing cases with the structure of Prof. Procrastinate's situation, in a specific case where, for example, the requirement to not do y is owed to my wrongly failing to do x, there is also this morally prior and overriding requirement: "Do x AND y." Even if, because he will not Write, he ought not to Accept, he also ought to [Accept and Write]. This is an instance of what I will call "priming": converting the concessive antecedent of a conditional requirement into a part—a conjunct—of a requirement over a conjunction of actions, such as "Accept and Write the review," or "Build and Comply with the specified institutions."

So far, this is only to rehearse these points familiar from chapter 8, in order to set up some further ones. The immediate point is that the concessive/conditional dilemma can be transcended in cases where there is a morally prior, relatively nonconcessive, requirement to refrain from the conceded violation AND perform the act that is required given that morally compliant action. To match several of these points to some convenient terminology, let us say that: "Conjoining" is the syntactic operation of counting two actions under one requirement. "Priming" is the ascent, so to speak, to a superordinate or morally prior nonconcessive requirement.[4] "Plural" requirement is a special case of conjoint requirement (of a kind to be explained in Part 4) over actions by multiple agents. The concessive/conditional dilemma can be avoided by conjoining and priming. As we will see, in the context of social justice this raises the "culprit problem," which will call for an account of Plural Requirement.

In addition to my own moral failures, there is another kind of bad fact that bears on what I ought to do, not my own moral violations but those of others, and these are important for the case of social justice. All of the facts, including those interpersonal bad facts, bear on what I ought to do, but since this—again, but now in a structurally different way (one agent's requirements conceding violations by other agents)—yields only a concessive requirement, it is not fundamental, or not obviously so (we will push back against this impression shortly). We could again get beyond this inter-agential kind of concession in one way by noting that there is this *conditional* requirement: what I ought to do IF no one else does anything wrong. However, as in the intra-agential case we just rehearsed, that is not a requirement at all—nothing thereby gets required—in the (realistic) case where other wrongs are committed. Here, we do not have what we seek—a nonconcessive requirement—because we do not have a requirement at all.[5]

In the single-agent case we proposed to move to a nonconcessive requirement by priming—by understanding the requirement to cover a conjunction of actions. Procrastinate, who ought to Accept if he will Write, ought also to Accept AND Write. In order to follow that pattern, here we might wonder if there is a requirement of a collective or plural kind: what *we* ought to do. Let "we" refer to everyone in some specified domain: it might be all moral agents, or it might be members of a society (global or national). If there is such a thing as a collective form of requirement, then we can both get beyond the *concession* of others' bad behavior and also have an unconditional requirement rather than merely a conditional requirement. That is, there might be what we (not I) ought to do, namely: we ought to refrain from wrongs AND perform certain actions thereby called for. So, for example (familiar by now): even if we ought not to Build certain institutions because we would not Comply, it can yet be the case that—and this is both nonconcessive and unconditional in form—we ought to Build and Comply with those very institutions. It is important to emphasize that this is not merely a statement of what we ought to Build IF we will Comply. It is, rather, a requirement that applies whether we will Comply or not. It is a requirement "for" people like us. We accomplish the priming maneuver by appeal to an essentially collective mode of requirement, and this raises a number of issues we will consider closely. I will sketch such a view below and develop it later, but let us suppose for now that there is this mode of requirement over all agents in the specified domain.[6]

In one natural understanding of the ascent to relatively less concessive requirements we come to the ideal of a global prime requirement and the fragment of it that bears on the basic social structure—prime justice. That is, if there is such a thing as Plural Requirement, then there would appear to be the maximally nonconcessive principle requiring all agents conjointly to act rightly in light of each other's actions.

The global prime requirement clearly and unapologetically goes well beyond what is recognizable as social justice, comprising moral requirements of all kinds. Still, part of what we ought to do will, in ways that I will not try to make precise here, bear on our basic social structure, even though much of it will not. We could identify social justice as those features of the global prime requirement that do. On that view, they would not exactly be requirements, but parts of a requirement. That is different, because the 'ought' that ranges over all the conjoined acts cannot (or not obviously) be 'distributed' over the parts—the conjuncts in the prime requirement (as we have seen in chapter 8). This is not a technical anomaly or curiosity, but fits the intuitive idea that whatever social structures are required by full justice (allowing for multiple realizations of the requirements), whether they ought to be built or maintained depends on what the facts are. For example, if they would not be complied with, or if they would trigger some tragic unjust reaction, then perhaps we ought *not* to build or maintain them. So they are not, according to the global prime requirement, themselves required except as a part or fragment of a broader requirement that covers them along with such things as compliance. (The requirement, we might say, covers *not each but all* of the several elements.) Still, there is content there, and this justice portion of the prime requirement bearing on basic social structure, we might call "prime justice." It is a candidate for the content of full social justice, whatever its content might be.[7]

3. Is Global Prime Justice Hopeless?

There are big parts of interpersonal morality as we know it that are concessive to moral deficiency. It is wrong to leave a borrowed bike unlocked; there are thieves. It is wrong to vote for a candidate simply because of the value of what she promises; there are liars. It is wrong to pass along a secret received in confidence even to just one person; there are gossips. Each of these suggests large veins of concessive moral rules, and there are many more. None of them would be included in a prime requirement, since it is utterly nonconcessive (though in no way incompatible with concessive requirements). So, in the same way that much of the content of a prime ethics (as we might call it) would be inappropriate in real concessive conditions (Prof. Procrastinate ought not to Accept even though Accepting is part of what he nonconcessively ought to do), it might be that prime justice, that portion of the global prime requirement, would similarly be like a duck out of water. Indeed, I have framed the discussion so far around the idea that prime justice might be hopeless, in the sense that the standards are so high that there is strong reason to believe they will never be met. Since prime justice is meant to be the standard of justice that is appropriate along with such morally pristine individuals, it might seem that it, too, is somehow either highly unlikely in its own right, or profoundly inappropriate as a standard for morally more concessive conditions of individual morality. But this, as it turns out, is far from obvious. Consider the two questions in turn.

First, is it guaranteed that the standard of prime justice—the right standards for basic social institutions in a world of morally flawless agents—is far beyond what we might ever hope to achieve (partly, perhaps, because we will not do all that we could)? That answer is no. Granting that there is no reasonable hope of achieving the environment of morally flawless agents, that says nothing directly about the hope of achieving a basic social structure that meets the principles that would be appropriate in those unrealistic conditions. In general, many standards that would be appropriate there are not, on that basis, somehow made hopeless (whether or not they would be appropriate) in more realistic conditions. That is an entirely separate question. For now, the point is a formal one: posit some standard for social justice that you think is plausible and not hopeless to achieve in realistic conditions. It could, in principle, turn out that this standard is also appropriate under the assumption of morally flawless agents. This shows that the hopelessness of the global prime require-ment does not establish that prime justice is, itself, hopeless.

Of course, simply because a certain standard appropriate for highly ideal conditions is (or, that is, might be in principle) within our reach in nonideal conditions does not show that it is an appropriate standard for these less ideal conditions, and that is the second question. The right thing for the basic social structure in realistic conditions might be only an essentially concessive re-quirement, one dictated by the presence of various shortcomings of morality and justice. Prime justice might not be hopeless, but it might be right only in remote imaginary conditions.

That might be so, but it might not. It is also possible, for all we know at this abstract level of inquiry, that prime justice is precisely what is required in re-alistic conditions. To explore this, we might consider some putative standard of justice that we (or just you) find plausible—both appropriate and not hope-less—either for people as they are, or at least people as they realistically might be. Next, we should ask whether its grounding or justification is contingent on concessions to violations of morality or justice. If so, then it is not a candidate for prime justice, and is *essentially concessive*. But if not—if it is not contingent on any such concessions to violation—then it is a candidate for prime justice even as it is the right standard in flawed realistic conditions as well. If there is such a standard let us call it *robust prime justice*.

Robust Prime Justice
Prime Justice is robust if the requirements of justice in realistic mor-ally deficient conditions are not different from the nonconcessive prin-ciples of justice (namely, Prime Justice). (More precisely, it is robust relative to a particular specification of realistic morally deficient conditions.)

Rawlsian justice, to take a familiar case, is famously tailored to the ideal-izing assumption of full justice-compliance. Justice-compliance is not full moral compliance, but is it tailored, on that view, to moral *non*compliance in any way? I do not see any respect in which it is. It might, instead, be robust, tailored neither to moral perfection nor to imperfection but applicable to ei-ther. (For one thing, as I have argued in chapter 4, the circumstances of justice do not limit the idea of justice to cases involving individual moral deficiency.)

The method of Rawls's original position does apparently expose the deriva-tion of the principles of justice to information about how and to what extent people are likely to behave immorally, as I pointed out earlier.[8] But the ques-tion here is different: Do the facts about likely immoral behavior actually drive any of the reasoning in favor of Rawls's proposed principles of justice as against the alternatives he considers? Although I will not investigate the ques-tion, it is at least not obvious that they do. That alone is enough to illustrate the larger point, which is that principles of justice might be non-hopeless and appropriate in real conditions even if they are also principles suitable for the prime requirement in which there are no moral violations.

So, prime justice might be hopeless, but that is far from guaranteed, and something like Rawlsian justice throws this into serious question. Prime justice might, finally, be dismissed by some as a standard (however high, however hopeful, and however just) that is not appropriate in realistic conditions of moral deficiency even if it might be realistic. Again, we have seen that there is no general reason to believe that this is reasonable. What is justice for the flawless might be justice for the flawed.

It is right, or at least less severely wrong, to build and maintain the basic social structure that is called for given that we will tend to misbehave in various ways, and there is not some structure that would be more right under those conditions. In what sense, then, would it be fortunate or desirable if prime justice were robust—if meeting it were not only right in concessive conditions but would also be right in nonconcessive conditions? The following analogy, while only rough, may be suggestive. The mathematical problems used to test proficiency will be different for college students from those for elementary school students. In that respect, different standards apply. Suppose a grade-schooler were to ask in what sense the college standard is a better or higher standard. After all, a correct answer in grade school is no less correct than the correct answers in college. All are fully correct. Still, we might answer by pointing out to the grade-schooler that the standard appropriate for her is the appropriate standard only because she lacks certain knowledge and skills that the college students have. While it is the proper standard, and if she meets it she performs flawlessly by the appropriate standard, nevertheless, it is a lower standard though not lacking at all in correctness. Something similar would hold for a concessive standard of justice if it is different from prime justice. It is right only because something is wrong. That is precisely to say that if it is *not* different, if prime justice is robust, then meeting the appropriate standard in concessive conditions is not only fully correct, it is also not in any way the meeting of a lower or reduced standard. There is, then, also this kind of distinction enjoyed by robust prime justice, if there is such a thing: it is right not only for flawed people like us (though it is fully right also in that way given how we are); it is also not altered or bent to fit our crooked shape, since it has the same shape it would have even if we were morally straight.

PART B

4. Getting Specific

In this second part of the chapter, I want to look closely at a way of resisting the identification of social justice with that fragment of the Global prime requirement (I will herein capitalize Global and Specific to keep the back-and-forth as clear as possible): Why associate justice with the broader condition of full moral compliance generally, rather than more narrowly with compliance with those parts of the Global prime requirement that are constitutively relevant to a rightful basic social structure—that is, social justice? The challenge itself is somewhat elusive, though I try my best to address it. It is, in any case, somewhat arcane—likely to animate only someone who is already quite drawn to the promise of Prime Justice as a general idea. Others could safely bypass this discussion without any significant loss of the book's main claims and arguments.

The satisfaction of the Global prime requirement is highly idealistic and even hopeless, of course: full compliance by all agents with all moral requirements including those of social justice. It does not follow, as we just saw, that prime justice—that part of the Global prime requirement—is so unrealistic, but still, given this irrealism of the broader requirement within which Global prime justice is embedded, a central question is whether full social justice would be better conceived as responsive in some way to the real moral deficiencies of human life. It is worth considering what such an alternative might look like, and whether it looks philosophically viable.

There is a limit to how much can be conceded—no viable conception of the content of social justice concedes all real and expected human moral violation.[9] One reason is that while practical proposals for rules of social regulation must accommodate all the facts, including facts of moral violation in the presence of the rules, this is not a recipe for principles of social justice. Practical proposals must be concessive even to injustice itself where it is expected to endure. Not all moral violation is social injustice, however. Consider cheating at poker, neglecting one's friends, or infidelity in a romantic relationship. So it may seem that at least those other violations could be incorporated into a realistic approach to social justice, suggesting a partially concessive approach. However, since social injustices would still be fictitiously assumed away on that mixed account, the requirements that would be appropriate *conditionally* on that mixed assumption will still not be appropriate in nonfictional reality. If the requirements in question are merely conditional in that way, they will not, as we have seen, require anything in (most or all) real societies, societies in which the "if" clause—which includes full compliance with justice—is not met. In that case, all or most real societies would be left to count as neither just nor unjust.[10] The consequent, or "then" clause, is the requiring part of the conditional, and it will not apply since society ought not to act *as if* the facts were, in the hypothesized way (in the antecedent), better than they really are.

The goal of letting a principle of justice be concessive, to any degree, then, faces a dilemma: it may seem that either it is fully concessive, incoherently accommodating injustice itself, or it is merely conditional in light of its hypothesizing away the facts that count as unjust. This *concessive/conditional* dilemma could be avoided, as we have seen above, by an unconditional principle requiring basic structural features, along with behaviors that are in compliance with justice. (That is, by conjoining and priming.) A Global prime requirement would require, conjunctively, compliance, by all agents in the relevant domain, with all moral standards, not just those concerning social justice. This conjoint requirement avoids both horns of the concessive/conditional dilemma: it is not, as practical proposals must be but principles must not be, concessive to all facts good and bad. Nor is it merely conditional, having application only in certain (as it happens, unrealistic) conditions. It is unconditional, constituting a requirement in real conditions. It is unrealistic only in the untroubling sense (philosophically speaking) that it, like so many genuine requirements, is unlikely to be complied with.

This Global prime requirement, ranging over acts by multiple agents, will face a serious difficulty, however—the culprit problem: injustice is not, by this accounting, necessarily a wrong by any agent. In the account I will propose in Part 4, this mode of requirement turns out not to be a requirement on any agent, but rather a hybrid of conditional agential requirement on one hand, and unconditional but non-agential evaluation on the other. It is fair to say that we escape the two horns of concession and conditionalization by landing on a third horn: the culprit problem. It is, perhaps, not a dilemma, then, but a trilemma. I will confront the culprit problem and argue that we ought (!) to live with it.

There is, however, a second complication to consider, and its proper treatment is not independent of the culprit problem and the idea of Plural Requirement. We need to compare the full or global kind of priming, to a more limited, as I will call it, *Specific prime requirement*. This would be one according to which we focus on the requirement over all justice-constituting structure and behavior, but which takes everything else, including what I shall call "justice-neutral" moral noncompliance as given. A requirement on a set of individuals to Build and Comply with certain structures and institutions, even while conceding no injustice, might take various other bad facts as given, such as all moral noncompliance that does not (even in aggregate) count as social injustice. This, of course, is to be contrasted with the Global prime requirement we have been considering. Since this Specific alternative is, in an obvious sense, partly concessive—namely, to moral violation outside of justice—it may seem that it can only be a subsidiary principle, driving us to go on in any case to articulate the fully nonconcessive, or Global prime requirement. In that case, there would be good reason to reject the Specific prime requirement as the setting for the identification of full nonconcessive principles of justice. (Even there, the reasons would not be, as they might seem to be, that Specific prime justice is a more realistic requirement. Indeed, that plays no role, as we will see.) The question we turn to is the choice between these two theories of prime justice: Global and Specific.

The Specific prime justice account can equally avoid the concessive/conditional dilemma, but by priming only over social structure, *given* known and expected other behaviors be they morally good or bad. It is still not merely conditional, since it says what to Build and Comply with not if, but *given the fact that*, there are certain other moral violations.[11] Specific prime justice, then, is unconditional—prescriptive in real conditions, just as the Global version is even without any such concessions.

5. Realism Is Not the Point

Since the principles of Specific prime justice are shaped, or relative to, more of the realistic facts than Global prime justice, it is, in that sense, more realistic. It is important, however, not to be misled into thinking that this is any part of the (provisional) case for its superiority being considered here. It is not, as we can see in two different ways. First, and somewhat formally, it is evident that the case I have provisionally sketched makes no appeal to that consideration of realism as a desideratum or virtue in a theory of justice. The appeal, rather, is to the fact that they are violations, arguably, of a justice-irrelevant kind. Second, and more tellingly, since we have distinguished clearly between the task of choosing principles for social regulation on one hand, from the task of understanding the content of social justice on the other, we see that (except for the very thin postulation of circumstances of justice, which do not so much vary the content of justice as identify the very concept)[12] there is no evident rationale for thinking the principles should be responsive or relative to realistic factual assumptions about behavior. In response, it is often replied (I have found) that all this provides is wholly irrelevant principles for wholly unrealistic imaginary social worlds. As should be clear by now, however, this is a demonstrable mistake. The resulting principles are not conditional in that way, i.e., having application only in unrealistically compliant conditions. They apply, unconditionally, to societies here and now, in all their realistic glory. They do not directly settle what institutions such societies ought to build, but that is no objection since that is not their task, as important a task as it is in its own right. Perhaps they would provide some guidance in that task, perhaps not. Either way, they do have application without being conditional on unrealistic assumptions: they say that society ought to Build and Comply with institutions that meet the principles (whatever they might turn out to be).

If there were some strong reason for shaping principles of justice to realistic assumptions about behavior, then we might explain the superiority of Specific prime justice as follows: letting injustice facts in would be contaminating but letting other immorality in would not. But there is no such pressure toward realism, as I have argued, and so that does not yet explain what advantage there is in letting either of them in. Letting both kinds of deficiencies in would be the exactly right approach for the case of designing rules of regulation. But we do not somehow partake of that virtue by letting some of them in but not others. That makes no sense even for the case of rules of regulation, which must accommodate all the facts. By bracketing at least justice noncompliance, we are cleanly outside of the project of designing rules of regulation, and there is no longer any rationale for taking actual and expected bad behavior as given.

Now, if that much is right, doesn't this show even more, that when we come to the question of principles of justice rather than rules of regulation there is no rationale for taking *any facts at all* as given, so that morally bad facts are not to come in for special treatment? This sounds close to the Cohen view concerning the fact-freedom of fundamental principles. But we are not confronting quite the same issue. We can stipulate that the prime requirement in either the Global or Specific version ranges over behaviors *given all known and expected neutral facts*, those not subject to the form of moral evaluation involved in the requirement. The Cohen view insists that if any facts are playing this role as parameters or stipulations, then there is a more fundamental principle that is independent of those facts, and according to which they have their significance. But we can simply grant this for the sake of argument. As I argued in chapter 9, "Bad Facts," even if this metaethical claim of Cohen's is correct, such an unearthed fact-free principle is not of any normative significance. It still gives the same facts the same significance. So, the Cohen claim would have no bearing on our present question, namely whether the content of justice ought to take into account realistic facts of moral noncompliance so long as they are not themselves cases of injustice.

Specific prime justice has this form: "we are required to Build and Comply with a certain basic social structure given the (other) facts including justice-neutral moral violation." It builds in sensitivity, so to speak, to moral violation in that way. However, owing to the justice-compliance fragment of the Specific version the basic social structure that is part of the requirement is not meant or guaranteed to be appropriate in realistic behavioral conditions. Realistically, there might be significant noncompliance with those institutions if built, and these might even stem from deep human motivational proclivities, but that does not disqualify them from Specific prime justice. The priming move (albeit, here, only "specific" rather than "global") allows a strong answer to realist critics of the full compliance assumption. Full compliance with a just basic social structure is here "assumed" in the sense that it is part of what is required, and the institutions are not said to be required without such compliance.

We can now briefly notice a counterpart to a point made earlier about Global prime justice, namely that its content, derived in a highly unrealistic setting of full moral compliance, is not guaranteed to be inappropriate or hopeless under realistic conditions, and it would be significant if it were robust in that way. In the case of the Specific prime requirement there is a similar point:

the irrealism of the Specific requirement's satisfaction as a whole does not imply irrealism or inappropriateness of the institutional segment. That very institutional structure (again, allowing for multiple realizability) could, in principle, turn out to be required in realistic conditions of partial compliance, even though that is not implied by its being required along with full compliance. The basic institutional structure that is required along with full compliance is not guaranteed to be unrealistic or inappropriate in more realistic conditions of partial compliance, and it would be significant if it were required even there and in such a robust way.

6. Global or Specific Prime Justice?

Specific and Global prime justice might differ substantially in their content—in what they say is necessary and sufficient for social justice. While the content of Global prime justice will be social structural conditions that are valuable in a context of full compliance with morality and not only with justice, the content of Specific prime justice will be conditions that are valuable taking actual levels and patterns of moral noncompliance as given where these do not constitute social injustice. To illustrate this, suppose that individuals were inclined, and in a robust transhistorical way, to favor, more than is morally permissible, members of their own family. And define "simple nepotism" as any case of hiring or admitting one's own family member to an open position. Now consider a possible anti-(simple)nepotism principle (I will call it anti-nepotism for short)—not a rule of regulation or a practice that might or might not be implemented, but a principle whose plausibility is to be investigated—according to which it is a violation of social justice if certain offices and positions are with some frequency granted, by some who are in power, to members of their own family.

The *practice* of anti-nepotism (which is different from the principle) has a certain obvious downside, of course, namely that except in special cases a candidate's familial relation to the hiring agent is not plausibly a disqualifying consideration, not bearing on the fairness or effectiveness of their receiving the position, and yet it is made salient by a rule against nepotism. It is plausible that in the absence of any rationale for an anti-nepotism rule or practice, denying employment on the basis of kinship would be a kind of unfairness to the candidate who is a relative of the employer in addition to being inefficient.

Principles of Global prime justice might not contain an anti-nepotism principle, since under full moral compliance (which is admittedly unrealistic) employers would not abuse their power to favor family.[13] Indeed, it might include a principle according to which systematic discrimination by employers against family members is a social injustice. That would depend on details about how such a practice might substantially shape the basic social structure, drawing it into the question of social justice rather than only other areas of morality.

Suppose that case could be made. Global prime justice might plausibly require, along with moral compliance generally including no impermissible family-favoring, no family disfavoring. Under different, more realistic morally imperfect conditions, of course, practices of anti-nepotism might plausibly be required. Global prime justice (in the imagined scenario) would count such practices—practices of *anti*-nepotism—as a violation of social justice, though plausibly ones that are concessively required given the fact that people often violated the requirement not to unduly favor family. By contrast, Specific prime justice would plausibly include a principle according to which nepotism would count as unjust irrespective of whether those hired had otherwise been chosen in fair and effective procedures. The resulting discrimination against family members would not count as unjust in any way on that account.

This rough comparison is not meant to place either alternative in a more or less favorable light—and indeed neither strikes me as strongly favored or disfavored intuitively by this sketch—but only to show how they might differ at the level of principle even if not at the level of practice. Some might be inclined to focus on the evident similarity of the two approaches when it comes to practice, and to suppose that this renders the distinction between them unimportant. But it should hardly be a surprise, by this point in the book, that justice might differ at a level of principle even if this (in a certain way) has no practical implications. I have been arguing throughout that the question of what to do in practice is a flawed way of reasoning about what the content of principles of justice is. We might wonder, then, what other factors there might be to decide between them (to decide, that is, what to believe about justice). I have explained why the Specific version's being calibrated to the more realistic condition of considerable foreseeable moral deficiency is not an advantage—no reason to regard it as a more credible account of what full justice requires. However, Global prime justice has not been shown to have any particular advantage of its own either. Once the danger of defining justice in a way that already capitulates to injustice is avoided in the way the Specific account does, it is not clear how to choose between that and the Global version.

Now, it is important to be very clear: each of these is well-defined and unless some further difficulty turns up for one or the other, there simply are standards that can be defined in both of those ways. Deciding we would rather call one of them justice changes nothing and leaves both of them in place.

Here are a few considerations to consider to see whether either version is favored. First, both are in the plural requirement mode. So, in case that is thought to be a disadvantage, neither one is favored in any case. Second, both need there to be some account of which aspects of behavior and practice are included in basic social structure. This also does not favor either. Third, the Specific version needs it to be possible to say something much more specific: which moral wrongs are social justice- or injustice-constituting and which are not. It is clear that some are, as the example of a racist society can show.[14] But it is also clear that some are not, as the earlier examples of cheating at poker, neglecting one's friends, or infidelity in a romantic relationship show. The line between those categories bears a lot of weight in the Specific version, however, whose whole point is to avoid taking injustice-constituting facts as given and bending the standard of justice to fit them. Maybe this can be done in a sufficiently precise way. I note only that doing so is not necessary for Global prime justice, only for Specific. Insofar as this turns out to be problematic, that would favor the Global approach.

That potential advantage for the Global version of prime justice is not answered by any advantage for the Specific version that I can see, but this is hardly a complete study of the question. Suppose we have no particular way to choose between them. It is important to appreciate that either way justice is a standard that is not adjusted in any way to either individual or institutional realities that would themselves count as social injustice. What might first appear as ubiquitous deficiencies that are limited to the evaluation of individuals and their behavior—we have been focusing for simplicity on undue selfishness and other partiality among a few other things—may turn out when considered on a social scale to count the social structure as unjust by any plausible pre-theoretic or intuitive measure. If so, the Specific account must not bend justice to accommodate them, but must subject them to evaluation at the bar of justice. When we appreciate that various kinds of individual moral failings can, if sufficiently prevalent or virulent, count a society as unjust, in which case obviously standards of justice cannot be designed to bend to them rather than criticizing them, then it becomes clear that standards of social justice stand above and condemn much in human social life that may never be overcome. This must be so for the Specific as well as the Global version of prime justice.[15]

The common suggestion that this risks absurdly putting justice beyond politics has been addressed already,[16] and there is nothing to add here. To connect our conclusions here to broader themes of the book: it is often suggested that the idea of justice ought to be molded so as not to demand more than we will ever see in human life. Certainly, we do want a concept that applies in real life conditions—at least sometimes that is what we want. We have certain questions about real conditions, and we need conceptual resources if we are to work toward answers. The idea of "circumstances of justice" is, as I have said, best understood as containing conditions for the applicability of standards of social or distributive justice. The demand that justice must also be a standard that is not only applicable but also actually, or not improbably, satisfied has no similar warrant. I know of no plausible rationale for that demand. Prime requirement and prime justice, either Global or Specific, are applicable to our world whether or not there is much likelihood of their being satisfied, whether or not they provide practical guidance given what else we will actually do, and even though they do not exhaust the set of questions that should concern us.

7. What Can We Know of Prime Justice?

If justice is the standard for basic social structure that would be required along with either full moral compliance or even only an absence of injustice-constituting behavior, it may seem that it would be very difficult to determine much of its content. One question is whether this is so ("oh yeah?"), and another is whether this would be damning ("so what?").[17] Sidgwick, in the epigraph for this chapter, suggests that there is no "scientific" way to determine practical conclusions for radically unfamiliar and unlikely conditions, such as, presumably, full moral, or even full justice compliance. It is important to appreciate that the truth of a requirement does not depend on whether we would be able to know much about its content. Sidgwick seems to me to be too impressed with the epistemic difficulties. It is a bit like, upon realizing that we can never know all the digits in the decimal value of pi, we stipulate that it is a rational number after all, since that would be more tractable. The problem, of course, is that its guidance would be erroneous. Or, as noted in the introductory chapter, we might search for our keys under the street light, far from where we dropped them, because the light is better. Of course, if it is held that the content of the requirements of justice are not, as those examples are, independent of the investigator's discretion, then focus would shift to the strength of the case for that metaethical position that, in some form, thinking makes it so. While something like that is at least sometimes true of what we have been calling social rules of regulation, it is far less plausible—certainly not obvious—that we can also make the standards of justice (also prudence? logic?) as we choose.

There might very well be multiple nonconcessive or "prime" equilibria, so to speak, answering to Global prime justice—combinations of satisfied standards on people and institutions such that each such requirement is itself morally correct given the satisfaction of all the others. For example, it might be that property regime A, along with pattern B of moral compliance, along with full justice compliance is flawless with respect to justice, but then property regime C along with pattern D of moral compliance might also be so. So there is plausibly a disjunction at that level (in addition to whatever options each of the standards would themselves permit, as in the case of imperfect duties, etc.). It might seem that this gives rise to massive indeterminacy, but that is not clear. There may be enough determinacy about a sufficient number of standards—since many of them may be robust with respect to the normative environment—that the remaining indeterminacy would be relatively modest. For example, requirements against cruelty, and requirements against domination or subordination might not depend on facts about other forms of behavior. In any case, even if the indeterminacy in the standard's content were massive and hard to know in any detail, there is the more abstract point, as I have said, that this could nevertheless be the true structure of obligations and requirements even if its content would be hard to understand. In many areas of knowledge, we know of vast regions and categories of truths that are, and may even always remain, unknown to us. Math and cosmology are like this, and it would hardly be surprising if moral and political philosophy were too, even if we are inclined to hope not. Even if it is insisted that morality could not coherently be wholly unknowable, it might be partly unknowable. For just one way this might happen, the content of prime justice might consist of a set of implications (of one kind or another) of certain parts of morality we do or at least can know. The implications might be too complex for us to discern or fully explore, just as we do not know all of math by knowing the axioms.[18]

8. The Question of Reconciliation

It cannot be taken for granted, *a priori*, that our condition—the human condition, we might say—even considered over time, is hospitable to social justice on any recognizable conception of its content. If it is, presumably, it would be momentous to discover this good news, but it would be equally momentous to discover that—contrary to our hopes perhaps—the news is bad. An inquiry can be an important one, then, in that sense: the question is momentous because we very much hope the answer is one thing and not another. But the inquiry remains important, of course, whatever the answer might be, good or bad. If justice is Global prime justice, then unless prime justice is "robust"—the same content for realistic conditions as for the condition of full justice-compliance—I think it fair to say that the human condition would turn out to be fundamentally inhospitable to true justice—not because it is beyond our abilities, but because it is beyond our proclivities. For those who deeply hoped things were otherwise, that would be bad news, in which case the inquiry is of some moment. Perhaps the news will be good and, for example, prime justice is robust after all. However, even if it is not—if the requirements in realistic conditions are essentially concessive—this does not mean that people or societies cannot respond to injustice, even their own injustice, in ways that are fully right and proper, even, for example, against their self-interest and with moral worth. If, in practice, the human condition sadly presents us with nothing but the essentially concessive questions about social justice, and even if this is our own doing, we might, despite being flawed, yet respond flawlessly to that challenge and do fully and exactly what we ought to do in that circumstance.[19] We might find some, even if not wholehearted, reconciliation to the human condition in this: whether or not full justice is something for humans to strive for given what they know, humanity's moral failures do not preclude (which is not to say that they predict) successes that are, even if concessive, nevertheless complete and flawless, possibly even awesome, under the morally unfortunate circumstances we find, and perhaps place, ourselves in.

PART IV

The Culprit Problem

CHAPTER ELEVEN

The Puzzle of Plural Obligation

No collective responsibility is involved in the case of the thousand
experienced swimmers, lolling at a public beach and letting a man drown
in the sea without coming to his help, because they were no collectivity to
begin with.

—HANNAH ARENDT, "COLLECTIVE RESPONSIBILITY"

[T]hey are casting their problems on society and who is society? There is
no such thing! There are individual men and women and there are
families and no government can do anything except through people and
people look to themselves first. It is our duty to look after ourselves and
then also to help look after our neighbour and life is a reciprocal business.

—MARGARET THATCHER, INTERVIEW, 1987

1. Introduction

A familiar strand in traditional thinking about social justice ties it closely to
individual duties of reciprocity—the willingness to cooperate with others on
fair terms so long as others are also willing. So far as this goes, it promises to
ground at least part of the normativity of principles of justice in the normativity of individual moral requirement. However, it only goes so far, and comes
up short. An agent's duties of reciprocity are conditional on other people's motives and behavior, while, in a certain way, requirements of justice are not. If,
in an extreme case, no individual is disposed to cooperate even if others do,
then reciprocity does not require cooperative action by anyone. It is easy then
to construct less extreme cases to similar effect. Suppose each has an obligation of reciprocity conditional on enough others cooperating, but not *enough*
others will cooperate even if enough others were to do so. Again, no one's conditional obligation gets triggered and so no one does wrong according to reci-

procity even if no one does their part. Social justice, however, whatever its content, surely is not achieved by such mere reciprocity with its equanimity about universal defection. If no one does their part, then, at least often, perhaps no one is required to do her part, but this is not justice. And yet, what agent has violated the requirements of justice?

Perhaps social justice directly requires certain reciprocal motives and not only actions, so that the case in which all are disposed to free-ride is forbidden by justice after all. But on that view, social justice would be about what is in people's hearts, not about actual practices, institutions, or social structure. That seems to me to, so to speak, change the subject of justice. In this chapter, I will argue that the underlying philosophical problem, which I will call the puzzle of plural obligation, is not easily solved.

The idea of Prime Justice from the previous chapter, and more generally of Prime Requirement, brings us unavoidably to this puzzle, which is of interest even outside of our immediate concerns, namely whether there can be a moral violation by a set of agents even when there is no violation by any one of them. The Prime Requirement is, so far, formulated as a moral demand that a certain set of agents act in certain ways.

O(*Society* Build and Comply with just institutions, AND each *individual* behave in certain ways respectively)

But what is moral, or even normative about this? The worry is that it is not clear who is obligated. We have seen reasons to reject the idea that this can be factored into multiple obligations, some on society and some on individuals. As in the single-agent case of Professor Procrastinate, whether any of those obligations is actually obligatory is thrown into question in this multi-agent case, too, when not all of the actions are performed. The requirement would, in a way that is suspect, purport to apply to a collection of agents, but not to anything amounting to an agent—not even a group agent. Call this, as I say, the *puzzle of plural obligation*.[1] The idea of Prime Requirement happens to present the puzzle in a special form that can now be put aside, where one of the conjuncts itself—society's building and complying with just institutions— also involves thinking of a collective as an agent. That feature is incidental to the puzzle of plural obligation, which I will consider in the simpler form in which each of the conjuncts (or, later, disjuncts, as we will see) is a genuine agent/action pair.[2] The general form of the puzzling moral judgment, then, is this, letting S, T, and so forth refer to agents:

O(S does x & T does y & U does Z . . .)

It is required, ostensibly, that all of these agents, together, do certain things. We clearly cannot infer from this that each of them is required. The reason is that the value of the set of actions is compatible with its being pointless, or even a disaster, if only some do their part—even worse than if none did. An agent would not be required to act in that case. Here, again, the point is reminiscent of Professor Procrastinate, who ought to Accept and Write, but given that he will not Write, he ought not to Accept, which would be a bigger disaster than doing neither. We will turn to some multi-agent examples shortly.

I grant for the sake of argument that, even though there are other normative uses of 'ought,' the core normative sense of 'ought' says that certain agents have certain reasons.[3] This is an unnecessary concession for my purposes, since if that is not so, as some argue,[4] then the 'ought' in the plural obligation formulation may be unproblematic as it stands, and in need of no further analysis for my purposes. But suppose that it is so. In this chapter, I explore a number of failed ways to find an owner for the 'ought' associated with the intuitive idea of plural obligation. In the next chapter I propose an 'ought,' or a kind of requirement that is a sort of hybrid between owned and unowned oughts. Of course, there is a widely agreed kind of 'ought' that is non-agential, the so-called evaluative ought.[5] But this may be unsuited to the concept of a requirement of social justice, since injustice is plausibly some kind of wrong, not merely some kind of bad. On the other hand, while it is tempting to think that victims of social justice might appropriately feel not only disappointment, but also something akin to resentment (this being a marker of a moral consideration), it is a nonstandard kind of resentment that is not directed at any agent at all. The question is how justice and injustice are to be seen as more tightly bound up with the agentially moral than the merely evaluative ought would account for.[6]

In the next chapter, I will develop an account of Plural Requirement. The name marks the fact that it is not a case of plural obligation—entailing any instance of what I have called agential requirement. It is non-agential in that sense. In short, the idea of Prime Requirement, upon which the idea of Prime Justice depends, is committed to there being such a thing as a moral requirement of some kind over multiple agents even where they are not a group agent, and even apart from whether any of those agents is thereby under any moral obligation. For that reason, the puzzle of plural obligation is an important challenge, which I take up in this chapter.

I emphasize that the problem does not arise particularly from the idea of Prime Justice, or from its being a high, or nonconcessive, or unrealistic standard, but is entirely independent of those features. The problem arises for the very idea of social justice: if requirements of justice—be they idealistic or concessive—require members of society to do or refrain from certain things, the puzzle of plural obligation raises its head, since their all acting that way is not something that any agent can perform. What agents are under requirements of social justice? If no agent is then what kind of requirements are they? So, we now step back to consider this general problem in moral philosophy, keeping in mind that how it is to be best handled will apply to the case of an 'ought' of social justice in general and to Prime Justice in particular.

Moral Collective Action Problems

Suppose each person ought to do her familiar part, so long as others do, in a criminal trial setting, supposing for simplicity that the laws themselves are basically just: defense attorneys ought to promote the defendant's interests, but without dishonesty or violation of procedural rules. Prosecutors ought to attempt to prove guilt when in their judgment guilt is sufficiently likely given the pretrial evidence, again within the limits of certain good procedural rules. Judges and jurors likewise ought to perform their assigned tasks with honesty and effort, convicting when and only when the presented evidence is beyond reasonable doubt. With all these conditional obligations in place, suppose that none of the participants would in fact do these things even if the others do. Suppose that the attorneys would, in any case, go beyond the rules and their spirit in order to get the verdict they think is right, and the judge and jurors would likewise ignore the procedural rules, standards of evidence, and so on, in order to get the verdict they personally believe is probably correct.

Given this behavior, let us suppose that far more innocent people would be convicted and punished, and far more guilty people acquitted and freed, than if all did their assigned parts. Nevertheless, with some work on the details (the reader is encouraged to work with the example to make this satisfactory) it seems that many or all of the participants may be acting permissibly, or even as required—reverting to their own best judgment of guilt or innocence in each case—*given* how all the others would in any case—and yet also permissibly in the circumstances—behave. Surely, nothing guarantees that this could not be the case, and seeing that is all we need in order to ask our question: Would that be enough to persuade us that such a practice is not a social injustice? For my own part, I think it would be a travesty, and designing the example to rid it of individual moral violation, as I have roughly done, does not change that response. I expect that many will agree, pending some thought about the following puzzle: How can it be wrong if there is no agent doing anything wrong?

To think more about this, it will be helpful to move to some simpler cases. What a person morally ought to do on a given occasion often depends on what others will do. It may be that under the circumstances Dr. Slice, a surgeon, ought to make an incision and remove a tumor if and only if Dr. Patch (or someone) will be there to stitch up the wound. If Patch will not be stitching, then, since neither will anyone else (suppose that Slice is incapable of stitching and no one else will do so), Slice is not required to cut. (She is also probably required to not cut, which is a separate point.) What Slice is required to do depends on what Patch will do. In its structure, if not in the stakes, this is familiar in daily life.

But the story (as laid out previously in chapter 2) might be a little more specific, and more puzzling. Here we add that Patch, too, will not stitch even if the surgery has been performed.

Slice and Patch Go Golfing

Suppose that unless the patient is cut and stitched he will worsen and die (though not painfully). Surgery and stitching would save his life. If there is surgery without stitching, the death will be agonizing. Ought Slice to perform the surgery? This depends, of course, on whether Patch (or someone) will stitch up the wound. Slice and Patch are each going golfing whether the other attends to the patient or not. It is clear that each of them, callous as they are, is morally deficient in her motives, then. But, does anyone act wrongly?

Patch ought to stitch the patient if and only if Slice will perform the surgery. Stitching is possible, but pointless and harmful if there is no wound that needs stitching. But suppose that Slice will not perform the surgery. Patch might as well go golfing. Ought Slice to cut? No, because no one, including Patch, will stitch, and so the surgery will only make the patient's death more painful. Slice might as well golf. Neither has acted (or omitted) wrongly, despite the fact that the patient will needlessly die.[7]

Many of us respond to this case with the intuition that there is some moral violation here, but the puzzle is to find an agent who has committed it. The intuition that something goes morally wrong here cannot be handled simply by saying it is a matter of conditional obligations: each should act so long as the other does. The antecedent is not met, so no such conditional obligation has been violated either. We will consider other proposals below. The intuitive reaction could, of course, be mistaken. But that is not immediately obvious, since there are other assumptions playing a role here, any of which might be wrong instead. I will consider several of them in turn.

We may call the sort of case I am considering a *moral collective action problem*.[8] First, recall the structure of the classic collective action problem:[9] there is some combination of individual actions that would be good, even perhaps good for everyone, and yet no individual's own contribution to that set of actions would be worth it for the agent or even for the group (two different problems). For example, one person's learning enough to cast her vote wisely may be more trouble for her than it is worth (for her or even agent-neutrally) given that, whatever other people do, the improvement in her voting decision has only a small chance of making any difference. Her time, then, might be spent more wisely elsewhere, and of course the same would be true for each other voter. We might need informed voters even though no voter is likely to do any good by being informed.

Unlike the classic collective action problem, nothing in our moral collective action problems is driven by agents' preference rankings, but only by what they ought morally to do given what others will in fact do, whether they care about that or not. It is unlike the classic collective action problem in not being meant to explain any actual empirical phenomena, though of course it might if agents are morally motivated in just the right ways. Its importance is not mainly as a practical problem in the social world, but as a problem in moral thought, though of course that is one of our fundamental ways of understanding the social world.

2. *Whiff and Poof Plus*

Donald Regan's famous "Whiff and Poof" example has the same structure as Slice and Patch, though he, and Gibbard, who first sketched the example, used it for narrower purposes than mine here.[10] Here, suppose, are the agent-neutral values of the consequences if either or both push their buttons:

Whiff \ Poof	Push	Not-push
Push	10	0
Not-push	0	6

Regan demonstrates that it can be used to show that act utilitarianism—and indeed many forms of consequentialism more generally—lack a feature that Regan and others thought such moral theories should have. The feature is this: if each individual complies with the theory, then all agents together produce the best outcome available to them collectively. It is clear from Whiff and Poof, and Slice and Patch, that each person's producing the best consequences open to her—the act required by act utilitarianism—will not produce the best consequences open to the set of agents because of cases like these.

The Slice and Patch case has some advantages over the more schematic Whiff and Poof matrix. For one thing, it adds a story to the numbers. For another thing, the particular story makes it especially vivid that—intuitively, and obviously—neither agent is required to act unilaterally. It does so by building into the story that they are, plainly, not even permitted to do so. Finally, the puzzle emerges from the Slice and Patch case without presupposing (as Regan did) that we are operating within a consequentialist moral framework. Regan confronted cases with this structure as a challenge to utilitarianism, and offered a complex alternative utilitarian theory which he argued had the desired feature. However, the issue is more general than this suggests. First, as Parfit remarks,[11] the issue would be present within many moral theories according to which the consequences *among other things* matter to the rightness of action. You don't have to accept any form of consequentialism to think that, owing to the consequences attached to each agent's options, neither Slice nor Patch should do their part of the surgery under the circumstances.[12]

Second, it is possible for the general issue to be present even if the consequences that morally matter are not effects on anyone's bodily or mental states. The relationships between the values of the possible combinations of action can clearly have the Whiff and Poof structure regardless of what values are attached to what states of the world. To illustrate:

Stash and Burns
Two offspring of a famous, and recently deceased do-gooder, Andre, discover a stack of horrendously slanderous letters about their father. A biographer will find and publicize them if they are not burned, though the damage to Andre's reputation will occur only after the offspring, and anyone else who would be upset, are dead. What's needed is for Stash to deposit the letters in the incinerator and for Burns to ignite it. Either action unilaterally will be a disaster leading to either discovery of the letters, or to an explosion, respectively. As it happens, neither person is going to do their part even if the other would.

No one is physically or mentally harmed by the inaction, and yet many will think it obvious, in some sense, what they ought to do, and that their allowing the ruin of Andre's legacy is wrong.

We might try to go further, to concoct an example in which there is intuitively a collective wrong, but in a way that is not owing to the agent-neutral value of the acts' (expected) consequences. I will not pursue this, and I am not sure it could be done. For one reason, some familiar moral theories in which there are consequence-independent wrongs tend to be Kantian in that the moral disvalue rests on deficiency in the agent's will. But if that is the only way to explain agent-relative (and in that way, consequence-independent) wrongs, they will be a bad fit for the idea of plural obligation, since there is, by assumption, no genuine agent who commits the wrong in question. But I will not pursue this.[13] I rest with the fact that the Whiff and Poof structure poses a puzzle not only for consequentialist theories, but for theories in which wrongness can turn on (perhaps among other things) consequences. And the puzzle's relevance is not limited to theories in which the consequences that matter are only effects on someone's physical or mental state (such as health, longevity, suffering, or other experience) as the case of ruined reputation illustrates. (They might yet be held to be facts about individuals' well-being, since some authors contend that a person's well-being can be affected even if the person is not alive, though others contest that.)

Even if the best or only illustrations turn on consequences, what they show is that individual rightness does not entail what we will confidently recognize as collective rightness. Of course, the central question about this is whether there is any such thing as collective rightness, and I will defend a mixed answer. For the moment, however, I'm focusing on the fact that in order to generate the puzzle with the Slice/Patch case it is not necessary to assume that what is right is wholly a function of the consequences. The question arises, then, what it might mean for that set of actions to be wrong even if none of the individual actions is wrong. That is not a question specifically for consequentialism, and can be pursued independently. It may be that writers like Regan would agree with this, as when he says that, "No doubt it is obvious in some sense what they should do."[14] That is, he might be taken to mean that this observation is obvious prior to any commitments to particular families of moral theory. It is clear, at least, that he means that it is obvious prior to any commitment to act-utilitarianism, since his point is that that theory cannot account for this judgment. Still, he might have been assuming that what is right is, in some way, a function only of the consequences produced, which is not entirely pre-theoretic in the way we are wondering about. The same goes for Jackson, and Parfit, who also acknowledge pressure to explain how the collection of actions is, as they seem to think it plausibly is, morally wrong: that conviction, though, might be owing to their broad sympathy with consequentialist moral theory. As I say, my concern is not with consequentialist theory in particular and I do not presuppose that it is correct.

3. Qualifications about What the Agent Knows

I want to put aside two complicating issues about what the agent knows or believes about the case. First, if Slice does not perform the surgery she shows something morally bad about herself unless she had sufficient uncertainty that Patch would be there. There is controversy about whether the right thing (in at least one sense of "right") for an agent to do depends on what she believes.[15] It might be that it does not so depend, that what she ought to do depends on what is actually the case, something a properly motivated agent will hope to get reliable beliefs about. Or it might be that it does depend on her beliefs or evidence: that the right action is for Slice to cut so long as she (reasonably, or whatever) believes Patch will be there. I want to explain how I will avoid this issue, since it is not germane. In the examples I present, I will not normally mention what the agent knows or believes about the facts, and I will proceed as if the obligations depend on the facts themselves. Readers who doubt this, though, can easily modify the examples in the following way: assume that the agent in question has the beliefs or evidence that would generate the same obligation that I am considering. So, when I proceed as though Slice is not obligated because Patch will not be there, it is fine to substitute the point that Slice is not obligated because she reasonably believes Patch will not be there. The point of the example survives in the following formulation: suppose that each doctor reasonably and truly believes that the other will not be there to help the patient. Then neither commits any wrongful act or omission, even as the patient is left on the table needlessly to die. It is puzzling if we think, intuitively, that there is some moral violation here, since it is not clear that there is an agent who has violated any obligation.

A second complication about the agent's knowledge concerns its connection to the agent's abilities. I will assume for present purposes, as I have throughout the book, that an agent is not required to do anything that is beyond her ability. And sometimes an agent's ignorance is part of what puts certain actions beyond her abilities. This emerges clearly on the conception of ability that I considered in chapter 6: "Mitigating Motives." Roughly, you are able to do something when trying would tend to succeed. If I do not know and am unable to find out the combination to a lock, then I am unable to open it. The ignorance alone is not ability-blocking, since if I know that the combination is written on the back of the lock, or if other basic efforts to discover it would tend to succeed, then opening the lock is not beyond my ability. Here is how I can open the lock: first, find out the combination, then dial it in. But if the combination is not something I could (tend to) discover by trying, then opening the lock is also something I cannot (tend to) achieve by trying, and so it is beyond my ability (to that degree). Or at least that would be supported by that particular conditional analysis of ability (to which I do not need to commit myself).

In order to focus on a certain puzzle about obligation, I will try to put aside these questions about what the agent knows in the following way. I will limit myself to examples in which the relevant agents know (or could easily come to know if they tried) what they need to know in order to perform the action in question. So, for example, I assume that Slice knows or could know whatever she would need to know in order do the surgery, and Patch has the requisite knowledge to stitch.[16]

So, the puzzle again is this: If Slice is not required to cut, and Patch is not required to stitch, then how is there any moral violation when, as a result of their going golfing instead, the patient worsens and dies? The puzzle is that apparently neither of the individual agents has a requiring moral reason to act otherwise, despite the sense many will have that something has gone morally wrong. Here is a view that might be lying in the background of the intuitive reaction to the case:

Violations Are by Agents
If moral wrongness is present, then there was an obligation on some agent to act or omit other than as they did.

I will assume that a moral obligation is a species of practical reason. We could generate the puzzle in other ways. For example, we might leave reasons out and simply observe that there seems to be a moral violation in the case, even with no agent having an obligation, and that is puzzling. The formulation in terms of reasons is useful, though, since it identifies one basis that is often thought to explain why there are no moral obligations without a required agent: obligations must involve practical reasons, and there are no practical reasons without an agent whose reasons they are. In any case, this is how I will formulate the puzzle: If moral obligation is always reason-providing for some agent, then how can there be a moral violation when neither Slice nor Patch has reason to do their part?

Here is an inconsistent triad. Which proposition ought to be discarded?

a. *Violation:*
   It is morally wrong if the patient is left to die.
b. *Violations are by agents:*
   If something is a moral violation, then there was an obligation on some agent to act or omit other than as they did.
c. *No violating agent:*
   There is no agent in this case who is morally required to act (or omit) otherwise.

If we hold on to Violation, then we must believe either that moral obligations are not always normative for any agent, or that there is, in fact, an agent under an obligation. If there were a good general account of how to resolve this as a general matter, it would resolve that issue as it applies to the idea of Prime Justice. After critically surveying several attempts to resolve the puzzle, in the next chapter I will propose a conception of what I call "Plural Requirement," which is a hybrid between agential and non-agential kinds of moral standard. First, though, I will look closely at cases that tend to evoke the apparently moral reaction, and rebut some arguments that they can be accounted for in terms of violations of agential obligations.

4. The One-Person Case

Sometimes what an agent ought to do depends on what else that very agent will do (or so we are assuming, in actualist formulations as explained in chapter 8). Since this is structurally similar in a certain way to our puzzling multi-person case, we should look here for clues. Consider Doctor Divot.

Doctor Divot
He will golf at noon even if he has made the incision in the patient who needs surgery, and so he will not be stitching the wound. It is his job to do both, he could easily do the stitching, and nobody will if he does not. We can assume that he ought to cut and stitch. Given that he will not stitch, he is not required (and incidentally, probably not permitted) to cut. Also, as it happens, he will not cut, and given that this is so, it is not the case that he should stitch.[17]

The structure of the case is by now familiar from Professor Procrastinate, and the name is changed only to resonate with the more puzzling case of Doctors Slice and Patch. Divot is evidently quite right (at least permitted, but pretty clearly also required) not to cut given that he will not stitch, and he is also right not to stitch given that he has not cut.[18] So far, so good. Has Doctor Divot done anything wrong in this case? Yes, since he has violated his obligation to cut and stitch.

In the one-person case, our intuitive reaction that there is a moral violation is easily explained because there is a single agent of both of the prospective actions. In the case of Slice and Patch, there is no such single agent. Unlike the case of Dr. Divot, neither of them is required to cut and stitch, and so neither of them has violated such a (putative) conjunctive obligation. That was the obligation whose violation we could appeal to in order to point out what had gone morally wrong in Dr. Divot's case, but it is not available in the case of the two doctors. Even as the patient's condition worsens unto death for lack of the doctors' care, neither doctor acts wrongly. What, if anything, is the moral violation in these cases?

5. Group Agents?

Some groups might count as agents, and if that were true of the small group consisting of Slice and Patch, this would resolve the puzzle. It would be natural, as I have said, to think that something is not an agent unless it could have the mental states that are part of what it is to produce intentional action, including beliefs, desires, and intentions. Maybe Slice and Patch are a small group agent of this kind, a surgical team. Even if they are, the puzzle can still arise in cases where group agency is far less plausible. Consider a less coherent group:

The Stranded Ambulance
A group of adults is standing outside smoking, something that is not allowed inside the nearby bar where they have been hanging out. An ambulance with lights flashing rolls by, slips, and careens into the ditch. It would not be difficult to free the ambulance to continue on its way if the smokers would work together. As it happens each of them is a slacker— none would be moved to help even if some or all of the others were to be willing to work together. If any one person were to try alone, the risk of killing the driver as well as the patient would be high. The ambulance sits stranded as the coronary patient inside expires for lack of emergency room care. Suppose (in case it matters) that the smokers are each aware of all the facts I am describing.

In this case, in addition to generalizing the case beyond two acts to many acts, the individuals involved seem unlikely to meet whatever criteria would normally be imposed on some collection's counting as an agent. They are too ragtag for that. (If you disagree, adjust the example so as to remove satisfaction of the conditions of group agency that you accept.) It would not be enough to have an account of a group action. There are several notions of that kind that

have use in certain contexts,[19] but what is needed to support a group requirement is for a group to have what it takes to be subject to a requirement even
when it is not acting. We could allow that whenever a group is acting in any of
several senses, then it is, in an associated sense, an agent. This adds nothing
but a network of terminology. However, we are trying to capture cases where
a group is under a requirement to act even if they don't act, which requires
what we might call latent agency. The group of smokers is not performing any
group act, so that is no route to showing they are an agent in any case. If that
group of smokers 'ought to have helped' then we must confront the inconsistent triad.

Frank Jackson handles cases like this by allowing any collection of actions
to count as an action.[20] Then, the compound action might be wrong whether
or not any of the ingredient actions are wrong. For example, he defends the
principle that an act's rightness or wrongness depends on the difference that
it would make. Neither doctor's inaction makes any bad difference, so each
individual omission is not wrong. But Slice's and Patch's joint inaction makes
the momentous difference that the patient dies, so the compound (in-)action
is wrong.

Jackson seems to avoid the inconsistent triad presented earlier by denying
the third element, the proposition that there is no violating agent in such a
case. He does not directly say whether the set of agents associated with any
random set of acts is an agent, although he clearly says that there is an action
by the set of agents.[21] In any case, I think we can insist that where there is an
action there is an actor, an agent of that action. It would be the pair of doctors
on Jackson's kind of view. I believe that this view runs afoul of the attractive
principle that,

No Agent without Subjective Reasons
Nothing is the agent of a given action unless it has the capacity to represent both options and their value in ways that systematically (whether or
not perfectly) cause behavior promoting or in accord with value as
represented.

First, keep in mind that if it is easier than this for a group to count as an agent
then there may be no culprit problem, which would only make things philosophically easier for my view that there is a broadly moral violation in such
cases. But the view would be fragile insofar as it is thought plausible that
groups are not agents unless they have what it takes to have subjective reasons.
So, I propose to grant this for the sake of argument and develop an account of
broadly moral requirements that can apply to groups even if they are not
agents.

Now, if the only groups that are subject to requirements of social justice are
the ones that are genuine agents in their own right, then the normativity of
requirements of justice could, without philosophical complication, be what I

have called deontic moral requirements: requirements of a certain agent that the agent do a certain thing. There would be no need for the difficult idea of plural requirement. However, it is at least difficult to confidently insist that this is so. To see this, consider how the question takes shape in the account of group agency developed by List and Pettit.[22] They argue for a number of ways in which not just any set of agents, or even a group (an entity whose identity can survive changes in the individual membership), counts as an agent. Nothing is an agent, on their view, unless it has motivational states, representational states, and ways of intervening in the environment in pursuit of its motives given its representations.[23] They argue at great length that some groups can meet these conditions, though that requires, among other things, a highly constrained and modally robust relation between group outputs and the attitudes of individual members (closely akin to Arrow's conditions on a "social welfare function" adjusted in ways that avoid the alleged impossibility; see chapter 2). Whether this latter claim, that some groups can meet the three basic desiderata of agents, is correct or not, it is obvious that very many do not.

So far then, the class of moral requirements I am calling "deontic" will fail to apply to a lot of groups because they are not agents in the right way. This would not yet establish a further claim I wish to make, namely, that some groups are subject to standards of social justice even if they are not agents. To see the general plausibility of this, it is important to see that their further conditions for a group to be an agent are saliently similar to, even if not fully as strong as, conditions on a group's being roughly democratic or at least responsive equally to every member's relevant attitudes (as their quasi-Arrovian account shows). Even if their account is subject to difficulties, the broader idea is plausible, namely that a group is not an agent if its outputs are not determined in certain systematic ways by aggregating certain preferences, judgments, or choices of the group's members. But then it is hard to deny that many societies that fail to meet that very general idea of responsiveness might (for that and/or for other reasons) be unjust. A good illustration is a dictatorship—a society in which the group's relevant outputs are determined largely or wholly by the attitudes of a single person. List and Pettit deny that this is a group agent[24] rather than a certain setting for the dictator's agency, and yet we should continue to think that a dictatorship is (or at least can be) an unjust society. Surely we want to criticize not only the person in charge, but the basic social structure itself, as unjust. If so, a society can be subject to moral requirements of social justice even if it is not an agent. As I say, this result is not tied to List and Pettit's specific account. The general idea is that social structural injustice can be present even in societies that lack the features necessary for them counting as agents.

Suppose that the advocate of "easy agents" were to adjust and insist that while it may be that the group is not an agent, and that there is no action without agency, nevertheless, in these cases there is the agency, one by one, of the set of individuals. They are clearly agents, after all. It is not nearly so obvious, he might continue, that there is no action without a *single unified* agent of that action. I think this leaves considerable strain. It introduces a moral requirement that does not require anything of any agent at all, and so an unfamiliar kind of requirement that would need more explanation (as I will provide for Plural Requirement).

Suppose we object, next, that a requirement is, among other things, an objective (or evidence-independent) reason. Parfit employs a distinction between subjective and objective rightness in a way that might allow the following reply: whether the agent acts as it has reason to do is the question of subjective rightness: it has (let's say) reason to act in light of what it would be reasonable to believe about the morally relevant facts. Objective rightness, which is what one ought to do were one's morally relevant beliefs to be true, is not itself reason-giving.[25] So, the fact that there is no agent with a reason in these cases does not show that there is nevertheless no objective moral requirement, a requirement which is violated if the set of required actions is not performed.

I think this does not avoid the problem. Suppose we allow, in that spirit, that to say that something is objectively required is to say that there is someone for whom the objective requirement is a requirement—an agent such that they *would have reason* to do it were they to reasonably believe the relevant facts. Call such an agent a "reason receiver." Grant that there might be such a reason receiver even if there is not, given her actual beliefs, a reason. The problem in our plural cases is not only that there is no agent with a requirement-given reason, but also that there is no agent in this position—no reason receiver. I think this insistence on a reason receiver as a necessary condition for objective requirements is attractive, and would defeat the Jackson/Parfit gambit. I am not confidently declaring against them on this basis, only pointing out how surprising it would be if they were correct: any old set of agents would count as an agent, at least any that might figure in cases like our examples. This entails either that there can be an action without any individual or collective agent who performs it (very surprising), or that a random collection of agents is always a thing with the capacity to have reasons (very surprising), or that a thing can be an agent of a given action even without any such capacity (very surprising). My objection is not, of course, to the claim that there is a morally significant sense in which the set of agents ought to do a set of actions. I will develop such an idea in the next chapter. What I have been arguing here is that there is nothing fitting the description of an agent and so any sense in which they ought to do it must be very different from even the objective ought familiar in moral obligation. Jackson and Parfit have not said enough to support the suggestion that there is a morally significant requirement of any such kind.

It might seem that these are the options in response to cases like Slice and Patch:

Deny that there is wrong (perhaps wrong to the patient) in those cases, thereby abandoning the initial appearance, or,

Accept that there is wrong done, supporting this by stipulating or arguing that the relevant collectives are moral agents after all, apparently lowering the bar for something to count as a moral agent.

Recall some terminology: agential requirement comprises evaluations of an agent's motives, or of her actions, the latter being what I shall call "deontic." The account I will propose in the next chapter explains how to save some of the apparent moral significance of such cases, partly by incorporating (a) a tight connection to agential, and indeed deontic requirement, and (b) an analogous principle to 'ought implies can,' increasing the resemblance to deontic requirement. Plural Requirement steers between the Jackson/Parfit easy agents (as I will call that strategy) on one hand, and a merely evaluative, but non-agential and non-deontic notion of what the group "should" do, on the other.

Note that I am making trouble for myself in doubting that their accounts are adequate. If they were found acceptable—if the reader rejects my objections or accepts any similar account to theirs—then that would suffice for my purposes in understanding Prime Justice as moral. Here again, I suppose for the sake of argument that they are wrong, and could happily proceed without these complications if they are right.

Edmundson, who is one of those who thinks that states are agents, argues that states can have obligations that "distribute" to members in the form of unconditional obligations to do one's share of what is required of the collectivity. This is most plausible in "incremental" examples notably unlike Slice/Patch cases, in which each person's doing her part adds value in the direction of the value of the discharge of the collective's full obligation.[26] His argument is suggestive even if it remains unclear what is thereby required of members. (For example, what value is each to promote, and how does the expected value of their alternative actions figure into how much they owe?) In incremental examples where each individual has an unconditional obligation to do her share, we don't have the same puzzle about how there could be an unconditional requirement without an agent who is thereby required. There is the possibility in which these individual requirements stem from a requirement at the collective level. That bypasses the puzzle of requirements without agents if the collective is an agent. But there remains the conceivable case in which owing to a requirement at the collective but *non-agential* level there are unconditional requirements on members to do their share. This should not be described as "distributing" to the members, since the requirement on the collective is, we have stipulated, non-agential, whereas the ostensibly quite different kind of requirement, viz., agential, is what attaches to the members. As I define "plural requirement" this case would not be an instance of it, because it is defined in terms of conditional obligations, not the unconditional ones in question here. So, is there a counterpart to or variant of plural requirement (for incremental examples) defined in terms of the unconditional agential requirements of members? This bears more thought but it might be unnecessary to posit any requirement at the collective level here except as a summary of the individual requirements. Edmundson argues that there are cases in which there would not be the individual obligations if it were not for the apparently morally prior or explanatory obligation at the collective level, which he believes is fully agential. If such cases are plausible even for collectives that are not agents, it is not clear what is wrong with holding that the requirement that first appears to us as if it is collective is just the sum of the members' individual unconditional requirements, though this bears more thought. In any case, for present purposes, it is not obvious that such cases involve any unconditional mode of requirement even without any unconditionally required agents, which is what Plural Requirement is intended to do.

6. Unilateral Compliance

Should each smoker have pushed on the ambulance, even though no one else would push? Some moral theories would be led in this direction, but this seems to count decisively against them. This would evidently imply that smoker A ought to approach the ambulance and push whether or not others will, and the same goes for B and everyone else. Leave aside difficult questions about what a given smoker is intending or trying to do, or about how hard he should push, or whether he should do something else like shout out the timing to coordinate the would-be pushers ("On three!"), even though there are no other pushers. Those problems aside, suppose that unilateral pushing risks tipping the ambulance over the edge of a cliff, while coordinated pushing would be entirely safe. Is each smoker wrong for having not unilaterally pushed, with no hope of success, and thereby risking killing the driver as well as the patient? More simply, consider the unilateral compliance view in the case of the doctors. This would apparently imply that Dr. Slice is required to cut into the patient, even though no one will be around to stitch up the wound, worsening the patient's painful death. A moral theory could hardly go more badly wrong than that.[27]

In a related suggestion, suppose we held, with Derek Parfit, that each of the doctors' (or smokers') omissions is itself wrong because each is a (relevant) part of a collection of acts or omissions that made things so much worse.[28] This would be a way of avoiding the conclusion that neither of the doctors is wrong. Frank Jackson, however, gives the following argument against that move of Parfit's.[29] Consider two people L and M who act in ways that together cause a patient's death. But suppose that if either of them had refrained, the other would still have acted, and the death would have been preceded by much worse pain. The patient dies if either or both of them acts, but the suffering is much worse if only one of them acts. Parfit's principle, saying that an act is wrong if it is part of a collection that together make things worse than otherwise, makes L's action wrong, even though, given that M was going to act, L's action only makes things better. L ought to act in such conditions. And, of course, the same holds for M's action. Given that L was going to act anyway, M ought to act and make things better than they otherwise will be. Switching acts for omissions, this is just like the doctor case. Parfit's principle would count each doctor's inaction is wrong, but surely, given that the other doctor will be golfing, inaction is morally right. So the principle apparently gives the wrong answer.

7. Prospective Agency?

Here is an alternative way to try to account for the intuitive sense that something goes morally wrong as the patient is left to die: there is some temptation to count any such group, however ragtag, as a collective agent just so that the normative obligation has a place to land. This approach—call this "prospective agency"—seems to me quite close to the "easy agents" approach with the explicit addition of the claim that no independent basis is needed for regarding the set as an agent. A moral obligation might befall this group and *thereby* change its status into that of a prospective group agent who could and should free the ambulance. If groups become agents or prospective agents in this way, with obligations attaching to the group agent as such, then the normativity gap would be closed in those cases. However, this seems *ad hoc* if there is nothing else sufficiently agential about them such as attitudes that are patterned or causally or semantically interlocking in certain ways (again leaving open just what it takes to be a group agent). If the only basis for attributing agency to the group is that there seems to be a moral obligation present, then inventing prospective agency seems to be no more than rejecting the principle that moral requirements must always be requiring for some (real) agent. In the end, I do recommend rejecting that principle, but the point here is that this is different from a plausible account of how a group is an agent.

8. Nonmoral Disvalue

We could retreat and say there is disvalue here but not of a moral kind after all. We avoid the inconsistent triad by rejecting (1), the claim that there is a moral violation in this case. But this route is not free of difficulties either. It is fine to say that even though there is important "disvalue" in the ambulance case, not all disvalue is moral disvalue. That is surely correct. There is aesthetic value, epistemic value, instrumental value, prudential value, and so on. This proposal to explain the cases in terms of nonmoral value is only plausible, though, if we have some reasonably clear understanding of the kind of disvalue that is supposed to be present. The proposal grants that it would be good if the smokers pushed the ambulance out, and bad if they did not. But compare the smokers case to another that is just like it, except that no one is around to help. The ambulance gets stuck and the patient dies. That is bad in the most obvious way. But does that exhaust the badness we are after in our feeling that in the smokers case it is bad if they do not help? It is not just the patient's dying that we think is bad, I submit. We think there is an additional bad (so to speak) in the fact that the smokers did not help. What kind of bad is that? It's not aesthetic. It's not prudential for any agent I can see. It's not epistemic, logical, or instrumental. If there is this bad in the fact that the smokers do not help—a bad additional to the patient's dying, and additional to the smokers' morally bad dispositions (which are present whether they are at the bar or not)—it might best be reckoned a *moral* bad. If not, *what is bad about the smokers not helping*—what kind of disvalue is that? Of course, this is our puzzle: In what way is this a moral bad, a wrong of some kind, even if no agent involved does anything wrong?

9. Subtle Wrongs?

We should consider several ways of trying to find individual moral violations in the examples of the doctors and the smokers. Consider some proposals that grant for the sake of argument that Slice is not required to cut, Patch is not required to stitch, and none of the smokers is required to push on the ambulance. What other obligations might there be that they are violating?

Maybe each individual is wrong not to have signaled a willingness to help. If there is some chance that others could be enlisted by signaling a willingness to help conditional on others helping, then maybe doing so is required. Is there a moral violation of that kind in these cases? It depends on how the cases are specified, which is as much as to say that this is no general solution to the puzzle. Suppose that no such signaling will have any effect on the others because they are not willing to do their part. In that case, it is hard to see what obligation there could be to signal.

Even so, if signaling is easy and risk-free then some might wonder what could justify refraining from signaling. This would be especially tempting for someone who thinks the individual's obligations depend on what she reasonably believes about what the others will do, and not solely on what they actually will do. But even then, this is no general solution since the case might be such that any signaling at all would be dangerous, and far from worth it unless it would (or were reasonably expected to) meet with success. For example, suppose any noise would risk bringing down a bridge hovering over the scene (and knowing this they've been quiet until now). Similar stipulations could be substituted to introduce risk for any action, even silent ones, that might be used for signaling. In those possible cases, signaling is not required (and not permitted), and it remains unclear who has done anything wrong.

The same difficulty attaches to any suggestion that some individuals should have taken any action at all, such as trying to push the ambulance, or trying to organize the others, or to form the individuals into a collective agent.[30] We can easily stipulate conditions where these should *not* be done given that the others are (reasonably believed to be) utterly unwilling to help even if others would. Each of them is unwilling to take up the example or invitation of others, and so each is also not required (nor permitted) to dangerously and quixotically try to produce such an example or invitation. And, of course, it is easy to set up the case so that none of the individuals is able to collectivize or organize the others (as distinct from signaling such a plan).

10. Bad People

One point to look more closely at, of course, is that the doctors, or the smokers, might be *bad people* if they are intentionally disposed not to join with the relevant others to help, and that might account for some of our moral disapproval. This does not locate any wrongful act or omission. It is plain from the start that the doctors are morally deficient in their callous motives, as we have said. There is a puzzle about the case only if it is initially tempting to think the patient is somehow wronged, which would be different. We are asking specifically whether there is any action whose performance or omission is wrong in the described conditions. No morally bad character or motivational state would, by itself, count. Nevertheless, the appeal to character or motivations might still be relevant in another way. Suppose that in noticing some bad character or standing motivations of the agents, this accounts fully for the intuition that there is something or other morally bad in the case. If so, the puzzle dissolves. Even if no agent has acted wrongly, some or all are morally bad in certain ways.[31]

On this view, the patient dies as a result of the bad dispositions of some bad people, though none of them was required to act any differently. For any one of them their having good dispositions or intentions would not have made any difference to the patient's fate. Their being bad at heart, and this having bad consequences, just seems to be a different feature of the case from the wrongness (if any) of not saving the patient. To see this, suppose I write a novel modeled on my two neighbors. They are bad people. If they had been good people my novel would have been a masterpiece that inspired some readers to forgo suicide and make good lives, but as things are those people die. They die as a result of my neighbors' morally bad characters, but this does not make the deaths of my suicidal readers a wrong of any kind, whereas we are trying to account for the sense that the death of the patient of Slice and Patch is a wrong of some kind.

The cases of the doctors and the smokers seem intuitively (I am assuming) to present us with a wrong that happens at a certain time, roughly *at noon*, as the patient's care is neglected. Even if there were such preexisting conditions as morally bad traits and dispositions in either or both doctors, the times during which those dispositions exist include many times other than the times at which the patient needed care. Maybe Patch is a selfish jerk, but if this is a part of his character he did not become a selfish jerk just as the surgery appointment (and his tee time) approached. So, on that proposal about character or dispositions, nothing went particularly wrong at noon. That does not capture the reaction that the patient is wronged by what happens at noon.

It remains for this dispositional approach to contend that the patient is wronged at noon by the admittedly preexisting immoral dispositions of the smokers or doctors. This would involve rejecting the principle that when someone is wronged, some agent was required to act or omit differently. As a substitute, it might be held that some agent was required to *be different*. I return to each of those possibilities below.

In a more complex proposal, we might say that each smoker has an obligation to form a conditional intention in this emergency.[32] They ought (unconditionally) to intend to ⟨help if there would be a helpful cooperative effort⟩. Granted, we do not need to see this only as a standing issue about their character or dispositions. At the moment help is needed, it could be that they have this obligation, and if they fail something goes morally wrong at that moment. The thought behind this is that our intuition that something goes wrong could be explained as our disapproval of the individuals' failure to form or have these intentions. Unlike actually acting to help, which would be pointless for any agent given that others will not cooperate, the conditional intention may be required whether or not it will be reciprocated. Each individual is to blame for their morally poor intentions at that crucial moment.

This suggestion falls in between the two suggestions that we found to fail. It is a bit like objectionable moral character, with the difference that it is meant to be a dateable failure that occurs at noon, the moment the patient is denied vital help. That would avoid the objection that the bad character predates the emergency and so cannot account for the idea that something morally goes wrong in the moment. In focusing on intention in the moment of need it is a bit like the suggestion that each individual ought to have acted, with the difference that the moral value of the intention, unlike action, may not depend on what others will actually do or intend.

In the end, the conditional intention proposal does not seem to avoid the dilemma. We could, somewhat arbitrarily, have tweaked the character point to say that each moment the person fails to have good character is a new moral wrong by the individual. But that is not satisfying, since it puts no importance at all on the appearance of the ambulance. It is not clear why the conditional intention is any different. Intention may strike us as more act-like, but this is not helpful since action by any of the agents would be pointless (and worse) given that there would be no cooperation in any case. What special value would there be in any of the individuals forming this virtuous conditional intention, beyond the value that such a motivational state would have possessed whether there were any patient in need or not? Call this,

> *The Missing Emergency Problem:* Since the moral deficiency of missing conditional motives could be present whether or not the patient needs, or is reasonably believed to need, the set of actions, it does not account for (by being meant to substitute for) the sense that some acts that were (or should have been believed to be) *needed* were not performed.

This point is actually independent of the preexisting condition problem: the possibility that the motivational defect might have occurred at a prior time, a possibility that really only makes vivid the missing emergency problem. Let the motivational defect be at the same time as the fatal neglect. Still, the kind of defect it is does not depend on whether there is anyone in need, so it is insufficient to explain the intuitive wrongfulness of the patient's death. For these reasons, I believe that the conditional intention approach fails to account for the intuitively wrongful death of the patient. The account I will offer in Part 4 of this book involves conditional intentions, but avoids the problem of the missing emergency, as I will explain there.

The puzzle of Slice and Patch is not to explain how something or other is morally amiss. It is stipulated in the example that they have morally deficient, callous motives. The puzzle is that while it may seem that something more is morally wrong than this, that turns out to be difficult to vindicate. What cannot be explained in that way is how the patient who dies at the hands of two such callous doctors is wronged. Recall, it might seem that these are the options in response to cases like Slice and Patch: deny that the patient is wronged at all in those cases, thereby abandoning the initial appearance; or, accept that there is wrong done by stipulating or arguing that the relevant collectives are moral agents after all, apparently lowering what might seem to have been the bar for something to count as a moral agent. The account I will propose explains how to save some of the apparent moral significance of such cases, along with (a) a tight connection to agential requirement, and (b) an analogous principle to 'ought implies can,' increasing the resemblance to agential requirement. It is a version of the deflationary position, since it is not agential requirement or wrong, but with less complete deflation.

11. Moral Luck?

We should consider the possibility that our intuitive disapproval in the puzzle cases is best explained as a case of moral luck—moral responsibility that derives from things that are out of the agent's control. The doctors are culpable, and so they wrong the patient, though not through any fault of their own. The very existence of moral luck is controversial. However, moral luck, even if you accept that there is such a thing, will not apply in a way that would explain our reaction to the puzzle cases. Consider several varieties of moral luck. First, circumstantial moral luck is where an agent did something wrong, but only because she landed, in a way that was out of her control, in circumstances that caused her to do so. Her doing wrong would, in a way, be outside of her control. In our examples, though, this does not apply, since we are stipulating for present purposes that no agent did anything wrong.

A more pertinent species of moral luck would be "resultant" moral luck:[33] a person is responsible for what happens, in a way that she does not control, as a *result* of what she does (or does not do). If two agents exercised the control they have in exactly the same way, one might unluckily cause harm that the other does not. Some believe this unluckily increases her culpability. There are two complications about applying this idea in our cases. First, causation is central here and it is controversial whether the nature of causation is such that any of our doctors or smokers causally contributed to the patient's death. It is a feature of the cases that given that the others are not prepared to help in any case, and given that the patient's survival requires combined efforts of multiple agents, no individual's omission makes any difference with respect to whether the patient would die as compared (counterfactually) with what would have happened had she acted. Some theorists, however, deny that causal contribution requires making that kind of counterfactual difference. Our cases are instances of individual omissions (not acts) which are evidently not wrong, and which make no relevant counterfactual difference. For the issue of resultant moral luck to arise here, it would have to be the case that omissions that make no counterfactual difference to some fact can nevertheless be causal contributions to that fact. Some theorists do, indeed, accept this.

Even if the omissions count as causal in the right way, however, a second and more serious obstacle to relying on resultant moral luck in these cases is that it is standardly invoked only as an amplifier when the agent has acted (or, possibly, omitted) wrongly. The question, normally, is whether she is subject to *more* blame if things happen to go especially badly after her wrongful act.[34] Resultant moral luck is not used to explain the presence of blameworthiness where, but for bad luck, there would otherwise have been none. It is used to explain the amplification of blameworthiness where there would have been some blameworthiness with or without the bad moral luck. Since the acts in our examples are not blameworthy at least if there is no bad luck, the standard notion of resultant moral luck has no application.

A third difficulty for the use of resultant moral luck in our cases is that it is not clear that our intuitive reaction really does depend on the lucky or unlucky results.[35] Suppose that the patient, against all odds, survives even though the doctors (or smokers) do nothing to help. It might still seem that the patient was wronged in some way, being left without help in conditions that would have led any responsible party to understand the risk of death. It may be natural to think that something has gone wrong at noon, even if there is no bad outcome for which responsibility is (somehow) to be ascribed. The puzzle of plural obligation is, roughly, that we have similar intuitive reactions as if the group of agents were itself an agent. If the assistance could be provided by a single person, and they did not provide it, we would harshly judge anyone who could have helped but did not, even if the patient happened to survive. Even in that case, however, we should not judge the person to have acted (omitted) wrongly. To see this, first note that the patient did not, as it turns out, actually need help. Rather, the patient only appeared to need help, and we judge harshly anyone who could have provided that (apparently needed) help but did not try. Nevertheless, it is not clear that anyone is wronged by the inaction. Suppose the ambulance case is varied so that the whole scenario is a ruse, with actors playing the roles of patient and driver. We harshly judge any individual who refuses to offer help if it appears to them that the person's survival depends on it. But in that case there is no victim, and arguably no one is wronged by the inaction. A decent person would have offered help, but that is compatible with saying that unbeknownst to the potential helper, no help was needed or morally required.

One lesson is that our judgment in these cases does not depend on how things actually go, and so it cannot be explained as a case of moral luck. A second lesson is that this judgment does not depend on anyone's being wronged. That is, if any of the agents believed or should have believed that the others would have helped, the fact that their belief that the patient needed help happened to be false would save them from actual wrongdoing, but not from culpability for their failure to do what appeared to be required. The bottom line is this: neither the idea of moral luck, nor the distinction between wrongdoing and culpability (blameworthiness) works in these cases to vindicate the judgment that any agent acted wrongly or culpably.

I hope to have shown that it is difficult to understand any way in which the patient's death that results from the doctors' refraining from necessary surgery is morally wrong. The case is structurally similar to examples of what we may regard as social injustice, where a bunch of people (think of the participants in my retrograde trial example at the start of the chapter) ought to do their parts, and yet given that others will not do theirs in any case, none is obviously wrong in refraining from doing her own part. In response, we might withdraw our initial thought that such cases are morally bad or wrong in any way, even if they are nonmorally unfortunate, as are epidemics and lethal hurricanes. In the next chapter, I resist such a complete demoralization of such cases, even though I see no prospect of fitting them under the category of agential moral wrongs. They are nevertheless morally significant in deeper ways than epidemics and hurricanes are. In that same non-agential way, then, social structural injustice may be a moral deficiency, not only an unfortunate condition in the way of natural disasters. The case for this is the business of the next chapter.

CHAPTER TWELVE

Plural Requirement

I mean not, . . . by any thing which I have here said, to throw any odious imputation upon the general character of the servants of the East India Company, and much less upon that of any particular persons. It is the system of government, the situation in which they are placed, that I mean to censure; not the character of those who have acted in it.

—ADAM SMITH, *WEALTH OF NATIONS*

1. Introduction

In the previous chapter, we saw the difficulty of understanding, in agential moral terms, the idea that a set of agents, where the set is not itself an agent, can possess, meet, and violate moral requirements. I argued that the idea itself, at least to many, feels like an integral part of the toolkit of moral reasoning. In that case we would like to find a tenable philosophical understanding. The puzzle arises very clearly, as well, for the account of justice as Prime Justice, as explained in chapter 10: "Prime Justice." In this chapter I propose a theory of Plural Requirement which allows us to vindicate much of its ordinary usage, but which does not count it as an instance of agential moral requirement. I will explain, however, that the links to the agential idea are significant nevertheless, in a way that allows us to understand the way in which Plural Requirement is, broadly, a moral idea. The remaining extent to which it is not a familiar agential form of moral requirement transfers to the idea of social justice as Prime Justice, which is a form of Plural Requirement. This implication is not a great cost of the approach, however, so long as it might have been plausible from the beginning that principles of social justice are not, or at least not obviously, action requirements on agents. What that leaves unclear is how social justice requirements are moral requirements at all (and if not, what kind of requirements are they?). Seeing how Plural Requirement is a broadly moral requirement will allow us to see how social justice requirements are broadly moral requirements as well.

Before introducing Plural Requirement, we should recall that there would be little need for it if all we needed to account for in cases of social injustice is the intuitive sense that the members of the relevant society have morally poor motives or intentions. That much is clear in the simple Slice and Patch case, but we see there that there is an additional moral salience to cases with that structure. Many, at first, believe that this extra salience is that the doctors did something wrong, thereby wronging the patient, though I have argued that this cannot be sustained. Nobody does anything wrong in the case suitably described. Shall we conclude that it was only a kind of illusion that there is a morally significant sense in which the patient not only dies, but is unjustly (shall we say?) left to die? Perhaps. But this is a larger retreat than is warranted, as I intend to show in this chapter. Putting the question in terms of our primary topic, social justice, we need only consider cases with a similar structure to that of Slice and Patch but where the individuals are members of a society and the actions in question concern, in the right way, harms or disadvantages to some that are results of the basic social structure—a structure of dispositions and behaviors. There could easily be cases of that kind wherein no one does anything wrong by refraining from doing their part, because doing so would have been pointless or worse given that others would not have done their part in any case. Yet, as a result, some are needlessly left with, for example, inferior chances for a good life. If the individuals lack the appropriate conditional cooperative intentions then this is probably a moral deficiency in them, but that is no more than a (partial) theory of good individual moral character or motives. Its judgment is notably independent of whether anyone's life prospects were actually harmed. This recapitulates my objection in the Slice/Patch setting to the alleged adequacy, by itself, of the conditional intention requirement—the problem of the missing emergency.

I do not propose to pull a rabbit out of a hat. What I will explain in this chapter is a common and distinctive structure of conditions which have a moral significance which, while not being an instance of agential moral requirement, are intimately tied analytically to certain such requirements. I then step back to note that, just as in a number of other cases many will hold that there is moral significance even if it is not agential, we have as much reason to say the same here. We do not, simply at will, christen these cases "morally significant," but bolster that judgment with the exhibition of the tight connections to agential, indeed deontic, moral requirement (and in this way the case for their being moral may be even stronger than the other examples I will mention). The idea of Plural Requirement is an account of one way in which there can be not only bad wills and bad outcomes, but social injustice, even where it is not an agential wrong. It is an account of one important form of *structural* injustice.[1]

It may seem that plural requirement is distant from ideas of what is right, since findings of injustice of this kind are not necessarily findings of moral failure of any agents at all. That is, not only is this species of wrongness not agential, it does not even imply any acts or attitudes by any agent that entail any criticism of any agent, not even those constituting the required plurality. That, however, is no additional burden for the idea of plural requirement. Even standard agential moral wrongness does not entail any blameworthy agents, since for a given wrong there might be a good excuse. That distinction between wrongness and blameworthiness is widely accepted, and Plural Requirement supports something analogous. As sketched in chapter 7, Plural Requirement explains how a basic social structure can be deficient in a broadly moral way, and how when it is it might be excusable, in a notable sense, not depending on whether it entails wrong actions or morally bad motivations on the part of the member individuals.

To begin, then, a Plural Requirement, as I will call it, ranges over a conjunction of two or more propositions stating that a certain agent does a certain act, as in:

It is a Plural Requirement that [S does x and T does y].

This is not an agential obligation, since it does not attach to any agent, and so is no agent's obligation or requirement.

We will continue to use the terms "requirement" and "obligation" advisedly, and not interchangeably. When I mean the non-obligation kind of requirement, I will capitalize, as in Plural Requirement, or Requirement. With that rule in place, it should be safe to continue to say that even agential obligations "require" (lowercase) things of agents. Plural Requirements require things of sets of agents in the way I will explain, but they do not obligate any agents, and their violation does not entail that any agent behaves wrongly.

I propose that to say that,

It is a Plural Requirement that (S does x, & T does y)

is to say that,

    i. If S does x, then T is obligated to do y, and,
    ii. If T does y, then S is obligated to do x, and,
    iii. It ought to be the case that (S does x, and T does y)

It is straightforward to formulate a structurally similar set of conditions for more than two agents.[2]

This is the conjunctive version of Plural Requirement, and we will encounter a disjunctive version below. The two conditionals alone would not capture the idea we are after, since they would be satisfied when neither x nor y are performed. (Recall my suggestion at the opening of the previous chapter that justice requires more than reciprocity.) We are trying to capture cases where there is an intuition that those acts ought to be performed. Thus, we add the third condition, (iii). The occurrence of 'ought' in that condition is neither agential obligation nor Plural Requirement, but merely evaluative. Notably, as discussed earlier,[3] it is in the mode that Sidgwick called "the political ought," an ought about how things ought to be, not about what anyone ought to do. There is really nothing political about the idea Sidgwick is identifying, and he might better have called it the ought of general desirability or goodness. Of course, the third condition alone would also not capture the idea we are after, which is something more than evaluation of a state of affairs as good. Only by adding the other two conditions is Plural Requirement tied to deontic obligation, though without being an instance of it.

We might formalize Plural Requirement statements as follows, letting ⊙ stand for "It is a Plural Requirement that . . ." and reserving "O" for deontic obligation:

⊙(Sx & Ty)

That is, it is a Plural Requirement that S does x and T does y. This does not entail that,

⊙(Sx) & ⊙(Ty)

because each of those conjuncts is undefined for that plural mode of requirement, neither being a conjunction of actions.[4] If S and T constituted a group agent, then there would be a question about whether a deontic ought that requires their two actions "distributes" to produce individual deontic requirements on each to do her part. But Plural Requirement is not deontic requirement, as we have seen. We could certainly ask whether Plural Requirement, as it were, decomposes into individual deontic obligations, but then the answer is clearly "no," this being the point of the design of our examples of Slice/Patch and the Stranded Ambulance. For these reasons, the debates about actualism and possibilism, discussed in chapter 3, do not arise.

As I have said, putting it now into this notation, in conditions (i) and (ii),

⊙(Sx & Ty) →
[(Sx → O(Ty)) & (Ty → O(Sx))]

That is, if it is a Plural Requirement that S does x & T does y, then if S does do x, then T is deontically required to do y. Also, if T does y, then S is obligated to do x. This uses a principle we might call "triggered distributivity," which can initially be defined for the case of deontic obligation, call it,

Individual Triggered Distributivity
O(A&B) & A→ O(B)

It says that if an agent is required to do two certain things, and the agent will do one of them, then it follows that the agent is required to do the other.

Whether or not this is valid as a general principle, it will be correct in a wide range of cases. When philosophers object to the Distributivity principle, which would allow us to move a requirement holding over a conjunction to a requirement over each conjunct (see above at p. 154ff.) the most common objection is that even if an agent ought to do both (such as Accept and Write), whether they ought to do either (Accept; Write) sometimes depends on whether they will do the other. (Whether Professor Procrastinate ought to Accept depends on whether he will Write.) This should be familiar from our earlier discussion. Triggered Distributivity steps back and says that, in any case, if the agent *will* do that other thing (Write), that particular worry about inferring a requirement over the first thing (Accept) lapses.

I do not assert the principle of individual Triggered Distributivity. Rather, I define Plural Requirement such that it is present only in cases where a plural version of Triggered Distributivity would be valid—that is, excluding any cases where, owing to some special circumstance, this inference rule would not be truth-preserving.

Plural Triggered Distributivity
$\odot$(Sx & Ty) & Sx → O(Ty)

This use of it mimics the deontic version syntactically with the only change being that the outside operator is "$\odot$" rather than "O". So, to conclude this explanation using the new terms, for it to be Plural Required that S does x and T does y is for a plural version of Triggered Distributivity to be true (which gives us (i) and (ii)). For reasons given above, we then add the third condition (iii) which is not at issue just here.

Now, moving on, in (i) and (ii) we see, as the consequents of those conditionals, "T is obligated to do y," and "S is obligated to do x." Notably, those embedded atomic deontic obligation statements will, if 'ought implies can,' entail, in turn, that,

(Sx → CAN(Ty)) & (Ty → CAN(Sx))

Pronounce "CAN(Ty)" as "T can (or is able to) do y." That is, if S does x then T is able to do y, and if T does y then S is able to do x. So, in that case those ability statements are implications of the initial Plural Requirement statement. This is a refinement of the "bridge principle" I asserted in chapter 7: "Justice Unbent."[5] That was stated on the preliminary supposition that there could be agential obligation over a society itself. Here I simply state the same bridge principle but for the case of what I have now defined as "Plural Requirement," which is not a case of agential obligation.[6]

What about defining Plural Requirement so as to hew closer to the moral by insisting that $\odot$(Sx & Ty) → CAN(Sx) & CAN(Ty)? This is going beyond noting the link between the deontic obligations (mentioned in the consequents of the conditionals) and ability. This would be stipulating a connection between

Plural Requirement itself and individual ability. Just like the agential 'Ought,' what we might call agential 'Can'—ability of an agent—is undefined over the whole plurality of agents and acts in such cases. Still, I leave undecided, for the moment, whether $\odot$(Sx & Ty) entails some sense of POSSIBLE(Sx & Ty). Now, as *against* the distributed Can, it seems too strong. All that is plausible is that each agent Can do their part given that all the others do their stated part (which they are not thereby required to do (at least) unless all the others do). Call this *reciprocal ability*.

What we do not yet have is a counterpart notion of ability that applies at the level of groups that are not themselves agents. For example, we could define plural ability of a group to mean just this: each of the conjunct actions in the scope of the ostensible Plural Requirement Can be done if all the others are done. Then Plural Requirement would entail a certain kind of plural ability. By involving a counterpart of the deontic 'ought implies can' principle, this would elegantly resemble agential moral obligation in yet another way. But whether that account can be maintained raises further issues, and having flagged this question I put it aside until I can consider it in detail later in the chapter. (See the section "Feasibility as Plural Ability" below.)

Plural Requirement, then, is a hybrid of non-agential evaluation, on the one hand, and agential obligation (embedded in conditional contexts) on the other hand. In addition to it engaging with agential obligation insofar as it implies those conditionals (i) and (ii) about obligation, it also has the following important tie to agential obligation (as follows quite obviously from the conditionals):

Satisfaction Triggers Obligation
Plural Requirement does not entail any agential obligations. But in the case where the Plural Requirement is met, each individual has and satisfies an agential, deontic obligation.

Plural Requirement, then, is built to a large extent out of conditions in which there would be deontic obligations. It is more closely related to deontic obligation than other forms of evaluation that assert only that certain things, or even actions, would be good in some way, resting with only a condition like (iii).[7] It involves a connection to agency that is left unexplained by accounts such as those of Jackson and Parfit in which sets of actions are treated, without further explanation, as morally and deontically required.[8]

Non-Deontic Moral Requirement

Perhaps the central question raised by this idea of Plural Requirement is the very idea of a moral ought or requirement of some kind even though it is not itself any agent's obligation. When violated there is a wrong without a culprit. This is, unfortunately, initially an obscure idea. We can bring it into better focus in several ways. First, consider some cases that strike most people as moral judgments, but which do not obligate any action. These apply to agents, but not to their actions—in our terminology they are agential but not deontic. While the nature of such an 'ought' is a difficult matter, we are familiar with apparently moral oughts of that kind, as seen in the following two cases:

Marcus ought to be more sympathetic.

This is intended, often, as a kind of moral judgment. Sometimes, of course, it means to claim that some actions are required, but the point here is that it needn't always mean that. Consider also,

Lori ought to have suffered for what she did.

Not everyone shares this kind of "retributive" intuition. But those who do are not directly addressing the question of any obligatory actions. The "requirement" might be satisfied if Lori's business fails, and so forth.

There are also a number of contexts in which the use of the idea of social justice seems to involve a non-agential, and yet evidently moral, notion of ought. For example, on some views, distributive patterns of social goods can be unjust whether or not there is anything anyone ought to do about it. The idea of Plural Requirement has an advantage over the already quite intuitive case of culprit-free wrongs by distributive injustice, when the question is whether it is really a moral kind of disvalue. Both distributive injustice and Plural Requirements countenance wrongs without culprits. Plural Requirements alone, though, maintain a connection between such wrongs and acts. In the case of Plural Requirement, there is a moral violation unless certain agents each, and all, do certain things. It is a species of violation that is constituted partly by certain actions or inactions, unlike the case of distributive injustice. It is conceptually more like—though it still does not consist of cases of—standard deontic wrongs in that way. I take this to bring it closer (in case this is necessary) to the standard moral case of wrongs by culprits. This point may not be necessary since, as I have suggested, wrongs by distributive injustice might plausibly be fully fledged moral wrongs with neither culprits nor any relevant acts or omissions. But it can't hurt.

In another case of evidently moral judgments that are not directly deontic obligations, there are familiar statements such as, "One of those two people ought to help," where this is meant not to ascribe an obligation to any particular person, but only to a disjunction of persons (so to speak). Here is its form:

It is (plural) required that (Sx OR Ty)

As some hold in the conjunction case, but more obviously here, we cannot distribute the requirement to each disjunct, and so no non-disjunctive ought statement is entailed—no deontic requirement follows. These cases seem to be closely related to my cases of Plural Requirement, yet different. What they have in common is that no agent is obligated by this "requirement," and yet something is said to go morally wrong if the enclosed disjunctive statement is not true—if the requirement is not met. Violation takes place without a culprit, just as with the conjunction case of Plural Requirement.

Since there is no deontic obligation involved, the deontic 'ought' is unavailable. Accordingly, I propose to add to the account of Plural Requirement a disjunctive variant, as follows:

Disjunctive Plural Requirement
To say that it is Plural Required that (Sx OR Ty) is to say that,
iv. ~Sx → O(Ty), and
v. ~Ty → O(Sx), and
vi. It ought to be the case that either (or both) Sx or Ty.[9]

Notice that without that third condition (vi), when each does the action neither of the conditionals brings agential requirement into play. Since we want it to be a requirement even in the case where both act, we need (vi). [10] However, (vi) alone would leave us without any analytical tie to agential moral requirement, and the broadly moral significance that lends.

Now it may appear that this is somehow committing us to the controversial rule of Factual Detachment discussed in chapter 8.[11] However, all that is being said is that there is a certain mode of (non-agential) requirement when and only when those three conditions are met. This claim is not vulnerable to claims such as that Plural Requirement holds in some cases where one or the other of those conditions is false. That is how Factual Detachment is attacked. By definition Plural Requirement does not hold in those cases. I am hereby giving the name Plural Requirement to all and only cases that meet certain conditions. We have two varieties: the conjunctive variety is where conditions (i)–(iii) are met, the disjunctive variety is where conditions (iv)–(vi) are met. I have formulated these for the case of two agents, but it is a trivial matter to restate the conditions for sets of any number of agents.

There is a notable symmetry here. Recall, that in the conjunctive case of Plural Requirement I remarked that there is a tantalizing analytical tie to agential deontic requirement in that when all of the agents in the plurality do their part, each is agentially required to do so in light of the others doing so. Here, in the disjunctive case there is kind of symmetrical connection to deontic requirement in that if neither acts, then both violate deontic agential moral requirements. But neither is under an unconditional agential moral requirement.

Compare the Plural Requirement approach to Jackson's easy-going approach to actions. As we have seen, Jackson lets any set of actions be an action. That way there can be a wrong action even though none of the individuals has done anything wrong, a feature shared with Plural Requirement. I have objected that this implausibly counts utterly disorganized sets of agents as group agents, and many sets of agents should not be so counted. The Plural Requirement approach does not count the set of actions as an action, and so it is under no pressure to treat the set of agents as an agent. So far, that is an advantage over Jackson's view. But of course, Plural Requirement involves wrongs without culprits, whereas Jackson's view cooks up culprits easily. For what it's worth, I believe that I could revise my own intuitive view of moral wrongness in order to make culprits unnecessary more easily than I could accept either that there are acts without agents, or that there are agents so randomly constituted. The main point is that either route is disruptive. It would also be disruptive, however, to accept that, as the smokers shuffle back into the bar, or as the doctors practice their golf swings on the first tee, and the patient is needlessly left to die, the only thing that goes wrong is that, as if it were of natural causes, someone dies.

2. Are Plural Requirements "Practical"?

As should be clear by now, there is an important respect in which Plural Requirements are not practical requirements: there is no agent who is thereby subject to any obligation. This is a difference from the individual case of conjunctive obligations. There, the conjunctive requirement is straightforwardly practical for the agent. Even there, it is not a requirement that addresses a different question: whether to do either one of the actions. It does not address that at all, and surely it is not "practical" with respect to questions to which it is not addressed. But it is practical on one thing: the agent ought to do all of the conjoined actions. In the Plural Requirement case there is no counterpart, because there is no agent subject to its requirements. We should not exaggerate this: it does say to a set of agents that a certain set of actions is required. Still, this is not, and will often not entail a requirement on any agent. There remains the set of conditional requirements that we surveyed: for example, if all but one of the actions will be performed by the others then that action is indeed obligatory. Also, as we have seen, it follows that if all of them will be done, then each of them is obligatory. This is all relevant to practice, of course. But there is no agent who is obligated *to do them*, and so there is no unconditional practical requirement on any agent owing to a Plural Requirement itself.

This way in which Plural Requirement, and so the requirements of justice, are not practical may cast doubt on whether understanding what they require would be of any value, and this brings us into engagement with the stark view I will call "practicalism," about normative moral and political philosophy:

Practicalism
There is little or no value in studying or learning about how things ought to be unless this has practical implications (and valuable ones).

If requirements of social justice are a form of Plural Requirement, and Plural Requirement does not have (unconditional) practical implications, practicalism denies that understanding justice would be of any value at all. To be clear, there is no dispute about whether there are plenty of requirements of a very practical sort regarding such things as building and complying with certain rules and norms for the basic structure of society. On my view, there will be plenty of concessive requirements: given that certain ingredients of justice are missing, certain agents will be obligated to do certain things. But the standard of justice does not address and may or may not contribute to answering these questions (for example, it is a fallacy of approximation to suppose that justice's ingredients ought to be produced piecemeal; see chapter 14: 'The Fallacy of Approximation'). The practicalist might very well wish to argue that justice itself is misconceived by me, and turns out to have unconditional practical implications. I have given arguments for conceiving of justice as "prime justice," according to which that is not so, but no doubt more would be needed to foreclose those criticisms. What must be avoided, though, is the lazy identification of full justice with some relatively relaxed standard simply in order to get it to have practical implications of this kind. At least, before doing so we should contend with the arguments presented earlier that such bent standards will often be patently concessive to injustice.

3. The Case of Good Motives

Here is an important variant of the case of Slice and Patch. It meets the criteria for violations of Plural Requirement, even though in this case no agent even has any morally bad motives.

> *Good Motives Slice and Patch*
> Suppose Slice and Patch *are* each disposed to do their part if and only if the other will (and owing to the fact of the first agent's acting).[12] That seems to be the morally right disposition, and yet if neither acts, each abides by that good motive by not acting.

Why might they not act? The explanation might be that each, or either, believes that even if she acted, the other would *not* act. That might take different forms. (i) Either might falsely, but rationally, believe that the other is not disposed to cooperate. Alternatively, (ii) even if either does correctly believe that the other is cooperatively disposed, each might think truly or falsely that the fact that she will herself act would, blamelessly, not be known to, or believed by, the other. In either of those blameless cases, neither of these well-intentioned agents would act. And, each will have done the morally right thing, not just relative to her beliefs but relative to the genuine fact that the other does not, for one of the above reasons, act.

This case is important for the following reasons. The original version involving bad motives evokes intuitive moral disapproval in many people, but then it is difficult to vindicate philosophically. Among the most tempting vindications are those that locate the moral wrongness in the morally deficient motives of the individuals, but this too proves difficult since (mainly) the opprobrium they warrant owes nothing to the needless death of the patient. The intuitive disapproval, however, at least for many people, targets the needless death, not (or not only) whatever bad motives and dispositions the actors brought with them to the scene. There is something additionally bad, and bad morally speaking, about the fact that in addition to already being morally deficient in their motives, these several agents did not act to save the patient's life at the crucial moment. However, we never did find any moral violation by any agent that might explain the wrong of letting the patient die. If we conclude that there is none, we might revise the initial intuition and decide that, once it is clarified, the case of Slice and Patch only gives the illusion that the death is an agential, if somehow collective, moral wrong. This much seems probably correct to me, and consistent with the idea of Plural Requirement. Some might be tempted to add the following, however, though in the end it seems to be a mistake: we might add that the only morally salient unfortunate facts in the case are the bad motives of the individual agents. I believe that the Plural Requirement structure can fairly be said to display a morally salient structural failure that is not captured by noting the poor motives alone. As I have emphasized, it is still not a case of the violation of any classic moral obligation. It lies in between: it is a morally salient failure in a way that *makes no reference to* the moral deficiency of the motives, though it does not rise to classic moral violation. The case of Good Motives Slice and Patch illustrates this. Having explained the ways in which Plural Requirement is a morally salient phenomenon, we see from this case that these are still present even when bad motives are not.

Is there really anything moral about the way in which the doctors with good motives unfortunately do not save the patient? Is it, perhaps, simply unfortunate in some wholly nonmoral way? But what way is that? In case the issue is clearer when the stakes are higher, consider the case of,

Mutual Assured Destruction
Whether the other party also does this or not, each of two hostile countries threaten massively deadly and wholly pointless destructive nuclear response to any nuclear attack from the other. It is not clear that either is morally required to withdraw this threat unilaterally if it seems necessary and effective in order to securely deter a first strike attack. Suppose, in addition, that one or both countries reasonably, but mistakenly believes that the other country may attack either unprovoked or under a blameless misunderstanding, unless there is this deterrent.

It would be natural to say that "they"—the countries—ought to stand down, though neither ought to stand down given that the other will not. This natural judgment seems to call for action—a set of certain actions by certain agents. It is not a judgment merely of either party's prudence, but rather it presumes, I believe, to be a moral judgment of some kind. Finding no way for it to be an agential requirement, Plural Requirement is offered here as a good fit.

We might regard this, and parallel good-motives examples of failures of prime justice, as *blameless* violations of the Plural Requirement, where the bad motives version similar to Slice and Patch is a blameworthy violation. It is not clear whether we ought to recognize an essentially plural form of blame, and I merely mean to identify the issue. The poor individual motives are morally criticizable, though it may not be the agent's fault that they are present. In that case, there is nothing yet to blame them individually for. Perhaps we can recognize a kind of attitude similar to blame toward the set of agents, though not toward anything that is an agent, in our common responses to cases such as the Smokers, or Mutual Assured Destruction.

There is also a blameworthy case worth noticing that is *not* a violation of Plural Requirement, as when the set of Smokers failed to respond, but the patient scenario was a ruse, as mentioned above in the section "Moral Luck?" in the previous chapter. Importantly, of course, in all these cases there is no wrong, no unmet obligation, by any agent. In both the bad-motives, and the good-motives cases, there is (whatever else is going on) an essentially collective, morally salient, bad situation. In the bad motives version, it is appropriate to morally judge the poor motives of the individuals, even though that preexisting motivational condition does not fully explain the moral significance of the event (at noon, for example). In the good motives version, there are neither poor motives nor wrong or blameworthy actions by any agent. There must be an epistemic lapse or misfortune of one of the two mentioned kinds, but even if that is not morally or epistemically culpable on the part of any agent it is a kind of defect of the collective situation. Its moral significance is indirect, namely in the three-part structure of Plural Requirement.[13]

The account of plural requirement is not meant to suggest that since there is a wrong of a plural kind each participant is responsible for the wrong in some way or to some degree. It takes no stand on individual responsibility, except to say that, by hypothesis, each of the component acts is not wrong. Indeed, in certain cases that are used to pose difficult questions about causation and responsibility, we can see the structure of plural requirement in play. An example is the "thirsty traveler," discussed by Hart and Honoré among others. The Traveler is killed by a combination of Enemy 1 filling his canteen with salt, and Enemy 2 stealing the canteen thinking it contains water. Neither act by itself is objectively wrong given what the other enemy will do, and yet it is tempting to think that the Traveler is nevertheless wrongly killed by the two enemies.[14]

4. Feasibility as Plural Ability

Now, suppose I have persuaded you that there is a morally salient form of moral standard that is essentially collective and non-agential, but analytically inseparable from the agential, and appropriate for reactive moral attitudes in ways that natural disasters are not. It is arguably still a stretch to call it 're-quirement.' The problem is not only that it is not directly agential. It also seems that common judgments of justice and injustice have a notable feature that is associated with requirements, namely conditionality on some kind of possibility. The familiar version is 'ought implies can.' We don't easily understand something as analogous to agential requirement or a moral 'ought' if it does not, so to speak, imply something analogous to 'can.' We can call this the *plural ought implies can question.* And our apparently plural-formed judgments about justice display this. If a certain society is such that there is not (and never was) any way for it to achieve certain structural conditions—if even effort and perseverance by all members would not succeed—then we may be inclined to deny that the absence of those conditions is any kind of injustice rather than merely simply a kind of misfortune that faces that society, in the manner of natural disasters. (Of course, not all agree with this, but it is unclear whether justice, for them, is any kind of requirement.[15]) Roughly, it's worth considering whether something parallel to 'ought implies can' (hereafter OIC) can be ascertained for the case of Plural Requirement.[16] A desideratum of such an account, I will suppose, is that the notion of non-agential requirement is connected in this way to some counterpart of the idea of ability. I will use the term "feasibility" to name this notion: a counterpart to agential ability, but applicable to sets of agents and acts which there is reason to think are, in some way, collectively required. This would imply, plausibly, that something is a requirement of social justice only if it is feasible.

I propose to understand *feasibility as plural ability,* which I now go on to explain. For clarity, I stipulate, as a terminological decision, that feasibility is not ability, the latter being applicable only to agents. There is normally no error in speaking of what is feasible for an agent as simply a syntactic variant of discussing what the agent can, or is able to do. On that way of seeing things, if a group were an agent, then there would not be any distinct question of feasibility for the group—the relevant notion would be ability, even if that would raise distinctive questions in the case of group agents. But I will use the notion of feasibility to mark the prospect of a non-equivalent counterpart, for non-agential groups, of the agential notion of ability: feasibility is to groups as ability is to agents. There is then a rationale for using the idea of feasibility rather than ability, namely, that there is a significant counterpart to ability, namely plural ability, whose interest arises from the idea of Plural Requirement. Ability applies to actions, but what is plural required is not actions but certain sets of ordered pairs of agents/actions, which is crucially different. Feasibility, on the usage I adopt, has a subject matter of its own. In the swelling recent literature about feasibility, there may be more than one thing getting discussed under that moniker, but there is no need here to take up what feasibility "really" is. It will be valuable if we can devise a reasonably clear and explicit formulation of the idea of feasibility for groups interpreted as "plural ability" of the constituting agents.

In Parts 1 and 2, I provisionally treated social justice as an agential obligation on societies, postponing (with warning) the questions that arise from their not (ever or often) being genuine agents. In that mode, I also talked at length about when certain motivational features of an agent are requirement-blocking. This will not have any application at the level of the society's motives, since it is often not the kind of thing that has motives of its own, or so I presuppose. So I proposed bridge principles from individual inability to group inability, and from individual requirement-blocks to group requirement-blocks. (See chapter 7: "Justice Unbent.") We should briefly look back at these in light of the kind of thing I now argue that requirements of social justice are: Plural Requirements. The general idea, so far, is this, giving us only a necessary condition:

> *Plural Requirement Entails Individual Ability*
> Since there is no Plural Requirement on a group of agents unless, (a) each of those agents is required to do her part of the ostensibly required set of actions if others will, it follows from 'ought implies can,' that, (b) each is able to do their part so long as others do theirs.

As we have just noted, individual motivational features will—in some cases, but not as often as many suppose—constitute individual inabilities or blocked requirements. So, in some cases individual motivational features can block Plural Requirements. This would establish an elegant parallel: just as agents sometimes have their abilities or requirements blocked by certain motivations they have, so too groups, even when they are not agents, sometimes have (the plural counterpart of) their abilities or requirements blocked by motivational features—this time not features of them as a group, which may not have motives of its own, but of their constituent members. The piece that is, so far, missing is an explicit account of ability for the case of a group of agents which is not itself an agent.

We know, then, that Plural Requirement is partly a set of *reciprocal agential requirements*: each agent in the set is morally required to do her part if the others do theirs. (For compactness, I will now often use the following abbreviations: Plural Requirement (PR), Plural Ability (PA), agential Reciprocal Requirement (RR), agential Reciprocal Ability (RA).) Those are, as I say, agential requirements, though in a conditional context, so from OIC there must be reciprocal agential abilities (RA) in those same contexts. But that's just individual ability, and so not a kind of ability that attaches to the set itself—and of course agential ability does not apply to the set. So far, this much is clear on this account:

Plural Requirement → Reciprocal Requirements → Reciprocal Abilities

One question is whether there is an idea of group ability that has some special connection to abilities of the group's members. Call this the *feasibility/ability question*. We might think that just as PR will have these implications for RR at the individual level, PA has implications for RA. But this seems not to be so. A set of agents can apparently be able to do something even if there is little or no ability of any agent to do her part. That is, there are cases where there can be, intuitively, plural ability even without individual reciprocal abilities, so it is not clear that PA → RA. Here is an example:

Mastodon Hunt
A certain large group of agents might set out to kill a mastodon by each trying to do their part, namely hitting it with a spear. But even if no individual has a significant chance of striking the animal, it may be that enough individuals will tend (each improbably) to succeed that the group reliably fells the hunted beast.

We do not have an analysis of PA yet, but this looks like a case where we should believe it is present. Each of the individuals is unable to spear mastodons, despite some lucky shots. Still, since it only requires a few hits, the large group tends to succeed.

While it is notable that PA does not seem to imply RA, there is no obvious problem here, and so far this is all consistent: suppose some plurality is required to fell the mastodon only if the plurality is able to do so: PR → PA. (PA is used intuitively here, to be explained presently.) This implies that the individuals are, in the standard agential deontic way, reciprocally required and so reciprocally able, as we have seen. That's compatible with there being some cases where the plurality is able but individuals are not. If the individuals are not reciprocally able, then the plurality is, while able, *not* required. So the mastodon case can be a case of plural ability without reciprocal ability, but it is incompatible with plural or reciprocal requirement. Dropping the abbreviations for a moment, the link between Plural Requirement and Reciprocal Requirement means that some things for which there is Plural Ability may not meet Reciprocal Ability, and so could not be Reciprocally Required, nor therefore Plural Required.

However, if we cannot understand PA in terms of individual RA, then we need some alternative way of understanding PA. We saw that PA is apparently not a certain configuration of RA. However, even if it were, that relationship would not have exhibited any *similarity* between ability at the plural level and ability at the individual level. It would be all about ability at the individual level. To exhibit such a similarity or isomorphism I will take for granted that individual ability is well-understood by what is often called a "conditional analysis." There are objections to that approach to ability, but I will pass over them here. To have a conception of agential ability to work with, I will assume that, as discussed in chapter 5,

Conditional Analysis of Ability
Agent S is able to φ if and only if were S to try, S would (tend to) φ.

I want to explain how, supposing that is the idea of agential ability, there is a structurally similar conditional analysis of feasibility—the essentially plural and non-agential analogue of ability.[17] I propose to understand PA in a way that is closely parallel to that influential way of understanding individual ability, even though it must be a non-agential variant, like this:

Conditional Analysis of Plural Ability
A set of agents is PA to φ if that set would tend to succeed conditional on plural trying.

In considering a conditional account of plural ability similar to such an account of individual ability, I am again considering it as something that might be granted for the sake of argument to those who might wish, on the basis of claimed plural inability, to block certain ostensible Plural Requirements. However, it is also true that some adequate conception of plural ability would help in assimilating Plural Requirement, still incompletely, to the realm of moral requirement, and so I do pursue the conditional analysis approach in a sympathetic way, as one way in which this might be done.

This can only work if there is some definite meaning for "trying" in the antecedent of the conditional. This is initially problematic since we need the idea of Plural Requirement to apply to sets of agents that are not themselves agents, and so are not the kinds of things that act or try to act in the familiar agential way.

I will suggest that something can be found to do the trick for groups, a plural counterpart to agential trying that allows us a sensible interpretation of the dependence of PR on an understandable kind of PA. Notice that if that could not be done, then either (a) some other account of plural ability must be found, or, (b) without a notion of group ability/feasibility at all, Plural Requirement will not fit into any counterpart of OIC, increasing the conceptual distance between Plural Requirement and agential obligation. Recall that this is not a special problem for PR, but is arising as an effort to understand how, putting it very generally, social injustice is a wrong and not a natural disaster. That is not an idiosyncratic issue.

Recall, the conditional account understands individual ability as consisting in a tendency to succeed conditional on trying or setting out to do the thing. In parallel fashion, I propose the following account of such an antecedent at the plural level:

Plural Trying (or Setting Out)
For some φ that is plural required, *a group sets out (or initially tries) to* φ,
if and only if each (or enough) of the agents sets out to do her conditionally required part.

Plural trying plays the structurally identical role in a conditional analysis of
Plural Ability as trying does in agential ability:

Plural Ability
For some φ that is plural required, a group is plural able to φ if and only if
it is disposed such that IF it plural-sets-out to φ it tends to succeed (i.e.,
to φ).

Some will worry that this approach counts a group as being plural-able
even if it has no way of bringing it about that every agent sets out to do her
part, which might seem implausible.[18] This worry is also roughly parallel to
the 'can't try' concern about conditional analyses of individual ability (see
chapter 6: "Mitigating Motives"). That is, understanding ability as (roughly) a
tendency to succeed conditional on trying seems to count some agents as able
to do certain things even if they are (as the objection puts it) unable to try. Just
as something might virtually ensure that some individual will not 'set out to φ,'
something might guarantee, or at least probabilize, that not all members will
set out to do their parts. But the reply here is the same as it was there: that is
not properly seen as a case of inability, because it does not point to anything
interrupting any volitional (or in this case plural-volitional, so to speak) process of the individual or group. It shows that the act in question *will not* be
done (because the agent or plurality will not even initially try or set out to do
it), but it does not show that the individual or group *cannot* do it. The question
is not whether they are able, all together, to *set out* to do their parts. That setting out (or initial volitional process) is not something about which we are
inquiring whether the agent is able to do it. This point is similar to the fact that
the question is not, in important individual questions about ability to φ,
whether the agent is *able to set out (or try)* to φ. In both cases, it is not even
clear that ability is well-defined over the relevant kind of 'setting out' itself, its
not being properly an action in its own right. In any case, the question is about
the ability to φ, where ability is understood as a disposition to succeed conditional on setting out to φ.

In the group case (as we saw earlier in chapter 5: "Utopophobia"), it is especially easy to switch illicitly to the question of an ability of some agent to *get*
all the members to set out to do their part. That would presumably be a genuine action, more clearly so than 'setting out' to act is. Whether some agent has
that 'getting' ability would be a separate question (presumably depending on
whether *she* is disposed to succeed should she set out to do it). But showing
that one agent cannot get others to do something does not show that those

others cannot do the thing. As noted earlier (see p. 125), a parent may be unable to get his son to be at school on time, even though the son can perfectly well do it but consistently dawdles or refuses. Likewise, an agency, or government, or institutional designer might be unable to get the members of a society all to set out to do their parts in some scheme, but that might be only because those members dawdle or refuse.

With this conditional account of plural ability provisionally in place, there is now no reason not to accept that Plural Requirement implies plural ability—the counterpart to OIC. That is, we can grant it at least for the sake of argument, setting up the possibility of refuting requirement by refuting ability. There is no Plural Requirement on a group where it is not plural able to meet it. So: if it is not true that were each member of the group (or enough) to set out to do her part in the supposed plural-requirement of, say, justice, the group would tend to succeed, then it is not a Plural Requirement of justice after all. And I have just argued that it is no objection to a group's having a plural ability to do something (such as something putatively plural-required by justice) that it will never set out to do it, nor is it an objection that no one is able to get all or enough individuals to do their parts. There might be Plural Requirements even in those cases, since the group might yet be plural-able to meet them, and this line of response parallels what we should say in the individual case.

Recall the issue from chapter 11 about whether sets of agents can, relatively "easily" simply be regarded as moral agents in their own right. I have proceeded as if that is not so. However, by introducing plural analogues of requirement, trying, and ability it might seem that we are really treating these sets of agents as agents in their own right after all, as entities that perform intentional actions of their own and which in many cases do so rightly or wrongly. This would not be damaging to the overall argument of the book if that were so. Indeed, it would simplify and streamline the account significantly. We would treat requirements of justice as deontic agential moral requirements of a standard kind, applying to certain genuine agents—those made up of sets of other agents. The idea of Prime Requirement would have no need for the complex idea of plural requirement or for arguments that it is, in certain ways, sufficiently tied to agential requirement to explain the common sense that it supports a broadly moral kind of evaluation and reaction.[19] While that would ease the burdens of the account, it cannot be embraced on that basis alone. It is a hard and long-standing philosophical problem whether and how any collective of agents might have what it takes to count as an agent in its own right. I need not take a stand on that, but I proceed on the assumption—I grant for the sake of argument—that it is far from clear that the pluralities of agents that concern us do have what it takes. I proceed to develop an account that would not be deterred if they do not.

5. Prime Justice and Plural Requirement

We can now bring together the ideas of Plural Requirement and Prime Justice, in order to make a few important observations. First, it is a simplification to say, simply, that social justice is an instance of Plural Requirement. Since Prime Justice is only a fragment of the Global Prime Requirement, then it is required only conditional on the satisfaction of the other fragments. However, in that case the kind of requirement it is will be Plural Requirement. So Plural Requirement figures in two places: first it is the kind of 'ought' that ranges over the whole (Global or Specific) prime requirement. Second, in the case where the other fragments are met an 'ought' attaches as a Plural Requirement to the social structure fragment itself. Also, of course, at the level of Prime Requirement and at the embedded level of Prime Justice there are the conditional, in particular reciprocal, requirements on genuine agents associated with each conjunct.

Second, we can see from this that Plural Requirement is germane in two places. One is in the mode of requirement I have called the Global Prime Requirement (GPR). To recall, that is a requirement saying how all agents together ought to act. An issue that arises concerns whether there is something incoherent in this. If the GPR ranges over societies and other non-agential groups as well as individuals (and perhaps also genuine group agents) then it is not addressed to a set of *agents*. It may seem that it purports to be an incoherent heterogeneous blend of agential and non-agential requirements. The worry is that neither an agential nor a non-agential plural 'ought' can serve univocally to cover both the agents and the non-agents in the scope of the supposed requirement.

This *equivocal ought* objection seems to evaporate when the analysis of PR is borne in mind. GPR will indeed be a PR applying to individuals, to any group agents, and to any groups subject to their own PR's. Since PR does not entail requirements on the members of the Plural-Required set, as I have explained, there is not directly a problem of its equivocally issuing agential requirements to some, and non-agential requirements on others. It does neither. However, it might appear that the problem emerges in the conditional requirements that constitute much of that Global plural requirement, namely that each entity *ought* to act in their specified way if the others do so. That idealized 'ought' still appears to be equivocal. As applied to agents it will be a conditional agential obligation; as applied to certain groups, such as societies, it will be a conditional non-agential, i.e., Plural Requirement. So far, that is correct, but it does not appear to be troubling for the following reason: when those embedded Plural Requirements, such as those on societies, are in turn analyzed in the way proposed here we see that they either resolve into conditional agential obligations, or they still include further embedded Plural Requirements which eventually do. This is not quite exact, since there is, both at the global and at the embedded group level, the remaining element of Plural Requirement that is a broadly moral but non-deontic claim that the agents all doing their part would be good. Still, that is just to notice how Plural Requirement looks when it ranges over both agents and entities subject to their own Plural Requirements. I see nothing incoherent, and that is the only issue at the moment, in a requirement that is itself, in this way, a hybrid of agential and non-agential prescription or evaluation, along with embedded conditional requirements of the very same hybrid kind.

Second, we should check, as promised in chapter 8, whether once Plural Requirement is fully laid out it remains true that nothing I say has committed me one way or the other for or against actualism. Recall that I argued that, while I would go on to use actualist formulations in speaking of the requirements of justice, my commitments are weaker and that those formulations could be translated into the more complex terms of those weaker commitments without vitiating anything in the broader account. The translation in the standard agential case was to go like this: when we say that,

If Professor Procrastinate will not Write, then he ought not to Accept

All I really need is that,

his not-Writing and Accepting is more severely wrong than his not-Writing and not-Accepting.

Trying the same thing in the case of Plural Requirement, and keeping the negations in place for simplicity, when we say that,

If society S will not Comply, then it ought not to Build

all I really need is that

S's not Complying and Building is more severely Plural-wrong than S's not Complying and not Building.

There is no particular difficulty about this introduction of severity for violations of Plural Requirement. It would refer to any combination of more severe violations of the agential conditional obligations (each to do their part if the others do), and a more severe negative evaluation of the non-agential kind that fills out the analysis of Plural Requirement. There may be other formulations that also raise questions about their neutrality about actualism. Maybe what has been said here provides enough to show how to perform the translations in the other cases, but I will not pursue this further.

Finally, there is one further point that is, while rather technical, interesting enough (to me) to be notable. Recall from chapter 8 that there were various views about the issues raised by actualism, any of which would suit my purposes. One of them is an approach according to which the 'ought' according to which Professor Procrastinate ought to Accept & Write is not logically the same term as the 'ought' that occurs when we say (if we do) that since Professor Procrastinate will not Write, he ought not to Accept. The latter might be held to be, in some way to be explained, essentially concessive and so relativized to a condition in which certain other oughts are violated. This, if it could be worked out saves Distributivity, since it would still apply within any single level of 'ought.' I noted, there, an objection due to Kiesewetter according to which if these are two different oughts then at most one of them could be the "core" ought of practical deliberation. Whatever there is to say about that in the case of agential requirements, no such objection gains purchase in the case of Plural Obligation. Being non-agential, there is no case for supposing it is tightly connected with the demands of an agent's practical deliberation. Of course, this is one way in which it is challenging to associate it with the moral domain, but that's a separate issue. It is interesting that partly because of this feature, the Distributivity-saving idea of heterogeneous oughts, as I called such approaches in chapter 8, would not be subject to that challenge about which of the "oughts" is the core deliberative 'ought.'

6. Conclusion

It is important to remember (yet again) that the complications about Plural Requirement are not slings and arrows brought upon us by contemplating such hopeless ideas as a global prime requirement. The issue is unavoidable even for concessive thought about social justice, and it arises not from high or unrealistic standards but from the essentially plural agency of many groups where morally salient standards nevertheless seem to apply. From Slice and Patch, to the Smokers, to the citizens of a country, Plural Requirement is a structured set of facts partly about agential moral obligation, though not an agential obligation in its own right. None of this, of course, should be taken to suggest that individuals will not often, or even normally, have individual obligations to contribute to the improvement, production, or maintenance of social justice. The topic here has been the more fundamental one of what sort of requirements, requirements of social justice, are.

PART V

The Practical and the Idealistic

CHAPTER THIRTEEN

Progress, Perfection, and Practice

It's likely that should white supremacy fall, the means by which that happens might be unthinkable to those of us bound by present realities and politics.

—TA-NEHISI COATES, *WE WERE EIGHT YEARS IN POWER*

Until we bring ourselves to conceive how this could happen, it can't happen.

—JOHN RAWLS, "JUSTICE AS FAIRNESS:
POLITICAL, NOT METAPHYSICAL"

Man would not have attained the possible unless time and again he had reached out for the impossible

—MAX WEBER, "POLITICS AS A VOCATION"

*And because these daft and dewey-eyed dopes
keep building up impossible hopes
impossible things are happening every day!*

—RODGERS AND HAMMERSTEIN, "IMPOSSIBLE,"
FROM *CINDERELLA*

1. Introduction

In the foregoing chapters I argued that it is not a criterion of a plausible conception of justice that it be realistic, at least not in certain ways that are often demanded. I have allowed that it must not be utterly beyond our abilities, but that does not mean that it must be at all likely, or even congruent with deep, natural motivational proclivities (if there are any)—realistic in those ways.

None of that yet implies that justice *is* unrealistic in any of those ways. I have also argued that a strong candidate for the status of justice is "prime justice," in which the basic social structure meets the moral requirements (technically, requirement fragments) that apply to it as part of a package in which everything and everyone is morally in compliance. Now, while that "global prime requirement" is unlikely ever to be met (even if it is necessarily not beyond our abilities), this does not settle whether the standard of prime justice itself is also unrealistic or not, as I have argued. It might not be. However, it might be, and I contend that that would not count against it. As I have repeatedly emphasized, I do not offer any conception of justice at all, realistic or idealistic. Even prime justice is an abstract category of justice, not a conception of its content, and I have said nothing about what it would require. So, if someone were to doubt the value of understanding the content of prime justice they are not yet doubting the value of anything I have tried to do here.

Still, even if the reader were persuaded by my arguments that justice might be highly idealistic, and unrealistic in the specified ways, it would be natural to wonder what the point is of understanding either this point, or (which is different) the content of that impractical standard. I will resist, in coming discussions, the implicit "practicalism" that often lies behind such skepticism. However, first, in this chapter and the next, I consider several ways in which idealistic theories of justice could have value for practice, before challenging the strictures of "practicalism" in chapter 16: "Beyond Practicalism." To introduce the main points in this chapter: first, it is important not to foreclose the possibility of unbelievable moral progress. Second, even if the only value of a theory of justice were as a guide to social choice, in which case all we ultimately need from a theory of justice is comparative rankings of realistic possibilities, it does not follow that a practically adequate theory of justice could be developed without the idea of full social justice, or without a theoretical incorporation of unrealistic, idealistic standards of justice.

Looking ahead: in the next chapter I present a role for highly idealistic conceptions of justice in a certain kind of realistic practical deliberation, namely in order to defeat certain practical arguments for approximating unrealistic conditions, and also in some cases to countervail, from a value point of view, some deviations from the ideal with other further deviations. In the penultimate chapter I argue against practicalism in general and in moral and political philosophy in particular—against, that is, the view that the only value of theory (or "intellectual work") is its instrumental value, if any, in producing, in action and not only in thought, something else of independent value.

2. Dangers of Idealistic (and of Realistic) Thought

Recall the distinction between proposal realism and principle idealism (in chapter 3: "Anti-Anti-Moralism"). Nobody would defend proposing or taking action that is bound to fail. We are all proposal realists. The vocal opposition

we sometimes see to what we might call proposal-idealism would seem misleadingly to suggest that it has defenders.[1] A more substantial concern about
idealistic theory is that its principles might be publicly mistaken for proposals,
with the result that projects get taken on that are hopeless and possibly dangerous. That would not be any critique of the principles (or so I have been arguing throughout this book). It might, however, support a critique of the theorist. There can be circumstances in which certain idealistic principles are so
ripe for misappropriation as proposals that it would be irresponsible to openly
defend the principles.

Call this the *danger concern*. Here are two highly schematic examples, as
illustrations of this point, drawn from different normative perspectives: (A)
Some might think it irresponsible to elaborate and defend a relatively social-
democratic conception of justice (even if it is not a practical proposal) when
facts on the ground suggest that state agencies are bound to be captured by
special interests who could cynically exploit such a theory as a kind of ideological cover, reducing justice overall rather than enhancing it. (B) Some may believe it dangerous to defend the moral value of a package of arrangements including relatively unregulated markets along with certain safeguards (such as
high inheritance taxes) against the concentration of political power in the very
wealthy. A reason might be that the contemplated degree of economic inequality would already predictably lead to the prevention or dismantling of the contemplated safeguards against unjust political inequality. Again, the theory
might predictably be abused. The idea of the danger concern is that there
might be undue political danger, in some conditions, in defending certain principles even without offering them as practical proposals, and even if, at the
level of normative principle they are correct and defensible (and, in the mode
of Plural Requirement, even required).

An especially strong version of the danger concern might hold that circumstances are, in effect, always like that for all unrealistic principles of social
justice. This extreme view might have its best chance if it were also the case
that there is little or no value in understanding principles of justice unless they
are also apt as practical proposals. In that case, why take any risk at all? More
moderate versions of the danger concern would want to reflect on when ad-
vancing an unrealistic conception of what justice requires is too risky and when
it is not. Since my project in this book does not, even in a general way, advocate
any particular standards of justice, the danger concern does not apply here.
That is because my argument is about whether justice might be idealistic and
unrealistic in certain ways *whatever* it might require. I argue, of course, that it
might well be. (I will not pause here to consider the possible claim that even
this thesis is too dangerous to utter or defend publicly.) Whether or not there
is more to be said about what justice might require in substance, this point
alone—the point that defects in idealistic proposals are not necessary defects
in the underlying idealistic principles—would be an important response when
a conception of justice is criticized for being unrealistic.

Of course, reflecting on the more normatively substantial task of asking what justice requires: even if there were nothing at all to the danger concern, there might be a *pointlessness concern*—it might reasonably be asked whether understanding the normative requirements of justice, in the case where it is highly unrealistic, would be of any value. That concern is addressed in several ways in this and the following chapters.

Having just noted that in some circumstances defending even the principles might be dangerous, obviously in other cases perhaps not. Indeed (and I now turn to a new point) there is a certain danger in *avoiding* unrealistic political thought, and this danger must be weighed in the balance. To see this kind of danger in a general way first, think about great achievements of all kinds. Consider the perspective of an individual contemplating her possible futures. Young people are often urged to follow their dreams. Such advice is too simple for reasons that are now familiar. First, some of a person's dreams might be manifestly impossible, such as traveling back in time. Second, some might be possible but so difficult and unlikely that it would be irrational to gamble on them—such as becoming the country's president. Third, in some cases, even if there aren't other great obstacles, there might be a low chance of success stemming from the agent's own likelihood of giving up when the going gets tough—consider a supremely talented but lazy pianist contemplating a professional solo career. Fourth, while some unlikely ambitions might be worthy goals even if they will probably only be partially attained, others—perhaps the aim of being the first to swim the English Channel—might, at least for many people, contain drastically less value in any incomplete attainment.[2]

None of these points impugns, or even addresses, the value of the envisaged future life itself, but they raise questions about whether, even if it is highly valuable, it ought not to be pursued in practice. Nevertheless, even among these unrealistic pairings of dreamers and dreams, some do find a way. Some children born with physical disabilities become Olympic champions. Some born into oppression and poverty become world-changing scientists or artists. Even if not everyone should follow their dreams—and the occasional success stories obviously do not overcome that concern—it is also important to acknowledge that there are surprising cases where the most extravagant dreams turn out to be worth pursuing. Even if that is not the normal case, the unusual breakthrough cases are also important, and they would never occur without the dreaming. That, to put it succinctly, is the danger of not dreaming.

The anti-idealist about justice is cast here as the anti-dreamer.[3] I imagine the realist (so to speak) parent or teacher who counsels young people, rather than fastening on their dreams, to look instead, and only, at their real circumstances, the obstacles, the ways we know things normally operate, and to concentrate entirely on what would be moderate incremental hopes within those boundaries. These mentors do not just warn against reckless *pursuit* of unlikely dreams (the idealist agrees with that after all), but against even contemplating what would be a truly excellent life. They have their reasons for this caution: such personal ideals are often ideological or irrational, and even those that are not, are often quixotic distractions from certain realistic paths that are wide open even if they are not as alluring. Some are told that since the chances of their becoming, for example, a pioneering physicist are ridiculously small given their inauspicious social and historical location, there is no value and there is significant danger in contemplating such possible futures of high achievement.

What is distasteful about the cultivation of this kind of narrow-mindedness is that it would preempt much of what is best in human life and experience, and for no good reason. If dreaming were ineradicably dangerous, then that would be different. But a less crude stance is available, the encouragement of reflection on the very highest standards and aspirations along with a realistic approach to practice: close attention to costs and risks as well as benefits should one succeed; critical scrutiny of the ends themselves to guard against irrationality and manipulation of various kinds; saving part of one's energy for the less speculative, more certain, decisions and problems with which one is and will be faced; and so on. Nothing seems more foreign to the realist outlook than this injunction to take dreams seriously, and that realism can appear unreasonable for this reason.

No doubt, the analogy between having personal dreams for the future and contemplating possible social futures for a society is imperfect, but it is also, I think, telling. Something analogous seems right in the context of idealistic theories of justice as well. Even apart from the fact that they might be true and that understanding them might have some intrinsic value (about which more in chapter 17), this is one way in which they are practically valuable. Contemplating the high standards runs some risk, but so does not contemplating them. The risk of too much realism is that surprising breakthrough successes that idealistic reflection sometimes makes possible will not happen without it.

Across societies, and across time, there are many clear cases of what we might call *unbelievable moral progress*—unbelievable in the sense that their achievement would have been impossible to believe not long before it occurred. Judging great achievements to be impossible is a treacherous business. In about 1950, just twenty years before the first human walked on the moon, Ludwig Wittgenstein wrote, "We all believe that it isn't possible to get to the moon; but there might be people who believe that that is possible and that it sometimes happens. We say: these people do not know a lot that we know. And, be they [ever][4] so sure of their belief—they are wrong and we know it."[5] Even the smartest among us are often incapable of seeing the possibility of achievements that are then made real, often not long after they seemed impossible. When Robert Kennedy said in 1961 (the year Barack Obama was born) that "there's no reason that in the near and foreseeable future that a negro could not be president of the United States,"[6] many would have found it absurd. However, 50% already expressed willingness to vote for a black person for president, a dramatic change of 7% from only three years earlier.[7] Obama became president in the lifetime of Robert's brother, Ted Kennedy.

There is traditionally much debate about whether there has been something like on-balance moral progress, or, a different question: whether there is some underlying force or tendency in the direction of moral progress in human history. I am not claiming either of those things, but only that there are many instances of moral progress that would have seemed impossible not long before, and would not have occurred if no one had taken such unlikely possibilities seriously. Even if there is steady on-balance progress, that would not entail my claim that important instances often come as a surprise of the kind that matters for my purposes. On the other hand, there are certain stock examples that occur in those debates that can also be shown to have been unbelievable not long before they occurred. This is not the place to consider a broad list of examples from across history and around the world, though that would only strengthen my case. I limit myself to examples of social justice in my own country, the United States. Here are some standard plausible examples or indications of great improvements in social justice, each of which would have been believed by many or most people, not long before their occurrence, to be either impossible, or at least to lie much farther in the future: women's right to vote; legal abolition of slavery; legal marriage and other union rights for gays and lesbians; avoidance of world war for over 70 years and counting (as of this writing); and election of a black U.S. president.[8]

I am not claiming that it will be uncontroversial which, from a longer list of cases count as progress and which do not belong here or on a longer list. Rather, each reader is encouraged to add or subtract instances by their own lights. In addition to disagreement about which cases are progress, there will be reasonable dispute about which of those granted to be progress were facilitated partly by idealistic, unrealistic thinking about unlikely but worthy possible futures. We do not need cases where they would not have happened at all but for such idealism—though I believe there are many of those. It is enough if they were significantly hastened or improved by such thinking.

Here is a beguiling parlor game:

The Unbelievable Moral Progress Game
What unbelievable moral achievements might humanity witness a century or two from now?

The trick, of course, is that if you can seriously contemplate its occurring, you are thinking too small, or so history suggests. The fuller achievement of gay rights, or extensions of various rights and protections to people with various sexual identities and choices, or broader animal rights, or averting climate disaster, and so forth—none of these is eligible as "unbelievable" in 2019 because they are clearly already at least on the public radar and have wide, often optimistic, support. We are looking, rather, for the kinds of achievements that would truly surprise most of us now in the way abolition or gay rights would have surprised most people a century earlier. But then no eligible candidate can seem anything but absurd: the permanent end of major war, the eradication of hunger or poverty, the end of rape, of all significant racial segregation—these are the *kinds* of unbelievable steps forward—similar in the degree of incredulity they elicit—that have, in fact, been achieved time and again in history. It seems to be part of the human condition that we don't know our own strength. The point for my purposes is this: the actual historical examples I listed, and many other examples that might be added, normally came about partly as a result of the moral imaginations of some people. People's ideas are themselves shaped and constrained in many ways by broad social-structural, historical, and cultural causes, but no one denies that they are then also part of the causal order and have significant powers of their own, often indispensable.

Contemplating great achievements, even those that seem unlikely or even impossible, can and sometimes does contribute to their being achieved. Therefore, there is that kind of practical value in even highly idealistic theorizing about justice. It might be that even in these cases of success the odds were so low that much is owed also to luck. In that case it might be wrong to conclude that people were "able" to achieve these things, or that such achievements were "feasible."[9] The point here is only that they happened, partly through intentional effort, and would probably not have happened if all contemplation of their possibility had been stifled by their evident improbability. It should give us pause to wonder what other opportunities for great achievement have, so far, been missed because, seeming so improbable, they were not seriously thought about. Realism of that kind, as I have said, can be dangerously impractical.

It might sound as if my point is that idealism itself counts as a virtue in a theory of justice, if only because it keeps those possibilities alive. I do not mean that. I mean only that if we find independent grounds in support of a theory of justice that is highly idealistic, then even if it is granted that it might be correct, there are questions to raise about what value there would be—practical or otherwise—in understanding justice in that case. One answer to that question is that we ought to absorb the practical implications of the fact that we often do not know our own strength.

3. Critique of Pure Comparativism

I turn now to a very different issue about the value of understanding full justice if it is unrealistic. Suppose we put aside the point from the previous section that what seems impossible or unlikely at the moment might well be achieved, if history is any guide.[10] Suppose, instead, there are some conditions of excellent justice that we can safely suppose will never be achieved, and that merely approximating those conditions would be of little or no value. In that case, theorizing and other thinking about those high standards will not have the practical value of keeping them open as possibilities. Amartya Sen emphasizes this point with special attention to the idea of perfect or full justice. If it will never be attained, then understanding it will be of no use in making social decisions, since in making decisions between options that are or will be available there is no point in introducing unavailable alternatives. It might sometimes be valuable to achieve whatever elements of the ideal arrangement that we can, even if we will not achieve them all, but as Sen recognizes, there is no basis for assuming this is the case. Often, valuable elements only have their value in the presence of the full package, so to speak. This point, roughly the so-called problem of second best, will occupy us in the next chapter, but it is useful to acknowledge here that understanding ideals is not guaranteed to have that kind of practical value.

Perhaps, then, there is no practical value in the concept of (fully) "just" but only in the concept of "juster." And the issue this raises is not limited to full justice, but arises as well for any degree of justice (if any) that we can safely put aside as options we will never achieve in any case. Practicalism about justice is straightforwardly an answer to the fair question, "what good would such knowledge about justice be?" For present purposes I wish to grant a specific form of practicalism for the sake of argument. Assume, for purposes of this chapter,

Methodological Practicalism
We ought to theorize in exactly those ways that would best facilitate rational social choice.

I will refer to the division of possible societies into just and unjust as a "partition," following Sen.[11] One argument against employing the just/unjust partition—"[t]he grand partition between the 'just' and the 'nonjust'"[12]—is that it is of no use for purposes of choice between alternatives. I will call this argument the *sufficiency of comparisons*. I will return below to a second reason for doubting the value of a partition between just and unjust, namely the claim that full justice is not for this world, while practical choices between unjust and less unjust conditions face us all the time. Whatever full justice might consist in, the energy of political philosophers is better spent, on this view, contributing to clear thinking about the important comparative choices societies actually face now, or foreseeably. Let us call this argument the *practicality of comparisons*. I leave that line of argument aside for now. In both cases, the target is what I will call *partitionism* about justice: theorizing about justice in a way that relies on a partition between just and unjust social structures, and not (merely) on comparisons between the just and the juster. A binary or *bare partitionism* would include only the partition (and the comparisons that it supports) but no further comparisons with respect to relative justice or injustice. A *rich partitionism* would include both a partition and further comparisons. The approach that eschews the partition altogether is *comparativism* (weak or strong, to be explained).[13]

If understanding the partition adds no practical value to the comparative information in a theory of justice, it is fair to ask whether it adds anything of value at all. More starkly, if justice should admit of only the partition but no comparative information, we might wonder what good it is to understand justice at all. We will see how, even if partition information is of no use for purposes of choice over and above comparative information, this does not establish that a wholly comparative theory of justice is adequate—even for purposes of choice. The reason is that epistemology, surprisingly perhaps, might favor the richer measure, delivering a partitioned scale, or some information about the content of the partition, or at least partition-entailing judgments, in the first instance. In short, my claim is that even if practicalism were correct, and even though (as I will grant for the sake of argument) comparisons are sufficient for choice, the enterprise of a theory of justice does not somehow get to take such comparisons "as given," but it must generate many of them from its own resources. A wholly comparative conception of justice would limit itself to impoverished resources, and for no good reason.

Suppose that, while there is no appeal to any partition, we have good warrant for more than merely an ordinal ranking, but also for an ordering of degrees of justice on an interval scale. That is, we could not only rank states of affairs as to which is juster, but we could compare pairs according to which represented a greater difference in justice, and by what proportion. That is, we could say not only that A is juster than B, but also that the difference between A and B is greater than that between A and C. But suppose we were not in any position to represent how distant any arrangement was from full justice. This intermediate "interval" measure of justice would still be highly limiting intuitively, since it would not allow any meaning to be assigned to judgments such as that slavery is profoundly unjust, since that judgment entails a partition. Moreover, the interval ranking does not assign any meaning to the judgment that slavery is unjust at all. That is meaningless if there is no partition between cases that are just and cases that are unjust. I think this is such a big cost, intuitively, that I will regard this as decisive against what I will call *categorical comparativism*, the claim that justice does not (in reality or "metaphysically") admit of richer comparison than an interval scale allows: there is no partition between just and unjust societies. On that view, which I will now put aside, there is only "juster," to varying degrees allowed by an interval scale. It denies that a society organized around slavery (or any society at all, for that matter) is either just or unjust.

There remains a more nuanced kind of philosophical reticence about the just/unjust partition, and I will call it:

Methodological Comparativism
While there is or may be a partition in fact, we ought to theorize wholly in terms of comparisons.[14]

Here is an argument, which I will eventually reject, that methodological comparativism would follow from the sufficiency of comparisons, combined with methodological practicalism:

1. We ought to theorize in exactly those ways that would best facilitate rational social choice (*methodological practicalism*).
2. Comparisons are fully sufficient for rational choice (*sufficiency of comparisons*).
3. Therefore, we ought to theorize wholly in terms of comparisons, not in terms of a partition between just and unjust (*methodological comparativism*).

As noted earlier, I am accepting methodological practicalism for the sake of argument, in this chapter (only), and the same goes for the second premise, the sufficiency of comparisons, although I would also like to sketch what I take to be a strong case for its truth. Then, if all we want from a theory of justice is the structure and information needed to make the most rational social choices it may seem that there is no reason to build a partition into our working theory.[15] However, methodological comparativism does not follow from the sufficiency of comparisons along with methodological practicalism.

1. To see why, first, notice how restrictive comparativism is. Here are some familiar forms of judgment about justice that are obviously not available on an ordinal comparativist framework. To speak in a simple shorthand: if there is only "juster," then there is:

   a. no "just," no "unjust"
   b. no "much more just," no "much more unjust"
   c. no "highly just," no "gravely unjust"
   d. no "nearly just," no "far from just"
   e. no "nearly as just," no "nearly as unjust"

There would be no meaning to the claim that slavery is unjust, or that it is severely unjust. We could not meaningfully say that slavery is significantly more unjust than gender differentials in wages, only that it is more unjust. We could not argue that one policy would improve justice much more than an alternative. And so on.

There is more. Suppose that you are devoted to the cause of eradicating a certain source of corruption in the political process. Suppose, for example, that Supreme Court Justices are exploiting a loophole in the law and receiving highly lucrative favors and gifts from parties to cases they will hear. (Many examples would serve as well.) As strongly as you believe in this cause, there are other valuable causes too and your chances of success are uncertain. You should consider working on something else if this loophole-closing project is unlikely to succeed and other causes are not. For example, if one condition were twice as much more just (so to speak) than the status quo compared to another condition would be, then a 50 percent chance of attaining it would be as good as a certainty of attaining the other. If you take its chances to be less than that, you should work on the other cause, other things being equal. Allow for the obvious roughness of these numerical estimates, of course. However, on a simple ordinalist framework, that very form of reasoning is incoherent. The reason is that there is no measure by which the justice-difference of a certain improvement is any multiple, not even very roughly, of the justice-difference (from the status quo) of any alternative. Ordinal rankings contain no such information. In that case, the information about probability is of no use. Simple ordinalism, all things considered, is devastating to many of the purposes to which we hope to put our thought about justice. For this reason, I will put ordinal comparativism aside, and hereafter use the term "comparativism" to refer to approaches that include richer than ordinal comparisons.

An interval scale is one that contains not only rank orderings, but what we intuitively think of as *distance* information, on the model of points on a line. Some of the limitations in ordinal comparativism would be removed if interval information were available. On an interval scale we can meaningfully say that the improvement from x to z is greater than the improvement from x to y by some multiple. The rough judgment that z is "many" times further from x than y is would not be allowed at all by ordinal ranking because it implies an interval measure, even if only a rough one. So, if enough richness were available to support an interval comparison, this would support at least somewhat more of our standard reasoning about justice.

However, even an interval ordering would not allow any meaning for many of the standard judgments listed above. To see this, think of a line with no beginning or end, and each alternative state of justice lying at some point. Since the line segment defined by any pair is some fraction of any other line segment, the comparisons marked by judgments (b) and (e) are meaningful, but since there is no place to put the line between just and unjust (no "partition" as we are calling it), (a), (c), and (d) are meaningless. Merely comparative justice including ordinal and/or interval measures excludes many judgments that are at the very center of our thought, whether formal or informal, about social justice.

2. Second, even though there are many merely comparative "juster" judgments that are intuitively firm, many of these are pre-theoretic. That is, rather than being delivered by some theory (having not been evident until their support by a theory was understood) they are known or held prior to any general theory of justness. The only

method for arriving at them is, as we might call it, the "eyeball method": when presented with them we find ourselves (some or many of us) more or less spontaneously holding or forming judgments about which is more just than the other. That is a good start, as identifying a set of data points that a plausible theory will be expected to hit. But they are not yet a theory, and the question I want to pursue is how a theory might be arrived at. By a theory, I will mean an account of what it is in virtue which of some conditions count as juster than others, entailing rankings of, if not all cases, many cases that were not already covered by our "eyeball" judgments prior to having the theory.

3. Third, if firm intuitive judgments are to serve in the theory-building effort by providing data points, we would be deprived of a great deal of data if all partition-implying judgments were to be excluded, as is clear from (1). We would have to begin with eyeball judgments of *only* comparative justness.

4. The conjecture that identifying some societies as fully just will never (if full justice is very remote) inform any practical social choice (the "sufficiency of comparisons") does not address whether there is value in counting partition-implying judgments among the data with which to construct a theory. That is, it is no argument that they are not valuable or even crucial for that purpose.

5. Unlike in the case of utility theory (let the point be granted there for the sake of argument), there is no clear epistemological disadvantage attached to eyeball judgments that imply more than ordinal rankings. Many common judgments of what is unjust (rather than merely less just than something else) have as much epistemological warrant, however much it is, as those that imply an interval scale or a partition. In particular, there is not the "problem of other minds" that has led much of utility theory to prefer operating with merely ordinal rankings.[16]

6. There is not evidently any more reason for thinking that justice is bound to be at least comparative whether or not it involves a partition, than there is for thinking that it is bound to include a partition whether or not there are also further comparisons (such as between unjust cases). This would depend on what justice turns out to consist in, something that is not to be prejudged. For one example to illustrate this point, suppose justice consisted in the arithmetical equality of some social good to be distributed (such as income, resources, opportunities, rights, certain combinations of these, etc.). Since, except in the very simple case of comparing pairs of numbers for degree of inequality, there is no such thing as differing degrees of arithmetical inequality, such a theory would involve the partition between just and unjust distributions, but no further comparisons in either category.[17] (The same would arguably go for the sufficiency principle, some parti-

tion above which everyone has "enough" of some specified good.) Some measures have upper limits as well as subpar comparisons, such as purity or fullness. Others have comparisons with no such upper-bound or ceiling (which is also a partition), such as height or duration. But some measures, such as arithmetical equality, sufficiency, and many others, involve partitions with no other comparisons.

The main point for our purposes is that there is no evident reason for favoring our intuitive judgments of comparative justice over intuitive partitioned, or partition-implying judgments. That being so, it is legitimate and important to gather such intuitive data points as seem to be relatively firm, widespread, and so forth for the purpose of constructing and testing theories of what makes one case more just than another. Of course, the intuitive judgments, both the merely comparative and also the partition-implying ones, are often tentative and might fade in the face of the effort to find an adequate and compelling theory. But even if we are only concerned with the theory's practical value, and all we need when the time for social decision comes is the comparisons, this does not show that the best theory will not include the partition between societies that are fully just and those that are not.

It might yet be argued that while there is nothing wrong with theorizing with partition-implying judgments, still, doing so does not require theorizing about the nature or content of the partition itself, which might be more difficult.[18] One version of methodological comparativism could hold that we ought not to bother theorizing about the partition—seeking full understanding of the standard of justice involved—but might perfectly well draw on our partitioned eyeball judgments for their value in building a comparative theory. However, it is hard to see why, if such value is granted to those judgments, it would not be enhanced by theoretically elaborating and systematizing them in the manner of a theory of the standard. Since we have seen no strong reason to think such theorizing is either pointless or hopelessly difficult, there seems to be no point in eschewing the theoretical understanding of full justice even if (*arguendo*) all we want from the theory is comparisons to use in choice.

The argument in this section, so far, responds to the idea that a merely comparative approach to justice is favored by the (alleged) fact that full justice is too remote to be relevant for actual rational social choice. We have concentrated on the argument about the inclusion of a partition, but what drives the argument is the alleged remoteness of certain possible high degrees of justice, whether or not any threshold is involved: Why insist that our theory have anything to say about which societies are located in those remote high reaches of near justness, if we will never face them as real options? Call this,

Methodological Conservatism
The theory of justice ought to favor the investigation of standards whose achievement is not too remote in one of the following ways: too far in the

future, too dissimilar to the status quo (or to what has been seen), too unlikely, or too difficult or costly.

This is different from what we might call,

Practical Conservatism
Social changes that are remote in one of the above ways are, to that extent, less advisable.[19]

Methodological conservatism is a position about the merits of certain kinds of
normative theory, while practical conservatism pronounces on action. I will
briefly question one way of arguing for methodological conservatism before
turning to my main point, which is that even if it were a plausible view, it
would not provide the support it might seem to provide for comparativism.

Practical conservatism plus practicalism about political philosophy might
seem to support methodological conservatism. That is, if political philosophy
ought mainly to serve political or social choice, and such choice ought itself to
be conservative, then it may seem to follow (at least in a rough sense) that so
ought political philosophy to be conservative. To reject that strategy of argument, one must either reject practical conservatism (I will grant it for the sake
of argument), or reject practicalism about political philosophy (I reject it in
fact, but I waive that for this chapter), or deny that the conclusion of methodological conservatism follows from those premises. I deny that it follows.

We would need some reason to believe that wise conservative social choice
could not benefit from normative political theory's investigations of less conservative possibilities. For one example of how it might benefit, consider the
attempt to understand just how remote certain practical options really are or
are not (in time, similarity, likelihood, or difficulty). We can hardly rule out in
advance that this might be facilitated by reflection on a broader set of options,
including some that are patently remote. The case is similar to the failure,
noted earlier, of the argument that since comparisons are sufficient for *choice*,
theory ought to be comparativist. Here I point out the flaw in the argument:
even if *choice* ought to be conservative, it doesn't follow that *theory* ought to be
conservative. And this is so even on the concession (for the sake of argument)
that political theory ought mainly to serve political practice (a position I argue
against elsewhere in this chapter).

Whatever the merits of methodological conservatism, it is sometimes
thought to count in favor of comparativism about justice. Methodological conservatism is certainly no argument for comparativism as superior to partitionism. Suppose that meeting the partitioned standard, the standard of full social
justice, is remote (in some way). If standards of full justice are unworthy of
theoretical attention because of their remoteness (something I have just been
casting doubt on), then remote reaches of justness on a wholly comparative
scale must be unworthy too. There is no particular challenge to partitionism

in that. It is true that methodological conservatism's preference for non-remote comparisons would indeed count against theorizing with a justice partition if full justice is a remote standard. However, this is a count against methodological conservatism itself. As I have argued, reasoning with partitioned or at least partition-implying comparisons may be the only way to leverage our intuitive or eyeball convictions about justice into a set of comparative judgments that have any evidential support in normative theory. We can now add that if methodological conservatism rejects that method on the ground that it is contaminated by the remote (which we can grant for the argument) partition between just and unjust, then methodological conservatism, for no evident reason, bans the use of a wealth of ordinary convictions about the nature and content of not only justice but even of "juster." The point is exactly like the central point above about the pointlessness of comparativism's averting its eyes from partition-implying judgments. Whether those judgments are excluded on the ground that they are partitioned, or on the ground that they are remote, the exclusion appears to me to have no adequate justification.

For the reasons I have given in this section, neither methodological comparativism nor methodological conservatism is strongly supported by the assumption, were we to grant it, that the value of a theory of justice consists entirely in its providing guidance in social choice between alternatives we might actually face. Practicalism implies that if, at the time of social choice, we have comparative rankings of the practically available alternatives, we have no use for more than that. But this is not enough to show that theorizing about justice can generate the practically needed rankings if it were debarred from reasoning with threshold (e.g., fully just) cases and unrealistic desirable possibilities. Very little can be said in a general way (Sen does not address the question) about how a theory might arrive at a rich ranking of the realistic possibilities (which are surely many), but an important role must be played by efforts to exhibit such coherence and system—such theoretical structure—as might be implicit in intuitions and considered judgments about what is just as well as what is juster, allowing these fallible provisional views to evolve in the process of theorizing. That remains a very abstract point about how this might be done. Just one example that is slightly more concrete will concern us in the next chapter: when a single element of some high standard of justice is considered alone, say a certain basic liberty, it might or might not have the significant value that it would contribute when it is not considered alone—that is, in the unrealistic setting along with the other elements that make a desirable package. Whether the presence of that single element might warrant a higher ranking among practical alternatives can sometimes only be determined by investigating the more ideal case, in order to determine whether it has independent value or only the more interactive value along with the whole package. Idealistic standards (whether partitions or not) bear study in order to determine what sort of contribution is being made by their elements, and this will matter for determining the rankings of more realistic possibilities. This set of issues, which concerns us in the next chapter, is just one example of the general point of this chapter: to show both the sufficiency of rankings for choice, and the sufficiency, for realistic choice, of rankings of realistic options, is far from showing that the theory of justice could somehow generate the needed rankings if it kept within comparativist or realistic bounds.

4. Conclusion

In this chapter we have seen two ways in which an idealistic theory of justice might be thought to have practical value. There is the practical value of thinking big, since there is sometimes unbelievable moral progress. There is also the value of incorporating our considered judgments of full justice into theories even if all we need when it comes to choice is rankings of alternatives, since there may be no other way to theoretically generate and support any rankings that are not already obvious.

There is a third kind of practical value for the understanding of high idealistic standards, or even "ideal justice," that has nothing to do with any hope of meeting them. As we will see more fully in the next two chapters, it can be important to understand certain unrealistic ideals in order to work out whether certain value-contributing elements of those ideals would or would not still be worth having in the absence of the full package. That remains a "practicalist" argument for the value of unrealistic theorizing about justice. In the penultimate chapter I step back in order to challenge the "practicalist" proposition that there is no great value in a piece of political philosophy unless it provides practical guidance in political choice.

CHAPTER FOURTEEN

The Fallacy of Approximation

*In practice we must usually choose between several unjust, or second best,
arrangements; and then we look to nonideal theory to find the least unjust
scheme. Sometimes this scheme will include measures and policies that a
perfectly just system would reject.*

—JOHN RAWLS, *A THEORY OF JUSTICE*

1. Introduction

When political theory constructs models that are idealized in certain ways, it
is natural to ask whether they are of any use in practice. If there is hope of
fully achieving them, then they might serve as appropriate practical goals.
And even if they are not fully achievable, or not worth the cost or risk, they
will often be something to approximate. The value of approximating them
cannot be assumed, however, since the approximation might leave out something crucial. For an example in a different context, a car with a missing brake
pedal is approximately like a car with a brake pedal, but most of the value is
missing. Still, it is a valuable first step to *identify* the respects in which the
status quo differs from the valuable model or ideal, and that requires identification of the ideal. What to do in order to improve matters raises further
questions.

As Jürgen Habermas points out, on the question of the epistemic value of
political deliberation,

> In the final analysis, we are . . . confronted with the prima facie evidence
> that the kind of political communication we know from our so-called
> media society goes against the grain of the normative requirements of
> deliberative politics. However, the . . . empirical use of the deliberative
> model has a critical thrust: It enables us to read the contradicting data
> as indicators of contingent constraints that deserve serious inquiry.

[Those requirements] . . . can serve as detectors for the discovery of specific causes for existing lacks of legitimacy.[1]

Once we have identified the features of the democratic deliberative system that are responsible for reducing or destroying its epistemic value on political questions there are two ways to move toward improvement. One way would be to try to *remove* the offending features. As we have defined things, if all the offending features were removed, the epistemic value of the system would be improved and would be considerable. However, it cannot be assumed that removing only some but not all of the offending features would improve matters, rather than leaving them as bad or worse. The reason is the so-called problem of second best: when there is a list of features which together have a certain value, but some of them are missing, adding more of the features may or may not increase the value of the result. The reason is that the value contribution of any set of features might depend on the presence of other features that would still be missing. Adding features in that case might even do harm. For an analogy we will rely on throughout, you should not assume that taking two of your three prescribed pills is better than taking one, or none, since it all depends on how the chemicals interact.

Of course, just because it cannot be assumed in general that removing some but not all obstacles will help matters, it is also true that it might indeed help. If the other two pills are a vitamin and a dose of ibuprofen then they will probably still be good for you even without the third. Likewise, many ingredients of full social justice are likely to have value even if not all of the ingredients will be present. Even if they do, this would not yet show that understanding the full ideal was of any use, as something to approximate, since the independent value of some (or even each) of the ingredients might be fully known even without knowing the ideal. Structural approximation, as I will call it, approximation by having more rather than fewer of the ingredients in the ideal or model, will sometimes increase justice, other times not. It just depends on the case. The point I will be exploring in the first part of the chapter is that it is important to keep in mind that it cannot be *assumed* that it is, or even probably is, an appropriate practical goal to approximate the structure of an epistemically good deliberative system, or any other social ideal, since doing so cannot be assumed to approximate its epistemic value. So, the first way of responding to the offending features—namely, to remove them—is not as straightforwardly advisable as it might seem.

In this chapter, I explain this important general point which, for reasons I will explain, I call the fallacy of approximation (commonly known as the problem of "second best") in more detail. I explain the point in its most general form, explaining its unappreciated generality, before turning to its applicability to specifically political questions. In the next chapter, I turn to a second way to move toward improvement when the system has features that damage its epistemic value—not by approximating the ideal scenario but by countervailing some deviations with others carefully chosen for that purpose.

I will be focusing on two different cases:

- theories of full social justice,
- theories of an ideal system of free public political deliberation.

And in either case, I will suppose at least for the sake of argument, that this is a standard that is *unlikely ever to be met.* Suppose we had what looked like the best theory of justice, pending some concern about its being, in that way, "unrealistic." Whether or not it might be valuable in some other, nonpractical way, I want to focus on two ways in which it might be thought to be practically useful:

1. As a structural model to approximate.
   (I'll emphasize the limits of this.)
2. As a template for identifying what I'll call "countervailing deviations."
   (I'll emphasize the promise of this.)

If full social justice consists in the satisfaction of, say, three principles, then even if there is one that will not be satisfied, then it is, in one way, more in the direction of the fully just arrangement to have one or two of those that are available rather than none. The tempting thought that this is guaranteed to be an improvement in justice, however, rests on a fallacy, as I have said. In that thought there is a hidden general premise which is not true, namely that if you have some ingredients of a good condition, but you will not have all of the ingredients, having more of them would be better. More of the good set of ingredients is not guaranteed to be better rather than less. For our purposes the upshot is that a theory of full justice cannot be assumed to have value as a practical target of structural approximation (as we might put it).[2] This reopens the question of whether such understanding has any value at all, practical or otherwise. In this part, I want to acknowledge this challenge to the practical value of ideal theory, and to dwell more than is usual on this general point about value and approximation, putting the special context of political theory and democratic procedure off-stage for the most part until chapter 15.

In an economic setting, Lipsey and Lancaster famously claimed to demonstrate, with elaborate formal argument, the following point, as they described it, which has come to be known as the problem of second best:

> [I]t is not true that a situation in which more, but not all, of the optimum conditions are fulfilled is necessarily, or is even likely to be, superior to a situation in which fewer are fulfilled.[3]

With no technicality, here is another context in which that point, as naturally understood in ordinary language, is established by a simple counterexample:

Two Out of Three (Pills) Ain't Bad?
Suppose you are treating a serious medical condition with a cocktail of three pills daily. You have run out of one of the three medications, but you do have the other two. You cannot assume that taking those two would be better than your other options, which consist in taking only one or the other, or taking none.

They might be valueless, or even dangerous, without the third. The pill example, and plain English, are enough to establish the point that it is not always true that adding ingredients from the valuable set will add value. This, of course, does not mean that it will never add value, only that this inference form is invalid.

It is by no means clear that what Lipsey and Lancaster set out to prove is this lesson that is suggested by their gloss, and nothing I say takes any stand on that question. I now focus on the Fallacy of Approximation.[4]

The so-called problem of second best has a broader range of application than it might seem from the canonical treatment in economics. For one thing, it is by no means limited to contexts involving social outcomes, as we can already see from the example of the three pills. It is a very general point about value. However, even if we are especially interested in the context of social justice, it is important to appreciate several other respects in which the point has more general applicability than it might seem. First, I want to formulate the point more carefully, and then turn to several dimensions of its generality. Finally, we will note the significance of several of those points in contexts of normative political philosophy.

The issue is about whether having *more* of the elements is better. But there are two senses of "more." One sense of "having more" is having a larger number of elements. That is not the issue here. Obviously, having four coins may not be better than one if they are pennies and this is a dollar. A second sense of "having more" elements is having a superset: all of those that are initially considered, and more. Coins in a single currency do satisfy this version of "more is better": for any subset of the coins, having all of those and more coins is better (financially speaking). So, in the superset sense of "more," the question is whether, in general, having more of the elements from some good set is guaranteed to be better than having fewer. The answer is "no."

What I will call the fallacy of approximation is reasoning as if they are so guaranteed. The fallacy consists in supposing, in such reasoning, that the following principle is true, which it is not:

The Superset Principle
For any valuable set of conditions S, and satisfaction of any subset of it ss (including the null set), any subset of S (including S itself) that is a proper superset of ss will be more valuable than satisfaction of ss.

Insofar as it is systematically tempting to reason in that way, there is a

Fallacy of Approximation
It is a fallacy to infer (à la Superset) from the value-contributing conditions of any given model scenario, that among alternatives that lack at least some of those conditions, supersets of those subsets are better.

It may not be better to have more of the model conditions. ("More" in the superset sense.) We could just call it the fallacy of second best, but I will shortly explain why that name can be misleading. (While I do not expect my alternative name to catch on, I do believe it serves a good purpose in the present exposition.)

It is worth noting a certain similarity between the points underlying the fallacy of approximation and the view known as moral particularism.[5] The fallacy of approximation says, indeed, that the way in which an element "functions" to count as a reason in favor of something is variable according to what other features are present in the instant case. Notice that the fallacy of approximation's relevance goes beyond moral reasoning to practical or even evaluative reasoning of any kind. In that way it is more general than particularism. However, the fallacy of approximation does not make the strong claim that particularism does, namely that the value of a given type of consideration is always or normally dependent on the other present considerations. For all we have shown here, at any rate, the lesson is that the approximation form of reasoning has counterexamples. Nothing follows yet about whether they are the normal cases, or rare cases, or in between. Lipsey and Lancaster, as we saw, emphasize the point's agnosticism on this frequency issue.[6] If there is any temptation to think that the interdependencies that would block approximation reasoning are relatively rare, the arguments in support of particularism's claim that they are ubiquitous may be a useful corrective, but nothing is claimed here either way about how common counterexamples to approximation reasoning are, and it seems clear that it will vary from one domain to another.

I will not pursue the question of the fallacy of approximation's underappreciated generality in a formal way, but it will be helpful to introduce a few terms and ideas. Let us say that our subject matter is certain evaluative *standards*, and that they are met if and only if (and because) certain specified *conditions* are fully met. Call the case where they are all met the *model scenario*. We will speak of the model scenario and other scenarios in terms of which *subsets* of those conditions are met. For convenience I will speak of the *elements* of the model set, and of *contributing elements*, of the model set and of the various subsets.

Here, then, in my own words, is one familiar way of identifying the so-called problem of second best, closely following Lipsey and Lancaster's prose formulations, and making the Superset structure explicit. It characteristically includes several qualifications, which are misplaced, and I have highlighted them:

> *A Standard Formulation of Second Best*
>
> If there is some *social* scenario including multiple contributing elements that would, together, be *ideal or best*, but it is *impossible or infeasible* to produce or have all of them, it is not in general correct to assume that (as Superset would have it) the *second*-best option is to produce all of the available elements. Rather, the second-best option might be a scenario that does not have all of the available elements of the first-best option.[7]

I will go on to argue—or, perhaps, pause to notice what is now relatively obvious—that none of those italicized elements is essential to the underlying point, which means that its significance is broader than this formulation suggests.

That the point is not limited to examples in social scenarios is already clear from the case of three pills, as I have said. I will now briefly explain why it is not limited in the other ways suggested in that standard formulation: (a) it is not limited to cases involving any *ideal* or best. (b) It follows that it is not limited to cases of "*second* best" strictly understood. However, more generally, it is not even limited to cases involving a "*next* best." (c) It is not limited to cases involving *unavailability* or such related conditions as infeasibility, inability, or impossibility. Finally, though this issue does not show up in the standard formulation it is important to see that (d) it is not limited to cases where the value-affecting interactions between elements are *causal* interactions (the interactions in Lipsey and Lancaster's context of economic factors, and our example of the three pills, both being causal interactions).

a. Beyond Ideal or Best

Lipsey and Lancaster, even though this is not entailed by the math, explicitly tie their analysis to contexts in which there is an *unavailable first best* in the domain, and this has constrained later thinking which often follows the standard formulation. They pose the problem in terms of a condition free from certain constraints, and then consider questions about what would be optimal in the "second best" case, namely under those constraints.[8] My first generalization beyond the standard formulation, then, is this: there is nothing essential about focusing on the best scenario in the domain. I turn to availability next.

For one thing, in some contexts where the point seems nevertheless to apply there is no such thing as best. There is probably no such thing as a perfect painting, or a maximally pleasurable life. But my main point against "best" does not depend on that. A further point is this: suppose that some scenario S will not obtain, since at least some of its conditions will not be met. Someone might make the following inference, which would be a fallacy for the familiar reasons.

The fallacy without a best
S, while not ideal or best in any way, is good to some degree. Consider the domain of scenarios consisting of subsets of S's elements. For any subset, producing a superset would be better. The best available, then, would be to produce all of them that are available.

The fallacy is present here, even though there is no appearance of the best-but-unavailable, only a better-but-unavailable social scenario. So, the case where S is an ideal of some kind is just a special case. It is not in any way definitive of the fallacy.[9] In political philosophy, then, and even though we will specifically discuss ideals in much of what follows, the danger of the fallacy is present even in contexts in which best or ideal cases are not being considered at all.

b. Beyond Second or Next Best

The issue might, for all that, still be essentially about the *next best*, next to the "model" scenario in question whether or not it is a best or ideal case. A further point is that this is not so. First, there is no guarantee that the number of alternatives is not continuous, like speed. There is no "next fastest" speed. Call this a *continuity case*. The values of the alternatives to the model in some domain might be continuous in this way, so there would be no second best, or any next best to any model. In that case, the question cannot be seen as about how to identify the second or next best. In many value contexts, degrees of betterness, including perhaps degrees of justice, will be continuous in this way.

Even apart from continuity cases, the next best alternative might already be precluded by the same missing conditions that have ruled out the best or model scenario. Consider a model scenario that consists in the meeting of four conditions, A, B, C, and D. Suppose condition C will not be met, ruling out the best or model scenario. And suppose the alternatives are ranked as follows:

AB*C*D (model)
A*C*D
A*C*
C
ABD
AB
. . .

C, marked in bold and italics, will not be satisfied. Here, the missing condition rules out not only the model, but also the next best, and the next two best after that. This does not render the question about Superset moot in this case. There is still the question whether supersets of any of the subsets of the (ideal or nonideal) model are guaranteed to be better (and the answer is no). So, the terminology of "second best" is, again, a significant misnomer.[10] This is a terminological point, and yet it is important. The term "second best" has no real justification, I think, and can tend to suggest things that are not true. The second best option sounds like, in the whole scheme of things, something that must be quite close in value to the first best, and so pretty good. But the best under the given lack of some model conditions might, in addition to not structurally approximating the first best in the Superset sense, also be not nearly as good.

c. Beyond Infeasibility

Next, while many follow Lipsey and Lancaster in speaking as if the question only arises if some of the elements are *not available*, that is not so.[11] The underlying issue is more general and so more important than that. Whether or not the best or the model scenario is possible, feasible, or available, suppose it *will not occur*.[12] For example, it might even be that we could do it but, for some reason, we won't. This is not just a quibble. It is important, especially in moral and political philosophy, to distinguish clearly between a scenario's being one that will not happen, and its being one that is impossible or beyond the relevant agents' abilities. These are importantly different because, first, lots of things that people predictably will not do, they could do, sometimes easily. And, second, some moral evaluations might well hang on whether they were, nevertheless, within their abilities. Finally, even apart from the question of "cannot do" or even "will not do," suppose we are, for whatever reason, putting that model scenario aside in our thinking. The question remains, "We can and will establish the full ideal. But if we were not to do so, which would be the best of the remaining alternative scenarios?"

d. Beyond Causal Interactions

The thought that lies behind the critique of Superset reasoning is that the way in which satisfaction of one condition contributes to the value of the satisfaction of a set of conditions *depends on what other conditions are present*. We might say that the conditions "interact." In the classic economic setting the context is given by causal value interaction of elements of an economic scenario, such as levels of supply and demand, availability of resources, and so forth. The relevant context is also causal in several simple examples, like the pill case. There are many cases, however, in which there is a kind of interaction among the conditions that is not causal. Consider the aesthetic value of a certain combination of elements in a photograph despite the worthlessness of certain subsets of those elements. (We will see other examples.) It is natural to say that these elements "interact" in their contribution to the value of the whole, even though nothing causal is meant by this.[13] An example would be these two conditions:

1. Lee desires that his children are safe.
2. Lee's children are safe.

Plausibly, each of these has some value on its own. But when both are met (even if Lee doesn't realize it) there is, at least on some views, something more of value. Lee's desire is satisfied (whether he knows it or not), and this might be a new instance of value. Unlike the pills, the extra value here is not based on any physical effects of the co-presence of these two conditions. The satisfaction of Lee's desire is not a further event at all.

In some cases, then, the violation of Superset is due to noncausal value interactions. Consider these two conditions, illustrating not just noncausal interaction, but also a violation of Superset:

1b. Lou desires that his children be stars.
2b. Lou's children are stars.

When both are met, suppose this is good in a certain way to a certain degree, with each condition contributing to that value. But if not for 2b, 1b—a desire with that particular content—might arguably be bad—worse than its absence. In that case, Superset is violated. 1b's bearing on value changes in the presence of 2b. But this is not because of any physical effects of their co-presence. In these (Lou and Lee) cases, the valuable relation is desire-satisfaction. But there are plausibly other valuable relations such as fairness, justice, beauty, humor, and so on, that are instantiated but not caused by the co-presence of several conditions.

2. Positive and Negative Implication

The usual use of the point about second best or the fallacy of approximation is the negative implication that understanding some high standard is not useful for understanding value rankings where the standard is not fully met. It can be used against "ideal theory" about justice in that way: ideal theory cannot be assumed to be helpful in that particular way for "nonideal theory." However, in addition, for every negative implication of the Fallacy, there is, logically, also what I call a positive (or double negative) implication, namely: from the fact that some superset of conditions is not more valuable than a proper subset of them, it does not follow that this superset is not nevertheless a necessary part of the valuable model scenario. Here, then, is the positive result that is the flip side of the negative result: in light of the failure of Superset, just because something is not good by itself this does not entail that it is not a contributing and even necessary part of the valuable model scenario. The claim that meeting some set of conditions would be very good, or even ideal, cannot be refuted by showing that meeting only certain of those conditions would not be good.

To illustrate: consider steak sauce and steak, in the usual negative presentation—we cannot conclude that since the combination would be good having the sauce would be better than having neither ingredient. That is negative, in that this is no way to learn that having one of them would be good. On the flip side, however, there is the positive implication—positive in that it shows that this is no way to learn that something is *not* good: in a world in which you will not be having steak, we cannot conclude from the fact that having steak sauce would not be good, that having the combination would not be good. As it happens, it would be.

The point is quite simple, but the significance for normative reasoning is substantial. In normative contexts, the usual negative implication often bears (negatively) on the question of what to do, though not always, while the positive implication bears, instead, on what to think (about, for example, ideals like justice). Suppose we ought, morally speaking, not to build certain institutions because we will not comply with them in any case. It does not follow that building those institutions is not an element in what is required of us. We might be required to Build and Comply. The negative point is that, just because building is part of what is required, we cannot conclude that we ought to at least build even if we will not comply. That commits the fallacy of approximation. The positive point is that, just because we ought not to build the institutions, it does not follow that we are not required to build them along with complying.[14]

3. Moral/Political Examples

Shortly, we will look closely at a moral and political deployment of the idea that suggests one way in which understanding an ideal (or, more generally, a valuable but unrealistic) standard for social or political conditions might have practical implications even in nonideal conditions even though approximation cannot be assumed to be valuable. First, however, we can now, briefly, consider the fallacy of approximation in two moral and political contexts, just to illustrate several of the general points above.

As I have argued, the fallacy has application even if no ideal condition is under consideration. We can see that point in a context relevant to normative political thought in the following example. Suppose, plausibly, that military prisons are no part of a social ideal. We might still suppose that there could be ideal prison conditions, so to speak. At Camp Bucca, in southern Iraq, in 2004 it was reported that, "the detainee-guard ratio is 7 to 1, still above the *ideal* 5 to 1."[15] But put even that kind of ideal aside, since the fallacy of approximation is not limited to the consideration of best or ideal cases. Suppose only that a certain standard of adequacy, rather than any ideal, is met so long as there are,

a. 7 or fewer prisoners for each guard (not always ideal), plus
b. 50 minutes per day of outdoor time for each prisoner.

Superset would say that if we will not have (a), then having (b) is better than not having it. That is fallacious reasoning, and it might well go wrong in this case. If the ratio is higher than 7 to 1, it might be a disaster to have outdoor time for the prisoners, who might be difficult to manage. So here is a case of the Fallacy, with no unavailable *ideal* in the picture at all.

A second moral/political example can be found in Rawls, illustrating how the issue is present where the interactions in question are non-causal, unlike the usual causal settings for illustrations of the so-called problem of second best. Consider the principles that make up Rawls's conception of justice, according to which a society is just if and only if, in virtue of its basic structure, all three of the following conditions (simplified here) are met:

Equal Basic Liberties
A fully adequate set of basic liberties compatible with the same for all.

Fair Equality of Opportunity
Life chances not determined by class.

Difference Principle
Any inequalities benefit the position of the worst off, which is then maximized.

Notice that we have not yet needed to say anything about the famous lexical priority of certain of these principles, which figures importantly in Rawls's view. No such priority relation is relevant to a statement of the standard for full social justice. The three are individually necessary and jointly sufficient. We could have listed them in any order. As Rawls writes about lexical priority of the principles,

A principle does not come into play until[16] those previous to it are either fully met or do not apply. A serial [or 'lexical'] ordering avoids, then, having to balance principles at all.[17]

The other side of this coin is that lexical priority, which ranks certain cases of incomplete justice as more just than others, plays no role unless some of the principles are not met. It says only this: all arrangements in which Equal Basic Liberties are fully met are more just than any arrangement in which they are not. It has nothing to do with anything about what counts as fully just, though it obviously applies to the fully just case as an instance. It has nothing to to with what is to be done first. It says nothing about what to do in case of less than full equal basic liberties.

Now suppose the Liberties condition (let us call it) will *not* be fully met (however feasible or infeasible it might be). But suppose we can yet meet either or both of the Difference Principle and the Opportunity principle. Is Superset correct that meeting them both would be better than meeting only the Opportunity Principle? That is, would it be more just if we added satisfaction of the Difference Principle to Opportunity? First, as we know, this is not guaranteed, since Superset reasoning is invalid. Moreover, we can see how satisfying both principles (without the equal basic liberties) might be worse from the standpoint of justice. Consider a policy of keeping material inequality[18] within certain bounds, even if this reduces the absolute position of the worst off. This violates the Difference Principle, and yet it might be more just than meeting the Difference Principle in the absence of any other guarantee of equal basic liberties. That is, it remains an open question, and so this is a view that involves possible value interactions, and violates the Superset principle.

Having come to this conclusion, we see that one way to build this point into the theory (which starts with three unordered necessary and sufficient conditions) would be Rawls's way: to give some of the principles lexical priority over some others. Rawls gives Liberty lexical priority over Opportunity, both of which have lexical priority over the Difference Principle. That would block any implication that, even if equal liberty is missing, justice favors the Difference Principle. Now, there may well be *causal* value interactions that are important here. But it can plausibly be held that there are also *noncausal* value interactions: certain combinations of conditions *constitute* a more just condition, whether or not they cause one.

Appendix: Organic Unity and the Fallacy of Approximation

The fallacy of approximation (aka the problem of second best) will put some philosophers in mind of important discussions of the idea that value might involve "organic unity." In this Appendix, I briefly explain the relation between the two, and argue that in an important way the fallacy of approximation is more fundamental.

G. E. Moore argued that the value of a whole is not guaranteed to be equal to the sum of the values of its parts. In particular, he gave examples meant to show how certain things in combination had *more* value than that sum. One example is the combination of a mental state of aesthetic appreciation of some object, along with a beautiful object that is appreciated.[19] Moore argued that neither of these elements had much value on its own, but in combination the whole had great value. The position that Moore rejects, which I will call Summation, is not yet refuted, however. It is possible to hold that the value of each part increases in context—when it is combined with the other parts—leading to the enhanced value of the whole. Moore denied that a thing's intrinsic value ever changes with its context.[20] In that case, the only way to account for the enhanced value of the whole was to posit value that belongs only to the whole itself. Even without the parts having greater value in context, the value of the whole which combines the parts could sometimes be greater (or, presumably, less) than the sum of the values of the parts considered alone. Moore's examples do not concern causal interactions that generate the enhanced value of certain combinations of parts, but Summation is equally well refuted by causal examples such as the pills we discussed above. The value of Joe's taking pill A or pill B might be nil, but his taking them both might, owing to the chemical reaction in his bloodstream between the substances, be very great.

Before comparing Moore's view to what I have called the fallacy of approximation (the invalidity of Superset reasoning), it will be helpful to make some distinctions. We can define two kinds of holism about value, and two corresponding kinds of independence that they deny.

> *Contextual Holism*: Holds (what Moore denies) that the value of a thing can sometimes change in contexts of combination with other things.

Call the denial (along with Moore himself) of Contextual Holism, *Contextual Independence*. A second kind of holism, held by Moore, is,

> *Organic Holism*: A whole consisting of multiple parts might have a value different from the sum of the values of the parts considered in context.

It says that the value of the whole can differ from the sum even if the parts' values do not change in context. Organic Holism is equivalent to the denial of,

> *Contextual Summation*: The value of a whole is always equal to the sum of the values of its parts in context.

Let's use the term *isolated value* for the value of a thing considered alone rather than in a context of combination with other things. Even if, as Moore held, Contextual Holism were false (that is, if Contextual Independence were true), still, if Moore's Organic Holism were true the values of parts might yet interact so that the whole's value is greater than the sum of the isolated values of the parts.

There is an ambiguity in the meaning of "the sum of the values of the parts," since these values might be considered in isolation or in context. However, once it is assumed, as Moore did, that the value of parts in context is always the same as their isolated values (Contextual Independence), the kind of summation that is in question is this second version,

> *(Context Independent) Summation*: The value of a whole is always equal to the sum of the isolated values of the parts.[21]

Arguably, then, the fundamental kind of summation that is challenged by Moore is Context Independent Summation. Think of it this way: Moore adduces examples that appear to refute Context Independent Summation. Then there are two kinds of holism that could explain this, and he objects to one, Contextual Holism, and rests with the other, Organic Holism. *Inter alia*, Contextual Summation is also refuted, since it is inconsistent with Organic Holism.

Context Independent Summation is, arguably, also the simpler and more intuitive form of summation reasoning, since the possibility of Contextual Holism is somewhat exotic.[22] Hereafter, then, I will abbreviate Context Independent Summation to *Summation*, hence the parentheses in its title above.

That summarizes Moore's position among some of the options concerning how the values of wholes relate to the values of their parts.[23] The upshot for Moore is the rejection of Summation. I want next to compare Superset (which I have discussed above in relation to so-called Second Best) to Summation. They might seem to be very closely related, both asserting a kind of orderly relation between the value of parts and the value of wholes. This might tempt the view that the question of the truth of Superset is, more or less, the same as the question—much discussed by Moore and others—of the truth of Summation. However, I will argue (putting it imprecisely first for simplicity) that Superset is not ruled out by the refutation of Summation. Separate arguments are required to defeat Superset.

Superset's interest lies in two facts about it: (a) Superset is at least as salient as Summation in actual reasoning about the values of parts and wholes (exemplified in second best reasoning), and (b) the question of its truth is more fundamental than that of Summation in the following sense. While the refutation of Summation does not refute Superset, the converse is the case. Since Summation entails Superset, refuting Superset entails the refutation of Summation.

Recall,

The Superset Thesis
For any valuable model set S, and any subset of it ss (including the null set), any subset of S (including S itself) that is a proper superset of ss will be more valuable than ss.[24]

Before showing that Superset could be (though I argue that it is not) true even if Summation is false, I want to emphasize that this is not a merely technical point of dubious interest. While Summation is more simply stated, Superset is often more readily used in actual reasoning. This is because unlike Summation, Superset reasoning does not require reference to any specific quantities of value in any wholes or parts. Superset reasoning is available with much less information about the arithmetical values of the elements. By "available," I mean that, even though it is not a valid form of reasoning, its use does not require any arithmetical information (and, anyway, a restricted form of such reasoning is valid in some restricted domains, such as coins). It purports to apply whenever the value of each element is positive in the model context. Nothing more is needed. For example, recall our earlier example of the monetary value of some coins. You don't need to posit anything about their individual values in order to know that any superset of any subset of them is more valuable. By contrast, we cannot use Summation (except insofar as we can use Superset, which it entails) to compare the values of any of the subsets to each other without knowing the values of at least some of the coins. Summation reasoning is essentially about the precise arithmetical relations between the precisely quantified values of parts and wholes, so it is unavailable in reasoning about value in many concrete contexts (including many real and hypothetical scenarios). This way in which Superset reasoning depends on less information partly explains why it has the significance across the areas of moral and political philosophy that I discuss in the body of the chapter.

Having emphasized the salience of Superset reasoning, it is also notable that Superset could be true even if Summation were not. First, another definition:

> *Positive Synergy*
> Parts exhibit positive synergy if and only if the value of a whole is greater than (not only different from) the sum of the isolated values of the parts.

Positive synergy is one kind of case which, if there are instances, refutes Summation. (It is neutral as to which holism, Contextual or Organic, is the explanation.) Here is an imaginary but obviously realistic case of positive synergy: consider three things:

> *Element A*: S takes pill A
> *Element B*: S takes pill B
> *Element C*: S takes pill C

We know that the combination of all three elements could have a positive synergy, owing to beneficial chemical interactions among the substances in the pills. That is enough to refute Summation. But it would not refute Superset, since it might yet be true that (as Superset claims) any pair of the three pills is better than any of the pair's subsets (viz., zero or one of its members).

Simple cases of negative synergy, as I will call it, also refute Summation without refuting Superset. Whether or not the three pills have a positive synergy, we also know that pill B might have the following feature:

> *Negative Synergy* (or "less than the *sum* of the parts")
> For some elements A and B, they exhibit negative synergy if and only if the combination A&B[25] is *less good than the sum* of the values of A alone and B alone.

If there are such cases, they violate Summation. But they do not yet violate Superset, because A&B might yet be better than A and better than B, as Superset predicts. For example, the values could look like this, considering each element alone:

> Value of A = 3
> Value of B = 3
> Value of C = 3

Therefore, the sum of the values of A and B is 6. But it could be, because of how they interact, that the value of the combination,

(A&B) = 4

less than the sum of the values of the parts of A&B, a negative synergy, but greater than either part.

For a more robust case of negative synergies among the elements of a model set, suppose the same holds for other pairs: each pair has a value of 4, less than its sum of 6. Now we can add a negative trio synergy. Suppose that:

A&B&C = 8 (less than the parts' sum, which would be 9)

In this case Summation fails both for the trio and for all pairs. But Superset still holds: for any subset of the trio, any superset of it adds value. This is another case where Summation fails, while Superset holds. So either positive synergy or negative synergy can provide cases that violate Summation but not Superset.

It takes more than simple negative or positive synergy to violate Superset. Just to give an example, there is a kind of negative synergy, call it *strong negative synergy*, which will violate Superset. It could be that if you add B to A without C (C is strictly irrelevant to this example now), the result is worse than A alone (suppose A&B=2). (It might, as in this case, also be worse than B alone, a different feature.) A homely example might be having red wine with mint ice cream, the result being worse than the wine alone (and, incidentally, probably also worse than the ice cream alone). Call this kind of negative interaction:

Strong Negative Synergy (or 'less than *some* of the parts')
The value of the combination of several elements that are positive contributors to the model is less than the isolated value of at least one of the elements.

Strong negative synergy will always violate Superset, since by definition some of the supersets are less valuable than some of their subsets.

So, some positive synergies, and some negative synergies, will violate Summation. Even when they do, they may not violate Superset. *Strong* negative synergies are also possible, which violate Superset. So, Moore's claim—that Summation is false (even though, as he claimed, Contextual Independence is true)—does not refute Superset. His argument is thus not strictly relevant to the so-called problem of second best, which is, in its general form, equivalent to the falsity of Superset. Superset can indeed be easily refuted, but it is not the Moorean issue about Summation.

Having just seen that refuting Summation would not refute Superset, we can now see that refuting Superset does indeed refute Summation. This can be shown by demonstrating that Summation entails Superset. Suppose that Summation is true. Since Superset only considers the domain of positive contributing parts to, and in the context of, the whole[26] we know that the value of each part must also be positive regardless of context. This is because Summation, which we are, for the moment, supposing is true, stands for Context Independent Summation. The values of parts do not change with context. It follows that any subset of the model (which is to consider things out of the model context) differs from any of its proper subsets only by having additional value-adding parts. Superset must hold in that case: for any subset of a model's contributing elements, a (model-contained) proper superset of it is always more valuable. So, (Context Independent) Summation entails Superset.

Summation entails Superset but not vice versa. So refuting Summation (as Moore purports to do) leaves open the question of Superset. Refuting Superset, however (as I have purported to do following others), would also refute Summation. In this respect, the question of Superset is more fundamental than the question of Summation. We have seen strong counterexamples to Superset, in contexts of both causal and noncausal interaction among the values of elements. They count, *inter alia*, as counterexamples to Summation as well.

CHAPTER FIFTEEN

Countervailing Deviation

Two wrongs can make a right in the sense that the best available arrangement may contain a balance of imperfections, an adjustment of compensating injustices.

—JOHN RAWLS, *A THEORY OF JUSTICE*

1. Introduction

In this chapter I explore a second way in which understanding an ideal or valuable arrangement might be thought to be practically valuable even if it is not to be attained, sought, or approximated. The first, that the ideal gives a structural ideal that is to be approximated, faces important limitations owing to the fallacy of approximation. But there is a second appeal to the ideal (and also to partial ideals) and I will emphasize its promise. This happens also to be another way in which the fallacy of approximation can be illuminating in political philosophy. To begin with, we can bring the fallacy of approximation to bear on thinking about realistic practical political settings. Herbert Marcuse exemplifies the point in the context of what he calls "pure tolerance," which I will stylize slightly as the context of broad viewpoint-neutral freedom of expression. Marcuse grants to John Stuart Mill and followers that under favorable conditions pure tolerance will tend to promote progress toward the truth. Indeed, Marcuse insists that the point, or "*telos* of tolerance is truth."[1] Call this Marcuse's,

Epistemic Conception of Free Public Speech
The justification for a strong measure of toleration of and non-interference with expression is, in significant part, in order to foster the movement of thought toward true or correct views and convictions.

However, in a second step, Marcuse argues that this epistemic value of tolerance arises only if tolerance is combined with a social background in which, roughly, no point of view holds any strong nonrational advantage derived from, for example, economic or political power. That is, if one gender, race, or social class has the power to prevail in social debates irrespective of the quality of the reasons they can martial for their positions, he denies that "pure tolerance," in which all sides are equally left free to push their views without interference, will promote the truth. The background epistemology is one according to which the truth *would* be promoted if views prevailed according to their rational merits.

That is a contestable epistemology on which a view that better responds to epistemic reasons will be closer to the truth or more likely to be true, but I will not pursue that question here; I am not defending Marcuse's substantial view but pointing to his identification, in effect, of the fallacy of approximation in some familiar liberal thought: just because pure tolerance would be an essential part of a certain highly desirable condition does not mean it would be desirable without the other conditions.

I pause the Marcusean story here, and return to it shortly. Before turning to his practical proposal, which exemplifies what I will call "countervailing deviation," we can already see that use has been made of a certain social ideal or high standard, which may not itself be a realistic possibility. Nevertheless, it is used in a practically valuable way. By understanding the epistemic value of tolerance in its ideal setting, Marcuse is able to conclude that this is a value that tolerance will not have without that fuller setting and its other elements. This is an application of the idea we are calling the fallacy of approximation: free speech cannot be assumed to have the value it would contribute in the context of the ideal when some elements of the ideal are absent. In the absence of a certain kind of equal power (think of that as analogous to one of a cocktail of valuable medications), it cannot be assumed that free speech (one of the other medications in the valuable set) is still valuable rather than worthless or even dangerous.

The practical upshot so far is negative: the practical advocacy of a social ethos of tolerance even in the absence of the fuller setting of communicative balance is shown to be a poor argument. Understanding the ideal, then, has that direct, albeit negative, practical importance in realistic conditions. The result (if one accepts the ancillary premises) is not a small matter. Many have thought of the right to express one's views without political or social interference as implied by a certain morally mandatory kind of respect. But Mill, a utilitarian, did not see it that way, and neither does Marcuse. One could consider similar arguments about other traditional liberal rights, such as the right to vote, and so forth, and we will briefly do so shortly. Theories of basic liberties that defend a "system" of basic liberties, rather than each liberty on its own terms, will be less susceptible to the fallacy. Rawls defends basic liberties in that way, and we will come back to his case yet again in the context of campaign finance. Of course, some basic liberties might have great independent importance, while others may not. A right against cruel punishment probably does not depend on which other liberties are in place, for example.

Followers of Mill might seem to presuppose that the other preconditions for the epistemic value of free speech are in place. Idealistic theory runs a risk of that kind. There is a natural worry about people judging some idealistic scenario to be more feasible than it is and setting out to achieve it (call that the *danger concern*), but the present worry is slightly different. Sometimes idealistic theory is designed with a laudable attention to feasibility, in such a way as to tempt the impression that parts of it are held to be already fully or partly in place. Instead of rashness (as in the danger concern) this might lead to inappropriate quietism. Call this the *present-polishing concern* about idealistic theory. Roughly, it is what Marcuse accuses Mill of, and we find a similar concern more recently in some arguments of Charles Mills.[2] Both points are important—the danger concern and the present-polishing concern. Still, neither addresses the truth or soundness of the idealistic theories about which they raise warnings, and it is important to keep those questions distinct.

When an instance of the fallacy of approximation is identified in a normative political argument, the idea of a possible idealistic social condition is put to practical use in blocking bad arguments in favor of actual political proposals—those aimed at approximation. As I pointed out, the practical value is negative in a certain way, showing that a certain practical argument is a failure. Marcuse's argument about pure tolerance takes a second, more positive step, suggesting that certain carefully identified acts of "selective intolerance" might have a remedial effect. He appears to have in mind such forms of protest as interfering with publications and speeches that repetitively promote the views and interests of privileged classes. Before looking more closely at that particular context, consider the general idea of *countervailing deviation*.

Sometimes when there is a missing element from some valuable or even ideal condition A, we can ask what value is thereby lost in that condition B: what kind, and how much. For example, if one person regularly interrupts others at a meeting, we might conclude that this lets his power skew the course of discussion in a nonrational, or non-epistemic direction. His point of view may be influential for no good epistemic reason. We could restore that value without even thinking about the nature of the missing value if we could provide the missing element itself. But suppose that we will not or cannot provide it. In that case, only by thinking about the kind and extent of lost value can we think about whether there is some alternative way partly or wholly to restore that value. In some cases, the countervailing measure need not be a further deviation or at least it is indeterminate whether it is. However, we are exhibiting the importance of not fetishizing, so to speak, each element of the ideal, and so it is important to see that sometimes an appropriate countervailing measure might be to deviate even further from the structural model or ideal. That would make the resulting situation, call it C, *less* similar to the ideal scenario A than B is. Even so, in principle, the second subtraction—the further departure—could, in principle, partly or fully restore the lost value. That would be what I call a countervailing deviation.

It is important to point out that if a countervailing deviation were to *fully* countervail the first deviation (on balance or without any relevant costs of its own) there is no reason to suppose that this doubly departing scenario has any less claim to be ideal than the ostensible ideal from which it "deviates." It may be only that it would not have occurred to us except in this dialectic of deviation. On that view, the standards by which an arrangement counts as ideal may be multiply specifiable, and the idea of a deviation would be defined in relation to any one of the specifications.

Think again of pills. Suppose that pills A, B, and C would cure your ailment. But you do not have C. It may be that you should not take A and B alone (contrary to Superset, as discussed in the previous chapter). Suppose that in the absence of C there is a second way to achieve a cure, namely taking D along with A and B. Is the absence of C a deviation from the ideal? Deviation is only relative to a specification of the ideal. The absence of C is a deviation from the first specification (ABC). It is not a deviation relative to the second, equally ideal specification (ABD). Fully countervailing deviations from a given specification would take us to a second specification of the ideal. Imperfectly countervailing deviations from one specification might fruitfully be looked at also from the vantage point of some other specification of the ideal to which it might, in some ways, be at least closer, and so on.[3]

What counts as countervailing? It is not always a simple matter, of course, to determine what response would be countervailing in just the right way without, for example, entailing other moral costs that would mark it as overreaction. A further question then is whether, even if it is countervailing it is justified all things considered. We can notice these two questions by reflecting on the following example:

Traffic Jam
Suppose that patterns of political choice by non-black members of a community have intentionally led to policies (such as voter identification laws, and so forth) that suppress black turnout at the polls without solving any preexisting problem of fraud. Consider a plan by black activists to countervail this injustice by orchestrating traffic jams in non-black neighborhoods on election day so as to suppress levels of voting in a countervailing way.

We can see how this might be a candidate for a justified act of private countervailing deviation. Just because it would be good in a certain way if everyone had unimpeded access to the polls, in the case where one racial group has been deprived of that access *we cannot conclude that the value of others having access remains in place*. Logic alone blocks that inference, a case of the fallacy of approximation. In this case, the first step is to note and avoid the fallacy.

However, it is not a simple matter to inquire into whether the value lost by the triggering deviation—the lost access to the polls by blacks—would indeed be countervailed if there were a corresponding loss of access for non-blacks. Nothing follows either way about that simply from the failure of the approximation inference. Furthermore, even if it would be effectively countervailed, there remains the further question whether intentionally imposing the countervailing deviation would be justified. Not every act that would make things better (apart from whatever moral value the act itself turns out to have) is morally justified. The idea of countervailing deviation is not the crude principle that "turnabout is fair play." The profound disvalue of someone being raped is not, to any degree, restored by the perpetrator being raped in response, and the same will be true for many forms of wrong and injustice.

The Traffic Jam case is useful, then, for two reasons, and they point in opposite directions.[4] On one hand, it is not always easy to determine whether a putative countervailing deviation is actually countervailing in the right way, or, even if it is, such an action is justified on balance. On the other hand, the example calls, it seems to me, for reflection on a broader range of issues and tactics since it is suggestive of a line of reasoning in which countervailing deviation may sometimes highlight a consideration that makes the difference and renders an action permissible. For now, we are only observing that there is this consideration, a pro tanto reason in some cases for acting in pursuit of a countervailing deviation from a certain model or ideal.

Generalizing from the case of interfering with free public expression, it might also be that other acts that we have come to see as wrong in themselves might not be wrong, and the disapproving ethos might be explained in this other way. It so happens that both Mills[5] (not Mill!) and Marcuse deploy (as I read them) this set of ideas especially against liberal political philosophy—against Rawls and Mill respectively. Both can be read as pointing out that much liberal thought appears to commit the fallacy of approximation in advocating certain elements of a highly idealistic liberal scenario even in the absence of other important elements. They go further, arguing not only that this piecemeal value does not follow (which is an undeniable logical point), but also that as it happens, these detached elements do *not* have their claimed value outside of the aspirational (or even utopian) idealistic conditions. It is an interesting and important question, which I cannot pursue, whether liberal thought somehow defined is characteristically, rather than anecdotally, susceptible to this pattern of error. The idea might be that it fetishizes, as "rights," certain elements that would be an essential part of a describable ideal, failing to notice

COUNTERVAILING DEVIATION [293]

that unless the other elements are present (which, realistically, they often are not) the value of the fetishized elements goes missing. (Of course, this is not to say that there are not *any* rights that are, in that way, context-independent.)

Marcuse, then, argues that some kinds of (especially private, not governmental) interference with public expression might indeed be justified as a countervailing deviation when some other crucial elements of the ideal epistemic model of free speech are absent. This approach is entirely different from either (a) justifying disobedience to some norm,[6] such as "free speech," by showing that conditions of political obligation have simply been violated, leaving one morally free to disobey, or from (b) justifying disobedience on the ground that there is a certain outcome that would be good, which the disobedience aims at and will credibly promote. The idea of countervailing deviation makes neither of those claims. It claims rather that some value that the process would have had but for the triggering deviation would be restored by the countervailing deviation. The idea of countervailing deviation is proceduralist in that way. The value of the procedure itself might be instrumental, as it is in the epistemic context I have been using, or non-instrumental ("pure procedural," to use a term from Rawls).[7]

We can see this structure arise in certain settings of a kind that game theory considers. However, game theory analogies could easily be misleading, since unlike game theory the context for countervailing deviation is making no use of what choices would be instrumentally rational for individual players. Still, we can look at a familiar game theoretic scenario through the lens of an impartial standard of evaluation such as Pareto optimality or maximizing utilitarianism. In the following case, each player, A and B, might either do X or Y, and the best case is X/X. It is Pareto and utility superior to all other outcomes, so let it be our model condition. If one player, B, will not be doing X, then the smallest deviation from the model that is compatible with that would be where player B does not depart from the model but does X anyway. But then the outcome would be Y/X, with a score of 2/2. A better outcome, both by Pareto and by total utility, can be obtained by instead deviating further from the model, namely where both depart from X. Y/Y gives a score of 5/5 which is Pareto superior to the lesser deviation X/Y. B's doing Y would be a partially countervailing deviation given that A will do X. I emphasize that game theory, which is a branch of rational choice theory, is not doing any work here, since we are not asking what is rational for any player. Still, this matrix lays out the payoffs for each party and in some contexts that is enough to determine which outcome is impersonally best. Similar examples could be constructed if other standards of impersonal evaluation are preferred, such as equality, priority, and so forth. (Of course, some standards require more or other information than the individual payoffs.) Viewed in that way, this example gives a particular illustration of partially countervailing deviation.

A/B	X	Y
X	10 10	2 2
Y	2 2	5 5

There is also a variation, of course, in which the score for Y/Y is 10/10, which would be a case of fully countervailing deviation, though it is only a deviation relative to the postulation of X/X as a model. But X/X is no better than Y/Y so either has as much claim to be regarded as ideal.[8]

2. Is the Ideal Really Being Consulted?

The fallacy of approximation warns us against assuming that we should have as many elements of the ideal as we can. This is not a way in which the ideal is useful, but a way in which it might wrongly be thought to be useful. There is no attempt here to convince skeptics that there is a theoretical need to posit not only comparative relations of "juster than" but also a threshold or "partition" such that above that line a society counts as fully just.[9] For present purposes I take the availability of "just" rather than merely "juster" for granted. What I am hoping to show here is that an understanding of full justice can have a certain practical value even if it is not as a goal to achieve or even approximate. But, one might ask, what practical value? It is also not at all clear that consulting the ideal is any reliable guide to choosing a countervailing deviation. What use has the ideal been in a case like this? The answer, as I see it, is that it is only by thinking about the multiple elements in the ideal that one can consider whether and in what ways there is interaction between their values. However, the question of the value of the element in question such as free speech must be considered in the context of whatever other elements will be present and the absence of whichever elements will not, and this is so whether or not those other elements are parts of ideal justice. This might seem to make it doubtful whether the idealness of any arrangement is put to use here after all.[10]

In answer to that objection, recall that we are focusing on cases where it is reasonable to believe that element A is valuable. Our point is that this will not guide the agent's decision about whether to adopt A unless it is further determined whether A's value depends on the presence of any elements that will, as it happens, be missing. Often an agent will come to realize that their positive evaluation of A subtly took for granted the presence of a set of elements which together are good—a model or ideal condition. The usefulness of consulting the ideal, in that case, is not exactly that it is ideal, but that it happens to be the setting in which the element in question is thought to have value. Those, then, are elements upon which the value of A might depend, and if they will not all be present then that question must be considered. The reasoning that this triggers, again, is not specifically about idealness or full justice, but is set in motion because that is an instance, a model, in which the value of an ingredient is being assessed.

The point here about the value of consulting ideals of full justice, both for purposes of assessing an element's value in its likely setting and also for considering what might be countervailing, generalizes to the value of consulting whatever model, fully ideal or not, of a good set of ingredients might be operative in the tendency to think of one of the ingredients (such as free speech) as good. Put the other way around, that general value of consulting the operative model in which several elements are good together shows us how, often, the operative model is, or may be—thoughts about these things are not always precise on this score—an ideal of full social justice. In practice the point here might be put like this: "It is very plausible that this element is indeed part of a good set of elements when they are all present. For example, it would be good, and this element would contribute, if all the elements of full social justice were present, and that is a natural way in which to think of this element as good from the standpoint of justice. However, it is important not to fallaciously infer that this element is good whether or not those other elements are present." Ideals, or ideas of a just social structure, are merely special cases, though salient ones, of models in which a set of ingredients is held to be valuable. From there the points about the fallacy of approximation and the possibility of countervailing deviations from a model fall into place.

3. Institutional Countervailing

I have so far built on some examples of how individuals ought to conduct themselves in their political activity, introducing the possibility of permissible countervailing deviations from some valuable or ideal scenario including certain norms of behavior. But the idea of countervailing deviations is suggestive also in the context of institutional design, and that is the extension I briefly explore in the remainder.

Institutionalized countervalence is a model that can make some sense, in a distinctive way, of the device of legal restrictions on the finances of political campaigns. For present purposes, I put aside treatments of this issue that focus exclusively on procedural fairness irrespective of any epistemic value it might have. I do not mean there is nothing to it, but I want to focus on arguments about epistemic value. Rawls's important discussion of these issues emphasizes what he calls the "fair value," rather than merely formal equality, of political liberties. This might sound like an appeal to the non-instrumental or intrinsic moral value of procedural fairness, but his discussion explicitly invokes epistemic arguments. He writes,

[U]nless the fair-value of [the political] liberties is approximately preserved, just background institutions are unlikely to be either established or maintained. . . . [T]hese rules and procedures are to be a fair process, designed to yield just and effective legislation.[11]

With the goal in mind of a political procedure that is fair in a way that promotes just and effective legislation, he also famously argues that the package of basic liberties has a value that may not be compromised for the sake of non-liberty values (such as prosperity or economic equality)—that is, not even for the sake of promoting just and effective legislation. Any single category of basic liberty may, in some cases, be limited for the sake of other liberties or the proper set of liberties overall, though not for other reasons.

However, the political liberties are to be treated specially.[12] In the case of political liberties, the equal distribution of their usefulness or value—rather than the liberty or its extent itself—is an admissible rationale for limiting basic liberties. The reason is that a central part of the value of the political liberties is absent if their worth or usefulness is not also fairly (roughly equally) distributed, whereas this is not true for other basic liberties. In this case liberty can be limited for the sake, not exactly of liberty, but for a certain kind of equality—equal or fair *value* of the political liberties. He applies this reasoning to the U.S. Constitution.

[T]he aim of achieving a fair scheme of representation can justify limits on and regulations of political speech in elections, provided that these limits and regulations satisfy [certain conditions]. For how else is the full and effective voice of all citizens to be maintained? Since it is a matter of one basic liberty against another, the liberties protected by the First Amendment may have to be adjusted in the light of other constitutional requirements, in this case the requirement of the fair value of the political liberties. Not to do so is to fail to see a constitution as a whole and to fail to recognize how its provisions are to be taken together in specifying a just political procedure as an essential part of a fully adequate scheme of basic liberties.[13]

Here a basic liberty may be limited for the sake of fair value of political liberties.[14]

The form of argument behind Rawls's advocacy of campaign finance restrictions can be seen as a case of countervailing deviation. To see how, we need to identify a model or ideal, a triggering deviation from that model, and a partly or fully countervailing deviation. As we will see, this analysis need not be attributed to Rawls himself. Sketching such an analysis of this case serves several purposes. One is to help attune ourselves to the availability of such ideas in concrete cases. Another is to give an illustration of the earlier point that the operative idea of a deviation from a model or ideal is relative to a particular specification of the ideal, where there might be several specifications with equal standing.

As we saw in the discussion of Marcuse's critique of the idea of "pure tolerance," there is a conception of free expression in a collective that may indeed be one ingredient in a full instantiation of social justice. Even in the ideal setting it would be congenial to some forms of restriction, but incompatible with others. The terms "freedom" and "liberty" can be deployed in numerous ways, but the point I am after concerns the idea of a person's ability to express her views without interference (including threats, or harms) by public or private agents. That is what I will mean by a person's liberty of expression for present purposes. Liberty of expression or freedom of speech in a collective setting is not so simple though, since one person's speech can interfere with another's, as when shouting interferes with a performance, or one billboard obstructs another. Some restrictions on speech, then, would be speech-protecting at the same time. There is a pure model of free speech in which there is no restriction or interference with speech except to protect other speech in certain ways. Of course, this pure model is unattractive. Some speech causes or risks substantial harm to others in a sufficiently direct way that all agree that it may be restricted for the sake of protection, even if what is protected is not the other person's speech or freedom of speech. Taking that for granted (and acknowledging that it oversimplifies matters somewhat), there is a conception of freedom of speech in which, except for those harm-based cases, speech is regulated only for the sake of liberty of speech itself—within the bounds of harm-prevention, it advocates a maximal equal liberty of speech for each person: the most extensive liberty of expression—scope for expression without interference—for each that is compatible with equally extensive liberty of expression for all others. Here, then, is a recognizable and moderately sophisticated conception of freedom of speech:

Pure(-ish) Freedom of Speech
Except for cases of speech that directly risk harming others, speech is only restricted where necessary to increase freedom of speech in other respects and on balance.

The point in giving it this name is to resonate, at least loosely, with what Marcuse calls "pure tolerance," as discussed above. This model is not, of course, "pure" in the sense of eschewing all restriction. Nor does it even countenance restrictions only for the sake of harm-prevention. However, except for the special case of harmful acts that take the form of speech, the only value appealed to in shaping the domain of speech regulation is the promotion of freedom of speech itself. The liberty itself, conceived in a collective setting, generates grounds for restriction of that very liberty.

Campaign finance restrictions—such as limits on how much money people or corporations may contribute to campaigns or independently spend on campaign advocacy—commonly depart from the pure-ish conception of free speech. The departure is not simply in the fact that they restrict speech. Instead—and here is the point I have been laying the groundwork for—it is that campaign finance restrictions are restrictions on speech,[15] but they are often *neither* restrictions on directly harmful speech, nor aimed at reducing some people's liberty of expression in order to remove some restrictions or limitations on the liberty of expression for anyone. When wealthy agents are restricted from buying political advertising, this does not generally somehow remove some restriction or constraint on efforts by others to speak that were present prior to these new restrictions. Rather, it reduces everyone's formal immunity from interference without increasing anyone's immunity. In that significant sense, the restriction on liberty of expression that campaign finance restrictions represent cannot be said to be for the sake of anyone's liberty of expression. Campaign finance restrictions limit a central basic liberty in ways that are not grounded in that liberty, nor in protection from harm. Defenses of such restrictions that do not admit this will not be persuasive. It can fairly be said to depart from the pure-ish conception of free speech.

This might seem to be stated too baldly. Certainly, there may be contexts in which speakers with greater resources can capture a large fraction of a certain communicative space, such as the amount of time during the Super Bowl that is devoted to political advertising. This leaves less such "space" (in this case, time) for other speakers. Very broadly, the rise of cable television and then online media greatly weaken the suggestion that the communicative space is finite and might be filled by wealthy spenders.[16] In any case, regulations to mitigate that could broadly fall within the pure-ish model. However, the effect of wealth on the public communicative space is not generally like this. Those who can afford it can speak more, and often more effectively, but this does not always, or even normally, exclude other speakers from the public forum even if it does make it more difficult, as competing speakers often do, for other speakers to have their intended effect. There is more to say here, but I largely put it aside, only to say that there is a strong case for campaign finance regulation that can grant, at least for the sake of argument, that it is not in the interest of increasing anyone's freedom of or access to speech.

There is a traditional and telling critique of a tendency in some liberal thought to concentrate on the merely "formally equal" basic liberties, liberties that are formulated in a way that (merely) does not recognize any unequal status across individuals. What this leaves out, it is argued, is that such formal guarantees will be of vastly unequal value to individuals if they have vastly unequal resources, opportunities, or capacities (I will refer generally here to the "wherewithal") to exercise the liberties. Campaign finance restrictions might naturally be defended, then, as limits on how individuals with greater wealth will be permitted to use it to expand the exercise of their free speech beyond what is available to others. This is sometimes presented as a liberty-driven justification for those restrictions, now using a more substantive and defensible conception of the idea of equal liberty.

Then, even if freedom to speak without interference is to be limited, so long as it is limited in order to increase substantive freedom of expression in other respects, it would still be driven by the value of freedom of speech, now substantively conceived. However, this is still not a plausible characterization of campaign finance restrictions. They do debar (to some extent) those who have greater wherewithal from making greater use than others of their formally equal liberty. But they do not thereby increase freedom of expression in any respect, either formally or substantively. No immunity from interference is expanded, as we have already seen. Moreover, though, no speaker's wherewithal to exercise her formal freedom of speech is expanded either. No limits of either kind are reduced for anyone, even as they are tightened for some.

I am building to a defense (already intimated, of course) of such restrictions nevertheless, but it is important to emphasize the nature of what would thereby be defended: not the enlargement of deliberation or speech on any plausible understanding of that idea, but rather the *leveling down* of the amount of speech (or access to speech) available to each speaker, party, or point of view. The point of doing so is normally to *narrow the inequality* between the speech that is available to the various speakers, where that inequality itself, not some lack of or interference with speech, is held to be troubling.

The fuller model or ideal in view is not pure-ish free speech itself. Rather, that is an element that would have important value, including epistemic value, in an idealized condition in which there is also roughly equal wherewithal behind each person's freedom of speech. But in most modern democracies such wherewithal is very unequal. We can notice the salience of a hypothetical condition that is idealized in certain profound ways, a democratic arrangement with both equal wherewithal and pure-ish freedom of speech. Call this *Idealized Democracy*. Pure-ish free speech, to simplify, is a plausible element in the ideal or model of Idealized Democracy. (Obviously, that model specifies only a small part of what anyone could regard as a highly desirable arrangement, and others could easily be assumed by readers also to be included, giving us a model condition to work with.) Some readers may resist the appeal of what I am calling Idealized Democracy on the ground that equalizing wherewithal conjures the prospect of massive coercive interference with the operation of economic markets. But that is not essential, so such readers may include as part of that model that the equality of wherewithal arises, as it were, spontaneously and not as a goal of policy.

The unequal wherewithal we find in modern democracies is a triggering deviation from Idealized Democracy, rendering the value of the other elements (we have only specified Pure-ish Freedom of Speech) questionable in the way we learn from the Fallacy of Approximation. By thinking more about the model, we can hope to understand in what way the deviation represents a loss of value, and on Rawls's analysis, the unequal wherewithal along with pure-ish free speech changes the worth or value of freedom of expression from equal worth to unequal worth. With that as the loss, it can next be considered whether, rather than maintaining all the other elements of the model that we can, including pure-ish freedom of speech, removing one or more—thus *further deviating* from the structural model—might partly or wholly countervail the value-loss in the triggering deviation. Indeed, Rawls argues, judicious restrictions on the freedom to fund the purchase of political advertising is a limitation on the freedom of speech that can (at least partly) countervail the unequal wherewithal, restoring the roughly equal worth of the freedom of political expression. The limitation of that liberty is a further deviation from Idealized Democracy, but implemented in order to countervail the triggering deviation of unequal wherewithal brought to political speech. It countervails by restoring some or all of the value lost by the triggering deviation.

This pure-ish conception brings us close to the conception of freedom of speech that was invoked in the pivotal case *Buckley v. Valeo*. The Court wrote,

> It is argued . . . that the ancillary governmental interest in equalizing the relative ability of individuals and groups to influence the outcome of elections serves to justify the limitation on express advocacy of the election or defeat of candidates. . . . But the concept that government may restrict the speech of some elements of our society in order to enhance the relative voice of others is wholly foreign to the First Amendment. (*Buckley v. Valeo*, 424 U.S. 1 [1976])

The phrasing about enhancement could be misleading. The Court is not addressing restrictions meant to enhance anyone's voice, but is only addressing (and rejecting) the aim of, "equalizing the relative ability" of participants' influence. The view rejected here is a certain egalitarian one, and one that would depart from the pure-ish model. The Court rejects, as foreign to the First Amendment, any value in restricting the speech of some in order to equalize (to whatever degree) speech or access to speech—any leveling down of the freedom of speech. Restrictions on some that would *increase* access to speech by others are not addressed by this point, but as I say, campaign finance restrictions do not (at least not normally—certainly not always) have that aim or effect.[17]

Now, for my purposes, I do not have to say this is really a clear ideal of any kind, but it is notable that it is a decent interpretation of the Court since *Buckley*. We can grant, if only for the sake of argument, that the non-leveling down pure-ish conception has a place in a certain kind of ideal of democracy. My point, following Rawls, is that this single category of liberty should be seen as only one part of a broader ideal of equal basic liberties.

On certain strictly egalitarian views, of course, the wealth inequality in which some have more expressive wherewithal than others would be a deviation from justice all on its own. Then part of its bad effect might be counter-vailed by restrictions on campaign finance, though the unjust inequality would remain. That would be a clear case of partially countervailing deviations from a fully just system which includes both wealth inequality and speech free from interference except for the sake of speech. However, on some other less strictly egalitarian views the inequality of wherewithal, say money, need not be seen, in its own right, as a deviation from full social justice. (On Rawls's view, for example, some such inequalities can be just.) So in that kind of view, unlike Marcuse's argument as I described it earlier, and unlike a simpler kind of egali-tarian conception of justice, we do not yet have any deviation that needs coun-tervailing, and so that cannot exactly be what might justify restrictions on campaign finance.

However, there might be, as there is in both Marcuse and Rawls, a neces-sary condition of full social justice that requires a certain kind—at least ap-proximate—of equal power in the democratic political process. Where that is missing the question arises whether there might be a countervailing deviation available in certain speech restrictions. In the present case following Rawls, where the wealth inequality is not itself a deviation from justice, it nevertheless would be unjust if the potential that arises for unequal political power is not neutralized elsewhere. So campaign finance restrictions deviate from the no-tion of Idealized Democracy by withdrawing one of its elements, namely the pure-ish model of free speech: no interference with speech except for the sake of speech, roughly. But if there is a significant inequality of wealth, even if it is not itself unjust, then this is a deviation from Idealized Democracy too. It may need to be countervailed by restrictions on speech which violate the pure-ish model of that liberty. The deviation represented by the restrictions on cam-paign speech might be justified in order to countervail what would otherwise be a deviation from the roughly equal value of political liberties associated with significant (if not unjust in itself) inequality in wealth.

Now, this pair of deviations from Idealized Democracy may be thought by some to be wholly, not just partly, countervailing. In that case we would have an instance of a second specification of a certain overarching ideal. If we were to anchor our reflections around this specification of the ideal—call this speci-fication Regulated Inequality, and the overarching ideal Deliberative Equal-ity—neither the inequality of wealth nor the regulations on political expression would appear as deviations. As we saw above in a general way, this is a coher-ent possibility. For those who think the model of speech-regulated inequality (Regulated Inequality) is every bit as full a specification of Deliberative Equal-ity as Idealized Democracy is, the theoretical significance of that former speci-fication, which I have been concentrating on, might be less than clear. But there are two angles from which to see its significance.[18]

First, we can anticipate that some do believe that pure-ish freedom of speech is an element in a significant social ideal, however unrealistic. And it is not difficult to construct the fuller set of elements that would make this understandable, including equal wherewithal and the aspects of equal power that come with it. Even if it is granted, only for the sake of argument, that this Idealized Democracy is a fine social ideal (or "model" if only partly ideal), we can observe that in reality the equal wherewithal element is and will continue to be missing. It is a fallacy, as we have seen, to suppose that the other elements, such as pure-ish free speech, continue to be valuable when some elements are missing, and indeed that comes to look implausible. The withdrawal of pure-ish free speech that is represented by campaign finance restrictions is plausibly recommended as a measure to countervail the triggering deviation of unequal wherewithal. So the first way to see the point of positing Idealized Democracy as an ideal (specified in a certain way) or model is to conjecture that many will see it that way.

Second, for those who more naturally think of the relevant ideal as already including both economic inequality and speech-limiting regulations on campaign finance, namely Regulated Inequality, we can show how Idealized Democracy might naturally arise as a second, alternative specification of the ideal. If we begin with Regulated Inequality as the model, we can then ask what would be the right response if the regulations of speech were infeasible or simply not in the cards. A possible response in that case would be to induce, if possible, significant economic equality, perhaps even at the material expense of all in order to countervail the unleashed inequalities of power. And then, while it is hardly obvious, it might be judged that the result of these two deviations from this other specification of the ideal are perfectly countervailing, giving us Idealized Democracy as a second specification of the higher order ideal of Deliberative Equality. In objection to this thought it might seem as though the second deviation remains a loss even if it restores the other value. But that cannot be assumed, since we know only that pure-ish free speech has value in the context of all the other ingredients including the relevant equality of power. So, in principle, there might no loss at all.

Now, some might justify such restrictions on campaign finance by an appeal to fair or equal opportunity to participate for its own sake. That would be a case of leveling down. The countervailing deviation approach sketched here, by contrast, defends the restrictions on the epistemic ground that they are tailored to at least partly mitigate epistemically distorting tendencies of unequal opportunity to fund political speech—i.e., the irrational advantage this would systematically give to the views and preferences of the wealthy.

I believe there would also be many other examples in which the idea of institutionalized countervailing deviations would be a fruitful tool of analysis of existing institutional features, and also a way of thinking about institutional reform, under nonideal deliberative conditions. It makes use of the ideal, but not simply as an intellectual construction worthy of study (which I have nothing against), nor as a goal to be promoted or approximated, but as a template against which to identify offending features in order to use nonideal practices or structures for the purpose of countervailing the distortions. We have looked especially at ideas for countervailing certain kinds of unfortunate consequences of initial deviations, but the countervailing need not be justified always by consequences. Some deviations may constitute rather than, or in addition to, causing injustice. Some further deviation from ideal arrangements might fully or partly restore the lost value, again constitutively rather than by its effects. The example at the end of chapter 14 about forgoing the Difference Principle in certain cases where equal basic liberties are missing may be a class of such examples, though I cannot pursue the idea further here.

This exhibits an advantage of thinking of basic social and political liberties as a system rather than a list of rights each of which is itself inviolable. The system of rights or liberties can, as we know from Rawls, yet have a strong, even lexical priority over other values such as aggregate wealth or utility or even improvements to the well-being of the worst off. It can remain a distinctively liberal approach in that way, even if each liberty in the system of liberties might be far from absolute, departing from some liberal views on that score. The fallacy of approximation, as I have argued, can help us to appreciate the case for this more systematic approach to liberty and equality.

CHAPTER SIXTEEN

Beyond Practicalism

I felt the expectation that if I was writing or talking about problems, I should also be able to identify an immediately actionable way out—preferably one that could garner a sixty-vote majority in the Senate. There was a kind of insanity to this—like telling doctors to only diagnose that which they could immediately and effortlessly cure.

—TA-NEHISI COATES, *WE WERE EIGHT YEARS IN POWER*

I do not laugh at the content of our wishes that go not only beyond the actual and what we take to be feasible in the future, but even beyond the possible; nor do I wish to denigrate fantasy, or minimize the pangs of being limited to the possible.

—ROBERT NOZICK, *ANARCHY, STATE, AND UTOPIA*

1. Introduction

Philosophy is a natural target for critics who think intellectual work is worthless unless it is practical. Lots of philosophy does have practical value, but lots of it does not. It seems natural to ask, rhetorically: If it has no practical value, what good is it? Maybe it is sometimes taken for granted that nothing is valuable unless it is practically valuable. This very general *practicalism*, as I will call it (and which I will refine below), is dubious if not absurd, though less sweeping versions of it might be more attractive. We will see that it is very plausible that some things must be of intrinsic value, that is, apart from what they can be used to produce. A narrower practicalism might hold that intellectual work in particular is never of intrinsic value, and so is worthless unless it is of practical value. I will argue that this flies in the face of some robust views about the value of some intellectual work in science and mathematics.

(We could also consider the arts, but I believe that raises special questions that we need not go into.)

This leaves two problems of special interest here: first, so far, even if that point makes general intellectual practicalism appear implausible, it has no tendency to show that nonpractical *philosophy*, or in particular *political philosophy*, might be of intrinsic value. They might lack whatever it is about nonpractical yet important math and science that makes them important. This leads to the second problem, which is that even if those examples tend to refute practicalism, they do not yet provide any account of what is valuable about them. If we had that account we could consider whether some nonpractical philosophy had the relevant virtues, but it is difficult to find such an account. We will look briefly at some answers that many find tempting, in order to see that they are inadequate. I will have little more to offer on that question about the value of nonpractical intellectual work generally, or about many parts of philosophy. Rather, in the next chapter, I will offer a very local account: whether or not there is any general account of what makes some nonpractical intellectual work valuable, there is a good account of the value of understanding the nature of social justice that does not depend on the practical value of such understanding.

As I argued in earlier chapters, if we will not comply with a requirement, say, to Build and Comply with certain institutions, then (owing to further facts, such as the consequences of building dysfunctional institutions) it is probably not the case that we ought to build them. The truth about justice could conceivably be without practical implications in this way. There is, nevertheless, an important sense in which even a theory like this is practical—has practical significance—even if it lacks what we might call practical relevance. The egalitarian theory I sketched as an example in chapter 6, which included a Carens market, requires society to Build and Comply with certain institutions. The mere fact that people will not comply with those institutions hardly shows that they are unable to do so, as we have seen before. There are plenty of other possible explanations. Suppose society could Build and Comply. So suppose nothing impossible or unrealizable is being required by the theory, just something unlikely. The theory requires action, and not action that is beyond the society's ability (or so we assume). So, there is no basis for denying that it has the kind of practicality or availability for guiding action that any requirement must have if it is to count as moral or normative. Still, if society will not comply, then the theory hardly goes on to require that it should nevertheless build the ill-fated institutions. It says nothing either way about what to do in that case. It appears, then, to be a live possibility that the correct (or true, or best) theory of justice might be without practical relevance in that sense. This is where we confront the objection that drives this chapter: If a theory of justice has no practical relevance what good is it?

2. *What Good Is Nonpractical Intellectual Work?*

I begin with three brief points about the idea of truth as used in this chapter. First, I sometimes speak of the true theory of justice, and I use this for present purposes as interchangeable with the "correct" or the "best" theory of justice. It does not matter here whether there is one that is true or best for all societies in all times and places or not. Even if a true or best theory is a universal standard in that way, it could, for reasons sketched above, have no practical relevance given unfortunate facts about how people will actually behave.

Secondly, we can immediately put aside a simple account of the value an impractical theory of justice might have, namely the view that it is valuable simply because it is true. Truth is really not such a big deal, and so it is hardly an obvious source of significant value. The telephone directory is full of truths, but they are mostly of little importance. That is, they are not the kinds of things it is of much value to know.[1] If truths about the fundamental nature of justice are important or valuable to know, this must be for some reason other than their mere truth, since they share that with the statement of any given stranger's phone number. Both kinds of statement are true, but truth is not sufficient for importance or value.

A third point about truth is that, not only is it not sufficient for significant value, it is surely not necessary. As I defend the possibility of a valuable theory of justice even if it is impractical, I will often speak of the value of a true theory of justice. This is for simplicity. I do not think that the value of impractical theories of justice is likely to be limited to the true one(s). We could sidestep this issue by saying a false theory's value would rest on the value of the (true) understanding one might gain from it. For simplicity, though, I will suppose that our best hope of identifying the nonpractical value of theorizing about justice would lie with an evidently great achievement: a true theory of justice.

It will be important to focus sharply on the intellectual practicalist position I hope to rebut, and we can do that in several steps. As a convenience, call the intellectual product of some intellectual work a piece of "theory." It might be a proof (alleged or failed), or a set of arguments, or other things amounting to less than would normally be counted as a theory, but it will be useful to have a single name. Consider,

Practicalism
Even if true, a piece of theorizing has no value except in virtue of the product's availability for use in producing something else of value.

What might be said in support of practicalism? As one suggestion, here is a skeptical position about value, but it is untenable:

Instrumental Value as the Only Kind
The only kind of value there is (whether or not there are any instances of it) is instrumental: something's having as a consequence, or being a cause, or probabilizer, or available instrument for bringing about (or probably so) something else valuable, or being available for use in any of those ways.

That last clause about availability for use is important, because otherwise much of the medicine in my cabinet would not be counted as having instrumental value, since much of it will never actually be used. When we say the value of the ibuprofen is instrumental, we do not mean a kind of value that it will have only if it gets used. My new hammer has practical value whether or not I ever use it. It is true that there is also the different kind of value it has if it actually does get used. It was practically valuable in that latter way yesterday when I used it. We can call these *latent* and *occurrent* varieties of practical value, respectively. Latent practical value is availability for use as occurrently practically valuable, and is a derivative concept in that way. Still, when we ordinarily speak of something's instrumental or practical value we mean latent at least as often as we mean occurrent practical value. Surely, the practicalist is not withholding approval from a theory whose practical value is only latent, and approving only if it is actually put to use. So the kind of practical value of theory that is in question is the broader kind consisting of at least latent practical value, some of which will also be put to use and have occurrent practical value.

Practicalism privileges practice over theory, or action over thought, in the following way: theory (thought) is only valuable insofar as it facilitates valuable practice (action). This might be expressed this extreme way:

Action Is All: Nothing other than valuable action is valuable at all except insofar as it could be useful in valuable action.

This is an absurd preoccupation with activity or action. On this view, surgical correction of a congenital facial disfigurement or a chronically painful condition is not valuable except insofar as it facilitates further valuable *action*. The practicalist position I want to contend with would not imply these absurd things, and would accept that a piece of theory that led to a cure for cancer would be valuable quite apart from whether those who are cured go on to perform valuable activities. Their living longer and being free of pain would be enough.

An additional reason is that *Action Is All* does not quite get us to the issue I want to discuss. The reason is that it is too unclear whether theorizing might itself be a species of valuable action. In that case it would not need to be conducive to further valuable action after all. That ecumenical position is obviously not the practicalist view I want to challenge. So we can sharpen the position in this way:

> *Intellectual Practicalism:* No piece of theory is valuable except insofar as it could be used to produce something else (other than theory) that is valuable.

This is the target position, but I will henceforth call it *practicalism* for short.

As I have stated the practicalist view, it does not treat political theory as a special category, although that would be a narrower variant, practicalism about specifically political theory. Rather, it is a more general principle that might be offered in explanation of the practicalist view of political theory, and I will assess it first in this general form. Later, I will consider a narrow version limited to normative theory.

Practicalism (unlike *Action Is All*) allows that there might be valuable things other than activities. For all it says, the value of some physical activity, or some physical product, or a less pain-ridden life, could be non-instrumental (even intrinsic, which adds that it is non-relational). But not so for intellectual activities or products. This discrimination against intellectual activity and products would seem to call for some explanation. The idea that there is only instrumental value has been discarded, so that cannot be the charge against impractical intellectual work. If anything has value, some things have non-instrumental value. Why, then, couldn't some intellectual work be among these non-instrumentally valuable things? What support might be offered for intellectual practicalism? I confess, I do not know of any consideration that counts significantly in favor of this position. While this hardly refutes it, if it lacks any palpable support then it cannot be recited as if it poses a difficulty for the opposing view—the view that some theory, such as a theory of justice, may be valuable even if it has no practical relevance. This is the challenge I wish to pose for practicalism: unless some support can be marshaled, the practicalist ought to be chastened.

Even if it fails in that general form, there may be more to be said for a narrower form of practicalism limited to normative moral and political theory or philosophy. Call it,

> *Normative Intellectual Practicalism*
> No piece of normative moral or political theory is valuable except insofar as it could be used, in realistic circumstances, to produce something else (other than theory) that is valuable.

The fact that some theory is about normative matters, matters where conclusions must, in some sense, be practical or action-guiding, does not immediately imply that normative theory must itself be of any practical value or relevance. Suppose, for example, that understanding the theory would not help anyone do anything. In one such case, they might all be weak-willed. In another case, even if they are morally quite good, the theory might not be telling them anything normative that they did not already know or assume. So, the assumption that good moral or political theory is bound to be useful in practice in some way has no basis in the normativity of the subject matter. Its only basis could be the conjecture that good normative theory seems likely to conflict with many existing moral and political normative views, and that understanding the theory will tend to improve these views, and, finally, that improving these views will tend to change action for the better. None of this is guaranteed, and it is no condition on a sound moral or political theory that all these contingencies be in place. In light of these points I am not aware of any reason to think that intellectual practicalism has any special purchase on normative theory that it does not have on theory generally.[2]

There is a challenge for the nonpracticalist too. It is perfectly fair for someone with practicalist sympathies to ask, about an allegedly valuable piece of theorizing, *what is good about it*. Even if it is allowed for the sake of argument by the chastened practicalist that the answer would not need to point to the theory's practical value, it would seem reasonable to ask what practical *or non-practical* value it has. This is a fair challenge, and a difficult one. When the value of a piece of intellectual work does not consist in its practical value, it is hard to know what to say when asked in what this value *does* consist. I will eventually try to make progress on this in the case of a theory of justice. For now I want to make two points. First, an obvious but important point: even if no answer is forthcoming, that would not refute the value claim. The reason is that just because nothing can be offered in support of a claim of that kind of value does not show that the value claim is false, and it could be very plausible even so. There might be value of just that kind, and we have seen no argument to the contrary. Granted, if nothing more can be said in support of an alleged instance of valuable impractical political theory, even if it is not refuted, the theorist with that view should be chastened.

It might be thought that even if there could be such value, there could never be reason to believe there is. But we should not confuse two distinct challenges here. One challenge is the difficulty of saying in what the value of some intellectual activity consists. A quite distinct challenge is the difficulty of offering a reason to believe it has such value. To see how these are different, suppose that (at least innocent) pleasure is valuable in itself. When asked what is good about it, there may be nothing more to say, beyond "It just is." That does not show that there is no basis for believing it. To mark this point with some terminology, we can distinguish between *value support* for a value claim, and *evidence* for it. The fact that philosophers whom I judge to be brilliant and sensible believe it seems to be some reason for me to believe it. It is hardly proof, but that was not the question.[3] Maybe there are also other kinds of reasons to believe that certain things are good in themselves, or maybe not. My point is that none of this is ruled out even if there is nothing at all to say about what is good about them.

Without any value support, and in the absence of other strong evidence, this dead-end would leave the nonpracticalist (like me) with nothing to say against the practicalist. Neither has anything to say in support of their position, but nor have we seen any strong evidence or argument against them. Both ought to be chastened in that case. Even if this impasse is the end of the story, we will still have learned this much: neither position can support itself by pointing to the alleged absurdity of the alternative. Practicalism has, so far as we have seen, no basis on which to show that nonpracticalism is untenable, and vice versa.

I am not sure it is the end of the story, however. Even if there is no strong basis for practicalism as a general theory, this settles nothing about whether any impractical political theory has value. Even if some things might, in principle, have nonpractical value, what is good about *this*? It would be good to have a conception of what would count as an adequate answer, even if it is doubted that such an answer is available. If it is asked, "What is good about this instance of impractical political theory?" what sort of thing would count as an adequate answer?

I want to reflect on the case of mathematics. The reason is that it is a rich context for thinking about practical and nonpractical value of intellectual work whose truth is beyond doubt. What is valuable about mathematical research? Consider, especially, what is often referred to as "pure mathematics," those areas of the subject that are pursued for reasons other than any practical value they might turn out to have.[4] Perhaps even pure mathematics has practical value, a question I will consider. But suppose much of it does not, or at least that it seems to have a value that does not depend on this. In that case, it is fair to ask what is valuable about it.

If you think math can have nonpractical value then you cannot deny a piece of political theory value on the bare ground that it has no practical value. My aim in this section is only to argue that much math that is thought by many (including most of my readers, I suspect) to be important and valuable intellectual work has little or no practical value. In that case, either it has no value after all, or some intellectual work with no practical value can nevertheless be of great value. It is very difficult to say what is valuable about it, but we are not, I think, inclined to doubt, for that reason, that it has value. This ought to inform our approach to the case of nonpractical political theory.

Much of mathematics obviously has practical importance of the highest order. For one thing, as a general field, mathematics is inseparable from science, and most of the great practical accomplishments of biology, engineering, medicine, statistics, economics, and much else. However, there is more to math than its practical application. In wondering whether all valuable math is practically valuable, it is important to put aside several irrelevant meanings of "application." In one sense, of course, mathematics can apply to the world even if it has no practical application. The geometry of a sphere applies (roughly) to the surface of the earth. This means simply that it accurately describes or represents it. This does not yet mean that it has any practical value. It does have practical value, of course, but that is a different claim. Descriptive applicability is not the same thing as practical applicability.

Mathematicians also speak of applicability in several other senses that are not the one we are wondering about. One is applicability to the (other) sciences. This, again, should not be confused with practical applicability.[5] Also, much math is applicable to other areas of math. This is generally regarded by mathematicians as increasing the value or importance of the work, but, by itself, it is not practical applicability in the sense that concerns us.

The *field* of mathematics, or even of pure mathematics, certainly has practical value. But this is not our question, which is not about the value of a whole field, but about the value of particular instances of intellectual work that do not themselves have practical value. These are what the practicalist criticizes. The field of political philosophy or theory, even "pure" political theory—that which is pursued for reasons other than any hope of practical value—could be granted by the practicalist to have lots of practical value. This just means that many instances of that kind of theorizing turn out to have practical value, just as many cases of pure mathematics turn out to have such value. But, then, why not think that this is where the sole value of such work lies?

Consider the *basic research model* of the value of nonpractical theory in some field. As a strategy for producing research that has practical value, it will make sense to arrange for lots of basic research that is not practically motivated, since there will plausibly be unexpected practical discoveries. On this model, the value of a piece of intellectual or scientific work derives from the practical value of the larger enterprise of which it is a part. Basic research is sometimes defined as work that is motivated by curiosity rather than by any practical concern, and that parallels our working conception of pure mathematics.[6] Such work will sometimes turn out to have practical value even if this was not the goal.

It is important to avoid an obvious ambiguity. That is, the motivation for encouraging or facilitating lots of pure research is, on this telling, indeed wholly practical. We can mark that by saying that *externally* it is practically motivated. However, we also need to mark that the kind of research that is so motivated is pure or basic, and so *internally* motivated by curiosity rather than by any practical concern. Return, for a moment, to the question of the value of pure mathematics. Since so much practical value can be expected to flow from even pure mathematics, there is great practical value in promoting that kind of research—research that has (internally) no practical motive. If we ask about the value of a piece of pure mathematics, the basic research model answers this way: pure mathematics as a field of inquiry promises great practical value, and so it is a valuable field of endeavor. So consider this view:

> *Basic Research Model:* The value of any instance of pure research (such as pure math or political philosophy) consists entirely in its being a part of a practically valuable field of endeavor.

If there is a strong practical case of this kind for encouraging work in pure mathematics, is there an analogy in the case of pure political theory? If so, it must go like this: there are questions in political theory whose practical value, if any, is difficult to guess. Nevertheless, there is probably great practical value to be found in those areas in ways we cannot specifically anticipate. If the only kind of political theory that were done were internally motivated by the prospect of practical value these other areas would be underexplored, and much practical value will be missed. It would make sense, then, as a strategy for producing great practical value that could be produced in no other way, to also promote and encourage pure political theory—research not internally motivated by any prospect of practical value, but only by curiosity. And so on. On the basic research model, the value of any instance of pure political theory has its value simply as a part of a practically valuable field of endeavor.

Is there a plausible basic research rationale of that kind for the support of pure political theory, as there plainly is for pure mathematics? I will not try to answer that here. I will observe only that, for this purpose, we would not need uncontroversial examples. The argument does not depend on any claim about agreement. If you, the reader, accept certain examples, then let us work with those. Recall, too, that we also would not need examples that actually made a practical difference, since this is not the relevant criterion of something's having practical value. My practicalist opponent is not dismissing the value of all political theory that is not, in fact, put to successful use.

I argued in chapter 13 that high and apparently unrealistic standards of social justice have often turned out to be met (as a result of pursuing them), something previously unbelievable. For that reason, and maybe others, maybe there are good external practical reasons for promoting and encouraging even pure political philosophy, though I will not pursue the question further here. If so, that would be one important kind of defense of that kind of work. Pause for a moment to give this important point its due, and to recognize that it would answer, in a significant way, the practicalist critique of the kind of non-practical political theory we have been considering.

As important as that point is, I do not believe it is an adequate account of the value of pure intellectual work. To see why, return to the case of pure mathematics. The encouragement and promotion of work of that kind is said to be valuable because some work of great practical value will probably result only in this way. However, what about the many *instances* of pure mathematical research that do not themselves have any practical value? I do not just mean instances with no foreseen practical value, but work with no practical value, in fact. We cannot know for sure which work this is at any given time, since any instance might turn out to have practical value after all, but never mind; imagine some work that we stipulate has no practical value. On the basic research account this would be an instance of pure research that has *no value at all*. It is a part of an endeavor that, as a whole, has practical value, but it does not contribute to it. Encouraging even this instance of work may, indeed, have practical value insofar as it helps to encourage pure research more generally, some of which will turn out to have practical value. But none of this allows the basic research model to say that this instance of such work, lacking any practical value of its own, either directly or indirectly, has any value at all. The basic research model is not an adequate account of the value of instances of pure research unless this implication of the model is itself acceptable. I do not propose to settle it, but it would be important to test the idea intuitively, to see whether something seems to have gone wrong. It is clear, I think, that the idea that instances of pure mathematical research that themselves have no practical value have no value at all is inconsistent with natural and widespread ways of thinking. Maybe we should give them up (if, for example, there were some positive case for practicalism), but we first need to be clear about the tension.

It is quite clear, first, that what are generally regarded as great achievements in mathematics are often instances of pure mathematical work, pursued apart from any internal motive of their being of practical value.[7] Second, the practicalist effort to account for the value of these achievements as instances of a larger institution of basic research, deriving their value from the practical value (which is not in dispute) of the institution, would have no way to account for the value of the many individual mathematical achievements that are widely regarded as great whether or not they, themselves, have any practical value. The practicalist might insist that it is natural to treat these achievements as great, since praising them is part of the practically valuable project of encouraging such pure research. But the practicalist must add: these achievements really have no value, and our treating them as such is a white lie. If this is too much to swallow, then practicalism must be rejected. It is fair enough to point out that we have not explained what is valuable about such mathematical achievements, and this is admittedly a difficult task. But, even so, the dilemma for the practicalist remains: either they have no value at all, or practicalism is false.

Now, even if examples from mathematics (and similar examples could be adduced from science, such as some important work in cosmology or fundamental physics) persuade us that some nonpractical intellectual work has great value, this is still no account of what kind of value it might be. A general account of that kind might be extended to the case of political philosophy, if only one were available. As I argue next, several tempting approaches are inadequate. Maybe there are other more promising accounts, but I will not pursue that question, turning instead, in the next chapter, to a local account tailored to the case of philosophical understanding of social justice.

In his poignant reflection on the value of pure mathematics, G. H. Hardy claimed,

> [V]ery little of mathematics is useful practically, and . . . that little is comparatively dull. The 'seriousness' of a mathematical theorem lies, not in its practical consequences, which are usually negligible, but in

the *significance* of the mathematical ideas which it connects. We may say, roughly, that a mathematical idea is 'significant' if it can be connected, in a natural and illuminating way, with a large complex of other mathematical ideas.[8]

It is only roughly stated, but let us call this the *ramification account* of the value of nonpractical mathematics. It says that a piece of mathematics has a kind of nonpractical value if it has ramifications of certain kinds (to be specified by a fuller account) for many other mathematical ideas. There are many ways in which this might be spelled out. For example, ramifications might refer to relations of logical implication, or to something else altogether. Also, it might be that the work's ramifications, whether they are known or not, themselves give the work value, or alternatively the fact that such ramifications could come to be known. Still, I believe all versions of the ramification account will tend to face the following problem. If a piece of math is important because of some bearing it has on other pieces of math, this must either be because that other math is important, or because the relation itself is somehow important. Either way, the question of what kind of value we have on our hands has been postponed but not answered. The bearing of one chess problem (a kind of mathematical problem) on a thousand other chess problems would never convince Hardy that the first one is serious and valuable mathematics. A piece of math might well be important if it bears on an *important* math problem, but what makes that second math problem important?

If the value is meant to lie in the connection itself, where none of the connected things (certain instances of knowledge, for example) is assumed to be of any value, what kind of value is this bare connection supposed to have? Without answers to these questions, the ramification model does not appear to be a promising account of the value of nonpractical intellectual work, including mathematics, and including political philosophy.

In a separate vein, there is an impulse to point to the rarity, difficulty, or the display of prodigious skill in certain achievements as the source of their value. Group these together as *virtuosity* accounts.[9] Many have tried, and failed, to prove Fermat's Last Theorem, and then someone succeeds: Andrew Wiles in 1994. Let us grant that there is value in this virtuosity itself. The question is whether this accounts for the *great* value many of us believe that the proof has. Compare the proof to the performance of five aerial flips on the flying trapeze, something that has (I believe) never been achieved.[10] Suppose it was finally accomplished. Perhaps you think proving the theorem is even more difficult, but then we only need to add another flip or two to surpass its difficulty. Or you might think that they are not comparable because one is an intellectual achievement, the other physical. So compare the proof to the memorization of three hundred people's names in ten minutes, or to summing a huge string of numbers (or complicate it with whatever operations you please). Difficulty, rarity, or display of skill, as valuable as they might be, do not seem to account for the value that is present when they are deployed in order to do something more valuable than these. Such things might be a *great achievement* in one sense, and the achievement might be of *great value of a certain kind*. But it is not the achievement of something of *great value*. Two mathematical proofs might be equally difficult and elusive, with only one of them being of any importance, and the other being a brilliant case of "recreational mathematics" by Martin Gardner.[11]

Political philosophy can display virtuosity too. There might be great scholarly erudition, logical incisiveness, and so on. But consider a case in which these are displayed in the course of an arbitrary task, such as constructing the most defensible principles of justice that could be devised on the arbitrary supposition that that the earth contained only one species and one gender, or that the earth was flat and infinite in size. Certainly, this might be accomplished in a way that shows a kind of greatness, or even philosophical genius. But it would not achieve anything of great value. The value of nonpractical intellectual work is not made great by virtuosity of any kind, and so we have not yet identified the basis of its value.

I will not consider other general accounts about the intrinsic value of some intellectual work, in hopes that we could see how and whether it covers unrealistic political philosophy. If one is found, then that is no problem for my approach in the next chapter, in which I argue that since understanding justice is a constitutive component of a meritorious concern about justice, even practically irrelevant accounts of the nature and content of social justice might have great value *at least* in that way. The present chapter puts into serious doubt the very general assumption that no intellectual work has any value unless it has practical value. This is not yet enough to show the value of any particular intellectual work that might be challenged on that ground, such as a philosophical understanding of even the unrealistic requirements of social justice. I turn to that in the next chapter.

CHAPTER SEVENTEEN

Informed Concern

That no human being will ever act adequately to what the pure idea of virtue contains does not prove in the least that there is something chimerical in this thought. For it is only by means of this idea that any judgment of moral worth or unworth is possible.

—IMMANUEL KANT, *CRITIQUE OF PURE REASON*

One may or may not care about practice, but one may also care about justice, as such, one may be interested in what it is, even if one does not care about practice at all.

—G. A. COHEN, *RESCUING*

1. Introduction

I have argued in preceding chapters that even if full or excellent justice is an unrealistic goal, understanding it might yet have practical value. In some cases it might be appropriate to try to approximate it, though this is not guaranteed. In addition, understanding full justice can anchor practical remedial action in the form of what I have called countervailing deviation, which is not a form of approximating the fully just condition. And there may well be other practical uses of understanding unrealistic standards. But it is sometimes assumed, in effect, that the only value of understanding justice would lie in whatever practical value it has, and here I want to argue that that is not so. If I am right, then the value of understanding full justice, even if it is an unrealistic goal, is over-determined: it has several kinds of practical value, but its value does not depend on that in any case.

In turning to this question, we are not addressing the objection that conceptions of high or full justice that are unrealistic are false. Rather, we now suppose that it is allowed for the sake of argument that full or excellent justice

[316]

might well be unrealistic. Some will deny that, but we are not engaging with them in this chapter in order to focus on a separate challenge, which is this: suppose full or great justice is not a realistic expectation, not a standard people are at all likely or inclined ever to meet, and, moreover, that there is no other way in which understanding full justice would be available for the production of something of value. Here is the claim to be considered: in that case, there is no great value in understanding those upper reaches of justice, or in understanding whether it has such upper reaches. This is broader than the claim that such understanding is useless, which would leave the possibility of worth other than usefulness. Not only is it useless, on this view, it is, for that reason, worthless (or close enough). This is what I will argue against in this chapter.

Some admit that an arrangement's being "infeasible" (in at least some ways) is compatible with its being part of what justice requires.[1] Many political theorists and philosophers have come recently to argue that any set of restrictions on immigration that are remotely as strict as we currently find around the world are unjust. A certain kind of realist would infer that, unless such writers are confused about the nature of political philosophy, they must believe that "open borders" is a realistic possibility. However, Joseph Carens, perhaps the most influential philosopher in that school of thought, explicitly rejects the realist constraint. He writes, plausibly, "It is important to get clear first about what we think is right in principle before moving to the question of what we should do in practice. If one moves too quickly to the question of feasibility, one risks confusing elements of analysis that should be kept distinct."[2] Others, however, seem to be sympathetic to this this kind of realism, casting those who advocate for different positions as mere "dreamers," treating it as obvious that if some piece of political philosophy is useless in practice then surely it would not be of much value.[3] I believe that this is a perennial issue, but in any case it is presently a live one.

In the previous chapter, we saw how reflection on other areas of intellectual work suggests that it is far from obvious, and at odds with what many of us actually find to be valuable, to think that intellectual work can have only practical value. Still, as I have said, that point leaves open what kind of nonpractical value it might be. Putting aside those other intellectual fields, I focus now on political philosophy, and turn to a line of argument to the effect that understanding justice can be of significant value even apart from whether it has any practical value. I begin by presenting the line of argument in (reasonably) clear and succinct steps, but a number of questions arise and I turn to some of them next. The guiding idea is the oft-acknowledged value of appreciating how real social conditions measure up to, or fall short of, our highest standards. But what is valuable about this, and how valuable is it? The proposal I shall sketch builds on the more specific idea (also quite common if not always explicit) that an informed concern about social justice and injustice is a significant aspect of a morally good person, apart from any value the concern or the understanding might have for use in producing good action or anything else of value. Understanding justice is part of what would make such a concern count as informed. I begin with a detailed presentation, and then a further clarification and partial defense of the *informed concern* account, as I will call it.

Justice itself, I shall assume, is a great value, and I hope this first premise is common ground. Whether one prefers to speak only of some condition's being much more just than another, or also accepts that there is such a thing as full justice, these would be conditions of great value.[4] The thing that I am claiming to be of value here is not an abstract object such as a standard, a principle, or a concept, "justice," nor am I yet addressing the value of any knowledge or understanding, but rather the real condition of a social structure that is just or at least juster. That, I will assume, is valuable.

Some will think that justice is only a good thing if it is good for somebody, but I am not assuming that.[5] Consider a system of criminal law which applies an appropriate standard of proof to black defendants, but applies a higher standard to whites, acquitting them more easily. This may be unjust even if it hurts no one (although it probably also would). Justice might require even-handedness even if that is worse for whites and better for no one. We can leave that unsettled. My premise is that justice is a great value. I don't say that this is so because it is good for people, but I don't deny that it is either.

The violation of justice is something more than its absence, since it is absent but not violated whenever it is inapplicable. Justice is also different from some other values in that even where a standard applies and is violated this is not always bad, except in the sense of less good. I assume it is part of the concept of justice that its violation is (at least) agent-neutrally bad, in some way that goes beyond its being less good. (It is similar to the concepts of illness or tragedy in this way.)

Individual deontic moral violations, such as murder or assault, are naturally thought of as agent-neutrally bad in addition to their being agent-centered moral violations. We should hope they do not happen, even the ones in which we are not implicated. But this is disputable. It would not suffice for my purposes if the only thing agent-neutrally bad about injustice is, for example, certain suffering of the victims. Since the suffering could be present without any injustice that would not establish any agent-neutral badness of the injustice. Indeed, some may hold precisely this, that injustice and wrongness generally are entirely matters of agent-centered restrictions, with no residual agent-neutral disvalue.[6] If the account of Plural Requirement laid out in chapter 12, or something like it, is sound then injustice would be broadly a moral kind of wrong whose disvalue is agent-neutral rather than deontic. But for present purposes this does not matter. The important thing for the informed concern argument I am offering here is that injustice has a disvalue such that a morally good person will be disposed, in some way, to respond with certain attitudes or emotions such as sadness, indignation, and so on. What attitudes are distinctive of the proper response to injustice is an interesting question, but nothing here depends on the answer. Even if it is thought that the disvalue of injustice is wholly deontic, it remains sufficiently obvious for my purposes that a morally good person responds in her attitudes, and does so appropriately, to believed social injustice. It would not even matter, for this specific purpose, whether injustice is a case of moral disvalue (as I argue that it is, broadly speaking) if this claim about attitudinal response is accepted. It will be clearest, nevertheless, to proceed as though the response is to moral disvalue of a certain kind.

A first premise, then, is,

1. Justice is a highly morally *valuable* human social condition, and its violation is *bad*.

Next, a link between what is valuable in those ways, and appropriate attitudes:

2. What is morally valuable is morally *desirable*, and what is a moral violation is morally *lamentable*. That is, those attitudes are morally appropriate, and their lack is inappropriate.

Again, the argument does not depend on whether those are the specific attitudes that are appropriate, but they illustrate a certain element in the form of argument.

3. Therefore, justice (where it applies) is morally desirable, and its violation is morally lamentable. (from 1 and 2)

Some might even hold that there is nothing more to the greatness of justice except facts about appropriate attitudes toward that condition—say, its desirability, or its absence being lamentable. Others might think the justice of a condition is explanatorily prior to any facts about attitudes, which can be appropriate or inappropriate responses to that justice or injustice. Nothing here will hang on that issue, since both sides can (not to say that they must) agree with my next claim: that a certain concern for justice—tending to desire it and to lament its violation—is virtuous.

4. It is morally *virtuous* to have *concern* for justice in this sense: to desire or wish for it and to lament its absence. A person who does not care about the justice or injustice of social conditions is thereby morally deficient, lacking that virtue. (from 2 and 3)

(4) really just clarifies or sharpens the point of (3) for our purposes. Next, I propose that,

5. To have a concern for justice that is virtuous (or more virtuous) it must be *informed* by sound (or sounder) understanding of the nature of justice—what it is for a social condition to be just or juster.

It might seem that one could have virtuous responses to believed injustice even if one has a thin or even mistaken understanding of justice. Whether or not there is some worth in caring about social justice *de dicto*—that is, about so-called justice whatever it might be—(a question which is controversial), there is significant moral deficiency even in an agent with that concern, to the extent that their conception of justice is too rudimentary or mistaken or unsound. It follows from those steps that,

> 6. A sounder understanding of justice (whether or not that understanding is practically valuable) is a contributing constituent of having a concern for justice that is morally better or more virtuous. (from 4, 5)

Put another way, it is morally better to be duly concerned with justice and injustice in the world—with how just things were, are, and might be—and that depends on a sufficiently rich and sound conception of justice.

My main point is distinct from a subtly different one, namely that a person who has a sincere concern for justice (*de dicto*) *will be motivated* to understand justice better. That is, plausibly, also partly constitutive of such a concern. This is not a way of showing that such understanding is valuable, but only that it comes along with something that is. When someone asks what is so great about something, they might mean "show me," or they might mean "prove it." That is, they might be asking to be situated with respect to that thing in such a way that they come to value it or see its value. They might or might not then come to believe it is, apart from them, valuable, but that is a separate issue. And indeed, rather than asking to be shown how they might value it, they might be asking for some argument or evidence that it is, apart from them or you, valuable—"objectively" in that way. My informed concern account is an argument that understanding justice is objectively valuable in a certain way. It is not a way of coaxing anyone to value it.

There is a third way of addressing something's value, which lies, in a way, between those two, and that is to give an argument or evidence that any person who is herself good in certain ways *would value it*. Call this the *qualified appreciation* account of something's value. It can take two forms, and either would do. One is to use the (supposed) appreciation of any qualified person as indicative of objective value which they are *apprehending*. On that view, the facts about qualified appreciators are metaphysically extraneous to the thing's value. On a second version, for something to be valuable (maybe only for some things, maybe for all things) is to be such that a qualified person would appreciate it. Call this the *sentimentalist* version. There is no value that is apprehended by the appreciator in that case.

The value that is at stake here is not practical (even if there happens to be some practical value as well, which is disputable). The value of that understanding of justice that figures in this argument does not consist in the understanding's availability for the production of something else valuable. Rather, its value is that it is an essential constituent of a morally valuable condition of a person: their having an informed concern about justice.[7] That is, it is a constituent without which the value would be absent—it contributes value in that sense. That is the outline of the informed concern account of the value of understanding justice even if it is not practical. A number of issues are raised by this approach, and I address some of them in turn.

a.

The challenge I have been addressing is not to show that such understanding is more valuable than contributing to justice, or more so than any number of other accomplishments, but to refute the suggestion that it must have little or no value if it is not of practical value. Improving one's own virtue may not be as worthwhile as what one could do instead. Contributing to justice (supposing one's understanding of it is good enough) in practice might, depending on one's opportunities and chance of success, be the wiser and morally better choice. (Of course, improving one's understanding of justice could have practical value, contributing to one's ability to contribute to justice.) All of this leaves in place the value, so I have argued, of a better understanding of justice even apart from any practical value. That would refute the claim that it has none.

Next, however, how much? It might be objected that the nonpractical parts of understanding justice may contribute much less moral value to a person than practical sorts. To think about this it is important to put aside the separate question of what effort the person should make or should have made to understand this or that aspect of justice. The question here is which kinds of understanding contribute more or less to how good a person is, not how much reason one has to seek it. So we might simplify by considering cases where the understanding comes without effort, say by being exposed to experience, essays, conversations, and arts that bring such understanding unbidden.

We might be urged to change over to the question how much moral reason a person has to seek this morally valuable understanding compared to the moral value of other choices incompatible with that one. As is well-known, there are challenging questions of that kind that are not special to the activities of abstract political philosophy but which pose as much (or as little) threat to activities such as learning a musical instrument, hiking in the mountains, or buying a dog. In each case, there are normally ways in which one could have spent that time and those resources so as to better promote social justice, or reduce suffering in the world, or manifest respect for the dignity of one's fellow persons. If there is no good answer to such challenges, then the philosopher of unrealistic standards of justice is no better or worse off than many others, and so the question is not *especially* pertinent. If, on the other hand, many pursuits are morally permissible even if they do not (maximally, or even to any significant extent) promote justice or manifest moral worth, then perhaps contributing to the understanding of justice and injustice is permissible as well. And if the informed concern account is correct, then that activity may even have more going for it, morally speaking, than the other activities listed. If it is morally helpful that the musician or dog owner spend time on morally more pressing things *in addition*, then a similar dispensation must be allowed to the philosopher.[8]

b.

Does understanding the nature of justice have this value even if there is no disposition to lament injustice even roughly conceived? If the value is that it is actually concern-informing, then perhaps not. It is enough if we have established that it has value in anyone disposed to lament injustice, so I take no further stand on this. We have seen[9] that one element (the understanding) of what would be a valuable combination of elements (the understanding along with the concern) cannot be assumed to have any value when the other parts are missing.

c.

If injustice is a moral matter then it might be blameworthy, in which case that would be the attitude to focus the informed concern account around. The problem, of course, is that social injustice does not seem to entail any wrongdoing by any agent, as I have argued. I have proposed to understand violations of Plural Requirement as broadly moral, but not in a way that would identify any agent who might be subject to blame. Nevertheless, just as there can be plural counterparts to agential wrongness, agential trying, and agential ability (i.e., feasibility) it is worth wondering whether there is some significant plural counterpart to the agential distinction between an act's being wrong and its being blameworthy.[10] This is worth more thought, but the informed concern account does not depend on the outcome. Even if no counterpart to blame can be found, a morally good person will tend to respond in certain attitudes and emotions to cases of believed injustice as such, and that schematic point is enough for our purposes here.

d.

It might give one pause to hear that there is supposedly some moral value in a tendency to be sad—in this case, to lament injustice. But after a moment of thought, denying that would be the more radical and implausible view. Plausibly, at least for many or most people, it is a moral defect in a person if they are not saddened (in many cases) by another's suffering, or by a person's being unfairly taken advantage of. In that same way, a morally good person will, as a constituent feature of their goodness, tend to be saddened by social injustice. Now there are people whose suffering it would make me sad to know about even though it is not true that I have an interest in knowing how they are doing—most strangers. But the limited point for the moment is that their suffering is lamentable from my point of view even so, and entirely regardless of whether there is anything I can do about it. Should I be told about some stranger not that she suffers but that she is subject to great injustice (say she was lied to about something she very much cares about), if I am a good person I would tend to be saddened by that as well. It is lamentable in that sense.

David Miller, in his chapter, "A Tale of Two Cities: Political Philosophy as Lamentation,"[11] uses the religious setting of the idea of lamentation, which rhetorically casts this sort of view as mystical, perhaps an irrational vestige of discredited Christian metaphysics and dogma. Insofar as it does so cast it, the connotation would be unfair. The political philosophy in question is not itself the lamentation, it is the provision of lamentable information. It is not itself some form of sad feeling, or crying. It is a form of *critique,* a term which does not have the same florid ring as "lamentation" and fails to induce the ridicule that seems (I think it is fair to say) to be intended. Finally, "political philosophy as lamentation" might seem to refer to the view that the very subject of political philosophy is nothing but critique of irremediable injustice, which is of course not the position in question at all, and not one that anyone accepts. The accurate subtitle, of course, would not have served Miller's purposes as well: "Political philosophy as, among other things, critique of even irremediable injustice." There is, it seems to me, nothing ridiculous about that.

e.

The informed concern argument is not significantly committed on metaethical questions about realism, expressivism, and so on. My claims about the lamentability of injustice are normative, and could be accepted by an expressivist as well as by a moral realist.

f.

A moral virtue of a person is, for my purposes here, simply a morally valuable tendency to be responsive, in thought, feeling, or action, to certain actual or conceived scenarios. There are important questions about how exactly to understand this element of the moral domain, but we need nothing very specific here except my claim itself. I do not assume or deny that people exhibit stable traits of character that answer to traditional names like "honesty."[12] I do not assume or deny that virtue is the fundamentally explanatory category in moral theory, rather than, say, requirement.[13] I do not assume or deny that what is virtuous in one cultural or historical setting is (always, or ever) also so in any other setting. I simply take for granted that there is such a category as virtue in the sense specified, and I believe this is a fairly minimal and uncontroversial assumption.

g.

The debate about *de dicto* concern for what is morally right, more generally, is relevant.[14] Does it contribute to the moral worth of an action that the agent was motivated by a desire to do what is right, even apart from whether their understanding of what makes things right is at all sound? Or is that worthless except insofar as they also have some sound understanding of what makes acts right? As I say above, I do not need to claim or deny that there is any moral worth in that. A concern for what is just or right which is, as it were, maximally *de dicto* (there are limits to how extreme that can be) is a highly limited locus of moral worth. Without understanding anything about what rightness is, and/or more about which actual or possible choices are right, one's concern for what is right is morally paltry if not worthless. Similarly, although I do not need to take a position on it for purposes of my argument, as with rightness, there might be some virtue in caring for justice while not yet knowing very much about what would count. Still, a rudimentary or flawed understanding of what makes things just severely limits the moral value of one's ostensible concern for social justice to being also rudimentary or flawed.

I do not say that the more concerned a person is about justice the morally better he is. I assume only that some level of informed concern is morally important, and then I focus on what it means for that concern to be informed. I also do not claim that one is a bad person if one's understanding of justice is at all incomplete, but only that a person's concern for justice is more virtuous, other things equal, to the extent that the person's understanding of what justice is and requires is better.

h.

There are two aspects of understanding justice that are at issue for my specific purposes. One is the understanding that what it takes to meet justice might be unrealistic since it is not constrained by what is likely, or even by deep human proclivities that fall short of inabilities (the idea will be familiar by now). (Remember, that this is so is being granted to me for the sake of argument by the objector I confront in this chapter.) Failing to understand this would seem to be a profound flaw in one's understanding of the nature of justice. One's concern for justice, where justice is misconceived in that way, would be a deficient concern to that extent. A second kind of understanding of justice is knowing what it is that justice requires, and not simply the first, abstract (but important) point that it might include unrealistic requirements. Caring about justice, while misconceiving what justice requires, may be a deficient concern, though this is less clear than the first case. Consider an analogy with caring about truthfulness in people. It does not seem to render that concern less morally worthy if one does not know which things people believe, and so which statements of theirs would be truthful. Similarly, caring about justice might have most or all of its full value even if there is much one does not know about which things are just, or required by justice, and even if some of one's views about what justice required are mistaken. On the other hand, this has limits. If one's views about the content of justice are too badly awry—for example if one thinks that justice requires always favoring the interests of one's own social class—then it becomes unclear whether justice is the thing the person cares about. (Something similar must go for truthfulness.)

i.

To say that a person lacks some element of moral virtue, such as an adequate concern for justice, is not necessarily to say that this is the person's fault, or that she is responsible or to blame for it. Arguably, a person can be morally deficient through no fault of her own. The moral quality of a person's motivation, will, character, and so forth may be subject to a mode of moral evaluation that is not dependent on the agent's being responsible for her condition. There are considerations on both sides of that issue, and, again, I am not here taking a side. A similar issue came up in chapter 12, when we considered whether there could be any kind of moral significance to failures of Plural Requirement even though it is not a violation by any agent. There, as here, it is important to note the several ways in which the domain of moral evaluation might be broader than some agent's action being right or wrong. The case of virtue, or good moral will or character is a signal example.[15] A person might be callous as a result of having been emotionally abused as a child. Being callous is a moral deficiency, and so a person can apparently be morally deficient through no fault of her own. I do not need to endorse this view for present purposes, but it is helpful to note that I am not assuming moral deficiency is always the agent's fault.

j.

Recall (from our discussion in chapter 13) the position of Sen and others that there is little value in understanding full or even excellent justice, since all we need for purposes of social choice is a theory that ranks the available alternatives. This point is deployed against the usefulness both of any partition between injustice and (full) justice, and of even a comparative theory of alternatives that have little chance of coming true. Suppose it is objected that a person can have a perfectly sound conception of what makes certain realistically available social conditions more just than others, without any conception of what makes a condition highly or fully just. I argued that the prospects for a rich comparative theory of the kind that claim appeals to—even of feasible or available alternatives (as distinct from mere eyeball rankings of them)— were rather dim if no use could be made of the many judgments central to our familiar moral thinking that assert or entail a partition between just and unjust. That point matters even if the only goal is rational social choice among available alternatives. But suppose I was wrong about that, and that realistic rankings could be devised with no appeal to unrealistic rankings (so to speak). Here I am submitting a different consideration that would still stand, namely that a person whose understanding of justice was limited to that ranking of realistic possibilities lacks a degree of moral virtue (of morally good will, character, concern). Such a person cannot have an informed concern for—a tendency to lament—the degree of injustice or lesser justice that realistic conditions might exhibit. Nothing here depends on the idea that there is a threshold dividing full justice from injustice; excellent justice would work just as well, however one wishes to interpret it from a measure standpoint.

k.

It is important to recall a point from chapter 1. When I speak of understanding the unrealistic reaches of justice, I do not mean understanding "what a perfectly just society . . . would look like," as is sometimes said.[16] That is an inappropriate demand if, as seems likely, a just society would contain broad scope for free choice of social arrangements. There might be a million different things a fully just society could look like. The idea of high standards is often conflated with the idea of "blueprints," but there is no necessary connection. Justice, even full justice, might be a matter of meeting certain very general principles. The difference between justice as meeting general principles, and justice as meeting a blueprint, arises at all degrees of justice, and has nothing to do in particular with high or unrealistic standards.

l.

Some will say that this informed concern account gives the understanding of justice a practical value after all: the value of the understanding is for the purpose of making oneself a better person. This is an error, I believe. The value of the understanding, while not independent of the value of virtuous attitudes, is not dependent on its availability for use in producing anything of value. In addition, the moral value of virtue, or a good will, or good "character," is not held here to be instrumental to the production of good action. The good will of a political prisoner in permanent solitary confinement may have no such instrumental value, but it is a virtue of that person, and that is a species of moral value. I take that much to be widely acceptable to many views about the moral.

m.

Knowledge is generally agreed to be something more than, but including, true belief. For example, some true beliefs are lucky guesses or correct by some other happenstance, and those are different, in some way it is notoriously difficult to pin down, from cases where the belief's being correct is something more than happenstance or luck. There is a contemporary literature about the "value of knowledge," which is largely focused on whether and how knowledge is more valuable than non-knowledge cases of true belief.[17] This is not our question here. Our question is what the value is, if any, of (at least some) cases of true belief when having the belief is of no use in the production of some other valuable thing or condition.

Does the informed concern view distinguish between true belief and knowledge for purposes of assigning value? That is, does the moral value of the informed concern increase if the true understanding of justice is also a case of knowing, perhaps by not being, as it were, accidental in certain ways? This is a significant and interesting question, but neither answer is any threat to the validity of the informed concern approach. It is enough for my purposes that such understanding can have moral value even when it is practically of no use, and it is a fine question for others whether that value depends on its also being knowledge.

n.

I have argued that a concern for justice is more virtuous if it is more informed. The understanding is morally valuable as part of informed concern for the morally valuable thing, justice. There is no appeal to whether the understanding is desired. A separate point is that a desire to understand justice is also part of being concerned about justice. The understanding's value does not, in this connection, consist in its being part of informed concern, but simply as the object of a morally good desire. This does not say whether such a desire must be very strong with respect specifically to knowledge about justice that is of little practical value. But it is still the case that a person who cares about how just or unjust her society is (for example) will also care about whether she properly understands justice.

o.

Whether moral virtue requires it or not, there is a recognizable Socratic concern to understand not only what is just but what justice is. If you do not know what justice is, then it is impossible to care about instances of justice in virtue of their justice except (at best) in an attenuated *de dicto* way. That is a morally significant deficiency, even apart from whether it would have implications for your actions in realistic conditions. If you do aspire to care about instances of justice in virtue of their justice, you thereby value having a good—or at least better—understanding of justice. I am not offering a full account of what justice is, of course, and nothing at all about what specific things it normatively favors or requires. But I am offering an account of part of the nature of justice. Whether I am correct or not, one's understanding of what justice is would be deficient if one is mistaken about this part. This is a moral deficiency, rendering any concern for justice uninformed to some degree. And such understanding will be valued, necessarily, by anyone who aspires to care not about only instances of justice, but to care about their justice.

p.

It might seem as though the informed concern account only points to a form of practical value after all, the way in which a better understanding of justice makes a person's character morally better.[18] That is one measure of its practical value. There may be something to that instrumental conception of the value of investigations into the nature of justice, but it is not the value I am pointing to. While investigating or writing about the nature of justice might produce a superior condition of someone's character (one's own, or another's, respectively), that is different from the observation advanced here, namely that understanding the nature of justice—apart from anything that understanding produces or causes—can constitute a morally better character. We might say that this "makes" one's character better, but that is not a practical or instrumental value of understanding justice, even if inquiring or teaching about it might have practical or instrumental value as well. The informed concern account conflicts with "practicalism" as defined earlier. The practicalism that is hereby rejected is the view (as defined above) that such understanding—a possible product of theorizing—itself has no value unless it produces something else of value. With this all understood, it is not necessary to deny (or accept) the claim that investigating, or theorizing, or writing about full social justice might only have practical value in its producing intrinsically better moral character in those, if any, who come better to understand justice.

2. Conclusion

The informed concern account is offered as an answer to a very specific challenge, namely that if the requirements of social justice are not realistic, then it is unclear what value there would be in understanding them, or in understanding this fact about them—their irrealism. In reply, I have argued that it is a morally significant fact about a person whether they have a due and informed concern about certain things, such as the suffering of others, or their subjection to injustice. For this reason it is a morally significant thing to understand social justice, including whether it is the sort of standard that might require things even if they are unrealistic. One's concern for justice, to the extent that one has it, would misfire badly if that feature of justice were misunderstood. For example, if it is falsely believed that current social arrangements are not significantly unjust, and this is believed on the ground that there is no realistic prospect of much improvement, then not only would the belief be false, but the underlying concern for justice would itself be morally deficient owing to the profound misconception of the nature of its object. On this basis, even apart from any practical value there might be in understanding these features of justice, there is moral value in understanding it well enough to have an informed concern about justice. A person's morally sound orientation to justice is shaped by the fact that, and the ways in which, social injustice is lamentable.

EPILOGUE

[E]xcept all men were good, everything cannot be right, and that is a blessing that I do not at present hope to see.

—THOMAS MORE, *UTOPIA*

I NOW PULL SOME of the book's main threads together in order to frame their significance, and to make several further observations. The relation presented in this book between idealistic theory and real political practice is mixed: understanding justice, even if it is unrealistic, has some practical value in ways that have been neglected; it lacks some kinds of practical value that are sometimes assumed; it has a kind of novel practical value that I develop myself; and whatever practical value it does or does not have, there is also a nonpractical— yet still moral—value in having a concern for justice that is philosophically informed. Moreover, whether or not any of that is so—whether or not there is any of that value in understanding this—justice might yet be, in one way or another, an idealistic or unrealistic standard. Machiavelli and More (in the voice of his eponymous character) seem to say that it is, as do Plato and Aristotle.[1] Of course they could all be mistaken. We want to understand whether and how this is or is not so, not simply to defer to the daunting authority of such a foursome.

Clearly, practical normative prescriptions will need to be made in light of the best empirical suppositions about the motives and behavior to be expected. Knowing what we can about prime justice, even if that is the best candidate for the content of social justice, may or may not be a guide in that task. If it is "robust" then the proper prescription at the level of principles will be unbent by the shape of fallible humans. In that case justice is not guaranteed to be a practical guide, though it might yet be. It may be the sort of standard where approximating the just structure approximates justice, though this cannot be assumed as we know from the fallacy of approximation. Either way, understanding full justice may provide guidance as a template for judging where some ineradicable deviations might be partly countervailed by other deviations (or fully, in which case full justice would be in reach after all). There is also the possibility of expanding options by understanding their moral value, and finally the intrinsic value of not misunderstanding justice, thereby having a deformed concern about justice and injustice.

There is some appeal in dismissing this high-flying account of justice, especially if it is unrealistic. The alternatives to it are apparently only two: first, we might try to theorize about degrees of justness only, rejecting the very idea of full justice. As I have argued, it is not clear how such a project would proceed. Certainly, there are instances in which some conditions are patently more just than others. But the obviousness of those cases means no theory is being consulted to generate or explain that ranking. If we settled for those cases, this would mean not only giving up the idea of full justice, but also doing without anything properly thought of as a theory even of "juster than"—a theory being something that would purport to explain, ground, or generate the rankings. This does not show such a theory to be impossible, but now add the challenges that would come from eschewing any reliance, in developing the theory, on any judgments that entail that there is such a thing as full justice. As I argued, many of the judgments that normally figure in our reasoning about justice would be banished, such as that slavery is extremely unjust, and that unnecessary parking restrictions are not. Such a project raises these difficult questions, though as I say they do not prove it to be doomed.

The other alternative to a theory in which full justice might be a high and unrealistic standard would be to somehow justify relativizing its requirements to the range of human motives that we would have most reason to predict, should the full standard be put into practice. There are at least two things that are implausible about this approach. One is that some basis must be provided for the assumption that justice could not be a standard that, as it turns out, expectable human behavior is more or less sure to violate. It would need explaining how this is any more credible than stipulating in ethics that if lying for personal advantage is something that everyone will sometimes do then that settles that it is not wrong. As Cohen asks, in effect, what basis could there be for supposing *a priori* that societies are likely, or not very unlikely, to be just?[2]

The other implausible thing about stipulating that full justice is shaped to real expectable human behaviors, is not really a challenge to that general proposition (whereas the challenge in the previous paragraph is) but to the prospects of carrying it out. Prime justice faces the very same challenge, so my point is that the common assumption that a more realistic conception would for that reason be more tractable is far from clear. Unless the approach baselessly stipulates that whatever is the case at any given time is thereby just, it must suppose that whatever people and institutions might be like at any given time, there might yet be a suitably realistic standard by which things are, so far, unjust but could yet come to be just. All that could stop this from being a very remote and high standard of its own would be claims—claims in need of support—about which ostensibly high requirements for a basic social structure people will never meet. Let us allow that it is safe to assume that people will never all be perfect by sound standards of individual morality. How much more than that can be known with sufficient solidity to count as strong and clear limits to idealistic theory? Even if this kind of standard-bending were philosophically supportable, it is doubtful that it would prevent in principle the theory of social justice from being very high and remote from what has ever been seen or seriously hoped for.

A final thought about the politically idealistic as it figures in my approach in this book: things that are outside of collective human abilities are not, I have granted for the sake of argument, among the requirements of justice, so we are talking only about things that are, in that way, genuinely possible. There is a realm, then, of human possibility whose status as required or not required by justice is disputed in debates about realistic and idealistic theorizing. That realm does not disappear from the range of human abilities, just by counting it (as a certain realism might do) as beyond, or not required by, justice. Realism and idealism both attend to that same realm of possibility and take different views of its normative status. The dispute is also not about whether those possibilities are, putting it loosely, at least desirable. Of course, and notoriously, many utopian visions are not actually desirable, but that is not the dispute about realism and idealism. It is a dispute about the desirability of certain imaginable arrangements, which is entirely different. Nothing in this book can trigger that kind of dispute, since (and partly for this very reason) I stay completely out of debates about what, substantively, justice requires in principle or in institutional specifics. There is, then, this idealistic realm which both realism and idealism recognize, which both approaches can say is desirable, and about which both have characteristic things to say. I want only to note this difference between them: the realist view, or a strong interpretation of it, sees that realm as entirely outside of the enterprise of proper normative political thought. Those realists cannot deny that it is there, but on their view it is no more integrated with proper political thought than, say, the desirable possibilities that exist for musical composers. Real possibilities, yes, they must say, but generally unconnected (except in special coincidental cases) with the enterprise of political thought. Maybe so, but reflection on desirable but manifestly very remote possibilities is a perennial feature of thinking about social and political life. Prime Justice can explain why this should be so: certain of those desirable but remote possibilities anchor the idea of full social justice, an idea that is implicated in much of our thinking even in realistic practical contexts. How far it provides practical guidance is a different issue, though as it happens it can do so in at least the several ways I have described. Still, if the final chapter is correct, the value of understanding the idealistic reaches of justice does not depend on such practical value as it might have. And, as I hope to have shown, to contend that justice might be quite idealistic, its requirements going even beyond what we have reason ever to expect, is not to betray ignorance or naïveté about people and the world. Of course things are not as they could be. But they could be.

Preface and Acknowledgments

1. Leif Wenar ("Is Humanity Getting Better?" *New York Times*, February 15, 2016) uses the metaphor of using two eyes to see both how bad the world is and how much better it has gotten, and I slightly repurpose that device here.

2. Aristotle, *Politics*, book 4, part 1. Jowett translation, available at *The Internet Classics Archive*: http://classics.mit.edu/Aristotle/politics.html.

3. *Laws* 739A3–740C3, from *Laws*, 739a and following, Aristotle, *Laws*, ed. Malcolm Schofield, trans. Tom Griffith (Cambridge: Cambridge University Press, 2016).

4. *Notes of a Native Son* (Boston: Beacon Press, 2012), 112–13.

5. See the epigraph to chapter 2.

6. Some of the philosophical issues about these matters have been discussed recently around the idea of "effective altruism." See, for example, Jeff McMahan, "Philosophical Critiques of Effective Altruism," *Philosophers' Magazine* 73 (2016): 92–99.

Chapter One. An Unrealistic Introduction

1. In a passage I use as chapter 7's epigraph, irrealist extraordinaire, G. A. Cohen, argues that in one way his critics are more optimistic than he is. G. A. Cohen, *Rescuing Justice and Equality* (Cambridge, MA: Harvard University Press, 2008), 430.

2. Consider hopeless but not unduly costly measures that almost certainly will not, but just might, avert a massive disaster. In some dire cases even apparently futile measures ought to be attempted, as many examples would illustrate. But that observation plays no further role in the arguments of the book.

3. Currently scholarly investigations are being undertaken about whether either More or Machiavelli knew of each other's work when they wrote, respectively, *Utopia*, and *The Prince*. See William J. Connell, "Machiavelli's Utopia," *Times Literary Supplement* (November 30, 2016), https://www.the-tls.co.uk/articles/public/machiavellis-utopia/.

4. *The Prince*, chapter 15, quoted more fully in the epigraph to chapter 2. Niccolò Machiavelli, *The Prince*, trans. and ed. Quentin Skinner and Russell Price; revised trans. Quentin Skinner (Cambridge: Cambridge University Press, 2019).

5. Jean-Jacques Rousseau, *Emile: or On Education*, trans. Allan Bloom (New York: Basic Books, 1979; originally 1762), 34.

6. Jean-Jacques Rousseau, *On the Social Contract*, any edition, book 1, paragraph 1. Many quote Rousseau to justify their tailoring justice to the people they see around them. If Rousseau meant to take "men as they are" now, as we find them, it would be inexplicable why he would not also take laws "as they are," rather than as they might be. The difference can be explained if he meant only to take men as they always will be, or must be. Of course, this suggests that he did not believe there is a way laws must or always will be. The point is that the constraint is not what people are like under some specific historical or institutional conditions, but what they are like in their nature—what they will be like under any conditions at all, or any conditions that are possible from here. That is a far less restrictive operating assumption, and I believe Rawls, for one, follows Rousseau's maxim under that more

liberal interpretation of what people's nature is. He thus proposes to take "People as they are (by the laws of nature), and constitutional and civil laws as they might be, that is, as they would be in a reasonably just and well ordered democratic society." John Rawls, *The Law of Peoples* (Cambridge, MA: Harvard University Press, 1999), 13.

7. John Rawls introduces the idea of realistic utopianism in *The Law of Peoples*, 4. In published correspondence he makes it explicit that even very unlikely conditions count as realistic in the intended sense so long as they are possible. "I am not happy about globalization as the banks and business class are pushing it. I accept Mill's idea of the stationary state. I am under no illusion that its time will ever come—certainly not soon—but it is possible, and hence it has a place in what I call the idea of a realistic utopia." To Philippe van Parijs, 23 June 1998. In *Autour de Rawls*, special issue of *Revue de philosophie économique* 7 (2003): 7–20.

8. John Rawls, *A Theory of Justice* (Cambridge, MA: Harvard University Press, 1971), revised edition, sec. 2, 8. Henceforth referred to as *TJ*.

9. Herbert Spencer, *The Data of Ethics* (Cambridge: Cambridge University Press, 2012), section 102 (in chapter XV).

10. I raise questions about this epistemological challenge later, in chapter 10, "Prime Justice," in wondering whether there is much to know about the content of "prime justice."

11. Henry Sidgwick, *The Methods of Ethics*, 7th ed. (London: Macmillan, 1907), book 4, chapter 4, 474, quoted at slightly greater length in the epigraph to chapter 10.

12. Spencer, *Data*, section 105.

13. See Bertell Ollman, "The Utopian Vision of the Future (Then and Now): A Marxist Critique," *Monthly Review* 57, no. 3 (July–August 2005): 78–102 . For another excellent critical discussion of Marxian anti-blueprint arguments, see David Leopold, "On Marxian Utopophobia," *Journal of the History of Philosophy* 54, no. 1 (January 2016): 111–34. (Leopold borrows the term "utopophobia," while explaining that its meaning in his usage is somewhat different from mine.)

14. Charles Fourier, *The Social Destiny of Man, or Theory of the Four Movements* (New York: R. M. Dewitt, 1857), 81.

15. Michael Frazer describes the target of his criticisms in this way throughout his paper, "Utopophobia as a Vocation." See Michael Frazer, "Utopophobia as a Vocation: The Professional Ethics of Ideal and Nonideal Political Theory," *Social Philosophy and Policy* 33, nos. 1–2 (2016): 175–92. The idea shows up in the title of a recent collection of papers about ideal theory, *Political Utopias: Contemporary Debates*, ed. Michael Weber and Kevin Vallier (New York: Oxford University Press, 2017) though none of the views under discussion there involve the kind of theoretical construction of detailed ideal social worlds that the term suggests.

16. Gerald Gaus explores the range of theorizing about justice within (roughly) these limits, in Gerald Gaus, *The Tyranny of the Ideal* (Princeton: Princeton University Press, 2016).

17. I say more about this in chapter 13, "Progress, Perfection, and Practice."

18. Jeremy Bentham, *The Book of Fallacies* (Oxford: Oxford University Press, 2015; originally 1843), part 4, chapter 9.

19. A proposal, strictly speaking, is a speech act, and since a principle is not a speech act it is not a proposal. But even if we waive that, admitting that principles can be roughly understood in an imperatival mood akin to proposals such as "Do x," there is a further way in which nonconcessive principles are not utopian, as I explain in the text: no genuine requirements of justice are unrealistic—doomed to failure. Requirements depend on ability,

or so I assume throughout. Critics of that supposition may wish to defend even Utopian principles, though I do not.

20. Cf. my discussion of Enoch in section 7.

21. Much more on this in Part 2, and chapter 12.

22. "[O]ut of such crooked wood as the human being is made, nothing entirely straight can be fabricated." *Idea for a Universal History from a Cosmopolitan Point of View* (1784), "Sixth Proposition," trans. Allen Wood. From Immanuel Kant, *Anthropology, History, and Education*, ed. Günter Zöller and Robert B. Louden (Cambridge: Cambridge University Press, 2007), 113. Hereafter *Universal History*.

23. "[I]t requires correct concepts of the nature of a possible constitution, great experience practiced through many courses of life, and beyond this a good will that is prepared to accept it; three such items are very difficult ever to find all together, and if it happens, it will be only very late, after many fruitless attempts." Kant, *Universal History*, 113.

24. Such reasoning would be a case of what I call, in chapter 14, "The Fallacy of Approximation."

25. In his doctoral dissertation, Timothy Syme explores how the idea of basic social structure might be expanded in this way, as compared with a narrow focus on law or coercion. See Timothy Syme, "Everyday Life and the Demands of Justice" (PhD Diss., Brown University, 2015). See also Timothy Syme, "The Pervasive Structure of Society," *Philosophy and Social Criticism* 44, no. 8 (2018): 888–924.

26. Cohen, *Rescuing Justice and Equality*, 135.

27. Cohen, *Rescuing Justice and Equality*, 135–39.

28. Charles Mills, "'Ideal Theory' as Ideology," *Hypatia* 20, no. 3 (Summer 2005): 165–183. Hereafter "Ideal Theory." Reprinted in the collection Charles Mills, *Black Rights, White Wrongs* (New York: Oxford University Press, 2017), 72–90. Citations are from the journal version.

29. Charles Mills, "Ideal Theory," 172.

30. Mills, "Ideal Theory," 169.

31. Mills, "Ideal Theory," 181–82.

32. Mills, "Ideal Theory," 168.

33. Here are pointers to several more such passages, italics added, in Mills, "Ideal Theory": "One will need to work and theorize *not merely with the ideal*" (167); "In *never exploring* how deeply different this is from ideal-as-descriptive-models" (170); "Nor could it seriously be claimed that moral theory is concerned *only with* mapping beautiful ideals, not their actual implementation" (171); "*Abstaining from* theorizing about oppression" (171).

34. Mills, "Ideal Theory" (181).

35. I am grateful to Charles Mills for reading and responding (with approval, he permits me to report) to my interpretation in this section.

36. John Rawls, *Political Liberalism* (New York: Columbia University Press, 1993), 11–13.

37. Amartya Sen, *The Ideal of Justice* (Cambridge, MA: Harvard University Press, 2011).

38. Cohen, *Rescuing Justice and Equality*, 302.

39. Cohen argues that the Rawlsian method derives the results from several values, such as efficiency, or stability, that are not properly thought of as matters of justice. I look more closely at this issue at several points in the book (especially in chapter 9, "Bad Facts," and when discussing Sen in chapter 13, "Progress, Perfection, and Practice").

40. See chapter 9, "Bad Facts," on Cohen's argument.

41. I will look closely and critically at Cohen's position in chapter 9, "Bad Facts."

42. This comes up again in chapter 5, "Utopophobia."

43. This is more fully explained and discussed in chapter 5, "Utopophobia."

44. I discuss this "problem of second best" and its underappreciated generality in chapter 14, "The Fallacy of Approximation."

45. David Enoch, "Against Utopianism: Noncompliance and Multiple Agents," *Philosophers' Imprint* 18, no. 16 (September 2018): 1–20.

46. Enoch, "Against Utopianism": "Asking about the actions required of one agent given realistic assumptions about the level of compliance of others is also a worthwhile project" (5). "And there is no obvious sense in which this project—the one of nonideal theory—is posterior to or less respectable than the project of ideal theory" (5–6).

47. Enoch, "Against Utopianism," 4.

48. Making both of these points, he writes ("Against Utopiansim"), "Estlund is right in insisting that the likelihood of noncompliance *by an agent* is irrelevant to the truth of the ought judgment *about the same agent*. . . . But he doesn't notice (in this context) that often in political philosophy the ought judgment is about one agent, and the noncompliance is that of another. And then, his insistence against utopophobia is just beside the point" (4–5); and, "Estlund's main line against utopophobia is rendered irrelevant by this kind of multiplicity of agents" (5, note 13). See also "But he doesn't notice (in this context) that often in political philosophy the ought judgment is about one agent, and the noncompliance is that of another. And then, his insistence against utopophobia is just beside the point" (5). "But political feasibility worries are much better seen as primarily about multiple-agent cases" (5).

49. In David Estlund, "Human Nature and the Limits (If Any) of Political Philosophy," *Philosophy and Public Affairs* 39, no. 3 (2011): 207–37, I write, "[A]ny institutional proposal that ignores the facts about how people will actually tend to behave is worthless" (215). As stated, it does not discriminate between the one-agent case—should society implement institutions that society will not comply with?—and the multiperson case—e.g., should the state implement institutions that citizens won't comply with? As stated, it covers both.

50. As I write, in Estlund, "Human Nature," 226: "The rules and institutions that should be constructed given what is known about everyone's likely compliance are hardly guaranteed to be rules and institutions that qualify a society as just."

51. Enoch, "Against Utopianism," 5.

52. Enoch, "Against Utopianism," 4.

53. I realize the individuals making up the state may also be citizens. I don't believe that complication harms the point here.

54. Enoch, "Against Utopianism," 3.

Chapter Two. Overview

1. Charles Mills explicates several further, and deeper, relationships between Utopias and the dystopian in, "Through a Glass, Whitely: Ideal Theory as Epistemic Injustice," Presidential address for the Central Division, delivered February 23, 2018, in *Proceedings of the American Philosophical Association* 92 (November 2018).

2. The human nature constraint is, in effect, a version of what I call the "bent view" that standards of justice are shaped in order to ensure that people could, at least in due course and without oppressive control, bring themselves to behave in ways such that justice is achieved. (See chapter 1, p. 13.) Here I highlight the idea of "human nature" understood in the way I explain.

3. I paraphrase an example from Frank Jackson and Robert Pargetter, "Oughts, Options, and Actualism," *Philosophical Review* 95, no. 2 (1986): 233–55.

4. There are questions about the logic of such requirements. For example, the nonconcessive and the concessive requirements in this case could not be jointly satisfied, so how could they both be required? I treat such issues more fully in chapter 8, "Concessive Requirement."

5. I draw here on my brief introduction of this puzzle in "Prime Justice," in Vallier and Weber, *Political Utopias*.

6. See chapters 11 and 12.

7. For recent discussion of the pros and cons of a "person-affecting principle," and some references to literature, see Derek Parfit, "Future People, the Non-Identity Problem, and Person-Affecting Principles," *Philosophy & Public Affairs* 45, no. 2 (2017).

Chapter Three. Anti-Anti-Moralism

1. Bernard Williams has led the way. See Bernard Williams, "Realism and Moralism in Political Theory," in *In the Beginning Was the Deed: Realism and Moralism in Political Argument* (Princeton: Princeton University Press, 2009), 1–17. Alison McQueen instructively characterizes "political realism" as, "a distinctive family of approaches to the study, practice, and normative evaluation of politics that tend to (a) affirm the 'autonomy' (or, more minimally, the 'distinctiveness') of politics; (b) hold an agonistic account of politics; (c) reject as 'utopian' or 'moralist' those approaches, practices, and evaluations which seem to deny these facts; and (d) prioritize the requirements of political order and stability over the demands of justice (or, more minimally, reject any kind of absolute priority of justice over other political values)." Alison McQueen, "The Case for Kinship: Agential Realism and Political Realism," forthcoming in *Politics Recovered: Essays on Realist Political Thought*, ed. Matt Sleat (New York: Columbia University Press). McQueen also usefully cites passages where Geuss echoes Carr's view that morality is mostly rationalization. See Raymond Geuss, *Philosophy and Real Politics* (Princeton: Princeton University Press, 2008), 91–11, 85–92.

2. Since it might only be obvious once it is made more precise, I press the point at length in chapter 5, "Utopophobia."

3. Among many others, I count as representative examples, Carr, Morgenthau (note this chapter's epigraph), Williams, Sangiovanni. Generally, see authors discussed in "Realism in Normative Political Theory," E. Rossi and M. Sleat, *Philosophy Compass* 9, no. 10 (2014): 689–701.

4. Notice that this question of moralism vs. realism is entirely separate from the question whether political philosophy ought properly to investigate scenarios of full-compliance or high levels of civic or personal virtue. That question can occur perfectly well within either moralist or realist methods.

5. However, as I explain in chapter 8, "Concessive Requirement," the nonconcessive requirements that attract the charge of irrealism are still moral requirements that lie within the abilities of societies to meet them. The sense in which they might be unrealistic is that it might be unlikely that they will be met, and I argue at length that this points to no defect or objection to such requirements.

6. John Rawls, *TJ*, 3.

7. Rawls, *Political Liberalism*, xxxix and many other places in that book.

8. Rawls takes the basic social structure to be the subject of justice. See *Political Liberalism*, 257–89.

9. See Christian List and Philip Pettit, *Group Agency* (Oxford: Oxford University Press, 2011). If moral individualism is false then this threatens some forms of liberalism, a point

which might seem to resonate with some realist thought. But Rawls is regarded by those realists as the arch moralist even though justice is not a moral standard for individuals. And rightly so: he does say that political justice is a moral question, and realists often seem to deny it. What they are resisting then is not moral individualism, but, in some way, moralism more generally. For more about how liberalism is not essentially individualist in ways it is often thought to be, see my, "Liberal Associationism and the Rights of States," in *Social Philosophy and Policy* 30, nos. 1–2 (January 2013): 425–49.

10. Rawls proposes to "Use the two principles of justice as a part of the conception of right for individuals. We can define the natural duty of justice as that to support and to further the arrangements that satisfy these principles; in this way we arrive at a principle that coheres with the criteria for institutions" (*TJ*, sec. 51, 295). It is not clear that Rawls means to reduce the "criteria for institutions" to agential moral requirements, rather than merely to get them to "cohere."

11. For discussion and references, see Richard Arneson, "Egalitarianism," *The Stanford Encyclopedia of Philosophy* (Summer 2013 ed.), ed. Edward N. Zalta, https://plato.stanford .edu/archives/sum2013/entries/egalitarianism/.

12. See G. A. Cohen, "On the Currency of Egalitarian Justice," *Ethics* 99, no. 4 (1989): 906–44.

13. I will revisit these features of Cohen's view at chapter 9, "Bad Facts," for related but different purposes.

14. See Thomas Hurka, "Moore's Moral Philosophy," *The Stanford Encyclopedia of Philosophy* (Fall 2015 ed.), ed. Edward N. Zalta, https://plato.stanford.edu/archives/fall2015 /entries/moore-moral/.

15. Mark Schroeder, "Cudworth and Normative Explanations," *Journal of Ethics and Social Philosophy* 1 (2005).

16. I discuss a closely related point in chapter 9, "Bad Facts," where I consider what I call the "unearthed Rawlsian principle," and note that it normatively changes nothing as compared with what Cohen sees as Rawls's fact-dependent approach to justice.

17. See especially the discussion of "circumstances of politics" in Jeremy Waldron, *Law and Disagreement* (Oxford: Oxford University Press, 1998).

18. From Charles Larmore, "The Truth in Political Realism," in *Politics Recovered: Realist Thought in Theory and Practice*, ed. Matt Sleat (New York: Columbia University Press, 2018). See also his "What Is Political Philosophy?" *Journal of Moral Philosophy* 10, no. 3 (2013): 276–306.

19. This is not even "concessive" in my sense—not a question of what some agent should do given that this very agent will not do all that she should do—if the ruler is distinct from the immoral people. It is not even that special, but is simply standard moral thinking. But if, say, the people are the rulers, then there is still a perfectly moral question: what morally ought we to do given that we will behave immorally in certain ways? See chapter 1 (Introduction) and chapter 8 for my distinction between concessive and nonconcessive standards.

20. See Williams, "Realism and Moralism," 2; Andrea Sangiovanni, "Justice and the Priority of Politics to Morality," *Journal of Political Philosophy* 16, no. 2 (2008): 137–64; Enzo Rossi, "Justice, Legitimacy, and (Normative) Authority for Political Realists," *Critical Review of International Social and Political Philosophy* 15, no. 2 (2012): 149–64.

21. Cohen, for example, says this: "Asking what we think we should do, given these or those factual circumstances, is a fruitful way of determining what our principles are; and sometimes, moreover, responses to actual facts reveal our principles better than our responses to hypothesized facts do, because the actual facts present themselves more vividly

to us, and, too, they concentrate the mind better, since they call for actual and not merely hypothetical decisions (*Rescuing*, 247).

22. E. H. Carr, *The Twenty Years' Crisis 1919–1939* (London: Macmillan, 1939), 68.

23. Hans Morgenthau, "The Political Science of E. H. Carr," *World Politics* 1, no. 1 (1948): 127–34, at 134.

24. See Charles Pidgen, "Russell's Moral Philosophy," *The Stanford Encyclopedia of Philosophy* (Winter 2014 ed.), ed. Edward N. Zalta, https://plato.stanford.edu/entries/russell-moral/.

25. These are often regarded as species of moral anti-realism, but I will avoid that terminology to avoid confusion with the issue of political realism.

26. Maybe the modern idea of ethics as (in Geuss's terms, see Raymond Geuss, *Outside Ethics* [Princeton: Princeton University Press, 2005], 63) "the immanentist egocentric practical standpoint"—the fixation on the question "what ought I to do?"—is deeply mistaken, or at least a very incomplete picture of the normative landscape. How, exactly, that would be a special challenge to political moralism in particular is not yet clear from this formulation. Maybe the diagnosis would give some special role or primacy to politics in grounding some alternative form of practical or normative reflection. We await clear development of an alternative conception.

27. *Law of Peoples.*

28. Andrea Sangiovanni, "Justice . . . Morality"; Aaron James, *Fairness in Practice: A Social Contract for a Global Economy* (Oxford: Oxford University Press, 2012).

29. Rawls's famous limitation of his principles of justice to constitutional democracies has suggested such a view to many interpreters, though it does not mean that he takes this view. It does leave that possibility open, although there are other parts of his view that might be relevant to the question.

30. This must remain partly vague, of course, in light of the question discussed above about the boundaries of the moral.

31. Williams, "Realism and Moralism," 11.

32. "Realism and Moralism," 6.

33. It is simple to see what a minimalist moralism about justice would be: in its simplest form, it would hold that there is nothing to political justice other than minimalist moralist legitimacy. But, as we have seen, that is not implied by minimalism about legitimacy.

34. *The Prince*, chapter XV (quoted more fully in my epigraph to chapter 2).

35. I agree with Cohen that, "not all political philosophy questions are practical questions," a position for which he gives several arguments in the surrounding pages. *Rescuing Justice and Equality*, 307.

Chapter Four. Circumstances and Justice

1. This will be important in evaluating the idea of "Prime Justice," chapter 10.

2. For more on these ideas, see articles by Mark LeBar, "Justice as a Virtue," https://plato.stanford.edu/entries/justice-virtue/ and Alec Walen, "Retributive Justice," https://plato.stanford.edu/entries/justice-retributive/ both in the *Stanford Encyclopedia of Philosophy*, ed. Edward N. Zalta.

3. See also Rawls, "Unless these circumstances existed there would be no occasion for the virtue of justice, just as in the absence of threats of injury to life and limb there would be no occasion for physical courage" (*TJ*, sec. 22, 128). For a little fuller discussion of ways in which certain things fall in or outside of the applicability of (as she puts it) a predicate,

see Ruth Chang, "Introduction," in *Incommensurability, Incomparability, and Practical Reason*, ed. Ruth Chang (Cambridge, MA: Harvard University Press, 1997), 28. What's true of all predicates is true of moral predicates such as "just."

4. Some standards are essentially reciprocal, but not all.

5. David Hume, *A Treatise of Human Nature* (1739), ed. L. A. Selby-Bigge, 2nd ed. rev. P. H. Nidditch (Oxford: Clarendon, 1975), 3.2.2 (hereafter *T*).

6. The cases of rules and conventions might well involve a measure of moral motivation as well. What is distinctive of the case I call "moral motives" is that the coordinate behavior is not a product either of threatened sanctions or of an expectation of reciprocal behavior by others.

7. Karl Marx, "On the Jewish Question," in *Karl Marx: Selected Writings*, ed. Lawrence Simon (Indianapolis: Hackett Publishing Company, 1994), esp. 21.

8. *T* 3.2.2.

9. Gregory S. Kavka, "Why Even Morally Perfect People Would Need Government," *Social Philosophy and Policy* 12, no. 1 (1995): 1–18, citing Madison's famous dictum.

10. Something like this idea seems to be behind Hart's discussion of the minimal content of natural law, as a content common to all suitable "systems of mutual forbearance." See H.L.A. Hart, *The Concept of Law*, Clarendon Law Series, ed. Leslie Green (Oxford: Oxford University Press, 2012), 195.

11. John Rawls, *A Theory of Justice*, rev. ed. (Cambridge, MA: Belknap, 1999), sec. 22, 112. The existence of such a standard of eligible arrangements is not itself enough to guarantee that there is any act that is either forbidden or permitted in all such arrangements, so it is not enough by itself to count any actions as just or unjust.

12. Here I change the second condition from what was stated in the article from which this chapter descends, "What's Circumstantial about Justice?" in (special issue) *Social Philosophy and Policy* 33, nos. 1–2 (Winter 2016). There the second condition stated that the method was not Pareto inferior to any alternative. That seems not to be tracking what we are after here, namely a method representing a change to which no one would object. I now think the present condition captures that better.

13. The general line here is similar and indebted to ideas of Brian Barry, *A Treatise of Social Justice, Vol. 1: Theories of Justice* (Berkeley: University of California Press, 1989) and G. A. Cohen, *Rescuing Justice and Equality* (Cambridge, MA: Harvard University Press, 2008).

14. Hume and Rawls focus mostly on conflicts of interest, but Rawls writes, "A lack of unanimity is part of the circumstances of justice, since disagreement is bound to exist even among honest men who desire to follow much the same political principles" (Rawls, *A Theory of Justice*, rev. ed., sec. 36, 196).

15. Ibid., 126, emphasis added.

16. Ibid., 130.

17. As I understand Hume, "selfishness" cannot be seen as a moral defect for which justice might be the remedy. Our "natural" moral ideas prior to the invention of justice, would contemplate a due partiality with pleasure. "Our natural uncultivated ideas of morality, instead of providing a remedy for the partiality of our affections ["to ourselves," and "to our relations and acquaintance"] do rather conform themselves to that partiality, and give it an additional force and influence" (*T* 3.2.2).

18. Hobbes, *Leviathan*, chapter 13 (any edition).

19. Rawls, *A Theory of Justice*, rev. ed., 127.

20. Rawls, *Political Liberalism*, esp. 54ff.

21. *TJ*, 2nd ed., sec. 22, 129–30.

Chapter Five. Utopophobia

1. I discuss Rawls's remarks on these matters in the text around p. 87ff.

2. Peter Singer, *The Expanding Circle: Ethics and Sociobiology* (New York: Farrar, Straus and Giroux, 1981), 157.

3. William Galston ("Realism in Political Theory," *European Journal of Political Theory* 9 [2010]: 385–411) criticizes normative political theory that sets moral standards unlikely ever to be achieved. He writes, "Realists reject this account of political theory on the grounds that it is utopian in the wrong way—that it does not represent an ideal of political life achievable under even the most favorable circumstances. Tranquility is fleeting at best; conflict and instability are perennial possibilities. The yearning for a world beyond politics is at best diversionary, at worst destructive" (387). Theorists who Galston takes to accept this general stance include Bernard Williams, Stuart Hampshire, John Dunn, Glen Newey, Richard Bellamy, Geoffrey Hawthorne, Raymond Geuss, John Gray, William Connolly, Bonnie Honig, Chantal Mouffe, Mark Philp, Judith Shklar, "and her many admirers who endorse her anti-Utopian skepticism," and others.

4. Two articles that also provide references to many other recent treatments of feasibility are Juha Räikkä, "The Feasibility Condition in Political Theory," *Journal of Political Philosophy* 6, no. 1 (1998): 27–40, as well as Pablo Gilabert and Holly Lawford-Smith, "Political Feasibility: A Conceptual Exploration," *Political Studies* 60 (2012): 809–25.

5. For an excellent overview of this literature, see Zofia Stemplowska and Adam Swift, "Ideal and Nonideal Theory," in *The Oxford Handbook of Political Philosophy*, ed. David Estlund (Oxford: Oxford University Press, 2012).

6. The idea that requirements of, e.g., justice are somehow political but not moral is one we have considered and found wanting in chapter 3, "Anti-Anti-Moralism."

7. Later, at chapter 13, "Progress, Perfection, and Practice," I will consider this potential practical value of what may appear to be unrealistic theorizing about justice—its ability to sometimes induce achievements that would otherwise never have occurred.

8. As we'll see below in chapter 8, "Concessive Requirement," the concessive/nonconcessive distinction is wholly relative, rather than a pair of exclusive categories into which requirements are sorted.

9. When the issue is the probability of events more generally, it is widely accepted that possible events can have zero probability. Equiprobable events in an uncountable infinity of possible outcomes (such as all the places on the board the dart could land) cannot have more than zero probability, since any finite number of them would then absurdly sum to more than 1. But this is a separate issue from whether I might be able to do something even if there is zero probability that I will do it, or whether instead such an act is impossible for me.

10. Such a notion of impossibility is not conceptually incoherent, since even if being nearer to zero probability does not entail being more nearly impossible, being *at* zero probability could yet entail impossibility. To see how two variables could be related in that way, observe that if circle A and circle B have the same diameter and center point, then they are identical: one and the same circle. And yet, the center points of the two circles can get nearer each other without the circles getting (whatever this would mean) more nearly identical. I thank Josh Schechter for this example.

11. I benefited from comments on an earlier version of this section from Jerry Cohen and Nina Emery.

12. Inability apparently does not entail improbability if the conditional account of ability, discussed below, is correct. A person may amuse others often, but is unable to amuse them: trying tends to fail.

13. *TJ*, 455. I return to this natural but troubling feature of Rawls's contract-oriented method for determining the content of justice in chapter 7, section 7.

14. Elizabeth Anderson, *The Imperative of Integration* (Princeton: Princeton University Press, 2010), 3.

15. Thomas Nagel, *Equality and Partiality* (Oxford: Oxford University Press, 1991), chapter 3. Nagel's discussion was the spur to my own thinking about this problem, and my framing of the issue is owed largely to him. This set of quotes is all from the first few paragraphs of chapter 3.

16. "The danger of utopianism comes from the political tendency, in pursuit of the ideal of moral equality, to put too much pressure on individual motives or even to attempt to transcend them entirely through an impersonal transformation of social individuals. A nonutopian solution requires a proper balance between these two elements, and that requires knowing what they are and how they interact." Nagel, *Equality*, 24.

17. See, e.g., Joseph Carens, *Equality, Moral Incentives, and the Market* (Chicago: University of Chicago Press, 1981), 104. I discuss some aspects of Carens's view more fully in chapter 7, "Justice Unbent."

18. Nicholas Sturgeon reports this observation as lore among Cornell graduate students. See "What Difference Does It Make Whether Moral Realism Is True?" *Southern Journal of Philosophy* 24 (1986), Supplement.

19. Here I go through some points from chapter 14 of my "Utopophobia: Concession and Aspiration in Democratic Theory," in *Democratic Authority: A Philosophical Framework* (Princeton: Princeton University Press, 2008).

20. *Republic*, book 5, 457c–d.

21. Nicholas Southwood and Pablo Gilabert ("Ability and Volitional Incapacity," *Journal of Ethics and Social Philosophy* 10 [2016]) criticize certain views that employ the idea of what a person can bring herself to do (they cite Vihvelin, for example), which construe the "bringing" as some mental entity that is within or outside the agent's power or ability. My use of the term is entirely different.

22. Harry G. Frankfurt, in "Rationality and the Unthinkable," in *The Importance of What We Care About: Philosophical Essays* (Cambridge: Cambridge University Press, 1988), 184. Frankfurt is not here speaking about cases in which the internal forces are refused endorsement by the agent. They might call for a different account. Maybe in that case they are genuine obstacles in a way that interrupts moral responsibility for the choice. Keeping this open is analogous to my allowing for a category of clinical or pathological cases of 'can't will,' in which they do support 'can't do,' or at least block a requirement. Frankfurt's theory on which responsibility is tied to this higher order endorsement is subject to objections around the question of whether those attitudes are themselves under the agent's own control, or something she is responsible for. I haven't committed myself to it.

23. I say "at least" here since I will give a sympathetic elaboration of the conditional analysis, which I will have occasion to consider, in several other parts of the argument, as possibly correct. That is if it is correct about ability, then this will add support to certain other claims I make. See, e.g., p. 246.

24. For some discussion and references regarding conditional analyses, see John Maier, "Abilities," in *The Stanford Encyclopedia of Philosophy* (Fall 2014 ed.), ed. Edward N. Zalta, https://plato.stanford.edu/archives/fall2014/entries/abilities/.

25. Wiens (David Wiens, "Motivational Limitations on the Demands of Justice," *European Journal of Political Theory* 15, no. 3 [2016]: 333–52) offers, in passing, a different way to motivate the position contrary to mine, one that doesn't rely on a success conditional account: "Let φ be a generic action. If being motivated to φ is a precondition for doing φ and we can't be motivated to φ, then we can't satisfy a precondition for doing φ. Thus, we

can't φ" (6). Without further explanation, it is not clear what is meant by "can't be motivated." I doubt that motivations are the objects of abilities. If, instead, "can't" means not inability but impossibility, then the premise may be irrelevant to the pertinent cases. In what sense is it impossible that the person with interfering motives performs the act in question? After all, it is not a necessity that they have those motives, and it is not a necessity that they succumb or acquiesce. Finally, the inference displayed in the quotation is of doubtful validity in any case. For example, the causal order might guarantee that I do not and will not care in the slightest about drinking Mountain Dew. That hardly shows that I can't drink it (though it ensures that I won't do so).

26. More specifically: no agent is morally required to do anything that she is unable to do.

27. The conditional analysis has many critics, some of whom we will encounter. A recent detailed defense can be found in Joseph Mendola, *Human Interests* (Oxford: Oxford University Press, 2014), chapter 3.

28. J. L. Austin, "Ifs and Cans," *Proceedings of the British Academy* 42 (1956): 107–32, at 119. This example is especially important, since Austin grants later in the same piece that while certain conditional accounts of ability he finds in Moore and Nowell-Smith are subject to serious problems, these don't obviously apply to a conditional account in which the antecedent is "If she tries." The missed putt is his argument against that version.

29. Irving Thalberg usefully observes, "A surgeon, a third of whose appendectomies resulted in the patient's demise, scarcely passes our tests for surgical competence. But he would have been judged a wonder in Elizabethan times. A race-track tout, who has managed to predict one-tenth of the season's Daily Double winners, would rank as a skilled prognosticator by any standards. Whether or not our criteria for competence are detailed, closely analogous to the actions we expect of the practitioner, strict and comprehensive, is, no doubt, determined by the importance of his activity, the consequences of a faulty performance, the feasibility of duplicating the conditions of practice, and the availability of rival experts." "Abilities and Ifs," *Analysis* 22, no. 6 (June 1962): 121–26.

30. See David Lewis, "Finkish Dispositions," *Philosophical Quarterly* 47, no. 187 (1997): 143–58.

31. Kiesewetter makes a similar point. See Benjamin Kiesewetter, "Instrumental Normativity: In Defense of the Transmission Principle," *Ethics* 125, no. 4 (2015): 921–46, at 928.

32. This is Mendola's argument in *Human Interests*, section 3.2. In the context of a theory of feasibility, Gilabert and Lawford-Smith contend that "people can always try." See Pablo Gilabert and Holly Lawford-Smith, "Political Feasibility," 818.

33. The regress problem for acts of trying was pointed out by Gilbert Ryle, in *The Concept of Mind* (London: Hutchinson, 1949), 30ff. See also R. M. Chisholm, "J. L. Austin's Philosophical Papers," in *Free Will and Determinism*, ed. B. Berofsky (New York: Harper and Row, 1966); and K. Vihvelin, "Free Will Demystified: A Dispositional Account," *Philosophical Topics* 32 (2004): 427–50, at 443. The same objection applies to talk of 'can't intend,' and certain other notions that might be used in a conditional analysis. In the paper "Human Nature," I speak of what an agent 'can't will,' and this runs the same risk. I don't mean that willing is an action over which agents might have abilities or inabilities. That would lead to an infinite regress, but I'm not committed to any of that. Rather, the phrase is extremely useful in both capturing the appearance of 'can't' in the vernacular phrase, 'can't bring oneself to φ,' and also as syntactically parallel to 'will do,' 'can do' for purposes of asking what 'ought' implies. Ought does not imply will do, it does imply can do, it does not imply can will, so I argue. I don't mean that willing is an action. In effect, I just use 'to will to φ' as a shorthand for 'to bring oneself to φ.' Frankfurt, in "Rationality and the Unthinkable," also uses the phrase 'can't will' for similar examples, where willing is not an action.

34. Hornsby discusses this view in J. Hornsby (2010), "Trying to Act," in *A Companion to the Philosophy of Action*, ed. T. O'Connor and C. Sandis (Oxford: Wiley-Blackwell, 2010).

35. Keith Lehrer, "Cans without Ifs," *Analysis* 29 (1968): 29–32.

36. Mendola, *Human Interests*, investigates a set of issues around the idea of trying to try in chapter 3.

37. I'm grateful to Nic Southwood for pressing me to explicitly separate the trying and the persevering for a clearer analysis. (He is not, of course, to be seen as endorsing the analysis even so.) The account here aligns with Berislav Marusic, *Evidence and Agency: Norms of Belief for Promising and Resolving* (Oxford: Oxford University Press, 2015), in important respects. Portmore in his manuscript criticizes the Marusic approach, but unsuccessfully I believe. The argument hangs on a planning criterion, following others including Holly Smith. I think the planning criterion for being able is implausible in light of Messy Bill.

Chapter Six. Mitigating Motives

1. For a discussion of "Messy Bill," see pp. 28ff. and 99ff.

2. See the section on prerogatives in chapter 7, "Justice Unbent."

3. Douglas Portmore, *Commonsense Consequentialism: Wherein Morality Meets Rationality* (Oxford: Oxford University Press, 2011), chap. 3; Holly S. Goldman also endorses this view in Holly S. Goldman, "Doing the Best One Can," in *Values and Morals*, ed. Alvin Goldman and Jaegwon Kim (Dordrecht: Reidel, 1978), 185–214, at 194–95.

4. As Goldman explains, at some later point it might become true that were Bill to want to do it he would do it (though of course he won't want to or do it). That is not true early on—he will stop trying if he starts—and so he is off the hook. Of course, then, even having done nothing wrong, he may never get to the later point, thus eluding the obligation altogether according to this view.

5. We have seen it embraced even by Rawls and Nagel, whose views are of the sort regarded as insufficiently realistic by many other writers. This "human nature constraint" appears to be widely accepted.

6. Wiens, "Motivational Limitations," criticizes an earlier version of my argument, arguing that some cases of 'can't will' are cases of 'can't do' even though my account says otherwise, and I explain why I am not persuaded in, "Reply to Wiens," in the same journal issue: "Reply to Wiens," *European Journal of Political Theory* 15, no. 3 (2016): 353–62.

7. Williams argues that what morality requires does not have the overriding significance it is often claimed to have for what a person has reason to do even if it will often bear on the matter. Similarly, I assume only that what justice requires will often bear on what a society has reason to do. The connection between both what justice requires and what society has reason to do on one hand, and what a member has reason to do on the other hand, is similarly contingent and left unsettled here. The described view of Williams is present throughout much of his work, including throughout both *Moral Luck* (Cambridge: Cambridge University Press, 1981) and *Ethics and the Limits of Philosophy* (Cambridge, MA: Harvard University Press, 1985).

8. Here we could agree with a view such as Scanlon's (which is incompatible with Williams's) which does not tie the practicality of moral reasons to the agent's desires. T. M. Scanlon, *What We Owe to Each Other* (Cambridge, MA: Harvard Belknap Press, 2000).

9. Portmore defends such a view in *Commonsense Consequentialism*, chap. 2: "Which options have their normative statuses in virtue of their own goodness?" For a recent defense of a strong version of this view, see Peter A. Graham, "A Sketch of a Theory of Moral Blameworthiness," *Philosophy and Phenomenological Research* 88, no. 2 (2014): 388–409.

10. It may be that Nagel is pursuing two separate grounds for adjusting moral and political standards to certain human motives. Recall his unqualified statement that, "If real people find it psychologically very difficult or even impossible to live as the theory requires, or to adopt the relevant institutions, that should carry some weight against the ideal" (9). And yet, this comes immediately after his insisting on, "the relevance of what is motivationally reasonable to what is right." I hope to cover the ground by considering the "qualified" argument from reasonable resistant motives, as well as the "unqualified" argument from severe motives whether or not they are reasonable. See "Severe and Merely Insistent Motives" herein.

11. See the discussion earlier in this chapter of Messy Bill and the line that might form behind him.

12. Cohen, *Rescuing*.

13. Some philosophers deny that moral requirement (always or ever) implicates an underlying general moral principle. "Particularism" holds that a required act-token does not entail that there is a general principle requiring acts of the same type in the same circumstance. As Jonathan Dancy puts the view, "In ethics, a feature that makes one action better can make another one worse, and make no difference at all to a third." Jonathan Dancy, "Moral Particularism," in *Stanford Encyclopedia*, https://plato.stanford.edu/entries/moral -particularism/. That view rejects what we might call *circumstance-type generality*. But even a particularist view can allow that there are truths about what morality requires in counterfactual scenarios. We can reason about what ought to be done in some very particular set of circumstances, even if the case is entirely made up. In order to do so, we may or may not commit ourselves to any principles about what should always be done in similar circumstances. Extra-factual generality of moral requirements does not conflict with moral particularism.

14. To be clear: I will not here appeal to intuitive cases of what is often called a "prerogative" individuals might have to give more weight to certain considerations than they would get in a fully impartial view. I consider the relation of such prerogatives (if any) to our topic in chapter 7, "Justice Unbent," in the section "Are Prerogatives a Concession to Human Nature?"

15. The basic idea is best explained while supposing that requirements of social justice place requirements on individuals. As I have said, I will argue that this is not actually so (in chapter 12, "Plural Requirement"), and in that chapter I will return to the question of how to adjust the present point to fit my theory of Plural Requirement.

16. Quoted earlier, saying that sometimes interfering motives, "prevent [an agent] from performing an action that he had thought he wanted to perform, . . . only by virtue of the fact that he does not really want to perform it." Harry Frankfurt, "Rationality and the Unthinkable," in *The Importance of What We Care About: Philosophical Essays* (Cambridge: Cambridge University Press, 1988), 177–90.

17. If so, it has some of the structure of what I call "Plural Requirement," to be explored in chapter 12.

18. Recall, though, that I do not take a view about whether or when this is so. Rather, I simply bracket that category as raising special questions not relevant to the vast bulk of the case that lies at the core of the Bent View.

19. See Michael Brownstein and Jennifer Saul, eds., *Implicit Bias and Philosophy* (Oxford: Oxford University Press, 2016), 2 volumes; as well as Daniel Kelly and Erica Roedder, "Racial Cognition and the Ethics of Implicit Bias," *Philosophy Compass* 3, no. 3 (2008): 522–40.

20. "Rights and Duties in an Egalitarian Society," *Political Theory*, 14, no. 1 (February 1986): 31–49.

21. Ibid., 3.

22. Quoted above at p. 87, emphasis now added, *The Imperative of Integration*, 3.

23. Elizabeth Anderson, *The Imperative of Integration*, 3. I take her to implicate principles here by saying "just institutions must . . ." By contrast, "Institutions must . . ." would be unobjectionable in the present light.

24. Anderson, *The Imperative of Integration*, 4.

25. This point is commonly known as the problem of second best. The classic statement is R. G. Lipsey and K. J. Lancaster, "The General Theory of Second Best," *Review of Economic Studies* 24 (1956): 11–33. I consider it at more length in chapter 14, "The Fallacy of Approximation."

26. See discussions of the demandingness of moral theories in Peter Singer, "Famine, Affluence, and Morality," *Philosophy & Public Affairs* 1, no. 3 (1972): 229–43; Bernard Williams, *Ethics and the Limits of Philosophy* (Cambridge, MA: Harvard University Press, 1986); Shelly Kagan, "Does Consequentialism Demand Too Much? Recent Work on the Limits of Obligation," *Philosophy & Public Affairs* 13, no. 3 (1984): 239–54; Samuel Scheffler, "Prerogatives without Restrictions," *Philosophical Perspectives* 6 (1992): 377–97.

27. See below, 134.

28. John Rawls, *TJ*, 2nd ed., 1999. See, e.g., 7–8, 215–16, 308–9. See also A. John Simmons, "Ideal and Nonideal Theory," *Philosophy and Public Affairs* 38, no. 1 (2010): 5–36.

29. Onora O'Neill, "Abstraction, Idealization and Ideology in Ethics," in *Moral Philosophy and Contemporary Problems*, ed. J.D.G. Evans (Cambridge: Cambridge University Press, 1988), 55–69. See Alan Hamlin and Zofia Stemplowska, "Theory, Ideal Theory, and Theory of Ideals," *Political Studies Review* 10 (2012): 48–62, for more discussion of this point.

30. In a way that I have also encountered in others, David Schmidtz formulates his objection that way in, "Realistic Idealism," in *Methods in Analytical Political Theory*, ed. Adrian Blau (Cambridge: Cambridge University Press, 2017), 131–52.

31. See Gregory S. Kavka, "Would Perfect People Need Government?" *Social Philosophy and Policy* 12, no. 1 (December 1995): 1–18. Kavka argues that they would.

32. Adam Swift makes similar points in, "The Value of Philosophy in Nonideal Circumstances," *Social Theory and Practice* 34, no. 3 (2008): 363–87. This point is also important in assessing Rawls's claims about a theory of justice that is "moral but not political." See my discussion toward the end of the next chapter (7) at 140.

Chapter Seven. Justice Unbent

1. This difference between one agent's inability to get someone to do something and that second person's inability to do it is noted again in several different contexts later in the book. See the section "Feasibility as Plural Ability" in chapter 12, "Plural Requirement."

2. I take it as obvious that if citizens will not comply, then the state ought not to build the hopeless institutions. I go on to argue, of course, that this leaves open the possibility that the citizens ought to build and comply. See also my discussion of arguments by David Enoch in chapter 1.

3. Interestingly, some people are able to sing two notes at once, as in "overtone singing." I do not know about three notes. Obviously the example can be adjusted to whatever number of notes no one can sing.

4. On some theories of justice this will not always be so, as when a principle of distribution is not met but this could not have been remedied by anyone's choices.

5. See the definition of plural ability in that chapter at p. 247.

6. We will refine this later in chapter 12, "Plural Requirement," but briefly I will argue that the species of requirement that holds over a society (where it is not a group agent) is not agential obligation but Plural Requirement, and that kind of requirement over a set of agent-act pairs entails that each agent can do the act so long as the others do those acts each is paired within the requirement.

7. I do consider it briefly in chapter 12, to (only) float the possibility that the group's failure of plural requirement is, in an important sense, excusable if and to the extent that no agent does any wrong.

8. See the section below, "Excused Injustice, a Safe Harbor?"

9. The thoughts in this section stem from reflection on Sam Scheffler's comments on G. A. Cohen's *Incentives, Inequality, and Community: The Tanner Lectures on Human Values* (Ann Arbor: University of Michigan Press, 1995); hereafter *Incentives*. I am grateful to Scheffler for the chance to review the original, unpublished, written remarks. It should not be assumed that Scheffler agrees with what I say here.

10. Below I allow that sometimes a person is literally unable without the inducement. Then, of course, there can be cases where the only inducements that would do are oppressive or wrong.

11. As cautioned, I do not mean that the agent does not "have the ability," but only that without the incentive she is unable.

12. See his discussion of " 'ought' implies 'can,' " *Rescuing*, chapter 4.

13. *Rescuing*, chapter 6, section 13, "On Ought and Can," 250ff.

14. Though we will not look closely at this, a different route to a similar conclusion that the profoundly partial motives are requirement-blocking might appeal to what we have called their severity: the terrible psychological consequences of resisting them. This is different from supposing they somehow interfere with agency, but weighs the pain and distress heavily enough in some case to outweigh the reasons for resisting the motives.

15. Plato, *Republic*, book 5, 457c–d (also cited above in chapter 5). Charles Fourier, *Theory of the Four Movements*, ed. G. Stedman Jones and I. Patterson (Cambridge: Cambridge University Press, 1996), 1st ed. 1808. According to David Leopold, "Up to the age of four and a half, although they might be visited by their biological parents, children would be brought up by adults working serially as nurses (the latter drawn from the minority of adults attracted by nature to child care)." See "Education and Utopia: Robert Owen and Charles Fourier," *Oxford Review of Education* 37, no. 5 (October 2011): 619–35. See also the practices in Kibbutzim in Israel, as described in Daniel Gavron, *The Kibbutz: Awakening from Utopia* (New York: Rowman & Littlefield, 2000), chapter 7.

16. Carens concedes the point, and proposes a revised ideal in which people are obligated to contribute to the common good, but not necessarily as much as they can. See Carens, "Rights" 35.

17. Classic pieces include Samuel Scheffler, *The Rejection of Consequentialism: A Philosophical Investigation of the Considerations Underlying Rival Moral Conceptions* (Oxford: Clarendon Press, 1982), and Shelly Kagan, "Does Consequentialism Demand Too Much?" *Philosophy and Public Affairs* 13, no. 3 (Summer 1984). For some use of these issues in political philosophy, see G. A. Cohen, "Where the Action Is: On the Site of Distributive Justice," *Philosophy and Public Affairs* 26, no. 1 (Winter 1997): 3–30, and David Estlund, "Liberalism, Equality and Fraternity in Cohen's Critique of Rawls," *Journal of Political Philosophy* 6, no. 8 (March 1998): 99–112.

18. See esp. 103–8.

19. See 34.

20. "Morality and Reasonable Partiality," in *Partiality and Impartiality: Morality,*

Special Relationships, and the Wider World, ed. Brian Feltham and John Cottingham (Oxford: Oxford University Press, 2010), 106.

21. See the earlier discussion of justification vs. excuse at 104.

22. Pettit and List, *Group Agency,* plausibly suggest that democracy or something like it might be necessary. Supposing that is right, it is hard to believe that nondemocratic countries would thereby escape the charge of injustice.

23. I mentioned Rawls's insistence on motivational feasibility in chapter 6 along with a longer discussion of Nagel's similar view. See p. 141ff.

24. Cohen's distinction between principles of justice and rules for the regulation of society is a perspicuous way of thinking of this distinction. See Cohen, *Rescuing.* The distinction figures throughout the book but is introduced in the first few pages.

25. Cohen's more sweeping thesis is less plausible than this more limited argument. Letting justice be shaped by some facts is not initially troubling in the way that it is troubling to let justice be shaped by certain apparently justice-tainting facts such as the sort of talent-supremacist motivations I hypothesize. See chapter 9.

26. John Rawls, *Justice as Fairness: A Restatement* (Cambridge, MA: Harvard University Press, 2001), 185.

27. "We leave aside comprehensive doctrines that now exist, or that have existed, or that might exist," *Political Liberalism,* 40. Henceforth *PL.*

28. *PL,* 39.

29. The quotations after "My own reading" are from *The Law of Peoples,* 11–13.

Chapter Eight. Concessive Requirement

1. Alan Dershowitz, "The Torture Warrant: A Response to Professor Strauss," *New York Law School Law Review* 48 (2003): 277.

2. Thanks to Jackson and Pargetter, "Oughts, Options," one can illustrate and discuss several issues that had arisen in the preceding literature, including Howard Sobel, "Utilitarianism and Past and Future Mistakes," *Nous* 10 (1976): 195–219; Holly S. Goldman, "Dated Rightness and Moral Imperfection," *Philosophical Review* 85 (1977): 449–87; Richmond H. Thomason, "Deontic Logic and the Role of Freedom in Moral Deliberation," read to APA, 1977, and published in *New Studies in Deontic Logic,* ed. R. Hilpinen (Dordrecht: Reidel, 1981), 177–86; Holly S. Goldman, "Doing the Best One Can," in *Values and Morals,* ed. A. I. Goldman and J. Kim (Dordrecht: Reidel, 1978), 185–214; P. S. Greenspan, "Oughts and Determinism: A Response to Goldman," *Philosophical Review* 87 (1978): 77–83; I. L. Humberstone, "The Background of Circumstances," *Pacific Philosophical Quarterly* 64 (1983): 19–34.

3. For another example, 'ought' is often used in the philosophical literature to mean that there is some reason in favor, which is not enough to settle the question of requirement. I will not be using it in that way.

4. Though I will leave this next clarification aside, it may be that in some cases a person is unable to do A unless she does B, and/or vice versa. So a more general version would be:

Restricted Distributivity

O(A&B) & CAN(A) & CAN(B)→ O(A) & O(B)

Instead of saddling myself with that syntactic complexity here, it will suffice to hereby stipulate that in this chapter and book, in all cases of the form O(A&B), unless otherwise noted, I am limiting the domain to component actions A and B that are each within the ability of the agent.

5. See Kiesewetter, "Instrumental Normativity."

6. See chapter 5.

7. Nothing will hang on whether that is somehow fixed or certain, or only quite probable. Also, further questions arise about the identity conditions for the set of agents who do or do not Build and the set who do or do not Comply. I simply assume it to be the same set.

8. For the original formulation of the puzzle, see James Forrester, "Gentle Murder, Or the Adverbial Samaritan," *Journal of Philosophy* 81 (1984): 193–97.

9. For more on factual detachment and objections, see Paul McNamara, "Deontic Logic," in *The Stanford Encyclopedia of Philosophy* (Winter 2014 ed.), ed. Edward N. Zalta, https://plato.stanford.edu/archives/win2014/entries/logic-deontic/, especially the Appendix, "A Bit More on Chisholm's Paradox."

10. We will eventually need to explain how, as I will often suggest, it seems natural to hold that we ought to do something else that is incompatible with Building. How could that be required if Building is required? I address that issue below, under "Lesser Need 2."

11. A clear and seminal treatment of the issues is John Broome, *Rationality through Reasoning* (Hoboken: Wiley-Blackwell, 2013), chapter 3.

12. Michael McKinsey, "Levels of Obligation," *Philosophical Studies* 35, no. 4 (1979): 385–95, and Michael J. Zimmerman, *The Concept of Moral Obligation* (Cambridge: Cambridge University Press, 1996), chapter 4.

13. This sort of view occurs in Angelika Kratzer, "The Notional Category of Modality," in *Words, Worlds, and Context*, ed. H. J. Eikmeyer and H. Rieser (Berlin: Walter de Gruyter, 1981), 38–74.

14. Kiesewetter objects, in effect, that any such multiplicity leaves "the deliberative ought" unsettled. It is worth noting that in the non-agential mode of Plural Requirement (which I am mostly leaving aside here except for this note) deliberation is not obviously any part of the account, and so that concern would lapse.

15. Thanks to Doug Portmore and Jamie Dreier for discussion of this approach.

16. (B or C) should not be mistaken for meaning *necessarily* (B or C). It says that if you (will) do B or C, O(B), not "if you have no other choice but B or C."

17. Michael Walzer discusses this case in *Just and Unjust Wars: A Moral Argument with Historical Illustrations* (New York: Basic Books, 1977), 38–40.

18. The traditional "just war" doctrine holds that many acts by soldiers such as killing and imprisonment of enemy combatants are morally permissible in some contexts of war, so long as they are within certain limits of *jus in bello*, and Walzer defends a version of that position. Others, such as Jeff McMahan, dispute it. See his *Killing in War* (Oxford: Oxford University Press, 2011).

19. This point appears again in the chapter on Prime Justice.

20. Ralph Wedgwood, "Against Actualism," on PEA Soup, September 11, 2009, http://peasoup.typepad.com/peasoup/2009/09/against-actualism.html.

21. See the point about military prisons below in chapter 14, "The Fallacy of Approximation."

22. See Wedgwood, "The Meaning of 'Ought,'" in *Oxford Studies in Metaethics: Volume 1*, ed. Russ Shafer-Landau (Oxford: Clarendon Press, 2006), 127–60.

23. See Bernard Williams, "Ought and Moral Obligation," in *Moral Luck: Philosophical Papers 1973–1980* (Cambridge: Cambridge University Press, 1980), 118–19.

24. Sidgwick, *The Methods of Ethics*, chapter 3, section 3.

25. Sidgwick, *The Methods of Ethics*, 33.

26. See Mark Brown, "Conditional Obligation and Positive Permission for Agents in Time," *Nordic Journal of Philosophical Logic* 5, no. 2 (2000): 83–112.

27. Brown, "Conditional Obligation," 104.

28. Peter B. M. Vranas, "I Ought, Therefore I Can Obey," *Philosopher's Imprint* 18, no. 1 (2018).

Chapter Nine. Bad Facts

1. See chapters 4, 5, and 7: "Circumstances and Justice," "Utopohobia," and "Justice Unbent."

2. See chapter 7, "Justice Unbent." The quotation is from Kant, *Universal History*, "Sixth Proposition," 113.

3. Rawls, *Political Liberalism*, 103.

4. Freeman pulls together the main textual sources for roughly this list in "The Original Position," in *Stanford Encyclopedia of Philosophy*, ed. Edward N. Zalta (2019), https://plato .stanford.edu/entries/original-position/

5. *TJ*, 2nd ed., section 69, 398.

6. The pun is intended, though no part of my present point, in allusion to Cohen's incidental (so he argues) agreement, in certain respects, with Plato, discussed just below.

7. 262–63. My point here can allow that there would be even deeper principles required to "justify the use of the original position machine," underlying even the unearthed Rawlsian principle. The quotation is from Cohen, *Rescuing*, 262.

8. Several authors have explored the simplicity or triviality of the unearthing move, for example Thomas Pogge, "Cohen to the Rescue," *Ratio*, n.s., 21, no. 4 (December 2008).

9. See Plato's *Euthyphro*, trans. G.M.A. Grube, in Plato: *Complete Works*, ed. John Cooper (Indianapolis: Hackett, 1997), 1–16.

10. This is related to Valentini and Ronzoni's argument in "On the Meta-ethical Status of Constructivism: Reflections on G. A. Cohen's 'Facts and Principles,'" *Politics Philosophy Economics* 7 (2008): 403. They argue that the unearthed Rawlsian principle might be grounded in a fact, but a methodological one about how to construct justifications. Cohen would surely ask what it is that accounts for the particular moral significance of that method of construction, if not a deeper principle?

11. Cohen aligns himself with Plato in certain respects at 291. For Cohen's perspective about Plato's views more generally, including his "reactionary" political position relative to the sophists, see *Lectures on the History of Moral and Political Philosophy*, G. A. Cohen, ed. Jonathan Wolff (Princeton: Princeton University Press, 2014), chapter 1.

12. *TJ*, 2nd ed., 398.

13. That distinction is also right at the core of the line of argument of this book, which largely revolves around the danger (so I argue) of confusing the question what people ought to do with social structure given what they (or we) expect from people, with the question of what would be a rightful basic social structure.

14. For more on the distinction in Cohen, see 276–77.

15. Richard Arneson, by contrast to my reading, finds Cohen's "terminological" choice here to be undefended. "Justice Is Not Equality," in *Justice, Equality and Constructivism: Essays on G. A. Cohen's Rescuing Justice and Equality*, ed. Brian Feltham (Hoboken: Wiley-Blackwell, 2009).

16. See Cohen's more elaborate example at 308ff.

17. Another point of Cohen's is less persuasive. Notice that the consideration of some arrangement's overall expense is not an issue about anyone having more or less than others or with what justification. It is a non-comparative issue in that sense. Cohen tells us in *Rescuing* (323) that he rejects the view, "that distributive justice doesn't have a comparative aspect at all. And as long as it (at least also) does so, then [constructivism's sensitivity to the non-comparative issue of efficiency] will be (at least) in one way a deviation from justice."

That is a dubious argument, which resembles the following fallacious reasoning: having a crust is an aspect of what it is to be a pie. So pumpkin pie, by including pumpkin, which contains no crust, deviates from pie-ness "(at least) in one way." The fact that a certain consideration (such as Pareto efficiency or overall cost) is not a comparative consideration does not establish that an account in which it is one consideration among others is not comparative. We will return to this point shortly.

18. "An unequal distribution whose inequality cannot be vindicated by some choice or fault or desert on the part of (some of) the relevant affected agents is unfair, and therefore, pro tanto, unjust, and that nothing can remove that particular injustice" (7).

19. Indeed, it would be jarring for Cohen to call the choice of S2 over S3 an injustice, albeit a justified one. In the formulation of luck egalitarianism above (from his page 7) he seems committed to saying this. But he would not be forced to do so. "Unjust" arguably connotes wrongness, roughly meaning "wrongly not just." If not all deviation from justice is wrong, as Cohen believes it is not, this allows Cohen to say that S2 is not just, but, since not wrong, not unjust. I explain this point with respect to "fair" and "unfair" in *Democratic Authority*, 67. In an earlier draft, Cohen endorsed this gambit as we see in the following text, but that has dropped out of the final version. "I do not say, here, that deviations from equality are, just as such, *unjust*, but merely that they represent deviations from justice, where such deviations are *un*just (as opposed to: *not* just) only if they are *also* morally forbidden (because they are contrary to justice). So, for example, justice doesn't license a preference for saving my wife over saving a stranger, but doing so need not therefore be *un*just, a piece of *in*justice. My point that the Pareto Principle is sound policy but not a principle of justice tolerates each of the two possible answers to the question: are all deviations from justice injustices?" (Draft, September 2003, 35.)

This view, later abandoned, explicitly incorporates a suggestion I had made to him in correspondence which he cites. I am inclined to stand by it. But having apparently changed his mind about this, his mature view must have been that injustice (and not only non-justice) is not always wrong all things considered. But then it is no longer clear what the force is of showing (supposing he can) that Rawlsian principles countenance, as Cohen sees it, injustice. Note that my account of concessive requirement (see chapter 8) supplies a way of understanding how the injustice is wrong even if there is also a requirement to make policy in certain ways (à la Prof. Procrastinate). This fills an important gap that Cohen does not explain how to fill.

20. I briefly discuss a part of this question in "Human Nature and the Limits (If Any) of Political Philosophy," *Philosophy & Public Affairs*, 39, no. 3 (Summer 2011): 225ff.

21. 309 (emphasis added).

22. 311.

23. Cohen, *Incentives*, 263–329. There, he says that the Original Position, "Generates an argument for inequality that requires a model of society in breach of an elementary condition of community" (268).

24. At 178–80, Cohen trenchantly scrutinizes several short texts from across Rawls's career on this question, but still does not suggest that his (Cohen's) critique of Rawls's argument relies on the badness of the facts in question.

25. Leading contemporary examples include John Rawls, *A Theory of Justice*, whose approach derives especially from that of Immanuel Kant. Rawls writes, "The persons in the original position are to assume that the principles chosen are public, and so they must assess conceptions of justice in view of their probable effects as the generally recognized standards." See also David Gauthier, *Morals by Agreement* (Oxford: Oxford University Press, 1986), who develops an approach deriving from Hobbes and Hume. Speaking of Rawls, Scanlon, and Gauthier, Cohen writes, "All of these constructivisms agree in endowing the

legislator(s) whom they appoint with correct (or the best available) general information about human beings and human society" (*Rescuing*, 295).

26. Rather than denying the parties' knowledge, or installing false beliefs, constructivists might be interpreted as giving them the whole truth but then limiting their concerns in certain ways. I don't believe this affects any of my points. In either case, the parties are not seen as choosing in light of all the facts since either they are ignorant in certain ways, or they are assumed to ignore some of what they know.

27. The respect in which it is a bad fact gets complicated in a certain way if, as I will argue, the requirements of social justice are not requirements of an agential kind. See chapter 12, "Plural Requirement."

28. In the next chapter this "Build and Comply" formulation of the content of justice will be modified (the requirement ranges over a broader set of conjuncts), but not in a way that affects the present point, which is that justice does not directly call for certain institutions, and so justice is not a practical proposal.

29. I don't mean that this is *necessarily* a moral shortfall—it isn't if there can be adequate moral reasons of other kinds not to comply with social justice. I mean to say only that as it happens much noncompliance with justice will be morally wrong and not justified in any such way.

30. If, as I will argue in the next chapter, the bad facts include moral noncompliance generally, it is still possible, though not guaranteed, that justice noncompliance will still be included, and this objection would apply in that case.

Chapter Ten. Prime Justice

1. Compare the discussion in the Introduction with blueprint-like versions of utopian writing.

2. In chapter 1.

3. This is the way Actualism, as explained in chapter 8, "Concessive Requirement" sees it, and I am proceeding as if it is correct (though this is ultimately optional for my purposes as I explain in that chapter).

4. My language here about superordinate and subordinate requirements is meant only in Jackson and Pargetter's "Oughts, Options," sense, which is evidently weaker than the kind of hierarchical relations between McKinsean levels of requirement. I stay agnostic about whether the levels view is to be adopted, but the Jackson and Pargetter brand of primacy would stand either way.

5. Of course, we will tend to call it a "conditional requirement." Maybe that is a kind of requirement, maybe not. All that matters here is that nothing gets required unless the antecedent is true.

6. Getting past the conditional form is important for avoiding the objection that prime justice is no more interesting or important than what we should do IF we could fly, or were physically impervious, or immortal, and so forth.

7. Abelard Podgorski argues that theories that tie act requirements to evaluations of distant worlds are quite generally subject to serious problems. The threatened theories include all the main varieties of rule consequentialism, the Kantian universalization criterion, and the contractualist views of Scanlon and Gauthier. (See "Wouldn't It Be Nice? Moral Rules and Distant Worlds," *Noûs* 52, no. 2 [2018]: 279–94.) He notes that Rawls's specification of a society's requirements of justice by reference to distant worlds such as those containing full compliance is not subject to these problems. The reason is that the principles of justice are not requirements to act. For that same reason, my own way of tying what justice requires of an actual society to the distant world of full moral compliance (in

"Prime Justice") avoids those problems about distant worlds. Prime Justice does not say that we should build the institutions that are required by justice, since the value of doing so plausibly depends on whether people would in fact comply with them as they collectively should. (Saying this does not commit me to a normative theory that is consequentialist.)

8. See chapter 7, section entitled, "Rawlsian Realism Resisted."

9. This is different from the observation made earlier that normative theory cannot take all facts as given, leaving nothing to be normative about. See chapter 8.

10. Indeed, there is something incoherent here in the idea that some facts have been identified as constituting injustice, and at the same time no society counts as just or unjust since none meets the antecedent in the conditional. This is related to the circularity objection discussed above in chapter 9: "Bad Facts."

11. I interpret "x given the fact that y" as meaning both the conjunction of "if x then y," and the presupposition that x.

12. See chapter 4: "Circumstances and Justice."

13. I say "might," since there might still be reason for it, such as to ward off suspicion (erroneous as stipulated) that family-favoring is going on. It is not obvious to me one way or the other whether there would tend to be such suspicion in a world of full moral compliance, and I stake nothing on the answer. Also, even if simple nepotism were not forbidden I assume that what we might call biased nepotism still would be.

14. See my sketch of a certain racist society in chapter 7, p. 144.

15. As an anonymous reader has pointed out, we might think that the least 'specific' formulation of prime justice would proceed from an 'ought' that comprehends not only moral reasons but all practical reasons. On that way of seeing things, what I call 'global' prime justice is not an especially significant case. And then the title of true justice would go to the social structural parts of the global prime *practical* requirement. Perhaps so, and nothing else in my treatment would be damaged in that case. However, I believe that approach fails to reflect the supposition, which I am making, that social justice is a moral standard. The social structural part of the broader global prime requirement of practical reason would be a fragment of a nonmoral requirement, even if one that comprehends moral requirements too, as making up part or the requirements of practical reason. For that reason, I believe that what I call Global Prime Justice is favored.

16. Above at 122.

17. Recall the introduction of this common pair of questions in philosophy at 99.

18. For a thorough discussion of debates about such matters, see Steven Luper, "Epistemic Closure," in *The Stanford Encyclopedia of Philosophy* (Spring 2016 ed.), ed. Edward N. Zalta, https://plato.stanford.edu/archives/spr2016/entries/closure-epistemic/.

19. Here I speak of concessive requirements, as discussed in chapter 8, "Concessive Requirement," which can be translated, if necessary into rankings of moral severity.

Chapter Eleven. The Puzzle of Plural Obligation

1. A number of authors accept that there can be individual reasons to participate in a group action, the reasons stemming from good consequences the group action would have. Many of them, however, accept this only when other members would be willing to cooperate. See, for example, Donald Regan, *Utilitarianism and Cooperation* (Oxford: Oxford University Press, 1980); Parfit, "What We Together Do" (unpublished paper draft, 1988); Frank Jackson, "Group Morality," in *Metaphysics and Morality: Essays in Honour of J.J.C. Smart*, ed. J.J.C. Smart, Philip Pettit, Richard Sylvan, and Jean Norman (Oxford: Blackwell, 1987), 91–110. The cases I'm concentrating on do not meet that condition. For a discussion and a rejection of the "willingness requirement," see Christopher Woodard, "Group Based

Reasons for Action," *Ethical Theory and Moral Practice* 6 (2003): 215–29. If Woodard's own view is right that there are individual reasons for actions based on the consequences of possible group actions, even absent the willingness of the others, then my "prime require-ment" survives, albeit in a slightly different logical form. It names a pattern of action (ev-eryone behaves flawlessly) and assigns individual reasons of participation. That would suit my purposes even better than the compromise involved in my "Plural Requirement," de-scribed in the next chapter. Alas, I do not find Woodard ultimately convincing, though I cannot take his arguments up here. See also the discussion of this problem in Thomas H. Smith, "Non-Distributed Blameworthiness," *Proceedings of the Aristotelian Society*, n.s., 109 (2009): 31–60. Alexander Dietz also nicely lays out the ways in which alternatives to group obligations (he concentrates on reasons) do not seem to capture the intuitions. However, he then supposes they exist without confronting the difficulties, in order to ask what impli-cations such group reasons would have for individual reasons. I argue here that the difficul-ties are serious, perhaps insuperable. See Alexander Dietz, "What We Together Ought to Do," *Ethics* 126 (July 2016): 955–82.

2. The conjunct about society does not attribute an obligation to the society, but does treat it as an agent. After presenting Plural Requirement, it will be apparent that this is to treat Society as under a certain conditional obligation, but in this special case it would be a conditional Plural Requirement, embedded within a larger Plural Requirement.

3. Broome argues for this in *Rationality through Reasoning*.

4. See, e.g., Mark Schroeder, "Ought, Agents, and Actions," *Philosophical Review* 120, no. 1 (2011).

5. Recall the discussion of these matters in the final section of chapter 8, "Concessive Requirement."

6. Interestingly, the evaluative sense of ought, if it only states that something would be good, does not capture an element of the ought of justice (which may, I think, also be part of ought itself) of non-infraction, or non-violation. Some influenced by Sen-like points, may hold that there is no useful idea of full justice, only "juster," in which case that idea of infrac-tion would be out of place. But I argue in chapter 13, "Progress, Perfection, and Practice," that a theory of juster (so to speak) is ill-fated if our many threshold-entailing judgments are discarded. I will proceed on the assumption that the ought of social justice is, as we might put it, not just evaluative but *pro tanto* mandatory. That is, if not defeated it is an obligation.

7. In a recent discussion, Carolina Sartorio gives an example in which an explosion can be prevented by both of two people pushing their buttons respectively, but neither does. So, as it happens (unbeknownst to both), neither's pushing would have helped. However, in her case pushing does no harm even if it is unilateral. So she can plausibly (though not obvi-ously) say that there was wrong done by each, and so each is morally responsible for the harm (even though neither caused it, which is her main question). In Slice/Patch each is clearly *required* to refrain from the jointly helpful action, so neither acts wrongly. So the big difference is that Slice/Patch is a case where neither acts wrongly (and so, though that is not our main question, there is no basis for holding either responsible for the harm). Sar-torio is not explicit in saying that each acts wrongly in her case, but if she were to abstain on that question then her argument would apparently fail because then it cannot be as-sumed that there is a moral failure at all for which someone must be responsible. See "How to Be Responsible for Something without Causing It," *Philosophical Perspectives* 18 (2004): 315–36.

8. We can distinguish between "weak" versions in which each is not required unless the others comply, and "strong" versions in which each is forbidden when the others do not

comply (as in the Slice/Patch example, and the Smokers case below). The strong versions present the puzzle more vividly and so those are the examples I will present.

9. For a full treatment, see Russell Hardin, "The Free Rider Problem," in *Stanford Encyclopedia of Philosophy* (Spring 2013 ed.), ed. Edward N. Zalta, https://plato.stanford.edu /archives/spr2013/entries/free-rider/. As Hardin explains, the "Prisoner's Dilemma" is simply a two-person collective action problem.

10. See Regan, *Cooperation*. The structure of such a case has been discussed by a number of authors, perhaps beginning with Alan Gibbard, "Rule-Utilitarianism: Merely an Illusory Alternative?" *Australasian Journal of Philosophy* 43 (1965): 211–20, at 214–15. Gibbard's aim is to show that act-utilitarianism and rule-utilitarianism are not guaranteed to require the same actions. "Thus each individual may be doing the best he can do, given what the others are doing, but the society collectively may not be producing as much good as it could. While act-utilitarianism will sanction people's actions in this case, rule-utilitarianism will not" (216).

11. See "What We Together Do."

12. The idea of an act's consequences is conceived so broadly by some writers that it is not clear that there is any normative theory that could not be formulated as consequentialist. (For discussion, see Campbell Brown, "Consequentialize This," *Ethics* 121, no. 4 [2001]: 749–71.) That issue does not concern us here, and by speaking of the value of consequences of acts I will mean only agent-neutral value—where the value is not indexed to any agents or evaluators.

13. Elizabeth Anderson argues that justice is "part of the morally right," and that there is no violation of the right, and so of justice, unless some assignable agent has failed to give others what she owes to them. This identifies the domain of moral right, including justice, with what we are calling the deontic. She concludes that distributional theories of justice such as many forms of egalitarianism, which have no deontic content, have missed the concept of justice altogether. While this is a possible view, she does not, as far as I can see, attempt to argue for it. She endorses a contractualist account of the right, but even if that were established it is not obvious that its results must be deontic, at least if the Rawlsian version counts as an instance. When a social structure violates the principles of justice arising from the original position, there may or may not be anything that any particular agent can or ought to do about it, but it is a violation nonetheless. Either Rawls misses the concept of justice altogether, which she clearly does not believe, or the concept of justice is not essentially deontic after all. If one insists on that as a semantic constraint, there remains the non-deontic category which it is hard to deny is, in some broader sense, moral, such as a society's violating the principles of justice. Even distributive egalitarianism itself is said by Anderson to identify a condition that is, even though not deontic, "morally desirable." I share the impulse to include "moral" in that formulation, but it weakens her contention that such things are not matters of justice, limiting the latter (without argument, I think) to the deontic. Plural Requirement offers an account of the way in which such cases might indeed be properly regarded as broadly moral (and not only desirable *simpliciter*) without being directly deontic. It would not, incidentally, cover luck egalitarianism unless the relevant conditional requirements were added or meant to be implicit. See Anderson, "The Fundamental Disagreement between Luck Egalitarians and Relational Egalitarians," *Canadian Journal of Philosophy* 40, Supplementary 1 (2010): 1–23.

14. Regan, *Utilitarianism*, 21.

15. For a recent introduction and discussion, see Dale Dorsey, "Objective Morality, Subjective Morality and the Explanatory Question," *Journal of Ethics & Social Philosophy* 6, no. 3 (2012).

16. Stemplowska argues that Slice/Patch cases are not "feasible," because they don't know how to do it, which would count against a requirement. She seems to have in mind a case where one or both of the doctors does not know what her part would be and how to do it. I am assuming that each does know that. Zofia Stemplowska, "Feasibility: Individual and Collective," *Social Philosophy and Policy* 33, nos. 1–2 (October 2016): 273–91.

17. Some (following Jackson and Pargetter's position ["Oughts, Options"] about the similar example of Professor Procrastinate, borrowed from Holly Smith Goldman, "Doing the Best One Can," in *Values and Morals*, ed. Alvin Goldman and Jaegwon Kim [Amsterdam: Reidel, 1978], 185–214) hold that Doctor Divot ought not to cut. I have used the formulation "Given that x it's not the case that he's required to y." Formulated in this way, my statements are not in dispute as between "actualists" and "possibilists." The latter deny, however, that it's not the case that he's required—they insist that he is required. But they accept the more complex "Given" statements.

18. But see chapter 8, "Concessive Requirement," on how to translate so as to avoid commitments in the actualism/possibilism debate.

19. Joseph Mendola gives one in *Human Interests: Or Ethics for Physicalists* (Oxford: Oxford University Press, 2014), section 3.11.

20. A similar approach is proposed by Torbjörn Tännsjö, "The Myth of Innocence: On Collective Responsibility and Collective Punishment," *Philosophical Papers* 36 (2007): 295–314. Parfit, in "What We Together Do" takes a similar line. He lets a set of acts, as such, be morally required.

21. Parfit, in "What We Together Do," follows Jackson and adds that this does involve treating the group as an agent. Parfit, it is important to note, acknowledges that treating the group as an agent might be incoherent. For his polemical purposes, he argues that he does not need to decide this. For ours, we do, and I am arguing that it is indeed incoherent at least in many relevant cases.

22. *Group Agency*.

23. *Group Agency*, 19–20.

24. *Group Agency*, 59.

25. "What We Together Do."

26. Edmundson draws on Lawford-Smith for the idea of incremental cases. See William A. Edmundson, "Distributive Justice and Distributed Obligations," *Journal of Moral Philosophy* 15 (2018): 1–19; and Holly Lawford-Smith, "The Feasibility of Collectives' Actions," *Australasian Journal of Philosophy* 90, no. 3 (2012): 453–67.

27. A. J. Julius's view might seem to have this troubling implication, but I think it is not clear. He thinks there is a "shadow" reason to do it, but that it would not be "the thing to do." See *Reconstruction*, in progress. Julius's appeal to "shadow reasons" is a kindred effort to the account I offer in the next chapter, to identify a way in which these cases are broadly moral even without involving agential reasons for agents. However, I proceed without having found any reasons for agents on which to rest the account.

28. *Reasons and Persons* (Oxford: Oxford University Press, 1984), 70ff. He abandons this view in light of Jackson's objection in "What We Together Do."

29. Jackson, "Group Morality," 99.

30. Donald Regan, in his seminal treatment of such cases, took it up as a problem for Act Utilitarianism, and proposed a version that specifically required identifying cooperators and the best feasible plan for that group. Stephanie Collins, in "Collectives' Duties and Collectivization Duties," *Australasian Journal of Philosophy* (2012): 1–18, suggests that, "Each individual in the non-collective group has an individual duty to take steps to transform the group" (3). This won't help in cases where the act of coordinating has terrible consequences.

It's important to note that this kind of case is puzzling whether or not we accept act-utilitarianism, as I explained above.

31. Robert Goodin's focus on what each agent was *willing* to do suggests an approach of this kind. See "Excused by the Unwillingness of Others?" *Analysis* 72, no. 1 (2012): 18–24. In *Opting for the Best: Oughts and Options* (Oxford: Oxford University Press, 2019), Douglas Portmore argues that the failure to form (not as an action but as an exercise of non-volitional rational capacities) appropriate conditional intentions is not just morally bad but the violation of an obligation. Thus he does find wrongness in the story, though nothing more than the wrongness of the missing intentions. The patient, on his view, is not wronged, and so insofar as it was intuitive to think he was, Portmore agrees with me that this view cannot be vindicated. Bjornsson's instructive discussion of these kinds of cases leads him, too, to an account in which the moral weight of the idea of "shared obligations" falls on the individual agents' flawed "moral sensitivities." Gunnar Björnsson, "Essentially Shared Obligations," *Midwest Studies in Philosophy* 38, no. 1 (2014): 103–20.

32. Thanks to (especially) Sean Aas and Derek Bowman for helpful discussion of this suggestion in my graduate seminar, spring 2012. Portmore, *Opting*, develops an account of this kind, where the crux is whether one can be morally required to have or develop certain attitudes. Pending a clearer understanding of what, exactly, would be required, my reply here is applicable to his account.

33. The term is from Thomas Nagel's seminal discussion, "Moral Luck," in *Mortal Questions* (New York: Cambridge University Press, 1979), 24–38.

34. I find Michael Zimmerman's argument that even in those cases, one does not become more culpable—culpability being a matter of degree—plausible. If one is culpable, one might be responsible for more things (what Zimmerman calls "scope") if matters turn out one way rather than another, but that is different from being more responsible. "Moral Luck: A Partial Map," *Canadian Journal of Philosophy* 36, no. 4 (December 2006): 585–608.

35. Thanks to Sean Aas for pointing this out.

Chapter Twelve. Plural Requirement

1. For a description of cases that are naturally thought of as structural injustice see Iris Marion Young, "Political Responsibility and Structural Injustice," Lindley Lecture, University of Kansas, May 5, 2003. Her own project there is not, as it is here, to explain how anyone has been wronged even if there is no agential perpetrator, but to develop a forward-looking account of responsibility for social change. It would be problematic to think that is all there is to the idea of structural injustice, since whether the patient in Slice/Patch was a victim of injustice does not clearly depend on whether there are things that can and should be done going forward.

2. The formulation is more complicated for more than two agents, but we can see from the three-agent case how it is to go in all cases:

To say that it is a Plural Requirement that (S does x, & T does y, and U does z) is to say that,

If S does x, and T does y, then U is obligated to do z, and,
If T does y, and U does z, then S is obligated to do x, and,
If U does z, and S does x, then T is obligated to do y,
It ought to be the case that (S does x, and T does y, and U does z)

3. Chapter 8, "Concessive Requirement," "Appendix: Oughts Going Forward."

4. There seems no reason to deny that S and T could be the same agent, but in that case there is no obstacle to there being an agential obligation in the case. There is no trouble

finding an agent to own the obligation. I don't know whether to allow Plural Requirement over multiple acts by the same agent, though maybe it is harmless.

5. See 127.

6. So as to delimit the non-agential ("It ought to be the case that") part of Plural Requirement, condition (iii), we might want to add that where some conjunction of actions is plural-required, it must be possible that they all get performed. It is not clear to me that there is any good reason for this. But if that were contemplated, it would not be possibility in the sense of an ability at the collective level, because plural obligation is meant to cover cases where the group is not an agent. What variety of possibility might make sense there would require more thought.

7. The appearance of agential ought inside the conditionals is similar to conditionals discussed by Cohen that tell us what we ought to do if we can. In both cases this makes them importantly different from what we might call merely evaluative statements, such as that today's weather is much nicer than yesterday's weather.

8. See the previous chapter for discussion of Jackson's and Parfit's views.

9. It is straightforward to formulate the conditions for cases where one or another subset ought to do certain things—say, any pair among agents S, T, and U.

10. There is this complication: that would mean that if neither acts then each is required to act. I think this is OK as long as we note that agglomeration would not be valid over those two obligations.

11. See the discussion of "gentle murder" in chapter 8.

12. I say "the fact of her acting" so that that fact might have the fact of reciprocation as a "result" even before the act occurs. That is, it might be known at time t1 that at time t2 S will act. Knowledge of that fact could result in its being the case that at time t2 P will act. In that case it is not S's acting that has the result of T's acting, but it is the fact of her acting, the fact that she will act.

13. Björnsson proposes an account of a shared obligation for groups that are not themselves agents. His account, like mine, rejects desideratum (b) that there must be a violating agent for there to be a moral violation. Moreover, there is no link at all on his view between shared obligation and any agential obligation, as there is on the account I propose. I take this to be an advantage of my account. Rather, the moral failure is located in the deficient motives of at least some members: there is a group obligation to jointly act if and only if such a joint action would occur if not for deficient motives of some member. Thus, on his account the good motives cases under discussion in the text are not violations. Closely related, his account does not admit blameless violations. See Gunnar Björnsson, "Essentially Shared Obligations."

14. See H.L.A. Hart and T. Honore, *Causation in the Law* (Oxford: Oxford University Press, 1985, 2nd ed.). Thanks to an anonymous reader for this reference.

15. I have in mind, for example, G. A. Cohen in *Rescuing*.

16. Southwood considers related questions in "Does 'Ought' Imply Feasible?" *Philosophy & Public Affairs* 44, no. 1 (2016): 7–45, although using importantly different senses of 'ought' and 'feasible' than are at issue here.

17. Brennan and Southwood give this kind of conditional analysis of "feasibility," though they appear not to distinguish between feasibility and the agential notion of ability for individuals. See Geoffrey Brennan and Nicholas Southwood, "Feasibility in Action and Attitude," in *Hommage à Wlodek. Philosophical Papers Dedicated to Wlodek Rabinowicz*, ed. T. Ronnow-Rasmussen, B. Petersson, J. Josefsson, and D. Egonsson, https://www.fil.lu.se /hommageawlodek/site/papper/Brennan&Southwood.pdf. My conception of feasibility differs from Wiens ("Political Ideals and the Feasibility Frontier," *Economics and Philosophy* 31, no. 3 [2015]: 447–77), who lets strong dispositions not to try in a population count as

infeasibility. I think, though he may disagree, that this pulls the idea of feasibility too far from the agential idea of ability for it to be parallel in the way I am seeking. For our exchange (partly) about that see his article and my "Reply to Wiens," in *European Journal of Political Theory*.

18. See Stemplowska, "Feasibility: Individual and Collective."

19. Even then, it would not bypass the logical structure wherein the requirement applies to a conjunction or disjunction in which agents or pluralities of agents are conditionally required to do certain things. The idea would just be to treat that overarching 'ought' as applying to that set of agents considered as an agent in its own right.

Chapter Thirteen. Progress, Perfection, and Practice

1. For example, Gerald Gaus writes, "Ideal theorists who appreciate the difficulties of knowing their entire justice landscape, and who agree with Mill that actual experiments are useful, will come to think of ideal theory as less of a political program than as a research agenda," *Tyranny*, 90. This appears to take it for granted that ideal theorists tend, at least often, to be offering a political program. Surely some political programs are unrealistic, but all sides count this against them (as programs).

2. Cf. the fallacy of approximation, discussed in chapter 14.

3. See Gaus's discussion of "dreamers" in *Tyranny*, 12ff.

4. In brackets I substitute a corrected translation. Paul and Anscombe's version has "be they never so sure," which is clearly a mistake (perhaps it would have been "ever" but for a typo). Thanks to Tobias Fuchs for confirming this suspicion.

5. Ludwig Wittgenstein, *On Certainty (Über Gewissheit)*, ed. G.E.M. Anscombe and G. H. von Wright, trans. Denis Paul and G.E.M. Anscombe (Oxford: Basil Blackwell, 1969), 286.

6. See video of Kennedy's remarks, at: https://www.youtube.com/watch?v=0D7a8k5kyGw.

7. These Gallup poll results are presented in Howard Schuman, Charlotte Steeh, Lawrence D. Bobo, and Maria Krysan, *Racial Attitudes in America, Trends and Interpretations*, rev. ed. (Cambridge, MA: Harvard University Press, 1997), 102–8.

8. Some recent philosophical discussions of the thesis of moral progress, usually interpreted as on-balance progress over history, include Michelle Moody-Adams, "The Idea of Moral Progress," *Metaphilosophy* 30, no. 3 (1999): 168–85; Dale Jamieson, "Is There Progress in Morality," *Utilitas* 14, no. 3 (November 2002): 318–38 (tentative defense of moral progress, especially with the example of civil rights); Richard Rorty, "Dewey and Posner on Pragmatism and Moral Progress," and Martha Nussbaum, "On Moral Progress: A Response to Richard Rorty," both in *University of Chicago Law Review* 74, no. 3 (2007): 929–37 and 939–60 respectively. Two recent works on the topic are Philip Kitcher, *The Ethical Project* (Cambridge, MA: Harvard University Press, 2011); and Allen Buchanan and Russell Powell, *The Evolution of Moral Progress: A Biocultural Theory* (Oxford: Oxford University Press, 2018).

9. Southwood and Wiens ("'Actual' Does Not Imply 'Feasible,'" *Philosophical Studies* 173, no. 11 [2016]: 3037–60) say no, and use that against a kind of inspiration from history of the kind I'm pressing. I am not claiming the exemplar achievements were feasible or infeasible, since I find that concept to be vaguer than some recent writers believe it is.

10. This section draws on my "Just and Juster," in *Oxford Studies in Political Philosophy* 2 (2016): 9–32.

11. Amartya Sen, "What Do We Want from a Theory of Justice?" *Journal of Philosophy* 103, no. 5 (May 2006): 217.

12. 217.

13. The idea of a partition between just and unjust is only one kind of salient dividing point that might be present in an ordering of relative justness. I will not explore the possibilities, but will suppose, for simplicity, that if there is a partition, there is only one, the division between just and unjust. Also for simplicity, I allow and discuss the possibility of rankings within the unjust category, although I leave aside the question whether there might be orderings above the threshold as well (a kind of supererogatory justice). One possibility is that above the just/unjust threshold there are further degrees, with or without an upper limit. The issue before us, and addressed by Sen, is not whether we should posit such an upper limit in the space of zero injustice (though Sen's language of "what a perfectly just society . . . would look like" (*The Idea of Justice* [Cambridge, MA: Harvard University Press, 2011], 106) might mislead on this point). The issue is whether we should posit a partition between the unjust and the not-at-all-unjust, the "entirely just" (Sen, 216). Rawls interprets his own view as both admitting of a just/unjust threshold, as well as of degrees of betterness in the space of the just—a kind of supererogatory justice. See Rawls, *Political Liberalism* (Lecture VIII), 291. I discuss that passage in "Just and Juster," note 16.

14. Sen never denies that there might be a partition, and so I take his position to be that of methodological comparativism.

15. Sen writes: "Perhaps the most important contribution of the social choice approach to the theory of justice is its concern with comparative assessments. This relational, rather than transcendental, framework concentrates on the practical reason behind what is to be chosen and which decisions should be taken, rather than speculating on what a perfectly just society (on which there may or may not be any agreement) would look like" (*The Idea of Justice*, 106).

16. For some history of the avoidance of interpersonal comparisons, see Peter J. Hammond, "Interpersonal Comparisons of Utility: Why and How They Are and Should Be Made," in *Interpersonal Comparisons of Well-Being*, ed. Jon Elster and John E. Roemer (Cambridge: Cambridge University Press, 1991), 200–254. Interestingly, Jevons's early statement of the case for ordinalism did not make any use of the problem of other minds, but the elusiveness of measuring feelings, even our own. He wrote, "It is from the quantitative effects of the feelings that we must estimate their comparative amounts. We can no more know nor measure gravity in its own nature than we can measure a feeling; but, just as we measure gravity by its effects in the motion of a pendulum, so we may estimate the equality or inequality of feelings by the decisions of the human mind" (William Jevons, *Theory of Political Economy* [London: Macmillan and Co., 1871]. There are many editions, and the quotation is drawn from the Introduction).

17. I expand on this point in "Just and Juster."

18. Steve Wall usefully pressed this point with me, which is not to say he ultimately accepts it.

19. Gerald Gaus supports a stance of this kind, in *The Tyranny of the Ideal*.

Chapter Fourteen. The Fallacy of Approximation

1. Jürgen Habermas, "Political Communication in Media Society: Does Democracy Still Enjoy an Epistemic Dimension? The Impact of Normative Theory on Empirical Research," *Communication Theory* 16 (2006): 411–26, at 420.

2. This does not speak to the different view that its value may consist in orienting practice toward fully achieving it. That makes no reference to approximating it or its value. John Simmons discusses this approach to ideal theory in "Ideal and Nonideal Theory," *Philosophy & Public Affairs* 38 (2010): 5–36.

3. They say this particular passage expressed a "corollary," but this is the proposition (or

so it seems to me) that has attracted the ocean of references to their article, the main lesson that many have learned. See R. G. Lipsey and K. J. Lancaster, "The General Theory of Second Best," *Review of Economic Studies* 24 (1956): 11–33.

4. David Wiens, in "The General Theory of Second Best Is More General Than You Think" (unpublished ms, draft 2.1, April 2018), pursues this question carefully.

5. "Essentially the generalist demands sameness in the way in which one and the same consideration functions case by case, while the particularist sees no need for any such thing. A feature can make one moral difference in one case, and a different difference in another. Features have, as we might put it, *variable relevance*." Jonathan Dancy, "Moral Particularism," in *The Stanford Encyclopedia of Philosophy* (Winter 2017 ed.), ed. Edward N. Zalta, https://plato.stanford.edu/archives/win2017/entries/moral-particularism/. Thanks to Andrea Sangiovanni for useful conversation about this.

6. See "Or is even likely to be" in quotation above at 273.

7. Ng's formulation in an economics textbook is similar: "Given that some first-best conditions cannot be fulfilled, is it better to fulfill as many of the rest as possible? . . . According to the theory of second best the answer is a firm no." (Yew-Kwang Ng, *Welfare Economics: Towards a More Complete Analysis* [New York: Palgrave Macmillan, 2004], 188. See also 187.) Other examples that follow this pattern include Adrian Vermeule and Cass R. Sunstein, "Interpretation and Institutions," *Michigan Law Review* 101, no. 4 (2003): 914; Avishai Margalit, "Ideals and Second Bests," in *Philosophy for Education*, ed. Seymour Fox (Jerusalem: Van Leer Press, 1983), 77–90; Robert Goodin, "Political Ideals and Political Practice," *British Journal of Political Science* 25, no. 1 (January 1995): 37–56. Juha Räikkä, "The Problem of Second Best: Conceptual Issues" *Utilitas* 12, no. 2 (July 2000), is notable for having shown that the point is not essentially about feasibility. He does however limit the point's scope to cases involving ideals: "The problem of the second best potentially arises whenever one has to do with ideals" (206).

8. Suppose, "that the attainment of a Paretian optimum requires the simultaneous fulfillment of all the optimum conditions. The general theorem for the second best optimum states that if there is introduced into a general equilibrium system a constraint which prevents the attainment of one of the Paretian conditions, the other Paretian conditions, although still attainable, are, in general, no longer desirable." What they refer to here as the "general equilibrium system" in which none of the Paretian conditions is prevented, is the first best by comparison with which the constrained optima are "second best." When they say, "Specifically, it is not true that a situation in which more, but not all, of the optimum conditions are fulfilled is necessarily, or is even likely to be, superior to a situation in which fewer are fulfilled" (12) the first best is the "situation in which . . . all of the optimum conditions are fulfilled."

9. It is also not germane in the economic context. Take any condition that is optimal relative to constraints, even if it is not the fully Paretian optimal condition, i.e., free of those constraints. The reasoning all applies just as if this case were the first best, even if it is not.

10. At note 1 on page 11, Lipsey and Lancaster write, "The appelation [*sic*], 'Theory of Second Best,' is derived from the writings of Professor Meade; See Meade, J. E., *Trade and Welfare*, London, Oxford University Press, 1955."

11. In addition to their less determinate talk of "constraints," Lipsey and Lancaster, in "Second Best," repeatedly situate their proof in conditions of apparent infeasibility—where a "constraint . . . prevents the attainment [or "fulfillment"]" of the optimal conditions (11, 12), or some of them "cannot be fulfilled" (11, 15), "cannot be achieved" (16, 17), "cannot be obtained" (17), or where obstacles "for one reason or another . . . cannot be removed." This suggests, perhaps inadvertently, an inability or impossibility, but (whether that is what they meant or not) neither inability nor impossibility is germane.

12. Räikkä, "Second Best," makes this point.

13. This will put some readers in mind of what G. E. Moore called "organic unity." In the Appendix I explain how the present issues about Superset reasoning are different from, and may be more fundamental than, Moore's point.

14. For other reasons, as we saw in chapter 8, some doubt that we could be required to Build and Comply if we are not required to build. For one reason, that conjunctive requirement would seem to entail a requirement over each conjunct. Those complexities are beside the point if it is granted that, in some sense to be worked out, and in some cases, even though you ought to give your child all of three pills for his health, if, for whatever reason, you will not give the third pill, you ought not to give the other two. There are various contending ways of interpreting such cases to avoid difficulties, and some of them may even require carefully re-describing what is required. However, to put it roughly, any adequate account of these cases ought to suffice for our purposes here, and what I say is not committed on the main controversies. For more discussion of those issues, see Jacob Ross, "Actualism, Possibilism, and Beyond," *Oxford Studies in Normative Ethics* 2 (2012): 74–96.

15. "In Iraq, Detention Center Sets New U.S. Military Standards," Hannah Allam— Knight Ridder Newspapers, October 21, 2004. Retrieved, May 31, 2017 at http://www .mcclatchydc.com/latest-news/article24442234.html.

16. I believe the point is more clearly expressed if "unless" is substituted for "until," since lexical priority is not a point about the temporal order of the satisfaction of the principles.

17. *TJ*, 2nd ed., section 8, 38.

18. I use that compact phrase "material," simplistically of course, as a stand-in for the primary social goods, which gives us no handy adjective to modify the term, "inequality."

19. G. E. Moore, *Principia Ethica* (1903), any edition, chapter 1, section 18. Thomas Hurka cites precursors in "Two Kinds of Organic Unity," *Journal of Ethics* 2, no. 4 (1998): 299–320. Also, Michael Zimmerman and Ben Bradley, "Intrinsic vs. Extrinsic Value," *Stanford Encyclopedia of Philosophy* (2019), https://plato.stanford.edu/entries/value-intrinsic -extrinsic/

20. Moore limited his defense of this contextual independence to the case of intrinsic value of parts. Unless otherwise specified, when I speak of the value of a part or a whole I will mean its intrinsic value, its value irrespective of any role it might (actually or possibly) have in constituting, contributing to, or producing something else of value. The view (contextual holism) that the value of a thing might change when it is in combination with other things might be tempting when attending to the thing's value as, say, part of a certain whole that is valuable. That would not be an intrinsic value of the thing as defined here. Still, I have no need to concern myself with such claims. Some have held that even the intrinsic value of a part can change in context, and I discuss that possibility.

21. If Contextual Independence is true, then that plus Context Independent Summation would entail Contextual Summation as well.

22. See Campbell Brown's (limited) criticism of it in, "Two Kinds of Holism about Values," *The Philosophical Quarterly* 57, no. 228 (July 2007): 456–63. But see Hurka, "Two Kinds," on its perspicuousness in some contexts at 306–7.

23. Shelly Kagan ("The Additive Fallacy," *Ethics* 99, no. 1 [October 1988]: 5–31) argues that the model of "independent summed contributions" fails in the context of the factors that go into the moral value of actions. This goes beyond Moore, who argued only that there are at least some exceptions, and who never gave examples in that context. For our purposes here, though, Kagan's point is—in that particular domain—a denial of independent additivity, which, I am about to argue, formally leaves open the question of Superset in that domain.

24. If it's easier to grasp, this is equivalent: for any valuable set S, any subset, ss (proper

or not), is more valuable than any proper subset (including the null set) of ss. I prefer the one in the text because it focuses on the more valuable things by name: the supersets.

25. I am using the ampersand to denote either (as you like) a mereological sum, or a union of sets. We will also be engaging with arithmetical sums, for which I reserve the plus sign. The equal sign gives, on the right, the value of what is on the left, and context (the presence or absence of a plus sign) determines whether what is meant is an arithmetical sum.

26. Superset only considers value-contributing elements. This can make it seem less important than summation. But, whatever "important" might mean here, it doesn't matter for my purpose, which is to show that refuting it refutes Summation but not vice versa.

Chapter Fifteen. Countervailing Deviation

1. Herbert Marcuse, "Repressive Tolerance," in *A Critique of Pure Tolerance* (Boston: Beacon Press, 1969), 90.

2. Charles Mills draws attention to this danger in "Ideal Theory as Ideology," *Hypatia* 20, no. 3 (2005): 165–83.

3. I'm grateful to Richard Healy, Jason D'Cruz, and Tommie Shelby for helpful conversations.

4. Conversation with Amanda Greene helped me to clarify this.

5. Mills, "Ideal Theory."

6. The idea is not specifically engaged with questions about violation of law, since that wouldn't be a necessary feature of the kinds of countervailing deviation in question. Whether there is an obligation of some strength and in some cases to obey the law is a separate issue.

7. I consider a difficulty for this approach, what I call the "skew unit" problem in "When Protest and Speech Collide," in *Academic Freedom*, ed. Jennifer Lackey (Oxford: Oxford University Press, 2018).

8. I'm grateful to Ten-Herng Lai for suggesting examples of this kind. The matrix is structurally similar to the one about Slice and Patch in chapter 11, section 2.

9. I do make such an attempt in chapter 13.

10. I thank Aaron Bronfman for raising this point.

11. *PL*, 327. See also *PL*, 337, "[J]ust legislation seems to be best achieved by assuring fairness in representation and by other constitutional devices." Also *TJ*, rev. ed., 202, "The fundamental criterion for judging any [political] procedure is the justice of its likely results." At *PL*, 404, in "Reply to Habermas," Rawls adds that he does not take the political liberties to be *wholly* instrumental.

12. The political liberties include, "some form of representative democratic regime and the requisite protections for the freedom of political speech and press, freedom of assembly, and the like" (*PL*, 335).

13. *PL*, 362.

14. As it happens, the basic liberty that is limited is itself within the political liberties: freedom of political expression, though that is inessential to his point.

15. Some say it is not a restriction on speech, but only a restriction on spending money—and to spend is not itself to speak. It is true that what is *prohibited* is not speech but spending, but that is one way to *restrict* speech. A law that simply and directly forbade candidates from buying political ads (maybe only applying to opposition candidates) would also not forbid any speaking, but only buying. The fact that "money is not speech" is little support for the idea that regulating spending is never a restriction of speech. Rawls, for one, implicitly grants that liberty of expression is being limited by campaign finance

regulations of this kind, by locating the liberties he proposes to limit in the scope of the First Amendment (see below). He does not argue that freedom of speech is not being limited, but rather that it is being limited in a way justified by the aim of securing fair value of the political liberties.

16. Spencer and Wood present a detailed empirical examination in the several years after *Citizens United* took effect to test one interpretation of the "crowding out" hypothesis, namely that large spenders would flood the market reducing the chance of small spenders to make a difference, thus leading them rationally to withdraw. "We do not observe this behavior. Instead, we see evidence, at least for expenditures in the lowest five percentiles (less than $420), that the decision to spend money on political advocacy might be modeled more precisely as an act of consumption. Participants seem to gain utility by the mere act of participation. No existing theory, nor any that we can conjure, predicts that this kind of consumptive behavior would be altered by a decision like *Citizens United*." Douglas M. Spencer and Abby K. Wood, "*Citizens United*, States Divided: An Empirical Analysis of Independent Political Spending," *Indiana Law Journal* 89, no. 2 (2014): 315–72, at 352–53.

17. Later the court completes the rejection of leveling: "'Leveling the playing field' can sound like a good thing" but the First Amendment forbids it, they hold. *Arizona Free Enterprise Club's Freedom Club PAC v. Bennett*, 131 S. Ct. 2806 (2011). (A year after *Citizens United*.)

18. Thanks to Rachel Goodman for pressing me to be more explicit about the two-level structure that is needed to make sense of multiple realizability.

Chapter Sixteen. Beyond Practicalism

1. The phone book example is from Ernest Sosa, "For the Love of Truth?" in *Virtue Epistemology: Essays on Epistemic Virtue and Responsibility*, ed. Abrol Fairweather and Linda Zagzebski (Oxford: Oxford University Press, 2000). Turri, Carter, and Pritchard, "The Value of Knowledge," in *Stanford Encyclopedia of Philosophy* (2018), https://plato.stanford.edu/entries/knowledge-value/, cite several authors who argue that all true belief is intrinsically valuable: Alvin Goldman, *Knowledge in a Social World* (Oxford: Oxford University Press, 1999), 3; Michael Lynch, *True to Life: Why Truth Matters* (Cambridge, MA: MIT Press, 2004), 15–16; William Alston, *Beyond "Justification": Dimensions of Epistemic Evaluation* (Ithaca, NY: Cornell University Press, 2005), 31.

2. Adam Swift argues that there is no evident reason for holding political philosophy to a practicalist standard that would not appear to be appropriate in other areas of intellectual endeavor. See "The Value of Philosophy in Nonideal Circumstances," 366.

3. I have not here taken a stand on whether I should revise my degree of belief in the face of those apparent experts. That's a separate question. It's less contentious to say what I have said, that the fact that they believe it is some reason for me to believe it. On the further question about revision, see David Christiansen, *Philosophy Compass* 4–5 (2009): 756–67.

4. For several definitions of "pure math" see G. H. Hardy, *A Mathematician's Apology*, November 1940, 1st electronic ed., Version 1.0, March 2005, published by the University of Alberta Mathematical Sciences Society at: http://www.math.ualberta.ca/mss/. In section 23, Hardy appears to define it as math that is pursued in independence from any applicability it might have to the physical world. On the account I'm using, even "applied mathematics" in his sense might count as pure: pursued out of curiosity alone rather than for any hope of practical application. WordNet (copyright Princeton University 2006. See word-

net.princeton.edu): "Pure mathematics: the branches of mathematics that study and develop the principles of mathematics for their own sake rather than for their immediate usefulness."

5. In "Does Pure Mathematics Have a Relation to the Sciences?" Felix E. Browder (in *Mathematics: People, Problems, Results*, ed. Douglas M. Campbell and John C. Higgins [Belmont, CA: Wadsworth, 1984]) emphasizes how much of math has surprising application to the sciences. I don't deny that, of course, and much of what I'm saying about pure mathematics is granted by his regarding this fact as surprising.

6. See this short document on the idea of basic vs. applied research from the Lawrence Berkeley National Laboratory, entitled "Basic vs. Applied Research" (accessed March 21, 2018), http://www.sjsu.edu/people/fred.prochaska/courses/ScWk170/so/Basic-vs.-Applied -Research.pdf.

7. I defend this claim in more detail in, "What Good Is It? Unrealistic Political Theory and the Value of Intellectual Work," *Analyse & Kritik* 33, no. 2 (2011): 395–416.

8. *A Mathematician's Apology*, section 11. Philip Kitcher, in his book, *The Nature of Mathematical Knowledge*, notes his sympathy with Hardy, at least insofar as, "One would be hard pressed to explain the utility of number theory (one of Hardy's favorite fields)." Philip Kitcher, *The Nature of Mathematical Knowledge* (Oxford: Oxford University Press, 1984), 9.

9. I'm grateful for discussion of such suggestions with Matt Smith and Russell Hardin.

10. See four here: https://www.youtube.com/watch?v=MB4AbVgFHRE.

11. See, e.g., Martin Gardner, *My Best Mathematical and Logic Puzzles* (Mineola, NY: Dover Publications, 1994).

Chapter Seventeen. Informed Concern

1. See the brief discussion of feasibility, with references in chapter 12.

2. Joseph Carens, *The Ethics of Immigration* (Oxford: Oxford University Press, 2013), 201. This methodology plays a role throughout his book. We saw in chapter 6 how Carens also embraced a related "utopian" methodology in his previous book, *Equality*.

3. I believe this accurately represents the position of Gaus, in *The Tyranny of the Ideal*, at pp. 16, 39, 102.

4. See chapter 13, "Progress, Perfection, and Practice," for more on that question.

5. Derek Parfit, "Future People, the Non-Identity Problem, and Person-Affecting Principles," *Philosophy and Public Affairs* 45, no. 2 (2017): 118–57, and much ensuing literature.

6. I skeptically discussed Anderson's version of such a view earlier. See p. 355n13.

7. A view of this general kind is developed for the very idea of moral virtues, in Thomas Hurka, *Virtue, Vice, and Value* (Oxford: Oxford University Press, 2003), though I do not make that broader claim here.

8. Lest this sound like special pleading, it should be recalled that nowhere in this book do I, myself, explore in any depth what full or ideal justice might unrealistically require. In that sense of "ideal theory," I am not engaged in it in this book. Rather than doing it, I am, in various respects, defending doing it. Of course, if doing it is wrong, or worthless, then maybe the same would be true of defending it, though that does not seem obvious. Those who criticize doing it presumably think they are debating a worthwhile question, in which case they must allow that so am I.

9. In the discussion of the fallacy of approximation in chapter 14.

10. Stephanie Collins proposes a conception of blameworthiness for precisely this purpose: the case of sets of agents that are not themselves group agents. See "Oughts for Non-Agent Groups," unpublished draft, March 2018.

11. David Miller, *Justice for Earthlings: Essays in Political Philosophy* (New York: Cambridge University Press, 2013), chapter 10. Miller's discussion is cited approvingly by Michael Frazer, "Utopophobia as a Vocation: The Professional Ethics of Ideal and Nonideal Political Theory," *Social Philosophy and Policy* 33, nos. 1–2 (Fall 2016): 175–92.

12. There is controversy about this, with seminal critiques coming from Gilbert Harman, "Moral Philosophy Meets Social Psychology: Virtue Ethics and the Fundamental Attribution Error," *Proceedings of the Aristotelian Society* 99 (1999): 315–31; and John Doris, *Lack of Character* (Cambridge: Cambridge University Press, 2002). For citations and a critical overview of the literature, see Christian Miller, "Character and Situationism: New Directions," *Ethical Theory and Moral Practice* 20 (2017): 459–71.

13. For debate about that see, for example, Gary Watson, "On the Primacy of Character," in *Identity, Character, and Morality*, ed. Owen Flanagan and Amelie Rorty (Cambridge, MA: MIT Press, 1990), 449–70.

14. For an earlier discussion, see the discussion of moral "fetishism" in Michael Smith, *The Moral Problem* (Oxford: Wiley, 1994). For a recent piece that engages much of the literature, see Ron Aboodi, "One Thought Too Few: Where De Dicto Moral Motivation is Necessary," *Ethical Theory and Moral Practice* 20, no. 2 (April 2017): 223–37.

15. Gideon Rosen, e.g., argues that something might be a character flaw in a person even if they are not responsible, blameworthy, for it. Gideon Rosen, "Skepticism about Moral Responsibility," *Philosophical Perspectives* 18, no. 1 (2004): 295–313, at 302–3.

16. We find this phrase, e.g., in Sen, "What Do We Want," pp. 222, 225, 228, and *The Idea* (see "perfectly just societies") at p. ix, and multiple other times.

17. For an overview, see Duncan Pritchard and John Turri, "The Value of Knowledge," in *The Stanford Encyclopedia of Philosophy* (Spring 2014 ed.), ed. Edward N. Zalta, https://plato.stanford.edu/archives/spr2014/entries/knowledge-value/.

18. I thank an anonymous reader for the press for suggesting that I consider this objection.

Epilogue

1. See the quotations from Aristotle, Plato, and Machiavelli in the preface to this book.
2. See the epigraph for chapter 7.

INDEX OF EXAMPLES AND PROPOSITIONS

Note: Page numbers in italic type indicate where the example or proposition is explained.

A NOTE ON THE TYPE

THIS BOOK has been composed in Miller, a Scotch Roman typeface designed by Matthew Carter and first released by Font Bureau in 1997. It resembles Monticello, the typeface developed for The Papers of Thomas Jefferson in the 1940s by C. H. Griffith and P. J. Conkwright and reinterpreted in digital form by Carter in 2003.

Pleasant Jefferson ("P. J.") Conkwright (1905–1986) was Typographer at Princeton University Press from 1939 to 1970. He was an acclaimed book designer and AIGA Medalist.

The ornament used throughout this book was designed by Pierre Simon Fournier (1712–1768) and was a favorite of Conkwright's, used in his design of the *Princeton University Library Chronicle*.

CPSIA information can be obtained
at www.ICGtesting.com
Printed in the USA
JSHW050756050422
24617JS00003B/4